Paulsen

COMPUTATIONAL MODELS OF DISCOURSE

The MIT Press Series in Artificial Intelligence

Artificial Intelligence: An MIT Perspective, Volume I: Expert Problem Solving, Natural Language Understanding, Intelligent Computer Coaches, Representation and Learning edited by Patrick Henry Winston and Richard Henry Brown, 1979

Artificial Intelligence: An MIT Perspective, Volume II: Understanding Vision, Manipulation, Computer Design, Symbol Manipulation edited by Patrick Henry Winston and Richard Henry Brown, 1979

NETL: A System for Representing and Using Real-World Knowledge by Scott Fahlman, 1979

The Interpretation of Visual Motion by Shimon Ullman, 1979

A Theory of Syntactic Recognition for Natural Language by Mitchell P. Marcus, 1980

Turtle Geometry: The Computer as a Medium for Exploring Mathematics by Harold Abelson and Andrea diSessa, 1981

From Images to Surfaces: A Computational Study of the Human Early Visual System by William Eric Leifur Grimson, 1981

Computational Models of Discourse Edited by Michael Brady and Robert C. Berwick, 1983

Robot Motion: Planning and Control by Michael Brady, John Hollerbach, Tomas Lozano-Perez, Matthew Mason, and Timothy Johnson, 1983

COMPUTATIONAL MODELS OF DISCOURSE

Edited by Michael Brady and Robert C. Berwick

Contributors:

James Allen
Robert C. Berwick
Jerrold Kaplan
David McDonald
Candace L. Sidner
Bonnie Lynn Webber

The MIT Press

Cambridge, Massachusetts
London, England

PUBLISHER'S NOTE

This format is intended to reduce the cost of publishing certain works in book form and to shorten the gap between editorial preparation and final publication. The time and expense of detailed editing and composition in print have been avoided by photographing the text of this book directly from the author's computer printout.

Third printing, 1986
Copyright © 1983 by
The Massachusetts Institute of Technology

Printed in the United States of America.

Library of Congress Cataloging in Publication Data

Main entry under title:

Computational Models of Discourse

    (The MIT Press series in artificial intelligence)
    Bibliography: p.
    Includes index.
    1. Artificial Intelligence. 2. Linguistics--Data processing. 3. Speech processing systems. I.Brady, Michael, 1945- . II. Berwick, Robert C. III. Allen, James. IV. Series.
Q335.C56 1983   001.53'5   82-20402
ISBN 0-262-02183-8

CONTENTS

THE AUTHORS

James Allen
Assistant Professor
Department of Computer Science
University of Rochester
Rochester, NY 14627

Robert C. Berwick
Assistant Professor
Department of Elec. Eng. and Computer Science
Artificial Intelligence Laboratory
Massachusetts Institute of Technology
Cambridge MA 02139

J. Michael Brady
Senior Research Scientist
Artificial Intelligence Laboratory
Massachusetts Institute of Technology
Cambridge, MA 02139

David Israel
Research Scientist
Bolt, Beranek, and Newman Inc.
50 Moulton Street
Cambridge, MA 02139

S. Jerrold Kaplan
Vice President, Business Development
Teknowledge Inc
525 University Avenue
Palo Alto, CA 94301

David McDonald
Assistant Professor
Computer and Information Science
University of Massachusetts
Amherst, MA 01003

Candace L. Sidner
Research Scientist
Bolt, Beranek, and Newman Inc.
50 Moulton Street
Cambridge, MA 02139

Bonnie Lynn Webber
Associate Professor
Department of Computer and Information Science
Moore School of Electrical Engineering
University of Pennsylvania
Philadelphia, PA 19104

FOREWORD

Michael Brady

It should be noted at the outset that my personal research interests in artificial intelligence are in vision and robotics, not in linguistics. Two years ago, however, at the time that I was joining MIT, my general reading of the natural language literature in artificial intelligence suggested to me an undercurrent of change in computational linguistics analogous to that which has taken place, for example, in vision [Brady 1981]. This book on computational models of discourse stems from a series of conversations between myself and the other editor, Robert C. Berwick, that explored that change and the closeness of the analogy with vision.

What is the nature of the change? In a nutshell, it seems to me that artificial intelligence is crystallizing into more or less independent subdisciplines as an inevitable side-effect of maturing. Specialist journals have appeared, catering to specialized subdisciplines from linguistics to robotics. Even the field's traditional non-specialist journal *Artificial Intelligence* recently devoted a special issue to vision [Brady 1981]. It recognized that artificial intelligence researchers outside vision increasingly feel out of touch with work in that area. On the other hand, increasing numbers of perceptual psychologists want to become familiar with the computational approach to vision. Many artificial intelligence researchers feel similarly out of touch with other subdisciplines, notably robotics, search, and automated deduction.

Before exploring the symptoms of change, let us consider the state of natural language understanding research, say up to the time of the Schank and Colby's collection [Schank and Colby 1973], or the influential workshop on *Theoretical issues in natural language processing.* The vast expenditure of time and money on the machine translation projects of the 1950's and early 1960's, and the detailed formal mathematical study of parsing in the 1960's, provided little real insight into the problems of how natural language could be understood by, or through the use of, computers. The first wave of efforts in what is nowadays called computational linguistics had a considerable impact both on artificial intelligence and on a limited number of conventional linguists. The work of Schank, Winograd, Wilks, Woods, and their associates, suggested that it was possible to build a (huge) computer program capable of interesting linguistic behavior.

Although the emphases of different research efforts were in different aspects of language, they shared the characteristic that they resulted in entire (mostly) working systems. All the systems were required to deal with a wide range of linguistic challenges. They included a parser, a lexicon, and embodied proposals about the representation and role of semantic and pragmatic information in understanding and responding to an English sentence. The detailed interaction between the various subsystems was a central concern. In Winograd's system, for example, the fact that the sequence of processing could not be specified in advance was claimed as a major feature. The program SHRDLU contributed to the theory that sophisticated process interaction is central to modeling the flexibility of human thought, perception, and language understanding. In retrospect, however, these approaches to computational linguistics seem to be overly concerned with mechanism.

Inevitably, in order to achieve a total, working, natural language understanding program, early systems were forced to ignore, gloss over, or otherwise compromise on, many aspects of language understanding. The treatment of time, mood, purpose, theme, the determination of focus and reference, as well as many other issues, were accorded only a preliminary treatment. Some of the main insights which informed the construction of these systems were computational, and some of the main lessons which the authors claimed could be learned from their research, were about computational issues. the architecture of process interactions and the design of representations for semantic processing. For this reason, the detailed operation of the early natural language understanding systems and the issues they addressed were largely accessible to the general artificial intelligence community. At the interdisciplinary workshop on *Theoretical issues in natural language processing* [Nash-Webber and Schank 1975], six of the eight sessions concerned memory and knowledge representation. Most of the papers in those sessions could have just as easily been presented at a workshop on vision or reasoning (many were). Interestingly, only one of the forty papers presented at that workshop is referenced in this volume.[1]

What are the symptoms of change in computational linguistics that I referred to earlier? First, like vision, robotics, search, and formal reasoning, it has become

---

1. To be fair, some of the systems described at TINLAP-1 were refined and re-presented at TINLAP-2. Several references are made to TINLAP-2.

increasingly technical. In vision and robotics technical typically refers to sophisticated mathematical analysis. Although linguistics is, for the most part, (currently) less demanding mathematically than vision, there are, as always, exceptions. Berwick's grammatical analysis (and many similar analyses) of the Marcus parser and the McDonald generation program (chapter 4) is a model of precision. Similarly, Webber's (chapter 6) representation of the possible meanings of noun phrases fully exploits the power of the predicate calculus. Mathematics aside, technical refers to the precision and close attention to detail that is a feature of much current work in computational linguistics.

Second, though related to the first point, the problem with which any individual researcher is concerned in any particular project, seems to have narrowed considerably, with a corresponding increase in depth of analysis. The individual chapters in this volume restrict their attention to response generation, the determination of reference and focus, and the scope of quantifiers. In vision, people work on such problems as directional selectivity, the shape of subjective contours, and binocular stereo. The subject matter is primarily limited to what might be considered modules in the human's visual or linguistic system rather than being limited by a domain of application that potentially requires the deployment of the full panoply of linguistic or visual abilities. This does not imply that the epistemological base of a piece of work can always be completely unrestricted, as the paper by Allen in this volume illustrates. Domain restrictions are mostly a reflection of the lack of muscle and inappropriate architecture of today's computers. As the subject matter of individual research papers has become more restricted and specialized, so they in turn have become of less interest to artificial intelligence researchers whose primary interests are in other subdisciplines.

Recent papers in computational linguistics are also more demanding to read. One reason for this is immediately apparent to the casual artificial intelligence reader. Considerably more than lip service is paid to *non-* computational linguistics and vision. A more specialized background is assumed of the reader. Although the architects of early systems referred to the linguistics literature, they typically did so in general terms. Indeed it was even suggested by some authors that linguistics researchers simply had not uncovered ideas which were precise enough to constrain the detailed construction of a program or against which to evaluate its detailed behavior. There seems to have been an implicit assumption that the new conceptualizations introduced by computation were so radically different from anything that had been used previously in modeling language understanding that it was appropriate to make a completely fresh start.

In many recent papers, including those in this volume, extensive reference is made to detailed psychological and linguistic data. Results cited are used as evidence in support of the importance or appropriateness of a piece of work, as a source of constraint, or to justify some constraint or design decision, for example of a representation. Mitchell Marcus, for example, claims to have designed his parsing system PARSIFAL [Marcus 1980] to embody the constraints on human parsing which Chomsky has uncovered. The constraints are extremely detailed, concerning technical issues such as subject raising and embedded complements. Moreover, Marcus makes a number of detailed claims about program organization which he claims are implied by Chomsky's linguistics findings. The flow is not one way however. Computation contributes powerful ideas about representation and process, even if they are not omnipotent. While, the coupling of artificial intelligence with linguistics and psychology is not new, it has perhaps become more earnest and detailed.

One consequence of this change in computational linguistics is the tendency, remarked earlier, to publish in specialized journals, and to have the work recognized by the linguistics, philosophy, and psychology communities. This requires that computational linguists be able to discuss their ideas at least in part in terms that regular linguists are familiar with. A growing number of computational linguists have a formal qualification in linguistics, philosophy, or psychology.

The editors chose the contributions to this volume in part to illustrate the issues raised above, and in part to form a coherent whole. Jerrold Kaplan and James Allen provide rather different views of what is involved in understanding the meaning of a question in a discourse. An issue of deep and immediate concern for both of them is the need to generate responses, to participate in the discourse. David McDonald's contribution can be critically evaluated in the context of their work, and conversely. Also, they need to determine reference and focus, for, as both of them point out, much is left unstated in a discourse, and a participant has to exploit his or her knowledge to the full to keep talking. These are the questions studied by Candace Sidner and Bonnie Webber. Robert Berwick's introduction explores these interactions in more depth, and provides an overall context and critical review of the other five contributions. The overlap between the separate contributions is apparent even from the references cited; accordingly we have provided a unified bibliography.

PREFACE

David Israel

In the early days of Artificial Intelligence, researchers talked confidently about building fully intelligent entities, "robots", which could simulate (or emulate) any natural cognitive human achievement. Among such achievements, of course, is the (learning,) use and understanding of natural language. The early, semi-official view seems to have been that the human linguistic capacity could be duplicated by the application of perfectly general, non-domain specific operations to the admittedly special, but largely then uncharted, domain of language. This was, at the time, a perfectly reasonable position. It has ceased to be so and the essays in this volume bespeak the recognition of that fact by the vast majority of natural language researchers in Artificial Intelligence. They do so precisely by renouncing even a residual obligation to speak to the issue. Whereof we should no longer have to speak, we should pass over in silence.

Thus, it is no longer OK to "work in natural language" completely innocent of current research in syntactic theory. It should, by the way, be less than perfectly alright for people in syntactic theory to be as innocent of work in computational linguistics, especially in the theory of parsing, as many still are. The same point *could* be made about the inexcusability of ignorance of contemporary work in semantics; but nowhere near so glibly. I shall return to this difference later.

With syntax and semantics "covered", can pragmatics be far behind? Indeed not, but here the situation is very different. Certainly the source of the concepts deployed by AI researchers is to be found in the works of philosophers (especially Austin and Strawson, Grice and Searle). I think it can plausibly be maintained, however, that those concepts would remain "blind" without having to accommodate the "intuitions" that come from attempts to design computational artifacts capable of becoming language-users. (My apologies to Immanuel Kant.)

Imagine, for instance, that one wanted to build a thing which could reasonably be said to understand what you were talking about - at least when you were talking about some previously delimited domain; and to act accordingly, again within the limits of its sensors and effectors. (I shall limit myself to imagining a natural-language understanding system, leaving aside the difficulties of generation. See David McDonald's piece in the volume for a pioneering effort in production.) Imagine, further, that you have been given - free of charge - a perfectly adequate parser for English.[1] Close your eyes even more tightly and suppose you find, under your bed, say, a tractable algorithm which assigns a correct semantic representation to each unambiguous sentence-under-analysis of English and the right n such to each n-ways ambiguous sentence-under-analysis. (This last bit of fantasizing might require large doses of mind-altering substances.)

How much work have you got left to do? A whole lot, and one would have to be an unregenerate syntactico-semantic imperialist to think otherwise.[2] But it was only with the disciplined attempts actually to build such devices that one could see just how much and what. And more: for it is only with such attempts that one could appreciate the extent of feed-back, and feed-forward, across the heretofore largely insurpassable boundaries of **the sentence** and, independently, of the **black box**.

For notice that, a priori, it seems natural to elaborate the little daydream hinted at above by supposing that our parser-cum-semantic interpreter works on individual sentences in glorious isolation one from another; as if even a monologue (directed, though, at another presumably intelligent agent) could be thought of as built up out of independently intelligible units of meaning. The fully modularized dream, surely, is that one runs the sentences first through the parser, then through the semantic interpreter, and then passes the output of that stage to a module (or two or three) which, inter alia, keeps usable track of the previous sentences (their syntactic analysis and their meaning?) and of the "current non-linguistic situation". (Ah, but which aspects of this, and in what form?)

Dreams die hard; but not many are left who insist that the processing story, for individual sentences, must go the route traced by the little arrows in diagrams of the linguistic module; that is, who insist on reading high-level structural diagrams as flow charts.[3] Still, there is the matter of the assumption that one can, and should, do the syntactic-semantic analyses of individual sentences in principled

---

1. Mind you, there are interesting questions afoot as to the appropriate conditions of adequacy, let alone "perfect adequacy", on parsers.

2. There are radicals who wonder whether this package from the gods is necessary. In particular, there are those who wonder how much beyond the lexicon one really requires from semantics; such people might be characterized as syntactico-pragmatic hegemonists. We shall ignore them for the duration.

3. We shall return to this point shortly.

ignorance of the uses to which those sentences, now considered as members of a coherent collective, might be put in the situation at hand. This assumption may not do. Much of the best work on discourse suggests that it will not do.

Considerations such as the above, fleshed out, of course, with the study of actual data and the analysis of hypothesized computational regimens may seem to lead researchers in discourse phenomena to a dilemma of sorts. Remember what was said above about the importance of contact with research in linguistics and philosophy. Much of the best work from those quarters is based on and argues for a very strict modularity as among syntax, semantics and, well, the rest. There is a tension, isn't there, between the import of this work and the interactions among modules hinted at above?[1] Yes and no.

There is a tangle of issues here; and, fortunately, this is not the place to attempt to untangle them. (For an heroic and insightful attempt, see Jerry Fodor's "The Modularity of Mind" [Fodor 1982]. For a more circumscribed study, see Berwick and Weinberg's "The Role of Grammars in Models of Language Use" [Berwick and Weinberg 1982]) A first point to note is that, qua designers of natural-language understanding computational artifacts, researchers in Artificial Intelligence need not be bound by current theories of human cognition, in particular of psycholinguistics; although they may be, perhaps should be, and as a number of the pieces in this volume make clear, have been, influenced by such work. (And a little more vice-versa, please.)

More concretely, we should bear in mind the happy compatibility of theories of static modularity with processing models incorporating high degrees of dynamic interaction. (I borrow the two phrases, and much else, from my colleague Rusty Bobrow, who has thought long and well about these issues.) More concretely still, processing hypotheses which stress rich interactions between syntax, semantics and even pragmatics are not ruled out, for example, by any sane version of the thesis of the Autonomy of Syntax.[2] The crucial constraint imposed by acceptance of the Autonomy thesis is that the syntactic module have, so to speak, a mind - and rules and representations - of its own, that it not speak or understand semanticese, for example. Just so, the semantic interpreter should be untainted by acquaintance with the rules of conversation. There is no prohibition, though, against the autonomously specified syntactic component being guided, as it goes about its business of assigning syntactic structures to input, by requested output from, e.g. the semantic component - as long as use of that output requires

---

1. Note that here the insurpassable barrier is not the sentence, but the boundaries of the black box.
2. For some relief on this oft tortured subject, see Noam Chomsky's "Questions of Form and Interpretation" (in [Chomsky 1977]).

no "knowledge" on syntax's part of semanticese. As long, that is, as the communication medium between the two components is highly constrained, constrained enough to be "neutral" as between the concepts proper to syntax and those within the purview of semantics alone. Note, by the way, that it makes no sense to imagine that the semantic interpreter understands no syntactic concepts; structures describable only by use of them are, after all, its input. So again, highly interactive models can capture the "asymmetry" between syntax and semantics - the first can remain ignorant of the other's terms; not so, the second. Neither, of course, need know anything about the other's internal workings.

Things become much more controversial, and much more interesting, when we venture beyond the confines of the "linguistic system proper"; as, it seems, we must when we venture upon the treatment of pragmatics and discourse phenomena generally.

Now is almost as bad a time as any to make some terminological distinctions; or to confess to having ignored them in the foregoing. There is pragmatics and there is pragmatics. When I have talked of pragmatics, I have not had in mind the work of Richard Montague, David Kaplan, and others on the logic of indexicals or token-reflexive elements, expressions whose denotata are a function of specifiable aspects of the contexts of their use. Rather, as suggested earlier, I have meant the theory of the use of language in communication. This delimitation is irremediably vague and open-ended; and therein lies the rub. Formal pragmatics (as the work of Montague et. al. [Montague 1974] might be called) is an annex of formal semantics; hence, part and parcel of the study of the linguistic system. Communication-theoretic accounts, on the other hand, can respect no such departmental boundaries. Some discourse phenomena *can* be traced directly to syntactic and semantic features of the constituent sentences, taken one at a time as it were; some, cannot. Again, the rub of open-ended interactionism.

With the rub comes the challenge. Everyone agrees that the actual use of language in communication involves all manner of cognitive modules acting together. Researchers in language, from Linguistics, Philosophy, and Artificial Intelligence, hold that this interaction must not be understood as evidence against a high degree of (static) modularization, especially with respect to the linguistic system, taken now as a whole, as against the rest of the mental apparatus. The challenge is to think clearly and in a theoretically well-motivated and disciplined way about modes and media of interaction. It's dirty work; but somebody's got to do it. Past this preface, the reader will find evidence that some, at least, are trying.

And now for an anticlimax. I warned the reader that we would have to return to the issue of formal semantics for natural languages. Forewarned is forearmed. The papers in this volume are by and large silent on specific grammatical issues; the researchers in most cases assume the availability of parsers with usefully broad syntactic coverage. (It is no small praise of work in Computational Linguistics to note that this assumption is a reasonably safe one.) There are, of course, open problems in both syntax and parsing; but we are by no means completely at sea. Oddly enough, a bit of the same can be said for the theory of pragmatics and discourse. Here, building on the work of Grice, Searle, and others, and extending it impressively across hefty chunks of talk, researchers in AI have developed, at the very least, a habitable framework for hypothesis and experimentation. (See, for instance, the papers in this volume.)

With respect to semantics, it's sadly a horse of a different color. As one reads the essays, one may get the impression that there has been a principled decision to opt for extensional, first-order languages (usually sortalized) as generating the logical forms of English utterances and hence as the vehicles of semantic representation. My own view is that this decision is best seen as purely a tactical or pedagogical one; at something less than worse, it might be understood as forced on one, faute de mieux. With the tactics and/or the pedagogy, I have no argument. For the wistful longing for a better way, I have only sympathy. As for the principle, I deny it. I even have something of an argument.

AN ARGUMENT:

(a) All (both) programs for formulating formal semantic accounts for significant fragments of natural languages (fragments containing "interesting" semantic constructions) exploit formal languages quite different than the language of first-order logic. We have in mind Montague-style semantics and the Situation Semantics of Barwise and Perry [1982].

(b) In other words: to our knowledge, no significant fragment of any natural language has ever been semantically analyzed by way of a (systematic) translation into a standard first-order language. Indeed, again to our knowledge, no one has ever even seriously attempted it.

(c) The foregoing facts don't seem to be accidents of history and there do seem to be good methodological reasons for the history. The main consideration is the ad hoc and unsystematic character of attempts at semantic analysis of particular sentences of English by way of paraphrase into standard first-order languages. Crucial here is the source of this ad hoc character. Any account of the semantics of natural languages which exploits a formal language has a choice about where to be risk-taking. (Such choices go with the territory of deep and general unsolved problems.) It can be novel and daring in the specification of the formal language and its semantics. This is the route taken by Montague and Barwise-Perry.

Montague's language (the language IL in "The Proper Treatment of Quantification in Ordinary English") is a "throw in everything but the kitchen sink" omega-order intensional logic, with free use of lambda-abstraction and intensional operators of all degrees. To put it crudely, the strategy seems to have been to devise a construct in the formal language for each construct in the natural language. Moreover, Montague was at all times motivated by concerns for generality; indeed, his approach might be called "Pentagon Semantics". Look at the worst-case context in the fragment in which, e.g., noun phrases occur, and assign a semantic type to noun phrases accordingly. Despite this, the semantic account of IL is, in a sense, standard; it consists in extending Tarski-style treatments of quantificational languages of arbitrary order to modal and intensional languages, an extension pioneered by - inter alia - Montague.

Barwise and Perry's formal language ALIASS, on the other hand, is designed to be much closer in its syntax to the surface syntax of English. *Exactly* what its semantics looks like is not yet fully clear in that no treatment of a significant fragment has yet been (widely) published. (There is an underground literature; there is even a bumper sticker: Another Family for Situation Semantics.) In some thoroughly uninteresting sense, it too will be more of the same; that is, more set theory. But this may be quite misleading, as there are hints at a more properly recursion-theoretic treatment. Thus, special constraints may be put on the kinds of sets, and operations thereon, to be allowed. Classical Tarski-style semantics places no such constraints.

To return to our theme, then, the route taken by Montague and by Barwise-Perry has the advantage that the inventiveness is confined to an area susceptible to precise mathematico-logical treatment. It also allows (in theory at least) for simple (recursive) translation procedures between English and the target formal language.

The other, standard first-order, route focuses on the procedures for paraphrase (translation) from the natural to the formal language. It leaves such procedures, however, in just the state that they assume in introductory logic texts: imprecise, non-formalizable rules-of-thumb; heuristics based on appeals to intuition. The contrast is illuminating, and, on grounds of good scientific methodology, highly unfavorable, we think, to the "conservative" strategy.

(d) Once the set-theoretic semantics of a new, non-standard, formal language has been given, one can see *in general* how to "compile" that language into a first-order language, typically with a bloated ontology. Such compilation may make great practical sense if, for instance, one has a powerful first-order logic machine sitting on one's desk. Still, keep in mind that it just may turn out that the detour through the weird and wonderful is necessary; that it may just be (psychologically?) impossible to translate directly and systematically from a natural language into the language of first-order logic.

So much by way of argument; needless to say, more needs to be said. In the meantime, it's a pleasure to welcome the reader to this volume, to taste some of the first fruits of a happy blending of the sciences of language.

COMPUTATIONAL MODELS OF DISCOURSE

CHAPTER 1

Introduction: Computational Aspects of Discourse

Robert C. Berwick

1.1 Why computational models?

Talk, as everyone knows, is cheap. In stark contrast, a scientific account of talk is expensive -- we have no good theory, let alone a computational one, of this perhaps most facile human behavior. This blatant mismatch between superficial human ease and theoretical mechanical intractability agrees with the general experience of the past twenty years of research in artificial intelligence. Whereas "expert" problem solving behavior can be routinely duplicated -- there are programs that do as well or better than people in interpreting mass spectrograms or calculus -- the most mundane of human abilities remain beyond the reach of current computer programs. The following five chapters describe initial computational forays into the difficult territory of the cognitively effortless -- discourse.

The study of discourse begins with what talk is _for_. In this crucial respect, all five researchers share a largely unargued, but commonly accepted viewpoint: that linguistic behavior is basically about <u>communicative</u> <u>behavior</u>.[1] Packed into these two words, in fact, is the glue that binds together all five research efforts. The word "communication" is derived from the Latin *communitas*, to <u>share</u>, reflecting an intuition that the touchstone for communication involves, in some vague yet compelling sense, a notion of <u>sharing</u> -- be it thoughts, knowledge, or feelings. But what is even more remarkable about discourse is how this sharing comes about. The participants exchange mere <u>external</u> forms -- their utterances -- and yet manage to arrive at an <u>internal</u> correspondence, presumably one of partially shared mental states.

On the communicative view then, the job of a hearer is to somehow reconstruct a portion of the speaker's internal life -- namely, those the speaker wishes to convey (call this the speaker's message, or communicative intent, or

---

1. This view is not without its own problems: it (tacitly) assumes that "communication" -- whatever that is -- must have been functionally supreme in the evolutionary "design" of language. This may very well be true, but one must give some argument to this effect; it is not apodictic.

whatever) -- and the job of the speaker is to somehow facilitate this reconstruction. Thus, simply by adopting the usual view that language is for communication, all five researchers have embraced the following embryonic model of language use:

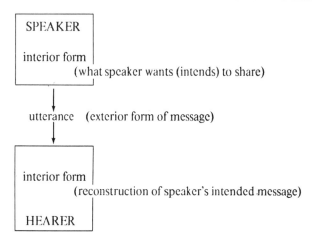

SPEAKER

interior form
                    (what speaker wants (intends) to share)

utterance   (exterior form of message)

interior form
                    (reconstruction of speaker's intended message)

HEARER

Figure 1 A model of language use.

What demands explanation is how this can all be made to work: Just what are the mysterious arrows that map a speaker's interior forms to utterances, and then back again in the mind of the listener? Somehow the hearer is able to infer part of the speaker's interior mental world simply by taking note of external utterances and their context. It all sounds like so much magic, or even a kind of telepathy; indeed it would be if nothing more could be said about the arrows connecting the boxes in our crude information flow diagram above. What makes the hearer's recovery of part of a speaker's inner mental life biological commonplace instead of magic is that there are significant constraints at every step of the process sketched above -- the relationship between communicative intent and utterance, between inner and outer form, is systematic. When I want to say that Discourse is like telepathy, not just any string of sounds will do. A whole series of regularities -- phonological, syntactic, semantic, and pragmatic -- intervene so as to dictate what can and cannot be counted as an utterance that properly conveys my intended message. It is the hearer's knowledge of these well-formedness requirements that permit the recovery of my intended message; similarly, it is my knowledge of these very same constraints (and my knowledge that my listener knows these constraints) that guides the exterior form that I produce. In brief, the hearer knows the rules of the game by which I produced my utterance, and uses these rules to infer inner form from exterior utterance. Shared knowledge makes further sharing possible, transforming the magical into the mundane.

From this vantage point, the study of discourse reduces to the study of these regularities. It should be no surprise, then, that this is the chief contribution of the research presented in this book: to provide a partial account of the systematic conventions of discourse. According to the work ethic of the artificial intelligence, the authors have for the most part exploited the discourse regularities they have uncovered by embedding them into working computer programs that actually aim to mirror the behavior of human discourse participants. A snapshot of which regularities each contributor has decided to focus upon looks something like the following, where the reconstruction of the speaker's communicative intent (as represented internally by the hearer) has now been broken down as follows:

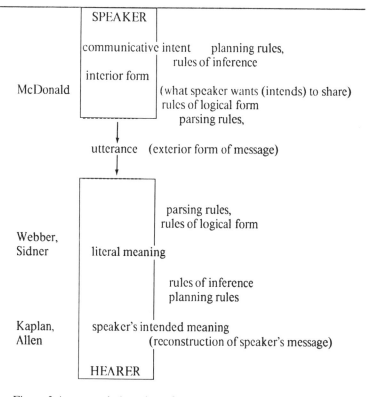

Figure 2 An expanded version of the model of language use.

As the diagram indicates, the work of each contributor to this volume has its own role to play in a full account of discourse behavior. Let us review these contributions, one by one.

First of all, it is worthwhile to point out that the discourse flowchart sketched above splits into two distinct parts. One is the translation from surface form to internal form: the input to a computer program is just some string of tokens, e.g., "Discourse is like magic", and our first task is to translate, or associate, these tokens with those of an <u>internal</u> language, typically tokens of some linguistic type. The internally-formatted counterpart of the input serves as the launching pad for further processing. What should this internal language look like? A trivial translation would be to simply add lexical category labels to each of the tokens of the input string; typically, however, a more sophisticated translation is assumed, such as a labeled bracketing representing a parse of the input string. Figuring out what this internal language should be like is Webber and Sidner's domain of research. As we shall see, Sidner and Webber adopt something in the spirit of modern generative grammar, if not its exact detail. Whatever the process, it is crucially a <u>formal</u> one. The input is a sequence of tokens, and the output is a string of symbols in some internal formal language. Crucially, the relation between surface and internal language is not one of identity -- some real work is done in the conversion to an internal language and so the computation that must be done is likewise not necessarily trivial. (We shall see precisely how non-trivial below.)

So far we are on familiar, if not altogether steady, ground. After all, philosophers since Frege have claimed that sentences of natural languages have "underlying" representations that are non-isomorphic to their surface forms. And they have used distinctions in the <u>form</u> of these representations to account for semantical distinctions. Kaplan and Allen, though, want to go this project one better. If differences in underlying form can be used to capture semantical differences -- the Frege-Russell program -- then why not expand the notion of "underlying form"? Kaplan and Allen do just that, and attempt to recover a partial representation of the speaker's beliefs and intentions. Now, a system that knows when and how to fix beliefs is a different order of beast than one that knows simply how to map tokens to linguistic types. Indeed, talk about fixing beliefs is part and parcel of what it means to talk about higher cognitive processes generally. It is not necessarily the province of the language processor, at least not in the conception of the language processor as ordinarily entertained in modern linguistic theory. Of course, to the extent that the mapping of tokens to internal form lays the groundwork for the fixation of belief, Webber and Sidner's theories provide the cornerstone for Kaplan and Allen's systems as well. (Entirely analogous, it would seem, to the way that early visual processing provides the representational foundation for calling a chair a chair.)

Returning now to our Cook's tour, Webber and Sidner's aim is to develop the right internal format in which to formally represent utterances, and how (in Sidner's case) to compute with that representation in order to keep track of the things talked about in a discourse. The purpose of this format is to define the domains of individuals or entities that are to be made available for further computational manipulation by the hearer. For instance, when I say, "I saw a Persian cat," then Webber's system is to make it clear that I am talking about a certain domain of individuals, namely, Persian cats. Webber's system pairs expressions in a formal language -- the language into which strings like "I saw a Persian cat" get mapped -- with an internal (presumably mentalistic) representation of sets of individuals

For the most part Webber is concerned only with a semantics for Noun Phrases. For example, Webber claims that the string (and Noun Phrase) three boys that ate a pizza "creates" two possible discourse entities reflecting the individuative and collective readings of this sentence. In one reading, a set of boys together eat a single pizza; in the other, three boys individually each eat a pizza. Crucially, Webber captures the difference in meaning between these two readings via a difference in the form of possible internal representations. A syntactic device -- the scoping of a SET operator -- is deployed to mirror the difference in meaning:

> (1a) $\lambda(v:\text{SET (boy)}) [(\exists y:\text{Pizza}) . \text{Ate } v,y \wedge |v| = 3]$
> (the collective reading: there exists one set of boys that
> serves as the argument to "ate")

> (1b) $\lambda(u:\text{SET}(\lambda(v:\text{boy}[(\exists y:\text{Pizza}). \text{Ate } v,y]))) [|u| = 3]$
> (the individual reading: each boy serves separately as an
> argument to "ate")

As we see then, Webber's approach to explaining different "readings" of sentences lies firmly within the Fregean "modern" tradition of the study of the "logical syntax" of language: some (not all) semantical differences are encoded as differences in the "shape" of a formal language into which surface strings are mapped.

Sidner's research begins where Webber's ends. It assumes a formalism roughly like Webber's, mapping surface strings into expressions in logical form (henceforth LF), but this is just Sidner's first step. The ultimate goal is to understand how the representations of discourse entities, for the most part reflexes of Noun Phrases, are manipulated over the lifetime of a discourse. It is this emphasis on manipulation, on how the discourse representation enters into language use, rather than just what the representation is, that marks Sidner's study as a quintessentially computational, rather than philosophical, analysis.

In particular, Sidner wants to be able to explain how people link together what is talked about in a discourse -- the foci of a discourse, in Sidner's terminology. Webber's formalism plays a key role here because Sidner must first be able to just represent what is being talked about. But there is an additional, computational story that must be unraveled, and that is how people "point back" to what is being talked about (via the use of anaphors like pronouns), how they compute this connection, and how, from time to time, they change what they are talking about. For instance, in the simple dialogue below:

(2) There were some strawberries in the fridge last week.
They were tasty, but didn't last long.
John found them, and that was the last we saw of them.
John has a penchant for fruit.

what requires explanation is (1) how it is that we know the first few sentences are about strawberries; (2) how the connection between they in sentence (2) and strawberries is established; (3) how a shift in focus -- such as to John by the end of the dialogue -- is computed. Sidner's theory accomplishes this by combining Webber's formalism for representing NP's with a push-down stack bookkeeping system for "what is being talked about." Thus it serves in effect as a part of a formal account of multiple-sentence logical form, a level of representation we might call "discourse structure". Just as there are rules of sentence grammar that tell us that he may -- but need not -- be linked with John in John thinks that he should win, Sidner's computational machinery is a first attempt to see how the structure of language determines this kind of linking over the domain of several sentences.

In short then, both Webber and Sidner are interested in the first stages of translating from surface strings to a purely syntactic logical form -- hence their placement in the discourse flowchart. But is logical form all there is to meaning? Clearly not: there is nothing in the theory of logical form as given so far that connects formally specified discourse entities to the world, nothing to provide an interpretation for the purely formal object "($\exists x$, x a Set(boy)..)". Webber and Sidner have offered an approach to the logical semantics of discourse (a syntactical semantics), and a way to pair LF expressions with other mental representations. How then are expressions in the LF language to be related to the "outside" world? Kaplan and Allen both take cracks at this most difficult of questions, though I believe that neither of them considered this to be one of their actual research aims. Kaplan's approach says in effect that people are connected to the world via a list of (observable) properties of objects -- an extensional viewpoint. That is, LF expressions are linked to objects in the world simply by listing the objects that fall under the predicate implied by the object; for Kaplan, the expression "three boys that ate a pizza" (or rather its logical translation) means a list of names of boys who either together or separately ate a pizza. In contrast, Allen's model centers on the causal connection between human actions and the world. It involves in an essential way what the speaker or hearer <u>wants</u> or <u>intends</u>. On different occasions, depending on the beliefs, desires, and party allegiance of the agents involved, one and the same set of formal objects (hence objects with the same properties, hence the same extensions) could have different intensions. Kaplan is aware of this distinction; as he observes, the "proper" answer to the question,

Which employees profit share?

could, on one occasion, be simply a list of employees -- the "extensional" meaning. But depending on what the speaker or hearer wants to <u>do</u> with the answer, it might be some description, such as, "the Vice Presidents".

In part this difference in approach is the result of the differences between the objects each has chosen to study. Kaplan opts for a relatively rich world of objects and properties, but an impoverished theory of belief and action: by fixing as his "real world" a relational database (DB) of objects with certain properties and reducing all human purposes to one, namely, finding out the answer to queries about the database, Kaplan can assume that extensions, now simply lists of database objects, fix meaning. With this theory about how formal objects connect to the database world, Kaplan can now build a system that constructs the proper response to questions that are pointless to answer when certain logical conditions obtain (such as the question "How many Bloody Marys did John drink at the party?" if no liquor was served at the party). Kaplan's program is able to deduce when such questions are pointless to answer because in his simple extensional world meaningless questions correspond to occurrences of empty sets in the middle of a search through a database to locate the objects that meet the description demanded by the question. Kaplan's system can detect these gaps, and then exploit a close correspondence between the surface syntactic form of the question and the database search it demands to generate an appropriate corrective or suggestive response (such as, <u>None, because there was no liquor served.</u>).

In contrast, Allen assumes an impoverished universe of properties of objects, but a rich theory of human action. Allen's basic idea is to conjoin a theory of linguistic behavior -- the theory of speech acts as developed by Austin and Searle -- with a largely AI-based approach -- a theory of planning complex tasks. Speech act theory provides a framework in which linguistic activity is "just another" kind of human action. But as a kind of action, a speech act must be planned, and it is then susceptible to explanation via a theory of planning. What Allen does is to show how a theory of planning can in fact be used to infer what plan or "action sequence" a questioner must have had in mind when a certain question was asked, and how that knowledge can be exploited to respond appropriately (it thus subsumes Kaplan's more specific case where the questioner's "plan" was to discover information about the existence or properties of certain objects). Allen also demonstrates that his theory of planning behavior is general enough to handle so-called "indirect speech acts", that is, cases where an intended meaning is not transparently encoded in the surface form of an utterance. For example, "I'm cold" can mean "Please close the window." The theory of purposive behavior embraced by Allen's system is thus quite broad. This universality in modeling planning is bought at a price: Allen's extensional world of objects and their properties is quite restricted. In fact, in his implemented system, one can only board or meet trains.

McDonald's work stands apart from the other four efforts in that it deals solely with the production of utterances rather than the recovery of communicative intent given an utterance. (Kaplan and Allen's work incidentally involves constructing adequate natural language replies in response to natural language input, but this is not their chief concern.) That is, rather than starting with external sentence form, McDonald is in the business of starting with an internal message and generating a corresponding external linguistic form. This dual effort is no less important than that of the other four contributors', since success of the enterprise of communitas clearly demands that the speaker adhere to the discourse conventions that the listener is expecting to use to "decode" the speaker's message. Like Allen, McDonald assumes that the ultimate structure behind a "message" corresponds to an action sequence, a plan. This plan -- hierarchically structured if the plan is composed of many parts -- is mapped onto surface string of words in two steps. The first lays out the general shape of the utterance, as defined by an annotated constituent structure tree -- the arrangement of Noun Phrases, Verb Phrases, and .the like as per the general dictates of a grammar and certain pragmatic constraints. The second step is a grammatical "polishing" operation that actually produces the words to be output, adds the finery of grammatical agreement, and so forth. The resulting machine is quite efficient; we shall see just how efficient below.

In effect McDonald's program must rely on many of the sub-components that have gone before, from Webber's to Allen's. It depends on Webber's logical form to enumerate the space of possible things to talk about, on Sidner's linking rules to say just when a pronoun or abbreviatory Noun Phrase may be used instead of a full Noun Phrase, and on Allen's planning theory to map out, at the highest level, what has to be said in order to achieve certain conversational goals.

The types of conventional discourse behavior explored in this volume are thus quite broad in scope. The regularities that have been probed range from patterns in the use of "abbreviatory" Noun Phrase expressions and pronouns (Sidner, Webber), to helpful responses to questions (Allen, Kaplan), to the production of utterances, given an intended communicative "message" (McDonald).[1] The constraints exploited by the contributors also run the gamut of linguistic and non-linguistic regularities. They include the purely syntactic (such as the knowledge that in the sentence Bill wants him to leave, Bill and him cannot be co-referential); semantic (such as the knowledge that the verb give has a kind of "argument structure" that requires a giver, a givee, and object to be given); pragmatic (knowledge that has to do with the context of the utterance, such as the knowledge that when I ask the question, "When does the train to New York leave?" I presume the existence of a train to New York, because otherwise I would already know the answer to my question); and inferential (such as the simple inference that if I know that A wants some action X to occur, then A wants the preconditions of that act to obtain, or more complex inferences grounded upon more highly structured bundles of information, like a causally structured action sequence plan for boarding a train).

It should be clear by now that this view of discourse as communicative behavior calls for a theory compounded of two parts: the first a theory of what is shared -- messages or mental stuff; the second a theory of how that stuff comes to be shared. A study of what the regularities of discourse are is, of course, part of the domain of many other fields -- psychology, sociology, among others. What distinguishes the contributions of this volume from these more traditional ways of viewing the subject (since all these fields also, by and large, adopt something like a communicative behavior view of discourse), is that they study the problem of discourse from the standpoint of computation. Part of this commitment to explanation via computation lies of course in the very fact that the authors all construct working computer programs that actually carry out the mapping from utterance to internal form or its reverse. More broadly, though, the contributors

---

1. All the contributors do add one important qualification to the "naturalness" of the input that is the assumed starting point for analysis: the actual input to the programs is in orthographic form, and thus omits such possibly important characteristics of the speech stream as stress, intonational contour, pauses, and the like, as well as those obviously "non-verbal" concomitants of communication like gestures. This is the usual qualification made in computational research of this kind, and it deserves some comment. In abstracting away from these well known properties of communicative behavior, it is important to keep in mind whether potential generalizations will be lost. Some of these features of speech -- such as fundamental frequency contour (the basic "pitch level" of the voice) and contrastive stress -- could be accommodated into the research presented in this book. In particular, it will be shown how contrastive stress might be factored into the approach that Sidner takes to the resolution of definite anaphors.

to this book are concerned with <u>how</u> it is that what the speaker has in mind comes to be reconstructed by the hearer, in short, with the study of (mental) <u>processes</u>. Implicit in this identification of computation with mental process is a key assumption of AI research with respect to the study of discourse behavior, an assumption that the five authors all take for granted, and one that in fact provides the cornerstone for their research and almost all cognitively-oriented AI work generally. This is the assumption that <u>mental processes are computational</u>, where by computational one may take Fodor's definition of computation: <u>operations defined over (mental) representations.</u>. [Fodor 1975] Computational processes are to be distinguished further in that their interactions with representations are purely <u>formal</u>. That is, it is the <u>structure</u> of a representation that dictates the course of a computation, and not its contents; a representation must wear its computational properties 'on its sleeve.'

A one-line summary of what the contributors to this volume are after ends up sounding very much like the goal of modern generative grammar: rules and representations. However, there is a crucial difference. As mentioned, since the contributors to this volume subscribe to the AI work ethic, they aim to do more than simply characterize the mapping between representational levels as some sort of <u>function</u>, they aim to characterize it as a <u>computable function</u>, preferably, an <u>efficiently</u> computable function. This added computational demand is the real spice of AI research, and is what distinguishes the research described in this volume from more standard approaches.

From a philosophical point of view, the incorporation of a computational viewpoint into the study of discourse appears to have had two substantial benefits. First, for whatever reasons, thinking hard about computational issues has led some of the AI research in this volume to actually anticipate certain developments in linguistic theory and philosophy. Second, the computational view as espoused in this volume leads directly to a more <u>modular</u> explanation of linguistic behavior. By "modular" I mean that part of observed surface behavior -- in this case, discourse behavior -- is to be accounted for by the interaction of two components, one based on the pure form of internal, mental representations, and the other based on computations defined over those representations. Of course, as any computer scientist would point out, representational and computational demands, data structures and algorithmic complexity, are intimately related. The presumed advantage of a modular account is that it allows one to factor out and state constraints for each module separately, with the interaction between components giving rise to the superficially complex surface behavior. In short, at least for the studies presented in this volume, the introduction of the additional demand of computability provides an additional source of explanatory constraint that can be mined.

In summary then, the computationalist has two unique contributions to make to the study of language: (1) an additional source of constraint, computability, with which to explain linguistic behavior; (2) an explicit concern with partitioning explanations of linguistic behavior into representational and computational components.

With this computational viewpoint in mind, let us take a more detailed tour of how the contributors to this volume fit into the discourse diagram and what discourse regularities they attempt to explain, placing special emphasis on what seems at stake from a computational point of view.

1.2 The Syntax of Discourse: Webber and Sidner

1.2.1 Creating and linking discourse entities

It is a familiar intuition that speech or written text "hangs together" in part because people conventionally use pronouns or abbreviatory Noun Phrases for previously mentioned Noun Phrases. For instance, in the sentence below, they is taken to stand for the Senators; the Senators is said to be the Noun Phrase antecedent of the pronoun they:

> (1) Speaker 1: I heard the two Senators argue yesterday.
> Speaker 2: Yes, they were in disagreement over extending the Voting Rights Act.

The problem to be investigated here can be illustrated by a simple example that Webber suggests. She observes that the same literal text string five dollars can be referred to anaphorically by either the singular pronoun it or the plural pronoun them:

> (2a) I gave Bill five dollars...It was more than I gave Bill
> (2b) I gave Bill five dollars...One of them was torn.

There are actually two separate puzzles to solve here. One is simply to figure out that five dollars can have two different "meanings", either as a collective entity or as a set of singletons. The other is to determine that it can be linked to the collective entity, and them to the singletons, and not vice-versa. The solution to the first problem is representational in character. The aim is to develop a language that can express the space of possible logical representations for the discourse entities implicit in a given literal text string. In the five dollars example, there would be two possible logical translations of the text: a collective reading and an individuative reading, corresponding to five dollars considered as a single entity and <u>five dollars</u> considered as a collection of five single bills. One must also supply a set of <u>rules</u> that say exactly how literal strings are to be translated into this language. This is the problem that Webber sets out to solve, and it is essentially a question about the proper representation of the syntax of logical form.

The second puzzle is more computational in character: with the possible array of discourse entities in hand, what are the rules that tell us which one (or more) of these possibilities is actually linked to subsequent pronouns and Noun Phrases that appear later in the text or discourse? The solution to this problem is Sidner's work.

Setting out to solve these problems is extraordinarily ambitious, in that Webber and Sidner aim to do for discourse what recent linguistic theory has accomplished only for single sentences. For single sentences there are various analogues of examples like (1) above. For example, the reciprocal anaphor <u>each other</u> can be used as an expression that designates a Noun Phrase that has previously appeared:

(3) The men seem to like each other. (each other = the men)

This kind of relationship is captured in several current linguistic theories by the notational device of <u>co-indexing</u>.[1] In the example above, one could represent co-designation by the simple device of subscripting the NP <u>the men</u> and the reciprocal <u>each other</u> with the same index:

(4) [The men]$_{NP_i}$ seem to like [each other]$_i$.

One may disagree about whether co-indexing is the right sort of notational machinery with which to express the indisputable fact that a text "hangs together." But whatever machinery one chooses, what is crucial from a linguistic and a computational point of view is that "binding relationships" are apparently subject to <u>syntactic</u> constraints:

(5) Every woman$_i$ thinks that the man she$_i$ married is wonderful.

---

1. See, for example, the Government-Binding theory [Chomsky 1981]; the Lexical-Functional theory [Kaplan and Bresnan 1981].

For instance, whether each other can designate one and the same entity as the men depends in part on the purely configurational aspects of sentences. For example, a lexical Subject of an embedded clause seems to block binding between each other and a possible Noun Phrase antecedent:

(6) *The men want John to like each other.

-- the so-called Specified Subject constraint [Chomsky 1973]. Similarly, if the quantifier every does not constituent command (c-command) a pronoun, then the two are not naturally interpretable as co-indexed [Higginbotham 1980]:[1]

(7) *The woman over-there who likes [every man]$_i$ in the room thinks [that [he$_i$] is too rich]. (every man = he)

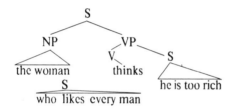

Contrary to first impressions then, it is not just the meaning of a sentence that determines what can hang together with what (though this is certainly yet another dimension of the problem). Further, whatever the interpretation of this array of facts -- and there is substantial dispute about the formulation of principles like constituent command -- one point is clear: to the extent that one can make binding constraints like the Specified Subject and c-command precise, one can replace vague intuitions about "text cohesion" with justifiable principles, a true theory of binding.[2]

A constrained theory of binding also offers substantial computational bonuses. For instance, as observed in [Berwick and Wexler 1982], the c-command

1. For our purposes here, a phrase α constituent commands another phrase β if the first branching category that dominates α dominates β. See [Reinhart 1976] for the original formulation.

2. Compare, for example, Halliday's unconstrained account (cited by Webber) of how cohesiveness in a text is obtained through "word substitution": substitution is "specified through the use of a grammatical signal indicating that it is to be recovered from what has gone before." This just restates the observation that pronouns and abbreviatory phrases are substituted for previously mentioned expressions. It is a description of what is to be explained.

constraint cuts down the computation that must be done in co-indexing expressions with antecedents (at least as formulated within a parsing framework like that of [Marcus 1980]); in the best case, it reduces the "search space" of possible antecedents by an exponential factor.[1] This is, of course, a familiar lesson in artificial intelligence research: by imposing appropriate constraints, one can eliminate the need for blind, combinatorial search. In short, the study of regularities in binding relationships within single sentences has led to the discovery of a set of representational constraints, and these constraints can apparently be exploited by computational models. To the extent that such constraints account for an array of linguistic facts and can be naturally incorporated into parsing and generation models, we advance towards the goals of characterizing what knowledge of language is and how that knowledge is put to use.

Now, this analysis is obviously just a start. So far, all we have said is that there seem to be two sorts of linguistic phenomena, those that obey some sort of constraints (and hence that one might say we partially understand) and those that do not (and hence remain mysteries). Relabeling the mysteries as "context-dependent" or "part of discourse" helps not at all. What is needed, as [Williams 1977] observes,

> is a careful articulation of the discourse component of grammar, on a par with what has been done for Sentence Grammar. If it is a theoretically valid entity, then it will be possible to formulate it as a set of rules governed by generally valid laws. It is not likely, in my opinion, that everything that has been named under the term "discourse grammar" will be explained by a single coherent theory; more likely, explanations will follow from the interaction of a number of distinct theories.
> [1977 page 138]

In Williams' scheme, rules like each other interpretation and certain cases of quantifier indexing apply at a level of syntactic structure, within individual sentences; they output a level of representation loosely called logical form (LF). In contrast, the rules that interpret they, the others, or ones (to cite an example that Webber is concerned with) apply after the rules of sentence grammar.

---

1. To see this, note that in the case of a full binary tree with n leaves and with a pronoun on the right-most branch, about n interior nodes have to be examined for co-indexing without the c-command condition, but only about log n nodes with the c-command condition.

What evidence is there that there are rules that operate on logical rather than syntactic forms? Consider an example that [Williams 1977] offers:

(8) Speaker 1: Bob left.
    Speaker 2: Bill will, too.

The second sentence has a missing Verb Phrase that is, intuitively, supplied by the first sentence:

(9) S1: Bob   [left]$_{VP}$
    S2: Bill will [empty]$_{VP}$ too

As Williams observes however, it cannot be that the VP of the second sentence is reconstructed by copying (or co-indexing) the <u>syntactic</u> VP of the first sentence, since the result is ill-formed:

(10) S1: Bob   [left]$_{VP_i}$.

     S2: Bill will   [empty]$_{VP_i}$ too.

     *Bill will left too.

In contrast, copying makes sense if it is some part of the <u>logical</u> form that is copied or co-indexed. Thus there are actual <u>data</u> that support Webber's insight that the anaphoric relationship between pronouns and NP's cannot be accounted for just by copying surface or text strings.

Adopting Williams' proposal about the representation of tense in logical form (open to dispute, but not at issue here), one would have the following:[1]

---

1. In more detail, Williams proposes that <u>Bill left</u> has roughly the following LF structure:
(11) [Past (Bill)$_{NP}$ [λx(x leave)]$_{VP}$]$_S$

While one may conceivably copy (or co-index) any part of this formula to the "empty" position in <u>Bob will too</u>, only copying the VP in square brackets results in a well-formed LF.

(12) S1:   [Bob   [left]$_{VP}$] (level of syntactic representation)

<---Rule of tense interpretation

[Past [Bob [leave]$_{VP}$ (level of logical form)

<---Rule of VP co-indexing
   S2:   [Future [Bill [empty]$_{VP_i}$ too] (level of logical form)

This example also points out the striking similarity of this approach to Webber's and Sidner's work: figuring out how how tense is represented at the level of LF is just the kind of question that Webber seeks to answer, while the rule of VP co-indexing (or copying) is just the sort of rule that Sidner wants to formulate. In the remainder of this section, we shall see in more detail just how close these approaches are.   In particular, one can show that Webber's representational language is compatible with recent proposals for the structure of LF, and that Webber's account of one anaphora is simply another Discourse Grammar "rule of construal", just like the VP copying rule. Importantly, one key finding that Williams' approach does not subsume is Sidner's observation that the co-indexing rules for pronoun interpretation appear to follow push-down stack discipline; as we will see, this is the Discourse Grammar analogue of the Specified Subject condition.   If Sidner's theory is correct, then the rules of Discourse Grammar are constrained in a computationally advantageous fashion, just as the rules of Sentence Grammar seem to be.

1.2.2 Creating discourse entities: Webber

Webber's research goal, then, is a logical precondition to Sidner's work. Discourse co-indexing involves co-indexing at the representational level of LF; therefore, before one can know which discourse entities are linked, one must know what the space of candidate indexable entities is. In the case of single sentences, one set of possible indexable objects corresponds to phrases that can be displaced according to a transformational movement rule:

(13) The officer arrested John$\Rightarrow$
     [John]$_{NP_i}$ was arrested [empty]$_i$ by the officer.

For Webber, the analogue of this task is the proper formulation of an LF syntax for Noun Phrases, or, as she puts it, the "combinatoric representation" of Noun Phrases "naturally evoked" by a text. Here we may take "naturally evoke" to be a gloss for an ⟨LF, domain of individuals⟩ pairing -- that is, each LF expression corresponding to an input string is paired with the set of individuals that it could denote. Webber's work involves specifying these three components: the LF language, the domains of individuals, and the pairing function. A key point of the work is that the mapping between LF expressions and sets of individuals is a function, not a relation. Therefore, alternative "meanings" derived from a single input string, such as the alternative collective/individuative readings of, "Three boys [each/together] ate a pizza," cannot hinge on the pairing function, which can only associate one denotation with an LF expression. The only alternative is to construct <u>different</u> LF expressions for different readings, one for each alternative.

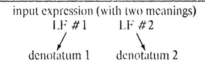

input expression (with two meanings)
LF #1   LF #2

denotatum 1   denotatum 2

Figure 3 A syntactic representation of differences in meaning.

Which distinctions in meaning are to be captured by logical form itself, as opposed to varying the domains of objects over which predicates may range? Recall what machinery is at our command for capturing such distinctions. All we can rely on is syntax: we can vary the order in which expressions are laid out in a line. This is how the ambiguity is "everyone loves someone" has classically been encoded: by reversing the order of quantification ($\exists\forall$ or $\forall\exists$). Similarly, all of Webber's meaning distinctions that are encoded via LF differences in form are done so by varying the scoping of various quantifiers. Webber handles the following distinctions:

distinction	operator/quantifier used to obtain distinction via scoping
collective/individuative	$\lambda u:SET -- SET(\lambda u)$
universal/existential	$\exists\forall -- \forall\exists$
definite/indefinite	$\exists! -- \exists$
cardinality	$|x|$

How are surface strings to be mapped to LF expressions? For the most part, this is not the subject of Webber's research. However, she makes the following rough-and-ready association between surface constituent structure (a representation that might be delivered by a parser) and LF expressions:

Phrase type	LF form
Verbs	Predicates
Relative clauses	lambda-abstracted predicate
Adjectives	Restriction clause in quantification
Nouns	Restrict domain of quantification
Prepositions	Predicates (e.g., On(x))
Articles, Determiners, etc.	Quantifiers as described in text
Number quantifiers plurals	Counting restriction on domain of quantification

Evaluating the Webber theory

How can Webber's proposals for LF be evaluated? The question to keep in mind here is why Webber has adopted this particular logical language in which to map surface phrases to LF expressions rather than some other. At first glance, uncovering evidence that would choose among alternative proposals would seem to be problematic: what we are talking about, at least for people, are differences in form that are not visible at the "surface". At best, we can observe only indirectly the effects of different choices for a logical form, and so there can only be indirect evidence that bears on our choice.

Pursuing this line of discussion, why should one an adopt a logical form that is different from surface phrasal form at all? The null hypothesis, after all, would be to simply assume that LF looks just like a surface parse of the input string:

(14) I saw John --> (I (saw (John)))   (surface parse = the LF)

instead of the predicate calculus formula:

(15) Saw (I, John)

It would certainly be computationally simpler to just adopt the former sort of representation as our LF; then no translation at all would be required. In short, one must furnish some sort of an argument for why LF should look like a prenex normal form rather than just its surface form.

As it turns out, however, there is evidence for adopting an LF in a prenex form, at least for sentences containing such quantifiers as every and some. This is the well-known evidence for an optional rule that moves quantifiers from the place where they occur in surface form and adjoins them to the front of the nearest "S" (sentence) node. (The rule of "quantifier raising" -- "QR" -- proposed in [May 1977]).

This model predicts that sentences in which there are two quantifiers and only one S-boundary, such as, "Everyone loves someone," should be ambiguous. The reason: since the rule QR can apply in any order to first move "everyone" and then "someone", or vice-versa, we can derive two structures, one in which "everyone" takes wide scope over "someone", and one in which it does not. And in fact such sentences are ambiguous in just this way. It is in this sense that QR accounts for the apparent ambiguity of such sentences. Similarly, the QR model predicts that sentences in which there are two quantifiers but one is embedded in such a way that the rule QR must cross two boundaries will <u>not</u> be ambiguous. This prediction too is borne out, accounting for the apparent lack of ambiguity in such sentences as,"Everyone believes that John loves someone":[1]

In short, by assuming QR to be a movement rule, we can use the same constraints on movement known to hold in other cases to account for the observed surface distribution of ambiguous quantifier readings.

Similarly, judgments about group vs. individual readings of sentences such as, Three boys ate a pizza seem to be conditioned by a rule of QR. In the reading where three boys separately eat a pizza, we may assume that the rule QR has applied to front the quantifier term three boys:

(16) [Three x_i, x_i a boy, [x_i Ate a pizza]]

When QR does not apply, we get a collective interpretation where the three boys as a group eat a pizza:

(17) [three boys Ate a pizza]

Webber's use of a SET operator in this case parallels the work done by QR; SET may be ordered either inside or outside the argument to the verb. Schematically,

---

<hr>

1. As it turns out, judgments when the quasi-quantifiers the or a are substituted for every are much less precise. But recall that this may be because these items are not "true" quantifiers at all, hence are not subject to QR.

(18) SET [x_i, x_i a boy] [x_i ate a pizza]
    (A set of three x_i's that each ate a pizza.)
SET [three boys],u [u ate a pizza]
    (A group of three boys that ate a pizza.)

Webber's use of restricted quantification, as in,

(19) ∃x: boy

to indicate that X has been drawn from the domain of individuals that are boys, is also fairly standard. For example, it follows the notation chosen by [Chomsky 1975]:

(20) Who did John kiss -->
    Wh-x, x a person,John kissed x

In sum, to the extent that Webber uses LF differences, particularly scoping differences, to account for different sentence readings, the representational format adopted by Webber stands squarely within twentieth century philosophical and current linguistic tradition.

1.2.3 Computing the Webber LF

We are left then with the question of computation. Given an input sentence, or a pre-parsed representation of a sentence, how hard is it to actually construct Webber's LF? Here we must be careful to distinguish between two aspects of the complexity of a system such as Webber's. First, there is the complexity of simply translating from surface strings to a prenex form. Second, there is the complexity of actually computing the predicates implied by the representations so constructed -- e.g., "Ate Bill, x". These are two different, though obviously connected tasks. The second depends on the predicates involved, how domains of individuals are actually defined, and so forth; it is thus difficult to make any claims about the complexity of this problem without a model. As we shall see, part of what Kaplan and Allen aim to do is to in fact propose simple world models for restricted domains so as to actually provide an interpretation for a Webber-type LF. We will restrict ourselves here to the complexity of just the translation of surface strings to a prenex form.

Even so restricted, interesting questions of computational complexity arise. Suppose that we adopt Webber's prenex form. It is relatively easy to show that if the input and output languages for the translation can be generated by a particularly restricted context-free grammar, then the translation will take only time linear in the length of the input strings, using push-down stack machinery. However, if we assume anything like a "real-life" phrase structure (with NP and VP nodes), then it can be shown that the translation will take more than simple push-down machinery.[1] In short, translating to a prenex form quickly is not necessarily a trivial task.

To gain some appreciation of the issues involved here, we will consider a simplified prenex translation and then show that even this minimal procedure will demand at least push-down store processing.

Suppose that the input language consists of English surface strings already translated into some kind of labeled bracketing -- a parse tree, like that provided by, e.g., the Marcus parser. Further assume that there is but one parse tree output for each separate input string -- an obviously false simplifying assumption, given the existence of structurally ambiguous sentences. The output language, the LF, is also assumed to be uniquely readable (unambiguous). A simple grammar for the input language, ignoring the existence of VP structure, might look like this:

$S \Rightarrow NP_1 \, V \, NP_2$; $NP \Rightarrow NP \, (S)$
$NP \Rightarrow$ Determiner(Adjective) Noun or Name
Noun $\Rightarrow$ boy, girl; Determiner $\Rightarrow$ a, every;
Adjective $\Rightarrow$ big, young,...
$V \Rightarrow$ loves; Name $\Rightarrow$ John, Mary,...

Given the input string, "John loves a girl", the desired prenex output is,

($\exists$x:girl) loves John, x

Even given these immense simplifications however the translation is still not computationally trivial. Why is this? Intuitively, the reason is that the order of the NP arguments can be reversed in the translation -- <u>John</u> precedes <u>a girl</u> in surface syntax, but the order is reversed in the LF. This suggests that one must either (1) abandon the prenex form; or (2) move to a powerful sort of computational machinery.

More formally, suppose that the mapping is effected by a syntax-directed translation. That is, for every context-free rule of the grammar for the input language, we associate a corresponding translation re-write rule. Each time that a re-write rule is used to build a portion of the input language parse tree, the

---

1. Though linear time translation is still possible on an augmented processor.

corresponding rule is triggered to build the tree for the output LF string. (Thus syntax-directed translation maps trees to trees.)

Given the input rule, $S \Rightarrow NP_1 \ V \ NP_2$ we therefore have a corresponding output rule that looks something like,

$T(NP_2) \ V \ NP_1 \ X_2$, where $T(NP_2) =$ the translation of NP_2, whatever that may be; and $X_2 =$ a new terminal element of the output language, a placeholder for the argument NP_2.

This is a so-called <u>non-simple</u> syntax-directed translation schema, so-called because the output rule has non-terminals in an order different from the order they appear in the corresponding input rule (here NP_1 and NP_2). But a theorem of formal language theory tells us this kind of translation may demand fairly powerful computational machinery: A syntax directed translation is <u>simple</u> if and only if it can be described by a non-deterministic push-down automaton. Therefore, we can conclude that even in this overly-simplified case, the translation demanded by Webber's prenex form cannot be done by a non-deterministic push-down automaton.[1]

Intuitively, the reversal translation cannot be done by a push-down automaton because all of the second NP must be constructed before we ever output the translation string, $NP_2 \ V$. But since NP_2 may be recursive, as in a relative clause, this could take forever, and we would have to process all of the input before ever constructing any part of the output LF. Even in this restricted case, then, the translation from surface string to prenex form can run into computational difficulties. There are two ways to proceed. First, as we did above, one could move to a non-simple syntax-directed translation. [Aho and Ullman 1973] show that an extension of a push-down machine, a <u>push-down processor</u>, can simulate all such translations.[2] Second, one could modify the Webber prenex form so that

---

1. See [Aho and Ullman 1972 page 230].
2. A push-down processor has the power to manipulate pointers to a directed graph, rather than just a list of nodes. It can also examine <u>k</u> nodes up its push-down stack, rather just one. The machine can add or delete directed edges to a graph, connecting nodes that it currently points to; it can also create new nodes and label them. Because it can connect new nodes to either the left or the right of old nodes, such a machine can permute the output tree (the graph) it constructs with respect to the tree specified by the input grammar -- hence its ability to handle non-simple constructions. Such a machine can, however still be quite efficient, operating in time linear in the length of input strings if the underlying grammar for the translation is LR(k) or LL(k). (See the section of this chapter on McDonald's system for a definition of LR(k) and LL(k) grammars. An LR(k) grammar is, roughly, one that generates a language that can be parsed deterministically, left-to-right, with the parse tree being constructed from bottom to top.) The Marcus parser is basically a push-down processor of this sort, operating with an extended LR(k)-grammar.

it is simple.

Consider option (2). Suppose that we adopt Williams' scheme in part, so that the translation of NP_1 V NP_2 is NP_1 NP_2 V^* X_1 X_2, X_1 and X_2 being placeholder elements for the arguments NP_1 and NP_2. For example, John loves Mary will now get mapped to the form, "$John_1$ $Mary_2$ loves X_1 X_2". Observe that this now is a simple syntax-directed translation -- the order of non-terminals in input and output rules is the same. We illustrate an example translation of John loves every boy:

stack:

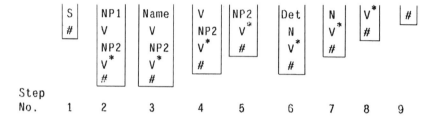

S	NP1	Name	V	NP2	Det	N	V^*	#
#	V	V	NP2	V^*	N	V^*	#	
	NP2	NP2	V^*	#	V^*	#		
	V^*	V^*	#		#			
	#	#						

Step
No.   1   2   3   4   5   6   7   8   9

(Recall that a syntax-directed translation requires that the symbols of the output translation grammar be interspersed with those of the input grammar. This is the reason for the appearance of the distinct V and V^* symbols.)

However, there is one problem with this method. Observe that this translation considers the verb as if it were a terminal item. That is, there is no VP structure as such. If this assumption is misguided, and we must have a distinct Verb Phrase, then the translation is again no longer simple, because the output grammar will have non-terminals in the order NP--V, corresponding to an input grammar order of V--NP. But then we need more than push-down stack machinery to carry out what needs to be done.

In short, our conclusion is that it is quite difficult to obtain a simple syntax-directed translation to cover anything like the translation involved in natural language. In any real case, we are likely to need at least the power of a push-down processor, rather than a simple push-down automaton. We see then that even when we restrict our attention to just the first step in the translation assumed by Webber's theory, interesting questions of computational complexity arise. In order to maintain computational feasibility, we must either modify the prenex normal form (perhaps in an unrealistic way), or else adopt computational machinery that is beyond what one might expect to require. Even in this case, if one demands linear time operation, it may well be that the underlying grammar for the input language must be LR(k) or LR(k)-like.

1.2.4 Linking discourse entities: Sidner

To see where we have gotten so far, consider following discourse:

> (21) There were some strawberries in the fridge.
> They were tasty, and didn't last long.

Webber's model provides us with a representation for a discourse entity evoked by the Noun Phrase some strawberries, or a representation for the clause as a whole. The first kind of representation results in an output something like:

> (22) $\lambda v:set(strawberries).in-fridge \ v$

Webber's model also can construct a similar representation for they. What it does not tell us, however, is that they and some strawberries are intended to pick out the same "objects" of a (presumably mental) representation -- that is, that these two NP's are co-indexed. Webber's rule give us a representation of all possible things being "talked about" in a discourse, but leaves us with the computational problem of picking out the right form to co-index with a subsequent pronoun or definite NP. Of course, there is a brute force way out of this dilemma. Since Webber's rules are supposed to exhaust the space of possible discourse entities, they are meant to exhaustively enumerate all representations for the NPs some strawberries and they. One could then simply try all possible anaphor-antecedent co-indexing combinations, subject to constraints of plausibility, meaningfulness, and so forth. The problem with this approach is two-fold. First, there can be an enormous number of possibilities to try. Let us call this the co-indexing proposal problem. As computationalists, we should worry about this. In the worst case, as researchers in computational linguistics have discovered, the possibilities explode so that exponential computational resources may be required.[1] Second, the predicate tests implicit in the terms

---

1. To see this, consider the case where there is some leading pattern of Noun Phrases, NP_1, NP_2,...,NP_n followed by a pattern of pronouns to which it must be linked, $Pronoun_1$,...,$Pronoun_n$. There are an exponential number of possible patterns of binding relationships between antecedent NP's and pronouns. If all of these must be explicitly investigated, exponential resources will be consumed.

"plausibility" and "meaningfulness" remain unelaborated. Let us call this second difficulty the co-indexing confirmation problem.

Sidner's research aims to solve just the first of these problems, the co-indexing proposal problem. Sidner's solution, not surprisingly, is to posit an additional constraint that cuts down the space of possible antecedent-anaphor pairs that must be examined. Out of all the NPs potentially available for co-indexing in a text at a given point, only one, designated the current focus is actually available as the "first choice" for co-indexing. The key idea is that what is currently being talked about, the so-called current focus establishes a local context of "first resort" for resolving anaphora relationships. In the sentences above, since "strawberries" is the current focus at the time they is encountered, by default they is co-indexed with strawberries. If for some reason the local binding fails, then and only then will alternatives be tried. For instance, if the second sentence was, "He....", then because the default antecedent strawberries is plural the default binding would be rejected.

How is focus changed? Simply by proposing and confirming a new potential focus, just as the very first focus of a discourse is computed. Note however that the current focus serves as the default co-indexer until it is dislodged by explicit disconfirmation. Thus the pattern for computing a new focus when a current focus already exists must be to (1) propose a new focus; (2) disconfirm the current focus; and (3) confirm the new focus. (Actually, (1) and (2) could be interchanged.) What happens to the old focus? Sidner claims that previous foci are available for later use. Indeed, there seems to be some evidence -- suggestive but not overwhelming -- that old foci are maintained in a last-in, first-out order.[1] As we shall see, this stack constraint, if true, has the effect of limiting the number of antecedent-anaphor bindings that must be investigated, and in certain cases entirely eliminates the combinatorial search for antecedents that marked earlier computational systems dealing with anaphora resolution. It is a kind of multi-sentence analogue of certain single sentence constraints such as the Specified Subject Constraint [Chomsky 1975] or Subjacency [Chomsky 1977]. Such a finding is of immense interest to the computationalist, because such constraints play a valuable role in restricting the amount of work that a language processor must do. For example, [Marcus 1980] has suggested that Subjacency and the Specified Subject Constraint are intimately connected to the design of a machine that can parse English fairly efficiently on-line without backup. If

---

1. Sidner says nothing about whether a "stack" of foci can be of arbitrary depth. Presumably, as is typically assumed, there is some finite limit to the amount of material that can be retained in such a manner.

Sidner's constraints on discourse can be maintained, they provide a similar and important wedge into the difficult task of constraining the computational complexity of multi-sentence interpretation. It is also of interest that Sidner's explanation is an essentially modular one; it blends a representational framework, basically Webber's, with a computational proposal. The result is an interaction that produces complex surface behavior from two quite simple, interacting sub-components.[1]

How exactly is the computation of foci carried out? If the focus machine is on virgin soil, then its first step is to make a list of what could be a focus -- what Sidner calls "potential foci." This amounts to an exhaustive case analysis. The expected focus (before confirmation) is:

> (i) The subject of a sentence in a be copulative sentence. ("There is a book on the table;" "John is sick." or

> (ii) The theme of the sentence (roughly, the "affected object", in Jackendoff's terminology), as in, "John hit the car." or the theme of the Verb complement, if the complement is sentential. or

> (iii) Other thematic positions (such as instrument, in "John hit the car with a hammer", with the agent last in this list. or

> (iv) The Verb Phrase itself.

However, there is really no need for this case-by-case definition of how foci are proposed. The reason is that the list just enumerates every possible thematic position in a sentence, and throws in the Verb Phrase to boot. It would seem more economical to simply replace Sidner's list with the following shorter definition:

> (23) FOCUS = a representation of the x such that P(x), where P(x) is a predication in x corresponding to the main verb.

There is one purpose, though, that is served by Sidner's list: it provides an

---

1. Below we shall see that by grafting an additional layer of structure onto Sidner's basic theory -- a theory of task-oriented discourse structure proposed by [Grosz 1978] -- the Sidner approach can be made to handle discourses that go beyond simple narratives.

order for checking potential foci. That is, the potential focus is first considered to be the Subject of a be copula sentence; if the sentence is not be copular, the theme of the sentence is considered to be the most promising potential focus; if the theme cannot be confirmed as focus, other thematic roles are checked, and so forth. If we translate this ranking into the "predication" formulation of focus, we see that this order simply makes explicit a set of heuristics for determining what the predication of the sentence is. This fact is relevant in that some independent work has been done in classifying the way in which the predication of a sentence is determined, and the results apparently re-state Sidner's potential foci heuristics. This coincidence thus provides some additional evidence that the re-definition of focus as "the x such that P(x)" is on the right track. It also extends Sidner's list, in that some cases are handled that are not covered by her original set of heuristics.

Let us sketch out some of the results of this linguistic work in more detail; the theory is that of [Williams 1980]. Let us say that there is a rule that builds predicate structure out of constituent structure by means of co-indexing, thereby associating predicates with arguments. The general co-indexing schema is simply,

(24) Co-index NP and X
    where X = an Adjective Phrase (AP), a PP,
    an NP, a VP, or an S

There is certainly not much in the way of constraint in this proposal. What is missing is the machinery telling us which NP's and X's are to be co-indexed, a matter which we will take up shortly. Assuming for now that the rules exist to properly co-index items, their effect will be to map a constituent structure like (i) below into structure (ii):

(25) (i) $[[_{NP}John]$ is $[_{AP}$ sick$]]$

Predication co-indexing

(ii) $[[_{NP}$ John$]_i$ is $[_{AP}$ sick$]_i]$

The NP John and the AP sick wind up with identical indices, corresponding -- perhaps -- to intuitions that sick is being predicated of John. Co-indexing thus has the effect of telling us which thing x is being predicated about -- that is, of pointing out to us "the X such that P(X)". Given proper co-indexing, a trivial rule of focus interpretation can then supply the right focus:

(26) $[[_{NP} \text{ John}] \text{ is } [_{AP} \text{ sick}]]$

Predication co-indexing

$[[_{NP} \text{ John}]_i \text{ is } [_{AP} \text{ sick}]_i]$

$X \qquad P(X)$

Focus interpretation

$\text{FOCUS} = X = [_{NP}\text{John}]$

In this sense the focus rule is simply a rule of interpretation, relating a representation at one level (that of constituent structure) to another level (that at which other "semantic interpretive" rules operate). Besides these cases of predication that are grammatically (structurally) based, there are examples of thematic predication control. As both Sidner and Williams observe, in such cases the NP that is the focus or Subject of the predication can be properly located if it is identified with the theme of the sentence, where theme corresponds roughly to the notion of "affected object." This approach is only as good as one's ability to identify the theme of a sentence, a problem that is fraught with difficulties of its own. (See, for example, the studies of "case frame" representations of sentences; [Fillmore 1968]; [Jackendoff 1972].) In any case, at worst (Williams notes) each verb can be individually marked so that it will indicate which NP is the theme. For example, the verb struck probably requires exceptional marking to handle a sentence such as,

(27) John struck Bill as foolish.

Here, John is the Subject of the predication of the sentence, hence the (initial) focus. In contrast, in

(28) John struck Bill.

Bill is the affected object or theme, hence the prime potential focus.

Let us now see how this revised definition of focus can subsume the original initial expected focus algorithm.

1. there-insertion and be copula cases.
(i) On the standard trace-theoretic analysis, the annotated surface structure of there insertion sentences is roughly like the following, with the lexical NP following the copula be co-indexed to there:

There are people in the room.

$[_{NP}$ there$]_i$ [be] [NP]$_i$ [in the room]

As a result, these sentences fall together with schema 1 of grammatical predication control, NP be AP, with AP = the remaining postverbal complement; the NP is the Subject of the predication, hence the focus, just as dictated by Sidner's algorithm.

(ii) Be-copulas fall directly under schema 1 of grammatical control: the NP subject is the Subject of the Predication.

2. Theme as focus: All cases where focus is the theme of a sentence fall under the heading of thematic control of predication co-indexing. Once again, the Subject of the predication (as determined by the co-indexing rules) corresponds precisely to the initial focus.

3. Other thematic roles: other roles marked by the verb (such as Instrument) are sometimes optional; that is why they are in general lower in the hierarchy of potential foci. There are two subcases: the additional roles can be either obligatory -- required by the verb -- or optional.

(i) Obligatory thematic roles: these are, e.g., the recipient of an action, as in double object constructions such as, Bill in I gave the strawberries to Bill.

(ii) Truly optional thematic roles: thematic elements that need not be present for the sentence to make sense, e.g., optional Prepositional Phrases, as in, I kissed Sue at sundown.

Note, as might be expected if focus is linked to the predication of a sentence, that such optional elements are less highly valued as potential foci; this is because these thematic elements do not play an essential role in the predication structure of the verb. By identifying focus with predication structure we thus obtain a simple explanation of the ordering of potential focus preferences that is observed but not accounted for by Sidner.

Having calculated the likely candidate foci, the second step in the focus co-indexing computation is confirmation. A potential focus is confirmed when it is known that a following pronoun or definite NP can be co-indexed to the potential focus. A potential focus is disconfirmed if it is determined that the individual or set of individual elements picked out by the focus cannot be the same set of individuals picked out by a following pronoun or definite NP. Once a focus has been confirmed, it is the current focus and serves as the first choice for any later co-indexing.

This reformulation of focus in the quantifier-like form, "the X s.t. P(X)" suggests that one can represent focus structurally, in a by-now familiar operator-bound variable form:

(29) John was hit by a car -->

$[[\text{John}]_{NP_i} [\text{was hit}] [\text{by a car}]]$ -->

$\text{John}_i [\text{a car hit } NP_i]$
the X_i such that $P(x_i)$

Note the similarity of this structure to that formed by the quantifier rule QR, discussed earlier. Indeed, as we shall see, there is evidence that the rule that forms "focus structure" is just the move-α rule in yet another guise. Moreover, the structure is quite close to that constructed by Webber's rules that build LF -- not surprisingly, seeing as the basic building block of Webber's LF is a move-α rule as well.

A confirming sentence will also be in this x--P(x) form:

(30) He was hurt badly -->

$\text{He}_i [NP_i \text{ was hurt badly.}]$

Taken together, the current focus along with its co-indexed pronoun determines a set of propositions, with each proposition saying something about the focused entity:

$x_i = \text{John}$

$P_1 = \text{a car hit } x_i$
$P_2 = x_i \text{ was hurt badly}$

Let us call this bundle of propositions about a particular focus a focus context.

How is a focus (or a focus context) changed? One can propose and confirm a new focus. Consider the following dialogue from Sidner:

(31) Wilbur is a fine scientist and a delightful guy.
He gave me a book a while back which I really enjoyed.
It was on relativity theory and talked mostly about quarks.
They are hard to imagine, because they indicate
    the need for elementary field theories.
These theories are tremendously complicated.

It is apparent that the last sentence is talking about elementary field theories, even if somehow it is still "embedded" in talking about Wilbur and the book. Indeed, this introspective sense that the intervening Noun Phrases such as Wilbur and the book are somehow still accessible can be confirmed by the addition of a single sentence with a pronoun:

(32) Anyway, I got it while I was working on the initial part of my research.

The use of an anaphoric it forces one to "pop back" to retrieve the (formally represented) description of the book. More importantly, Sidner observes that this behavior is stack-like, in that the intervening foci between book and field theories -- quarks -- are apparently "lost" when one accesses the book. A picture of the change in accessible Noun Phrase descriptions might look like this:

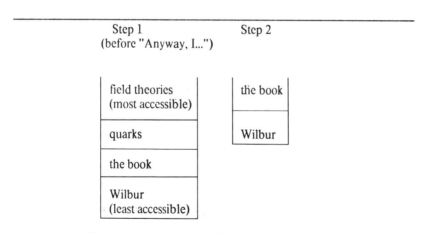

Figure 4 Accessible Noun Phrases in a stack model.

Although intuitions are not completely clear here, it is interesting to ponder what the force of the stack claim comes to. Consider a weaker, alternative hypothesis: that the "things talked about" in a discourse can be represented by an unordered list. To be concrete, let us say that items enter memory as they are mentioned, and then are available for anaphoric access subject to a decay limitation depending on the "time" since the item was last mentioned. (Let us ignore obvious objections about how "time" is to be measured, intervening effects, and the like; this "list" hypothesis is meant to be illustrative, not a serious suggestion about actual discourse behavior.) Note that with a decay factor added, the list is not <u>really</u> unordered, since items are ordered in an accessibility hierarchy depending upon recency of mention. On this alternative view, <u>Wilbur</u>, <u>the</u> <u>book</u>, and <u>quarks</u> are all still accessible after <u>it</u> is used to pick out <u>the</u> <u>book</u> in the "Anyway" sentence, but now <u>the</u> <u>books</u> is more accessible (since it was last "refreshed" by being pointed at by the anaphor <u>it</u>). This list hypothesis thus contrasts with Sidner's:

Step 1	Step 2
(Wilbur, the book, quarks, field theories)	(Wilbur, Q, FT, the book)
Increasing accessibility -->	

Figure 5 Accessible Noun Phrases in a list decay model.

Which structure more adequately reflects human discourse behavior? If the list decay model were correct, then we would expect either <u>quarks</u> or <u>field</u> theories to be (relatively) accessible for anaphoric contact after the "Anyway" sentence (20), just as <u>the</u> book was. However, this seems not to be the case, for sentences where one attempts to point back to either of these old, presumably accessible foci seem difficult to comprehend:

> (33) Wilbur is a fine scientist and a delightful guy.
> He gave me a book a while back which I really enjoyed.
> It was on relativity theory and talked mostly about quarks.
> They are hard to imagine, because they indicate the need for elementary field theories.
> These theories are tremendously complicated.
> Anyway, I got it when I was working on the initial part of my research.
> ?They [i.e., quarks] were named from a line in a James Joyce novel.

Instead, one is apparently forced to re-introduce such items by full Noun Phrases, as if one were "starting over again", e.g.,

> (34) Quarks were named from a line by James Joyce.
> They were first hypothesized in the early 1960's.

On the other hand, the old focus <u>Wilbur</u> -- an item that should have "decayed" as much if not more than <u>quarks</u> -- is easily accessible:

> (35) Wilbur is a fine scientist and a delightful guy.
> He gave me a book a while back which I really enjoyed.
> It was on relativity theory and talked mostly about quarks.
> They are hard to imagine, because they indicate the need for
> elementary field theories.
> These theories are tremendously complicated.
> Anyway, I got it when I was working on the initial part of
> my research.
> He's [Wilbur] a really nice guy for having given it to me.

Both aspects of this behavior are naturally explained by a stack, because if foci follow push-down store discipline, then <u>Wilbur</u> becomes the first accessible item after the discourse "pops back" to <u>the book</u>, and the intervening focus <u>quarks</u> is lost, thus forcing one to re-introduce quarks all over again. In contrast, an unordered or list decay approach cannot easily explain either the apparent loss of old foci or the apparently "refreshed" accessibility of other old foci.

1.2.5 Evidence for Sidner's focus theory

Intuitions about dialogues such as the one above, though suggestive, are shaky enough that one ought to cast about for other kinds of confirming evidence for Sidner's model. Here there are some general points to be made. First of all, Sidner's representation of focus mimics the rule of QR, with its Qx--P(x) form. Second, Sidner's representation is compatible with stress phenomena that are known to interact with focus. This is a particularly interesting property, since it hints at how one would begin to integrate properties of spoken language into a model of discourse. Finally, the stack-like behavior of foci is analogous to the more familiar case of syntactic opacity. Let us review this evidence in turn.

Syntactically, there are a variety of mechanisms that create structures of the form, "the x s.t. P(x)":

> Topicalization: Strawberries, I never liked [e]

> Wh-questions: Who did John kiss [e]?

> <u>It</u> clefts: It was John that [e] ate the strawberries.

In each case, the fronted item is intuitively the focus of the sentence. Thus, if the "x s.t. P(x)" form is in fact the right one for focus, then, as expected, syntactic operations that create this form also alter what is in focus.

Further, there is suggestive evidence (pointed out by [Chomsky 1976]) that stress interacts with focus via the machinery of variable binding or co-indexing. A focused NP acts like a quantified expression -- further support for the "x--P(x)" formulation. If this is so, then as a side benefit the re-formulation of focus as an "x--P(x)" structure would allow us to incorporate sentence stress into the focus model -- a feature that was not accommodated in Sidner's original proposal.

The key insight here is to observe that according to the "x--P(x)" formulation, the "s-structure" of a sentence -- roughly, its constituent structure augmented with an indication of moved constituents -- mechanically determines the focus of a sentence, or at least the primary contender for the focus. For example, consider the topicalized sentence:

(36) Strawberries, I never liked.

Assuming now that this sentence has an abstract constituent structure with an "empty" NP acting as a placeholder for the normal position in which "strawberries" would be found:

(37) [Strawberries]$_{NP}$ [$_S$ I [$_{VP}$never liked [$_{NP}$empty]]]

then the sentence is in X--P(X) form:

$$(38) \; [\text{Strawberries}]_{NP} \; [_S \; I \; [_{VP}\text{never liked} \; [_{NP}\text{empty}]]]$$
$$ X \qquad\qquad\qquad P(x) \quad \text{<--focus form}$$

The focus can then be mechanically recovered.

On the phonetic side, under the usual assumptions of modern generative grammar, s-structure also determines phonetic form (PF), in particular, stress. That is, there are rules that map s-structures to phonetic representations indicating stress:

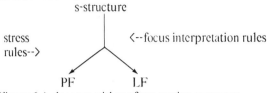

Figure 6 A decomposition of generative grammar.

It is important to observe that the stress rules do not interact with LF except in the sense that there is a common intermediary representation, s-structure, that serves as the base data structure for both the rules that form representations of stress and the rules that form representations of focus. Thus the hearer has an indirect route that can be used to deduce what focus must be, given stress, even though stress does not, in itself, determine focus. Namely, if the stress rules are invertible,[1] then s-structure can be recovered -- this is just part of parsing. Given s-structure, the focus rules may be applied to recover the focus.

To see how focus interacts with stress, consider the cases discussed by [Chomsky 1976]. The sentence,

(39) The woman he loved betrayed someone.

cannot be interpreted with he = someone. On the other hand, if someone appears to the left of the pronoun he, then co-indexing of he and someone is acceptable (but not necessary).

(40) [Someone]$_i$ was betrayed by the woman [he]$_i$ loved.

The reason for this follows from a more general restriction on co-indexing, namely, that a quantifier cannot bind a pronoun to its left. Compare, for example,[2]

(41) (i) *That he$_i$ was drafted shouldn't bother every soldier$_i$.
      (ii) That he$_i$ was drafted shouldn't bother Bill$_i$.

In (39) the quantifier someone cannot bind he for just this reason.

Now consider the stressed counterparts to these sentences. (41i) below, with

1. An additional assumption that must be justified: it is presumably not a necessary property of these rules that they are one-to-one, so that an inverse exists.
2. These sentences are from [Hornstein 1981].

<u>John</u> stressed, is just like (39) in that <u>he</u> cannot be co-indexed with <u>John</u>; in contrast, in (41ii), <u>betrayed</u> receives main stress, and <u>he</u> may be co-indexed with <u>John</u>:

> (42) (i) The woman he loved betrayed JOHN.
>   (ii) The woman he loved BETRAYED John.

Why is this? Following Chomsky, suppose that the focus structure for (42i) is as in (43):

> (43) John-- the x such that P(x)
> John-- Qx_i such that the woman he loved betrayed x_i.

Then the focused NP <u>John</u> is like a quantified NP, hence cannot bind <u>he</u>, just as in case (39). Similarly, if <u>John</u> is unstressed, as in (42ii), then we have the analogue of (40): <u>John</u> is not fronted, hence is not quantified, hence can now bind <u>he</u> as in (40).

Summarizing, there are two sets of structural facts that support a "Qx-P(x)" or operator--bound variable representation for focus. One is the variety of syntactic mechanisms that, blindly as it were, create a Qx--P(x) form that is interpreted uniformly as altering the focus of a sentence; the other is the apparent fact that a stressed NP that acts as if it were in Qx--P(x) form is likewise interpreted as indicating the focus of a sentence.

If discourse structure really represents the propositional structure of multiple sentences, then there should be no reason why it could not reflect some larger, overall propositional structure of a discourse. Significantly, there is some evidence that this is so.

Note first that Sidner's observations about the push-down stack behavior of discourse foci are drawn mostly from examples of narratives -- that is, stories that follow chronological causal sequences. As a result, the propositional structure of narratives tends to follow a sequencing determined by time: first P_1 happened, then P_2, and so forth. This time-determined structure is reflected in the basic stack-like behavior of foci.

But one can also imagine a more general situation where propositional structure is not restricted to simple linear order. Indeed, [Grosz 1977] has investigated just such a domain: a discourse about assembling a machine (a pump) from its parts. Grosz discovered that in this situation co-indexing defaults seem to follow the decompositional structure of the task itself. For example, if the pump could be assembled by first bolting on a sub-assembly, B, then a sub-assembly C, and B in turn demanded bolting on a bracket, turning screws, and so forth, then hearers seem to follow this tree-like task structure when figuring out what to co-index with what. Grosz' observations support the contention that it is the propositional structure of a discourse that shapes its syntactic form. Sidner's linear ordering, then, becomes just a special sub-case of task structuring where the task is linearly ordered by time. Observe that Grosz' more general tree structure subsumes Sidner's in that a sub-section of a tree may well be linear in appearance, and hence could act like one of Sidner's focus stacks.

It is interesting to observe that the computational advantage accruing from the Sidner stack focus model also obtains in the more general case of tree-structured foci. Suppose, for example, that a task imposes a natural tree-structured decomposition on a discourse. Adopting Sidner's focus accessibility constraint, only antecedents at certain sub-tasks would be available for co-indexing. Depending on the branching structure of the task, many co-indexing possibilities would thus be ruled out. (The exact savings would depend upon the task decomposition.) Now observe that a linear narrative task structure -- that assumed by Sidner --- actually obtains the worst possible savings, since under a strict linear order all preceding antecedent foci are potential candidates. We see then that Sidner's theory obtains only a lower bound on the computational savings to be gained by adopting a focus stack model. A more complex theory of task structure, if correct, would probably do better.

1.3 Kaplan: the world as database

So far, we have not yet provided any way to "connect" the representations of discourse entities or foci provided by Webber and Sidner to the world. One way to attack this problem is to create a simple artificial world. Kaplan's approach does just that: in Kaplan's system, the world of actions and intentions is boiled down to just one, that of asking questions; the external world of objects is reduced to that of objects and their properties in a database of relational attributes.

Formally, we could define such a database as a triple $\langle X, D_{i\in I}, U \rangle$. X is a finite set of database objects, like "John", "Mary" "Computer science 101". I is a finite set of attributes used to index the domain D such as "sex", "Grade", or "year". U is a function defined over attributes and their values that retrieves the set of objects that have a particular value of a specified attribute, e.g., U(sex,male) will return the subset of X that has the attribute "sex" with the value "males" -- John, etc. The crucial point is that a database is defined so that it has a quintessentially extensional semantics -- what U returns is a set of objects. A question asked of a database, a database query, is then simply some sequence of calls to the interrogating function U.

The goal of a database user in making a query is assumed to be simply to find out information about the attributes of objects. Consider a database that has information about students, the courses they have taken, their grades, and so forth. A typical query is, "Which students got A's in computer science 101?" The point of the query is to "find out about X", where X is the set of objects possessing the value "A", for attribute = "grade in computer science 101". So we have finally forged the last link in the discourse chain:

```
        1              2           3                              4
surface --->surface --->logical ---> <LF, Sets of individuals>--->Database
string      structure   form
(query)
            Sidner, Webber                        Kaplan
```

Actually, what Kaplan does is to telescope the process modularized by Webber and Sidner a bit, collapsing intermediate steps of recovering surface structure and constructing LF into a single computational step:

```
surface ---> hybrid logical form  ---> LF interpreted
string      syntactic structure       with respect to a database
```

Kaplan's hybrid syntactic/logical form is dubbed MQL for "meta query language". MQL has all the properties of a hybrid: it encodes the surface constituent structure of a query as well as a specification of which potential sets of objects in the database these surface phrases could denote. But how do we find out what objects these implied sets do pick out of the database? This is not difficult: given an MQL expression, with all its implied sets of objects and their attributes, we simply construct a query that does the actual job of "looking up the answer", returning the set of objects that meets the stipulations demanded by the MQL expression. After all, this is just what the database was designed to do in the first place. Thus, to interpret the question, "Who did John kiss?", Kaplan's system would first build a combined syntactic/LF representation,

> Wh-x, x a person, kissed (John, x).

and then simply query the database to see if, in fact, there were any objects X that have the attributes of being (1) a person and (2) being kissed by John. The program would return a list of names of such objects (probably people's names), or just "nil" if there were none.

How in particular is the syntactic representation of a sentence connected to the database world? In general, Kaplan's MQL assumes a straightforward relationship between objects of a syntactic type -- Prepositional phrases, Noun Phrases, Verb Phrases -- and objects of a database type. Thus it is the job of MQL to link syntax to the database, via the following associations:

Nouns -- correspond to database objects (users, advisers, accounts)

Prepositional Phrases -- correspond to restrictions on attribute sets; e.g., "Advisor with red hair" restricts the query to look at just advisors who also have the attribute red hair. Thus, the "meaning" of prepositions such as with and of is given via a specification of a corresponding database query that mirrors the restrictive intent of the preposition.

Adjectives -- are also interpreted as restricting some basic set, hence are also mapped into restriction queries.

(Restrictive) Relative clauses -- are another source of additional specification of what a basic NP refers too, hence are interpreted like adjectives.

Verbs -- are subfield links in the database, connecting one Noun to another. For example, the verb "sponsor" might be represented as a two-way table, with things sponsored on one axis, and sponsorees on the other. (The Nouns thus connected are the arguments to the verb, in the usual sense.)

Connectives and quantifiers (and, every, some...) -- are interpreted as requests for set operations, as one would expect from an extensional semantics. For example, "Who got A's in Computer Science 101 and A's in Computer Science 102?" simply intersects the two sets returned by the two halves of the full query. Similarly, quantifiers are interpreted simply as a series of queries, e.g., every x $P(x)$ is translated as $x_1 P(x_1) \& x_2 P(x_2)$...etc., iterating over each NP in the set returned by the non-quantified query.[1]

In the actual implementation, a dictionary entry for have or advise specifies what database paths and nodes correspond to the arguments of a verb. For example, "advise" might have the following template:

---

1. As Kaplan observes, there are some interesting questions to resolve here involving the scope of the and. Kaplan assumes it always takes wide scope: And(People who got an A in course 1, people who got an A in course 2).

Advise:

Advisors-->Database Field {Advisees/Projects}-->Projects
or Users

which would list the relevant database fields corresponding to the following
database representation:

Advisors
Smith, J.
 Advisees   <---Advisee subfield
  Jones, A.
  Charles, M.
 Projects   <---Project subfield
  Compiler Design

   The entry for advise would thus inform the system that to find out whether X
advises Y, look up the advisor subfield of the database, then trace through from
that point to subfields advisee or and return the objects listed there.

1.3.1 MQL and the interaction of syntax and semantics

As mentioned, MQL is a hybrid LF/surface syntax language. It is instructive to
compare it with Webber's LF. Consider the following example. Suppose the
query presented to Kaplan's system is: "Which users have accounts on projects
sponsored by NSF?" The MQL structure built from this query, reflecting the
surface syntactic structure of this question, looks like this:

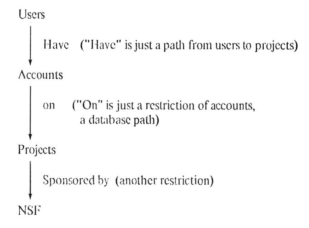

Users

| Have   ("Have" is just a path from users to projects)

Accounts

| on   ("On" is just a restriction of accounts,
          a database path)

Projects

| Sponsored by (another restriction)

NSF

That is, the structure of the query is that (Users have (Accounts on (Projects sponsored by (NSF)))). This structure is nearly a mirror image of a Webber-style representation for the same sentence:

> (wh-x:user)
> $\exists y:\lambda(y:Account)[\exists z:\lambda(u:Project)$
> [Sponsor NSF, u] .
> [On y, z]] . Have x, y

The bracketing reflects the restriction sets enforced by the MQL verbs and the prepositional restriction chains. [1]

Finally, we observe that Kaplan does <u>not</u> advance a rule like QR that "raises" quantifiers from their surface positions and adjoins them to the front of a sentence. MQL simply assumes that wherever a quantifier is found in the surface constituent structure of a phrase determines its scoping relationship to the rest of the sentence. But, as we have seen, this cannot always give the right answer, because it does not allow for the scoping ambiguities of, for example, <u>Everyone loves someone</u>. In these cases, MQL could simply be modified to incorporate a rule like QR.

In sum, to get an answer to a query in Kaplan's system we take the following steps:

> 1. Map the surface string to the MQL representation (roughly, Webber's LF, without quantifier adjunction)

> 2. Construct the database query by retrieving the database paths as indicated by the lexical items in the MQL structure and the bracketing of the MQL structure itself.

---

1. Aside: the use of the passive form <u>sponsored by</u> in the query raises one interesting point about the way Kaplan's system works. As we have described things so far, we would need a separate dictionary entry for the active form of each verb, e.g., <u>sponsor</u> and the verb's corresponding passive form (if any), e.g., <u>sponsored</u>. But this is wasteful. There is no need to store the proper database path for <u>sponsored by</u> if it can be mechanically derived from the entry for sponsor. There are two ways that this could be carried out in this context: (1) parse the passive phrase by converting it into active form; then use the database path specification for the active form, as usual; or (2) parse the passive as it appears on the surface, and then derive the right path by a uniform translation on the path specification for the active form. For example, if the database path for <u>sponsor</u> was "Foundation <u>sponsor</u> project" (thus specifying two database nodes, <u>sponsor</u> and <u>foundation</u>, the corresponding passive dictionary entry would be "project <u>sponsored by</u> foundation".

This lexical approach to the analysis of passives -- via so-called "lexical redundancy" rules -- has been proposed by several researchers in linguistics: see [Wasow 1977]; [Bresnan 1978].

3. Perform the query (or series of queries) as indicated by the MQL structure.

4. Return the set of objects satisfying the query.

Note that the set of objects returned by Step 4 could be empty.

1.3.2 The interaction of syntax and semantics

As we have seen, the syntax of Kaplan's logical form, MQL, in part determines the meaning of a question in the sense that the order of constituents determines the database path of the query, hence the set returned by the query, hence the meaning of the query given an extensional semantics. So syntax can influence semantics. For example, different syntactic (MQL) structures are built for the two questions, "Which professors taught students in computer science" and "Which students were taught by professors":

[Wh-professors [taught students in computer science]]

corresponding MQL structure:

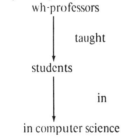

wh-professors

taught

students

in

in computer science

[Wh-students [were taught by professors in computer science]]

wh-students

taught by

by professors

in

computer science

Since the restriction sets specified by the two MQL structures are different --

in one, we ask about students in computer science, in the other, we ask about professors in computer science -- the meaning of these two queries is distinct. In addition, of course, the main queried set is different in the two sentences.

If syntax influences semantics in Kaplan's system, what about the other way around? Can database semantics alter syntax? The answer is yes. If the database path as extracted from a particular parse doesn't make sense, where "doesn't make sense" means that the query path selected was longer than the query path associated with another parse for the query, then the parse with the excessively long query path is discarded. For example, consider the question, "Which users work on projects in area three that are in division 3500?" This query has at least two parses: one where the sentential complement "that are in division 3500" modifies users, and one where it modifies "projects." The alternative database paths for these parses are as follows:

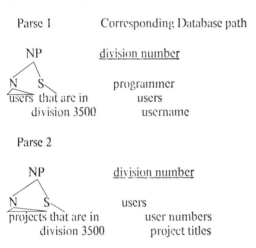

Parse 1   Corresponding Database path

NP   division number

N   S   programmer
users that are in   users
    division 3500   username

Parse 2

NP   division number

N   S   users
projects that are in   user numbers
    division 3500   project titles

Projects are further away from division numbers than are users. Hence, if we assume that database distance is a proxy for semantic relatedness, then the first syntactic structure is closer to the structure of the world (the database) than the second, because in the database "users" are closer to "divisions" than "projects" are. (It is interesting to compare this approach to disambiguating prepositional phrase attachments via distance along database paths with the approach of [Marcus 1980]. Marcus assumed a semantic relatedness "oracle" that could magically determine which PP attachment was preferred. Kaplan has simply constructed such an oracle for a database world.)

1.3.3 Questions, empty sets, and intentions

Given Kaplan's account of meaning, we can now return to our original problem of answering questions. What does someone intend when they ask a question? Kaplan assumes just what one would expect from a database semantics: a questioner want to find out what collection of objects, if any, meet the specification laid out in their question -- an LF of the form, "Wh-x, such that P(x)", where P(x) = some specification of x via a combination of attributes and values for x. The specification P(x) in turn determines what the query function U(attribute, value) must look like. Everything works fine if U returns a list of database objects satisfying P. But what should we do if U returns the empty set, if no object satisfies P? An analysis of this second possibility is what occupies the remainder of Kaplan's study.

All empty sets are created equal, but some are less equal than others. An analysis of why U happens to return an empty set is the lynchpin of Kaplan's analysis of "empty" questions such as "Who got A's in computer science 101". In this respect, the term "empty question" is well chosen.

To be concrete, consider Kaplan's example query, "Did Sandy pass the bar exam?" By assumption, the goal of the query is know whether Sandy passed the bar exam. (As we will see, this corresponds to a KNOWIF goal in Allen's more general system.) To proceed further, we must know what it means to "pass" a bar exam. As usual, the system's knowledge of "pass" is built into a dictionary entry that specifies its meaning with respect to the particular database at hand. Let us say that Y passes an X just in case X is an exam that Y took; that Y's grade was greater than 60; and that Y is a student. Thus pass defines a set of database attributes and values that must be satisfied if Y may be said to have passed an exam.

Evidently we have that Sandy passes the exam if Sandy takes the exam, and if Sandy gets a score of greater than 60, plus some other conditions that might be relevant. Symbolically,

$$A = \text{Sandy passes the exam.}$$
$$B_1 = \text{Sandy takes the bar exam;}$$
$$B_2 = \text{Sandy gets a score of 60 or more.}$$

More simply we have that $A \Rightarrow B_1 \& B_2$ (since if A is true, then B_1 and B_2 must be true; but if A is false, then we really can't say whether B_1 and B_2 are true or false, because we have not said whether they exhaust the conditions necessary to pass the exam.)

But for databases with a simple extensional semantics as defined earlier, a predicate that has an empty set as its extension results in a failure of the presuppositions behind a query. If A denotes the set returned by some query function U defined so as to specify Sandy's passing the exam, and if A, the set of exam passed by Sandy, is empty, then Sandy did not pass the exam. But why could A be empty? A is the empty set if either B_1 or B_2 are empty -- if Sandy either didn't take the exam or didn't get a grade above 60 -- then Sandy didn't pass the exam. But then we now have access to why A is empty. Since A implies $B_1 \& B_2$, $not(B_1 \& B_2) \Rightarrow not\text{-}A$. Thus if either B_1 or B_2 is empty, then A is empty. Let us call these the possible reasons for A's emptiness. Graphically, A is a subset of the B's, and if either of them are empty, then A must be:

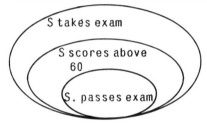

Figure 7 Subset relationships reflect the implicational
structure of a query.

Given an extensional semantics, the analogue of an implicational chain is simply a chain of database set inclusions.

There is one more complication, however. As in the example above, sets can form chains of inclusions -- A is a subset of B_2 (scoring above 60), and B_2 is a subset of B_1 (taking the exam). So it is really more accurate to say that $A \Rightarrow B_1 \Rightarrow B_2$, and hence that $not\text{-}B_2 \Rightarrow not\text{-}B_1 \Rightarrow not\text{-}A$. Translating implicational into subset structure, how can we find the reason for A's emptiness? We simply start at not-A and work backwards through the subset inclusion chain till we reach the first non-empty set. The set immediately before that one in the inclusion chain is the reason for A's emptiness.

Since subset chains are, in general, computed by the routines already required to look up database answers -- remember that database answers are just sets, and queries just a series of set specifications -- one can see that we are now in a good position to detect and respond to empty questions. The MQL structure in conjunction with dictionary entries provides the implicational chain. If as we are moving through the pathway specified by an MQL query we encounter an empty set before reaching the end of the query path, then the answer is empty and a pre-condition has been violated; we simply report back the first empty set along the chain, since it is the <u>reason</u> for the emptiness of the query. For example, consider the query, "How many students got A's in Computer Science 101?" Assume that this query has the following implicational structure:

students   --->   students   --->   course
getting A's   taking course   given

and the corresponding database subset structure:

<u>Course</u> <u>Given</u>

Computer Science 101
  <u>Name</u> <u>Grade</u>
  John   A
  Sandy B

Fine Arts

To find the students who got A's in Computer Science 101, Kaplan's system builds a query that runs down the list of courses till it hits computer science 101, then extracts the "grade" subfield, and finally, assembles into one set all those names associated with a grade of A. Given this procedure, it should be apparent that if the "Course Given" database object doesn't have the attribute value "Computer Science 101", the query procedure can immediately return an empty value. Since this was not the last step in the query procedure, we simply report this, by conjoining an empty set answer with the reason for the set's emptiness:

None, because the course was not given.

So far then, we have seen that the B_i's are necessary conditions for A to be non-empty. Plainly they are not sufficient conditions however, and this distinction is closely related to the possibility of appropriate "no" answers. To see this, consider the case where not-A (a "no" answer) can be a valid response to a question. By the above analysis, any of the B_i's being empty can make A empty. So it needn't be true that if A is empty, then a particular B_i is empty. (It is not necessarily true that not-A $\Rightarrow$ not-B_i.) This is the situation in which Kaplan dubs B_i a <u>presumption</u>; B_i is simply a necessary condition for A. Now suppose that a "no" answer demands that B_i be empty, i.e., that not-A $\Rightarrow$ not-B_i. But then we have that not-$B_i \Rightarrow$ not-A and not-A $\Rightarrow$ not-B_i, i.e., A iff B_i. Then whenever A is true, B_i is true; when A is false, B_i is false. This is the case in which Kaplan calls

B_i a <u>presupposition</u>. For example, if $A =$ "John takes piano lessons on Monday, Tuesday, Wednesday, Thursday, Friday, Saturday, or Sunday", then not-$A =$ "John doesn't take piano lessons". Let $B =$ "John takes daily piano lessons". Then A is equivalent to B; B is a presupposition of A.

Why can Kaplan's system be made to work so well? In brief, it is because the database world provides just the right narrow kind of semantical universe -- one in which the deeper problems of intentionality do not arise. For most purposes -- but not all -- the meaning of a database query is just the set of objects implied by the query. Thus restricted, there is a close correspondence between database paths and the syntactic structures provided by parse trees of English sentences, with the exact mapping mediated by specific dictionary entries particular to each database. But if meaning is not restricted to sets of objects, or if the goal of the questioner is not simply to obtain a list of database objects, then the enterprise becomes much less straightforward. Suppose, as Kaplan notes, that what the user really would like is some <u>intentional</u> description of the set of objects returned by the query -- e.g., the question, "Who profit shares?" might best be answered by the intentional phrase, "The executive Vice-Presidents." As an example of the same phenomenon on the question end, consider another one of Kaplan's questions, "Which model cars were sold last year?" Presumably, this question calls for a list of model types rather than a list of each car (along with its model type) sold. Kaplan's system has a crude heuristic to tell when such "abbreviatory" phrases might be preferable to a list of database objects -- it can take note when a list would be overly long, according to some metric of length, and attempt to re-interpret the phrase "which model cars" so as to obtain a shorter list. But to accomplish this feat in general would seem to require that the system have some model of the user's goals that goes beyond the desire for lists -- else, how could it know what the user really wants in the way of a description rather than a list? We will see in the next section that Allen's system is designed to accomplish part of this task, at least for well-restricted domains of objects and attributes. Allen's system assumes that the user has a set of three or more general goals, each of which is composed (hierarchically) of a well-organized set of sub-goals; in Allen's world, the super-goals are the everyday activities of meeting or boarding trains in railway station. Given that the system "knows" this much about the structure of these few human behaviors, it turns out that it in certain cases it can offer useful descriptions rather than lists -- all with respect to its stored knowledge, of course. It would be an interesting exercise to embed this more detailed models of questioners into Kaplan's more detailed world of objects and their attributes.

Besides this extension to a more sophisticated model of questioners, there are several other linguistically-oriented modifications to Kaplan's approach that would fill certain gaps in his syntactic analysis of English. As mentioned, Kaplan's syntactic analysis has no analogue of a QR rule. Therefore, it cannot capture ambiguous quantifier scopings, nor determine when such alternative scopings are prohibited. It would be a simple matter to add such a rule to the MQL parsing system, tailored directly after the QR rule of modern generative theories. Second, Kaplan makes no use of the co-indexing work of Sidner discussed above; there is no way for the MQL system to keep track of the introduction of discourse entities and their co-designators. Once again, this machinery could be lifted wholesale from Sidner's work; one need only add a co-indexing notation, and the same rules would carry over for the MQL structure. In fact, it would probably be best to split the homogenated MQL language back into the two representations from which it was distilled -- surface syntax, and logical form. Finally, Sidner's focus rules, as re-cast in the guise of predication , indicate "what is being talked about" in a discourse, hence, in a question. By incorporating the focus algorithm into the MQL structure -- via a representation reflecting a "x s.t. P(x)" form -- Kaplan's system could exploit Sidner's rules directly for determining what the topic of the question is.

1.4 Allen: meaning and plans

The gap between literal and intended meaning can be quite small -- an LF expression can manage to say pretty much what it means to say. Kaplan's database queries all wear their quizzical expressions on their sleeves. There is only one human intention in Kaplan's world: to find out the extensions of certain sets. But there may be thousands of objects and properties to find out about. In contrast, Allen assumes an impoverished world of objects and their properties -- a smaller database of objects and their attributes -- but a richer universe of intentions. His aim is to develop a more general approach human linguistic behavior by conjoining a Searle and Austin-type theory of speech acts together with other kinds of purposive behavior in a general model of planning behavior.

Speech act theory provides a framework in which linguistic activity is interpreted as just another kind of action -- I say "pass the salt" as part of a plan to get the salt. But so regarded, a speech act must be planned, and thus becomes susceptible to analysis by a theory of planning. Here Allen exploits what is known about planning as explored in the AI literature. The general notion is that in order to infer the plan of a speaker, one must first observe some external behavior of the speaker -- in particular, the speaker's utterance. Then one drives a inference chain forward from some (small) number of basic goals assumed to be mutually held between speaker and hearer. To take the setting that Allen uses, in a train station, the station agent may assume that people approaching him with questions only want to find out about boarding trains or meeting arriving trains -- and he may assume that the people approaching him also know that. Thus, agent and patrons share a small number of mutual beliefs; there are just two possible "top-level" goals. Each of these goals leads to a characteristic planning sequence: if one wants to board a train, then one must buy a ticket, find out what from gate and at what time the train leaves, go to that gate, and so forth. The key point is that different goals can expand into different planning sequences, hence eventually terminate as different speech acts. Thus the top-level plan of a questioner could be identified if the speech acts it leads to match what the hearer actually observes:

	Goals
	1. Board train
	Get ticket
Speech act	Find out about destination
The train to	Find out gate
Windsor?	Find out departure time
	2. Meet train
	Find out gate
	Find out arrival time

As is well known from the AI literature, "forward chaining" inference procedures -- like this one -- can be computationally costly: the number of possible ways a goal could be expanded into subgoals could be enormous. To help alleviate this problem, Allen's system drives an inference chain backwards from observed speech act to goal at the same time as all possible goals are expanded forwards. A plan is said to be identified when forward and backwards inference chains meet.

Given an inferred, plan, Allen's system then determines whether there are any obstacles in the plan that might cause its failure -- for example, the plan might be to board a train, but the person involved might not know from what gate the train departs. Allen's system detects these breaks in inference chains, thus determining what sort of information is to be supplied to the questioner: "Gate 7 at 9 PM"

Clearly this approach subsumes Kaplan's. A questioner's top-level goal in a database world is simply to find out information about some set. The planning sequence in a database world is just a path through the database designed to retrieve the desired information -- a sequence of calls to some query function, as we have seen. An obstacle in a plan is an empty set that interrupts this query chain. Thus, Kaplan's system is just Allen's restricted to the particular world of database queries.

Allen's more general approach to intentional behavior permits his system to make larger leaps of inference than Kaplan's. In particular, it can leap at least some of the inferential gaps corresponding to so-called "indirect speech acts" -- intentions of the speaker that are directly reflected in surface syntactic form. An example is the question "Can you tell me what time the train to Windsor leaves?" What the speaker presumably intends by this statement is to find out when the train to Windsor leaves, hence to get the station agent to tell him departure time. Thus the actual meaning of this query is "Tell me the departure time of the train to Windsor", even though the form of the query is a yes-no question, and thus could be literally answered with a simple "Yes."

This ability to reconstruct a questioner's beliefs and intentions from surface forms that do not explicitly indicate them is quite remarkable. It is purchased at the price of severely restricting the planning alternatives that can be considered. If one can only board or meet trains, then the opportunity to go astray is slight, and a combinatoric explosion in inference unlikely. It is not clear whether the same approach would work in a more realistic setting where there were dozens or hundreds of alternatives.

There are two classic ways out of the dilemma of excessive inference. One road to salvation might be called deus ex machina: invoke some computational machinery that can carry out the desired inference quickly. But for many AI researchers, the escape has been to adopt the working strategy of "divide and conquer" by simply assuming that knowledge about thousands of things can be organized into more modular units. Now, one can package either inference about plans and intentions, or inference about properties, or both. As for inference about intentions, it seems hardly likely that every time one hears, "Can you pass the salt?" one runs through in toto a long chain of deductions that ends with the conclusion that what was really meant was that someone wants you to pass the salt. The obvious alternative is to squirrel away commonly occurring deductions as little "lemmas" that trigger on an observed speech acts directly. Of course, this approach begs important research questions about the nature and organization of these lemmas. As for inference about properties, the AI literature of the past decade has been replete with several attempts at quasi-naturalistic classifications of human knowledge (including knowledge about human intentions) into organized packets. Perhaps naturally enough, for the most part these schemes hinge upon carving the world up in a way that is organized around human activities with intuitively discernible boundaries -- taking an airplane flight, ordering tickets in a train station, or ordering hamburgers in restaurants. Whether these efforts have carved Nature at her proper joints, I leave for the connoisseurs of fast-food restaurants to judge.

1.4.1 Allen's system: the details

In Allen's system there are, then, five steps to the analysis of a surface utterance:

(1) The surface utterance is parsed and mapped into a quasi-case frame representation, that is, a surface syntactic parse that annotates Noun Phrases with their thematic roles, such as Agent, Instrument, Location, and the like. (The syntactic parse is assumed useful only insofar as it aids in the recovery of proper thematic roles.) For example, a question such as "When does the train to Windsor leave?" is mapped into a thematic structure with a role of Destination filled by train1 (the train to Windsor). That the Prepositional Phrase to Windsor signals a Destination thematic role is a language-specific fact that must be known by such a system. In fact, Allen simply assumes the existence of parser that handles step (1); such a device might be tailored after the design of [Marcus 1980].

(2) The surface intention of the utterance is recovered. By this is meant simply whether the utterance is a command ("Tell me..."), a question ("When..."), or the like. Since all these sentence types are revealed by explicit syntactic signals, this can be done easily. Together with the thematic roles recovered in step (1), a possible set of requests (= what the speaker could want, given surface indications) is constructed. For example, the utterance "Does the train to Windsor leave at 4?" leads to the system to conclude that the speaker has made a request to be informed if the departure time for the Windsor train is at 4.

(3) The system starts expanding inferences forward from its two top level goals (boarding and leaving trains), along with a third, dummy, empty goal. The fringe of sub-goals currently expanded from higher-level goals are called the expectations. At the same time, the system starts expanding from the initial utterance backwards. So for instance, given the initial request that the speaker wants to know_if(departure-time (train1, 4)), the system fleshes out the possible goals that either the speaker wants the train to leave at 4; or the speaker doesn't want the train to leave at 4; or the speaker simply wants to know when the train leaves. The fringe of goals expanded backwards in this manner are dubbed the alternatives. An alternative is judged to mesh with an expectation according to a set of weighted criteria that are simply a way of expressing the likelihood of their compatibility. For example, if a top-level goal expands into subgoals whose necessary preconditions are incompatible with the preconditions of the alternative, then a mesh is unlikely; similarly, if the expectations being expanded forwards contains descriptions (like "boarding a train") that is compatible with the alternative being expanded backwards, then the two are more likely to mesh.

When the score of some alternative-expectation combination exceeds that of the dummy alternative by a certain amount, the pair is accepted as the most likely plan the speaker had in mind.

(4) Given a likely plan for the speaker (including a single "visible" portion, the observed speech act), the system traces out the steps of the plan to see if there are any gaps in preconditions such that the speaker might not be able to carry out the plan. For example, the plan of boarding a train demands that the speaker be at the departure gate, implying in turn that the departure gate was known. (Note that this means that Allen's system must have a set of rules for reasoning about actions, e.g., inference rules of the form, "To be at a place X implies that one knows the value of place X.")

(5) Assuming a model of co-operative behavior, the system responds so as to fill in the gaps in the speaker's knowledge that it has concluded are necessary to fulfill the speaker's plan. Here it can exploit the plan it has already inferred to construct a response, using the same thematic role mechanism of Step (1), but in reverse. Note that the system says nothing about how this linguistic realization would actually be carried out. McDonald's system, in fact, has been designed to handle exactly the problem of mapping from a plan description to an actual utterance. (See Chapter 4.)

As outlined, this procedure does not deal with indirect speech acts. Before tackling this more difficult case though, it might be best to illustrate the Allen system by comparing the way it and Kaplan's database system would analyze the same utterance, "Does the train to Windsor leave at 4?"

In Kaplan's system, there can be only one surface intention: a Request to Inform if P(x) is true. This is an appropriate choice given the goals that Kaplan had for his research, namely, to develop a cooperative database system that was also transportable. Kaplan's system assumes that there is only one goal of a database user: to know the value of some database object. In addition to this immediate goal, Allen's system contains several inference rules that immediately conclude that if someone wants to know the properties of something, then one wants one of the possible values of that property to obtain; further, one often wants to know the value of an object in order to identify it in the world. Thus Allen's system constructs four surface alternatives where Kaplan has one.

What about top-level expectations? Here too, Kaplan has but one: to find out about the properties of some data base object, X. In contrast, Allen has three: the board train plan, the meet train.plan, or the empty plan.

	Kaplan	Allen
Surface request	Inform if (Departure.time train_1 is 4)	Inform if (Departure.time train_1 is 4)
	Default Know_value	1. Know_value
Goals	Departure.time_e train_1	Departure.time train_1

2 & 3: The following inference rule expands (1).
If speaker wants to know some value,
then speaker wants either a
positive value (wants train to leave
at 4) or a negative value
(wants train not to leave at 4)
4. Inference rule expands (1):
If speaker wants to know some value
of some entity, then speaker wants to
identify the entity

	Kaplan	Allen
Expectation	Know_value plan	1. Board train plan
Goal	(Database object X)	preconditions: AT(speaker, location, time) matching template: Depart.location(train, location) Depart.time (train, time)
		2. Meet train plan precondition: AT(speaker, location,time) matching template: Arrival.location (train, location) Arrival.time (train, time)
		3. Null plan (empty)

Figure 8 A comparison of the Kaplan and Allen systems.

Next, the speaker's plan must be inferred. In Kaplan's system, there is no need for any inference: the top-level goal is to "know_value" and the speaker's surface intention is to "know_value" -- a match. In Allen's more complex world of intentions, one must first see that the goal to find out departure time (triggered by the knowledge that <u>to Windsor</u> signifies a thematic role of <u>departure</u>) meshes with the goal of boarding the train. It does: the board plan's structure includes a slot with the departure time, but the meet and null plans do not.

Note that the ease and simplicity of correct identification crucially depends upon the density of the space of possible plans. It is easy to imagine cases where finding the correct match is not so simple. For example, it is entirely plausible that one would want to meet a <u>departing</u> train -- in order to see someone off. This alternate meet train plan would be indistinguishable to the current board train plan -- at least as we have described boarding a train. Perhaps this is not a problem, however. The purpose of having alternate plans in the first place is to distinguish among different possible courses of action. If the plans for boarding a train and meeting a train to see someone off look exactly alike, then this is perfectly acceptable insofar as the actions the system must take are the same. (In this case, since boarding a train could require in addition that one have a ticket, a situation where the station agent also sells tickets could require a modification in the board train plan to this effect. Then the board train and meet departing train plans would be distinguishable. Allen has specifically ruled out this possibility -- station agents do not sell tickets in his universe.) But as soon as the space of possible top-level goals is expanded, even more complicated examples can be constructed. For example, suppose that one wants to delay the 4 o'clock train -- say by planting a bomb timed to go off as it rolls across a detonator. In this case, one would want to have the train leave at 4 even though the ultimate top-level goal is plainly to <u>not</u> have the train leave. Thus in this situation Allen's "know_positive" rule -- "know_if $(X) \Rightarrow$ know_positive(x) or know_negative (x) -- could lead to the contradiction of both wanting and not wanting the train to leave at 4. Examples such as this one show that, in general, a system incorporating Allen's theory would have to incorporate a more sophisticated logic of wants or beliefs.

Summarizing so far, in Kaplan's system the step from parsed utterance to plan inference is immediate; in Allen's, there is a significant amount of interpolation that is required:

	Kaplan	Allen
Observed	Request: Inform if departure.time	Request: Inform if departure.time
	Know_if	Know_if Know_value
Goal	Know_value departure time	Know_reference (speaker, time) where time = departure time of train Board train: know_reference (departure time, gate)

Figure 9 Summary of Kaplan and Allen example comparison.

Note that Kaplan's system has no model of the speaker's plan other than the simple one that the speaker wants to know the value of departure time.

What next? In Kaplan's system, the MQL structure (the parse) is mapped into a database query -- a sequence of queries that aim to find out the value of departure time. Suppose that the database structure is such that the following situation obtains:

Toronto train schedule
Arrivals
3 PM
Departures
1 PM

Windsor train schedule
Arrivals
1 AM
1 PM

Then the subset structure for the query looks like this:

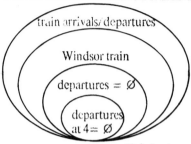

Figure 10 Subset structure for a database query.

There are no Windsor train departures. As usual, Kaplan's system reports back the largest empty subset in this chain as the reason for the empty set query response:

No, there are no Windsor train departures.

What about Allen's system? The analogue of the MQL query path for Allen is a trace through the plan of boarding a train. That plan includes a segment where the speaker must know when the departure time is, and what the gate number for departure is -- a gap that must be filled. Allen's system then attempts to bridge that gap by supplying information that it has. Assume -- as Allen does -- that the system has access to a table of departure and arrival times for trains so that it can find out these values for itself. Suppose that it consults this table and finds that there are no Windsor train departures. It then concludes that this is a gap in the speaker's plan that cannot be filled, and reports on the unbridgeable gap:

No, there are no Windsor train departures.

In sum, we see that Kaplan and Allen's system will perform in about the same way in response to database-like "empty" questions.

Of course, Allen's system can do some things that Kaplan's cannot, because it has a more complete model of the speaker's plan. For example, it can supply the gate number even if the user did not explicitly demand it -- since it too is a necessary precondition for the success of the inferred speaker's plan.

In a case like "Does the Windsor train leave at 4?", the surface form of the utterance matches the intention to find out when the train leaves. This is a direct speech act. If surface form does not directly reflect the speaker's intention, then one has an indirect speech act. Thus, to obtain the "true" intent of a speaker, no additional inference is necessary in the case of a direct speech act; the person means what he literally is saying. In contrast, in an indirect speech act, several layers of inference might have to be interposed before the "true" request is recovered:

	direct	indirect
surface form	Does the Windsor train leave at 4?	Do you know when the Windsor train leaves?
surface request	Inform_if (Departure time is 4)	Inform_if (Agent knows departure time)
underlying request	Inform_if (Departure time is 4)	Inform_if (Departure time is 4)

Figure 11 Comparison of direct and indirect requests.

Once the underlying request is recovered, the system can proceed as before, but how can one get from surface request to underlying request? Allen's answer is that recovering an indirect underlying request involves reconstructing a portion of a speaker's beliefs on the basis of observing an external utterance. Hence, recovering an indirect speech speech act is the same sort of process as recovering a speaker's ultimate plan -- only the inference chain can be longer, hence more difficult and error-prone. The extra step is simply to take the literal meaning of the observed utterance, obtaining a surface speech act as before, and then expand this alternative backwards by a series of inference rules dealing now with the speaker's desires with respect to what the speaker and the hearer (the station agent) mutually believe. In this case, what they mutually believe includes the information that the speaker wants the agent to tell the speaker whether the agent knows when the Windsor train leaves. It also includes the fact that knowing when the train leaves is the sole relevant precondition for telling the speaker when the train leaves, and further that the only possible effect of the agent's knowledge of when the train leaves on the speaker is for the speaker to come to know when the train leaves -- this since both speaker and station agent already mutually believe that the station agent knows when the train leaves. Thus the only possible plan that is advanced by asking the question is a plan where the speaker finds out what the departure time of the train is -- hence the inform-if underlying request.

If the context is constrained enough, the computational problems that could arise here do not seem to be insurmountable: if one can only meet or board trains, then the expression, "the train to Windsor" uttered without any surface indication of intent (as a request, say) can still be analyzed. However, this is simply because there cannot be many "deep" intentions. Indeed, given the tightly circumscribed train station world, a speaker would need but to approach the station agent and say, Windsor". The agent could then supply a response that met either the demands of meeting or boarding a train: a gate and a time. The power of Allen's system then is that in a constricted domain one can encode a sufficient set of axioms and inference rules to deal with a complete, but circumscribed, range of human actions and intentions. To extend this approach to the world at large would plainly require a way to restrict inference. Since people do somehow manage to get around in the world in general -- or at least they seem to -- one is ineluctably led to the search for those "natural" constraints on inference that people must presumably use. But therein lies the story of the future of cognitive science, a story that must wait for another book to tell.

1.5 McDonald: Saying What You Mean

So far, we have discussed models that "listen" to what is being said, but do not talk back. McDonald's model aims to plug this gap. In broad outline, McDonald's model of speech production is simple: It is a procedure that maps expressions in an <u>internal</u> language (generally assumed to be of a "conceptual" character, perhaps a "language of thought") to those of an external language, a sequence of phones or their written counterparts.

Properly blended, these ingredients are sufficient to meet the bare requirement of actually being able to produce output language from input messages. But as we have seen, if one is to take the computational view of mind seriously, one should strive for more than this. The ultimate goal is a <u>procedure</u> whose external behavior is causally connected to its internal organization in a fashion that mirrors that of the human cognitive faculty in question. This is a demand that goes far beyond simple extensional mimicry; crudely put, the computational "guts" of model and person are to be functionally equivalent.

Put another way, a theory of language generation that aims at an <u>explanation</u> of how people produce language must meet additional demands of <u>cognitive fidelity</u>. Some of these additional fidelity conditions are fairly obvious. For example, human speech is typically rapid and fluent, without excessive pauses; yet at the same time fluent speech is rife with certain characteristic errors; we will investigate some of these below. This blend of fluency and error is not surprising. Wherever we find a computational system working under severe resource constraints -- in this case, the demand to produce continuous, fluent speech -- we find cases where there has been an apparent sacrifice of perfect correctness for speed. As with any complex machinery, these "breakdown points" provide intriguing evidence for the internal construction of the language production mechanism itself.

McDonald's research into language generation lies squarely within this methodological approach. His basic goal is to develop a working computer program that can actually produce orthographic output from an input message language; one can therefore evaluate his work with respect to the (weak) milestone of Input/Output reproducibility. However, not only is the McDonald procedure designed actually to output orthographic text from message input, it is designed to output text quickly. In short, the major cognitive fidelity requirement that McDonald aims to meet is that of fluency, that is, the ability to produce language at a bounded rate without arbitrary pauses. This is a quintessentially computational demand, serving as a kind of "forcing function" to drive the design of the generation procedure. To meet the fluency requirement, McDonald advances a specific set of constraints on his input message language and mapping function. For instance, one of the message language constraints has to do with the order in which message sub-elements can appear in a complete message: it is forbidden to allow a sub-element that depends on some higher, more "abstract" message element to be expanded before that more abstract element. Then too, the generation procedure itself is restricted to do only a bounded amount of "advance planning" before it must decide what to say at any given step. (These vague terms like "bounded" and "advance planning" will be sharpened shortly.)

Together, the constraints on message language and mapping algorithm are claimed to be sufficient (not necessary) to obtain the desired result of fluent output. As in the case of other systems constrained so as to operate with limited resources, McDonald suggests that they conspire so as to prevent the generation procedure from correctly handling certain input messages properly. Although he does not provide a full characterization of which sorts of constructions can or cannot be handled, it will be shown below that a formal characterization of most if not all of the error-producing constructions can be given. In a nutshell, the fluency constraint is subsumed by a formal property of grammars known as the LL(k) condition [Lewis and Stearns 1968]. As we shall see, the LL(k) characterization provides a useful umbrella framework in which to unify the various constraints that McDonald proposes. One such framework is sketched below: it recasts the generation procedure as transduction guided by an underlying LL(k) grammar (and is consequently a variety of syntax-directed translation, a formalism more familiar from the realm of compiler design.) This re-interpretation of the McDonald model will allow us to investigate more carefully the claims of McDonald's research, and considerably sharpen the statement of his constraints.

Does the McDonald model mimic human speech production? There is some suggestive evidence that it does. It turns out that there are systematically produced "errors" in human speech -- ungrammatical sentences that are quite common in the spoken language -- that can be elegantly accounted for if one adopts McDonald's assumption of bounded planning during speech production. These are ungrammatical sentences (as noted by [Kroch 1981]) with so-called resumptive pronouns:

> The guy who I don't know whether he will come or not...

Such sentences are assumed to have a constituent analysis roughly like the following:

> $[_{NP}$The guy $[_S$ who I don't know $[_S$whether he will come or not...

That is, the resumptive pronoun he is embedded two sentential phrases away from the head Noun the guy to which it refers. Such sentences are produced apparently because the generation procedure cannot plan syntactic detail two sentences ahead and at the same time maintain the requirement of continuous output: the head Noun segment the guy must be "said" before the internal details of the second wh-phrase are worked out in full. As will be described in more detail below, the effect of such limited lookahead leads inevitably to ungrammaticalities in speech of the kind noted above.

Interestingly enough, these sentences are the production analogues of the well-known "garden path" sentences, such as,

> The horse raced past the barn fell.
> $[_S$ $[_{NP}$The horse $[_C$ raced past the barn $[_{VP}$fell.

> where C= a clause of a type to be determined by the parse, e.g., S or VP.

People cannot parse these sorts of sentences correctly,[1] presumably because of a limitation on the ability to "plan" a parse more than a few steps ahead into a sentence. This intuition has been given a computational grounding in Marcus' [Marcus 1980] model of sentence parsing, a model that also incorporates a notion of bounded lookahead driven by a "forcing function" of efficient operation. As it

---

1. Typically only when reading them, however. In normal speech, intonational effects seem to eliminate most garden paths by providing sufficient cues to direct the listener's parse.

turns out, forward planning of parsing in Marcus' model is limited to a lookahead of just one sentential clause -- just as in the model for the production of sentences -- and it is this restriction that forces the misanalysis of garden path sentences. It is not too much of an exaggeration to say that the McDonald generation procedure is the production dual of the Marcus parser.

1.5.1 The McDonald model

Before proceeding to a formal analysis of the McDonald approach and the cognitive behavior that it predicts, let us quickly review its central components as they fit into the general model of language production sketched above.

McDonald's message language, though never explicitly formulated, appears to be some variant of a standard quantificational language (capturing the propositional content of a message) along with (optional) sequencing and discourse information.

There are two features of the message language that are crucial to the exercise of developing a generation program. First of all, note that an expression in the message language is hierarchically organized as McDonald depicts it. Perhaps more importantly, the hierarchical structure encoded in the message language reflects to a considerable extent the phrase structure of the output form. As we shall see, the generation procedure makes crucial use of the nesting encoded by the parentheses in order to do its work.

Secondly, the input message language is fully disambiguated: the parentheses describe exactly one such tree structure. This uniqueness property will also play a crucial role in the efficient production of output from a given message.

A careful specification of the connection between message and output language is central to McDonald's research program, because the structural similarity between input and output language weighs heavily on the computational power required to perform the mapping from one to the other. For example, take the extreme case where the message language and the output language are one and the same -- that is, suppose that the "language of thought" were just English. Then the function required to take message language to "surface structure" would just be the identity mapping -- a rather efficiently computable function. In this case, there would be no surprise at all in the claim that the mapping procedure meets certain criteria of efficient computability.[1]

McDonald's output language is simply an orthographic representation -- a string of words. Thus, the output language does not include such features of the human speech stream as intonational contours or rhythm. Since some of these aspects of speech -- such as phrasing pauses and the like -- are known to be a significant part of speech output, it is important to consider just what their omission implies for the scope of the generation procedure. Later in this analysis we shall briefly investigate how intonational contour might play a role in a language generation model.

The function taking message strings to orthographic strings is described by McDonald as a finite state transducer that, tracing though the input message tree, outputs linguistic symbols (and sometimes new tree structure) as it goes -- thus producing the required output string. We might depict such a device as having a simple "read head" that traverses the message structure from left to right in a series of moves, noting symbols as it goes; access to a finite table of information that specifies its moves and the symbols to output (indexed by input symbol and machine state); but no storage tape on which to write symbols for later recall. However, this characterization of McDonald's generation procedure is not quite accurate, in that the automaton actually traverses the tree associated with the message structure, and thus does not exactly follow a left-to-right traversal through the message string. Actually, its traversal mirrors the hierarchical structure of the tree associated with the message.[2]

As will be shown below, this device has more power than a simple finite state machine; its traversal of the tree it is building gives it the power of a pushdown stack. However, it is still convenient for expository purposes to factor the computational power of the generation procedure into the finite tables of information the automaton accesses and the tree structure over which it moves.

---

1. Clearly, the McDonald procedure does not fall into this degenerate category. The generation procedure cannot be a simple identity mapping, since, trivially, a tense feature must be added to the output string. Still, the point about the importance of the input language remains the same: a precise characterization of the input message language is a logical prerequisite to the formulation of the generation procedure. To the extent that the message language remains unspecified, claims about the computational efficiency of the generation procedure are correspondingly vague and imprecise.

2. More precisely, the numbering traces out a so-called left-most derivation. Given a grammar G that generates a language L, a derivation of a sentence w of L is called left-most if, at each step in the derivation of L, the left-most non-terminal of the grammar is expanded. For example, consider the simple grammar S-->NP VP, VP-->V NP, NP-->John|Mary, V-->kissed. A left-most derivation of the sentence "John kissed Mary" would be: S-->NP VP-->John VP-->John V NP-->John kissed NP--> John kissed Mary. Note that this expansion order is exactly that of the top-down, left-to-right traversal specified by McDonald's automaton.

The tables of information are like the transition tables of a finite automaton -- they dictate what the next state of the machine shall be, given its current state and the symbol attached to the node of the tree currently being scanned.

In particular, the generation transducer has two finite tables that determine its next state and the symbol(s) that it should output: a dictionary and a grammar. The dictionary specifies an initial mapping from the non-linguistic message language to a structural linguistic counterpart. That is, the dictionary maps input messages -- such as "(lady-macbeth (persuade (macbeth (action))))(macbeth (murder(duncan)))" -- into the familiar structural constituents of linguistic theory -- clauses, subjects, and objects. By connecting propositions to linguistic objects, it is the dictionary that tells us which tokens are to serve as the predicates in the input message language, and which as arguments to the predicates. The dictionary is also the repository of information about what is called in linguistic theory grammatical relations -- for example, the information that, in English at least, the *Agent* of persuade is Lady-macbeth, and typically occupies a certain structural position in a phrase structure tree of the linguistic output -- the first Noun Phrase under a Sentence node (or the Subject, in familiar terminology); the dictionary further specifies Macbeth as the Object of the sentence, the first Noun Phrase dominated by the Predicate or Verb Phrase. In short, the dictionary provides a consistent way of associating grammatical objects (constituent structure trees) with the message objects, mapping thematic roles such as the "doer" of an action (the Agent) or the recipient of an action (the Patient or Goal) into positions in a phrase structure tree. Whatever the details of this process, and whatever one's particular tastes in grammatical theory, one thing is clear: a mapping from thematic roles (notions like Agent or Patient) to what are called grammatical relations (notions like Subject and Object) is something that almost every current linguistic theory advocates.

McDonald's grammar has the job carrying out such specifically linguistic work as deleting equivalent Noun Phrases in embedded constructions and actually modifying the structure of the constituent structure tree to produce a grammatical string of orthographic tokens. For example, in the Macbeth case, the grammar specifies the following series of alterations: (1) addition of a tense marker ("Lady-macbeth persuaded macbeth..."); (2) deletion of identical Noun Phrases (Equi-NP deletion) ("[Lady-macbeth persuade Macbeth [Macbeth murder Duncan]]$\Rightarrow$"[Lady-macbeth persuade [Macbeth murder Duncan]]"); and (3) interpolation of function words such as to (Lady-macbeth persuaded Macbeth murder Duncan$\Rightarrow$"Lady-macbeth persuaded Macbeth to murder Duncan"). The end product is a finished sentence, e.g., "Lady-macbeth persuaded Macbeth to murder Duncan". Thus the reconstruction of the surface string from message is broken down into several stages.

It is important to point out that this modular decomposition of representational levels from message to phonological form is part and parcel of modern generative linguistic theory, e.g., the work of Chomsky [Chomsky 1955]; [Chomsky 1965]; and many others. So for example, in the recent Chomsky theory, a level of representation at which thematic and predicate argument structure is expressed first gets mapped to a linguistic level that describes a constituent structure tree ("D-structure"), then, via grammatical rules (including "movement rules"), to a level of annotated surface structure ("s-structure"), and finally, to a phonological representation ("PF"). This is indeed roughly the block diagram of McDonald's approach. However, this logical decomposition does <u>not</u> specify a way of actually <u>computing</u> the phonological form, given an input message; this is the job of the generation model itself.

Furthermore, McDonald's actual generation procedure does not compute these stages separately, one after the other. Rather, the annotated constituent structure tree is built up piecemeal, left to right, in order that the fringe elements of the tree corresponding to actual orthographic tokens may be output as soon as possible. Thus, instead of building the entire tree for <u>Who kissed Bill</u>, the generation procedure actually first constructs only the fronted <u>who</u> portion. This node-by-node incremental output permits the generation procedure to actually "say" the token "who" before the remainder of the tree is completely built:[1]

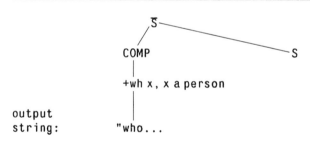

output
string: "who...

Figure 12 Producing a <u>wh</u>-question.

Turning now from questions of representation to questions of cognitive fidelity, we find that McDonald aims to account for a number of the obvious characteristics of human speech:

---

1. It also permits an efficient interleaving of processing: while the output tokens are being produced, the system can be constructing the next portion of the tree.

(1) Human speech production is <u>fluent</u> and <u>rapid</u>: whole clauses are produced without excessively long pauses; output proceeds at approximately a bounded rate.

(2) Human speech production is typically <u>error-free</u> and <u>well-formed</u> according to the rules of modern generative grammars, but with consistent exceptions.

(3) Speech is produced sequentially (an obvious physical constraint). (This does not exclude the ability to backup and restart the output of an entire phrase a common occurrence in everyday speech.)

(4) Speech is <u>planned</u> over representational units that are greater than one word in length.

The evidence for this last claim comes from well-established psycholinguistic phenomena. For instance, [Lashley 1951] pointed out that anticipatory errors such as, "The Patriots' number one draft <u>plunk</u> -- number one draft <u>pick</u>), Jim *Plunk*ett", are logically impossible unless speech is planned over expanses of greater than a single word. [Shattuck-Hufnagel 1979] Similar arguments also suggest that speakers must have some notion of how long a sentence must be before they produce it, since declination in fundamental frequency (the drop in baseline pitch of the voice corresponding to a decrease in the volume of air in the lungs)· is adjusted in order to comport with longer sentences. [Cooper and Sorenson 1977]. Finally, there is evidence for planning at a level that corresponds roughly to propositional units (whole clauses, such as <u>Lady-macbeth persuade Macbeth</u> (1 clause); <u>Macbeth murder Duncan</u> (a second clause) [Ford and Holmes 1978]. Below we shall provide evidence (as McDonald suggests) that such planning is strictly bounded, in the sense that the "window" over which the generator plans its behavior is limited in scope to approximately one additional sentential unit (one "S" node). (This is the production analogue of Marcus' [Marcus 1980] look-ahead limitation on a model of human sentence processing.)

McDonald's major computational thesis has to do with the observed efficiency of human language production and the constraints that this places on his generation procedure. Contemplating the apparent speed of fluent language output, McDonald stipulates that the output be constructed in <u>real time</u>, that is, at most k machine operations are permitted before the generation procedure <u>must</u>

take another step along the message tree structure and output a token.[1] This computational constraint, in turn, is used to motivate a series of constraints on (i) the input message language (the "well-formedness constraint"); (ii) the mapping procedure (it is deterministic, in that at any decision point a unique choice of next move can be made; it uses only limited look-ahead to determine its next move); and (iii) what the procedure can and cannot successfully produce (namely, it can successfully produce what people do and makes the same mistakes that people do). This argument is clearly run along the same lines as that of [Marcus 1980]: first, to assume that a strong computational (alias cognitive) fidelity assumption must be met -- namely, that normal fluent language is produced in real time without backup -- and second, to go on to deduce what machine properties are sufficient to achieve this computational constraint, while maintaining descriptive adequacy, all the while developing predictions about failure patterns of the generator that comport with human behavior.

How can these claims of efficiency be evaluated? The remainder of this section sketches an initial attempt to formalize the McDonald generation program as an example of a more theoretically familiar model -- an LL(k)-parser driven transduction, a top-down, deterministic, predictive parser that parses the input message string using a look-ahead of $\underline{k}$ tokens and at at the same time incrementally produces language output as desired.

Of course, this approach is not claimed to be the final word about how to formally reconstitute the McDonald approach. What is claimed is that the LL(k) formalization helps to expose the capabilities and limits of the McDonald generation procedure and at the same time admits a disciplined and rigorous evaluation of the constraints that he advances. Informal statements of the sufficiency of various constraints can be replaced by precise theorems. The LL(k) model, it is claimed, can capture all of the following properties of the McDonald model:

---

1. There is a slight difficulty using this definition straightforwardly, in that an output token can be a phonetic null element, i.e., silence. This is necessary for the generation of sentences where constituents have been displaced from their canonical positions -- e.g., so-called "movement" cases, as Who did Macbeth kill?. which is presumed to have the underlying form Wh-x, x a person, Macbeth killed x. A question then arises as to whether silences "count" in the time it takes to produce language output. Clearly they do sometimes: we have already noted that there are slight pauses at major constituent breaks. Finite phonetic adjustments will not affect any claim of linear time operation unless, there can be an arbitrary number of "pauses" that can pile up.

- Incremental node-by-node constituent tree construction and output.

- The message constraint. (If message element A makes reference to message element B, then B must be expanded before A.)

- A fully disambiguated message language.

- Deterministic operation.

- Traversal order of the constituent structure tree.

- Efficient (linear) execution time.

- Bounded lookahead for planning.

- Correspondence between violations of the fluency requirement in the model and (apparently) in human speech.

To check this claim in detail it will first be necessary to define a deterministic, predictive, top-down parser.

A top-down predictive parser with output and associated grammar G can be defined as consisting of the following components:[1] (1) a push-down stack; we shall denote the top-most element of this stack by T; (2) a finite parsing table (a two-dimensional array indexed by possible terminal items and top-most stack tokens); (3) an output string that is produced as the input string is analyzed; and (4) a finite control program that, in conjunction with the parsing table and input symbols currently scanned,[2] determines what the next move of the parser shall be. The action of the parser at any given step is determined by a transition function $\delta(T,w)$, where T = the symbol currently on the top of the push-down stack and w = the input symbol currently being scanned. The parsing table entry may also provide an appropriate symbol to output as well. There are three possible actions:

---

1. Actually, the parser described here can be constructed only if the grammar G has the property of being strong LL(k). This property will be defined shortly.
2. Only one symbol is scanned at a time in the network model presented above. We shall see how this may be extended to a lookahead of k tokens.

(1) If the stack and input string are empty (as noted by the presence of some pre-determined end of input marker as the top symbol on the stack), then halt and announce successful termination of the parse. (Acceptance is by empty stack and input.)

(2) If the top-most token T on the stack is the same as the current input token w, then remove T from the stack and go read the next input symbol; optionally, emit some output symbol.

(3) If the top-most token T on the stack is a nonterminal symbol, then lookup the entry corresponding to index (T,w) in the parsing table. The entry is either *error* (the string is not generated by the underlying grammar G), in which case the machine halts and announces rejection of the string;[1] or else a string of nonterminals XYZ that corresponds to the right-hand side of a grammar rule $T \Rightarrow XYZ$, in which case the symbols are placed onto the stack with the left-most nonterminal top-most on the stack (i.e., the topmost symbol on the stack becomes X, followed by Y, followed by Z, corresponding to a left-most expansion). Note that in this case we have "predicted" the expansion XYZ. Productions may also be of the form $T \Rightarrow \emptyset$, in which case the top of stack symbol is "erased."

The initial configuration of the machine is with its read head scanning the left-most symbol of the input string and its stack containing just S as the top-most symbol with the end-of-input symbol beneath:

---

1. Of course, one may do more than simply reject the input string: since an error is caused by the failure to find a predicted rule of the form $T \Rightarrow XYZ$, one at least knows what kind of phrase (left hand side of a rule) was being sought at the time the error occurred. and which sub-pieces of the right-hand side had already been constructed. This anticipatory context may in fact contribute to an explanation of planning errors of the Plunkett--pick type.

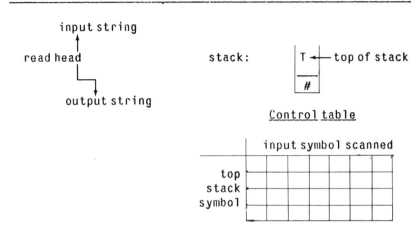

Figure 13 A predictive parser.

How exactly does the McDonald procedure simulate the behavior of a predictive parser? At first glance, there would seem to be an immediate paradox, in that McDonald asserts that his machine is a simple finite state machine "able to bind contextual variables but little else." But this paradox is more apparent than real. McDonald's controller is a finite state device, just as the controller (the finite control table plus controller) of a predictive parser is. However, both the McDonald procedure and a predictive parser operate in concert with stack-like data structures, implicitly in the case of the McDonald procedure and explicitly in the case of an LL(k) parser. Let us examine why this is so in more detail.

An LL(k) parser manipulates an explicit stack of activation records -- a list of non-terminal nodes. Stack discipline, plus the enumeration order of a left-most derivation, dictates which non-terminal will appear on the top of the stack next, and hence assist in the control of the parse. For example, consider again the familiar left-most derivation of Macbeth murder Duncan:

S⇒NP VP⇒Macbeth VP⇒Macbeth V NP⇒Macbeth murder NP⇒Macbeth murder Duncan

Suppose that one wrote down snapshots of the stack as it appeared during the LL(1) parse of this sentence. One would observe the following sequence of stack configurations (# is the end of stack symbol):

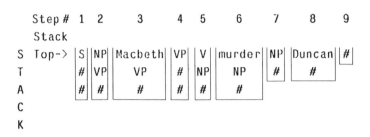

Figure 14 Stack configurations during a left-most parse.

Note that the top of stack symbols in this sequence correspond precisely to the order in which McDonald's finite state controller visits the nodes of the constituent structure tree that it constructs from the input message:

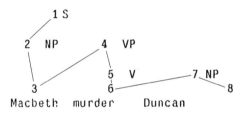

Figure 15 Traversal sequence of generation controller.

The LL(k) parser uses its stack simply to keep track of which non-terminal nodes are to be visited and the order in which they are to be visited. But this is precisely how McDonald's finite state controller makes use of its traversal of the constituent structure tree that is built. That is, instead of maintaining an explicit stack of activation records as an internal component of the parser itself, McDonald relies on a data structure -- the tree -- that is external to the generation procedure, maintained by the programming language in which his generation procedure is written. However, both methods perform exactly the same computational function: both internal stack and external tree data structure have the job of returning the correct next non-terminal node that will contribute to the next move of the parser. If one views the behavior of the stack or tree structure as a function that takes as input the current non-terminal, input symbol, and (fixed) finite parsing table, and produces as output a new non-terminal symbol, then stack and tree structures are extensionally equivalent; given identical inputs, they both return the same new non-terminal nodes for further computation.

Since an LL(1) parser's move is completely determined by the top-of-stack symbol and input symbol scanned, the equivalence between left-most tree traversal symbols and top-of-stack symbols in a top-down, left-most derivation means that the McDonald controller when driven by a finite table and using only one symbol of lookahead (the input symbol scanned) can be simulated by an LL(1) parser, and conversely.[1]

Let us consider just one simple example of the clarification this formal approach affords before reviewing all of McDonald's constraints. At first glance, one might think that in order to determine the proper expansion of some nonterminal -- say, the VP in our familiar leftmost expansion above -- one would have to keep track of the entire string parsed so far (that is, the entire prefix w to the left of the current input symbol being scanned) or even, worse yet, the entire parse tree already built. In fact, this is a worry that McDonald shares. He observes that this extended bookkeeping could lead to computational difficulties, since the sheer number of nodes in the parse tree to the left of some current expansion point can clearly be greater than a linear function of the input string parsed so far.[2] Since this computational burden might interfere with the aim of fluency, McDonald proposes a solution: the entire discourse history (input message scanned plus any relevant structure of the tree built so far) is to be stored, but in a random access list, so that items can be retrieved independently of their position in the list. In addition, McDonald notes that in some cases information must be "passed along" from node to node in the tree in order to aid with some particular expansion decision later on. However, it is not clear just what class of constructions would cause such problems; nor is it evident what or how much information must be "passed along".

With the LL(k) apparatus in hand, it is easy to make these intuitions precise. Consider first the puzzle of having to store all the words seen so far. This worry is a valid one, but it has already been ruled out by the LL(k) constraint. If the underlying grammar is LL(k), then we have already seen that one need not

---

1. More generally, a grammar is called strong LL(k) if the non-terminal symbol on the top of the stack plus the next k tokens of the input uniquely determine the next move of the parser. Thus, if a grammar is strong LL(k), then the simple parser designed sketched above can be straightforwardly extended to accommodate k tokens of lookahead.

2. In the worst case, if the length of the longest side of a re-write rule is l so that the "branching factor" of the tree is at most l, there could be l^{cn} interior nodes in the derivation tree for a string of length n.

remember all of the input seen so far in order to determine what to do next. More precisely, if a grammar is strong LL(k) then (current non-terminal, lookahead) pairs uniquely determine the next move of the automaton. In short, if the underlying grammar is LL(k), then McDonald's worries are groundless; there is no need for a random access list of previous discourse history in this case.[1] Moreover, the construction of complex category symbols for LL(k) grammars that are not strong provides a crisp characterization of what McDonald means when he says that information must be "passed along": it is exactly the complex category symbols (reflecting non-terminal-follow set combinations) that need to be saved on the stack for later reference.[2]

Let us now review the list of computational and cognitive claims that McDonald advances and see how the LL(k) property subsumes each of them.

Linear time production
It is a theorem that LL(k) parsing (with output) executes in time linearly proportional to the length of the input (message) string.[3]

Bounded lookahead and Top-down expansion
A necessary condition for LL(k)-ness is that top-down parsing can proceed using just bounded forward lookahead into the input string. Furthermore, by the properties of left-most derivations, the string of non-terminals to the <u>right</u> of some symbol A that is due for expansion is always more "abstract" than the material into which A will be expanded, in the sense that terminals will be derived from A before one ever proceeds to expand the non-terminals completely to the right of A.

Non-ambiguity
McDonald's input message language is fully disambiguated: the bracketing structure indicates exactly the scoping relations to be observed. As a result, there is only one derivation tree for an input message string. This is also a necessary condition for LL(k)-ness.

---

1. Except in the sense that the parsing table provides "random access" to a finite list of transition rules.
2. If a grammar is LL(k) but not strong LL(k), then the complex symbol approach constructs a new finite parsing table such that (complex symbol, lookahead) pairs also uniquely determine the moves of the parsing machine.
3. Reason: Since the grammar must be non-left recursive, any derivation A--> α must take only a linear number of steps. (This requires some proof.) Therefore, for a valid string in the language, there can be at most a linear number of steps before the stack is popped and an input symbol consumed; hence a number of steps linearly proportional to the input string in all.

Non-left recursion
If unaltered, McDonald's procedure must of necessity "pause" an arbitrarily long time before producing output for such messages as,

(((Mort's father's) cousin's) brother)

This is because if the finite state controller must traverse the message structure from node to node, then given a message structure such as the one above:

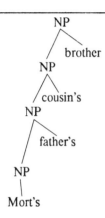

Figure 16 Left-recursive message structure.

an arbitrary number of nodes must be traversed before the first output token, Mort's, is ever produced, violating fluency. But left-recursion also violates the LL(k) condition. Hence, the LL(k) condition subsumes the left-recursion limitation.[1]

The LL(k) property and the message constraint
McDonald imposes the following constraint on the input message in order to guarantee that his production procedure meets the requirement of fluency:

---

1. If this is so, then one puzzle remains: just why are such constructions even producible in English? There have been at least several different explanations for this in the linguistics literature, but all seem to amount to much the same thing: it is assumed that the message input is somehow altered so that it is not left-recursive. ([Chomsky 1965] and [Liberman 1967]; [Chomsky and Halle 1968]; and [Krauwer and des Tombes 1980]) The proposals differ only with regard to how exactly the recursion is eliminated.

The Message Well-formedness Constraint (WFC) The order in which message elements will be realized must be such that any message element that will make reference to other elements in its realization must in fact be realized before any of those elements.
[McDonald 1980a]

As an example of this constraint, [McDonald 1980] offers the case of a message that violates the WFC by calling for the topicalization of an (arbitrarily) deeply embedded NP:

---

input
message: (topicalize (was reported(is likely(move...(the Shah)))))

desired
output: The Shah was reported to be likely to be moved...

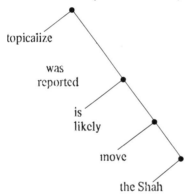

Figure 17 Input message that violates the well-formedness condition.

This message violates the WFC because topicalization requires that the deeply embedded element "the Shah" be expanded before it is "visible" to the tree traversal procedure. Since this element may be arbitrarily embedded, forward planning would have to be arbitrarily deep before the first output tokens, the Shah, could ever be produced.

Formally, the WFC is easily subsumed by the LL(k) condition. Consider the "Shah" case once again and let us assume an underlying phrase structure something like the following:

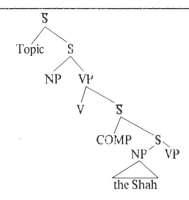

Figure 18 Syntactic structure for "Shah" sentence.

In the untopicalized version, the "Topic" node is expanded as the empty element, whereas in the topicalized case it is expanded as, e.g., "the Shah". However, the proper expansion decision clearly violates the LL(k) condition. The reason is simple. In order to expand the Topic node properly, the generator must have access to an NP arbitrarily far to the right of its current position.

Violations of the LL(k) condition comport with observed errors in human language generation.

As we have seen, the key constraints of McDonald's that ensure rapid output and hence fluent language generation can be succinctly described as constraints that guarantee that its underlying grammar is LL(k). However, as we also have seen, not all grammatical constructions can be parsed deterministically top-down via bounded lookahead; for example, left-recursive structures cannot be so parsed.

This connection between bounded look-ahead and the inability to successfully analyze certain constructions provides an opportunity for empirical testing of the LL(k) model of language generation. If language generation does make use of only bounded forward planning, then one would expect to find consistent failure on certain sorts of sentences -- namely, exactly those where the decision to expand a particular nonterminal cannot be made correctly without a lookahead that exceeds that used by the generation procedure. Evidence of such failures would provide strong support for the kind of model that McDonald proposes.

As it turns out, there is significant evidence of regular errors in everyday speech that are explainable if one assumes bounded lookahead, as observed by [Kroch 1981]. Kroch notes that people often produce ungrammatical embedded sentences with so called resumptive pronouns:

The guy who they don't know whether he will come or not...

In the example above, <u>he</u> is a resumptive pronoun, presumably co-designative with <u>the guy</u>.

Importantly, such sentences are generally judged ill-formed, even immediately afterwards by the speakers who have produced them; yet they are widespread in speech. The reason for the ungrammaticality of such sentences has been generally attributed to a violation of an "island constraint" [Ross 1967]: loosely speaking, <u>the guy</u> points to a pronoun that is "too far" away. Specifically, any binding relationship between <u>the guy</u> and <u>he</u> crosses <u>two</u> <u>wh</u>-S boundaries:

$$[_{NP} \text{ the guy}[_S \text{ who}.....[_S \text{ whether he}$$

Furthermore, the sentence is perfectly interpretable.

It is easy to show how bounded lookahead interacts with the requirement for continuous language output to produce the desired pattern of cases. Consider first how the McDonald procedure would plan a <u>wh</u> relative clause, such as, <u>the guy who I know</u>. At the input message level, McDonald expresses such a phrase by conjoining an <u>abstract</u> element, corresponding to the head Noun in question, <u>the guy</u>, and a <u>refinement element</u>, corresponding to some added (extensional) detail about the abstract element (e.g.,<u>I know the guy</u>).[1] Thus, there is an assumed underlying semantic grounding for the message description. As usual, McDonald's dictionary maps this quasi-semantic level of description to a linguistic level, assigning message elements to parts of a constituent structure tree. In this case, the abstract element gets attached to a <u>fronted clause</u>, soon to be realized as a head Noun, and the refinement element to some <u>matrix</u> phrase whose syntactic details have not yet been determined:

Clause

fronted phrase   matrix phrase

(the guy)   (I (know (the guy)))

Continuing, the generation procedure expands the fronted phrase into a full orthographic representation, so as to maintain the requirement of producing

---

1. Note that these items are unordered.

output as soon as possible. Note that one could not wait to do this until the entire matrix phrase were realized in detail, since the matrix phrase could be arbitrarily long. Thus the guy is produced without having decided upon the internal details of the matrix phrase:

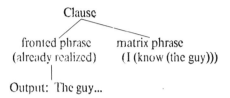

Clause

fronted phrase   matrix phrase
(already realized)   (I (know (the guy)))

Output: The guy...

Finally, the matrix phrase itself is expanded. First, the phrase is marked +wh (since it is known to be a matrix of some fronted clause). With the phrase so flagged, assume that the generation procedure has a rule that outputs the token "who" (as opposed to, e.g., "that'); exactly how this is done is irrelevant to present concerns. The generation procedure must now handle "I know the guy." Here, the wh flag plays a crucial role: it tells the procedure that when the NP "the guy" is finally analyzed, it is to be realized as a phonetically null element rather than, as would typically be the case, actual lexical items. (Otherwise, the output would be the incorrect form, "the guy who I know the guy.")

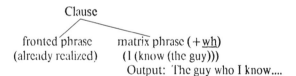

Clause

fronted phrase   matrix phrase (+ wh)
(already realized)   (I (know (the guy)))
               Output: The guy who I know....

The resulting output is just as desired.

The crucial point to observe about this example is that the syntactic details of phrases are worked out in advance only one S at a time; when the initial head Noun "the guy" is output, the syntactic "guts" of the wh-clause matrix have not been specified.

Consider then what happens when the refining clause contains a sentential clause of its own -- that is, when it contains an embedded element, as in, "I don't know whether the guy will come". The head Noun "the guy" will be output as before without planning the details of the syntactic realization of the message element to come -- as it must, if we are to assume continuous output. Then the procedure commences to output the wh-matrix phrase, just as before (turning on the wh-nullification flag):

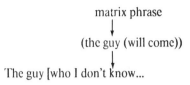

matrix phrase

(the guy (will come))

The guy [who I don't know...

Next, the embedded message element, (the guy (will come)) is processed. Suppose that this element is also realized as a wh-phrase, and a choice of "whether" as the lead-in wh-lexical item is selected:

The guy who I don't know whether...

What is to happen next? The wh-flag is still on, so the standard move would be to erase the message element "the guy", just as in a typical wh-phrase. But this would be an error:

??The guy who I don't know whether will come....

Note further that the ill-effect of "erasing as usual" can be locally checked; only the immediately surrounding context is required in order to tell that this structure is hopelessly bad.[1]

All seems lost. Suppose though, as Kroch suggests, that discourse NPs -- pronouns or anaphoric NPs -- are available to the generation procedure. Since the discourse machinery is already known to operate across utterances, then insertion of discourse items is clearly not subject to wh-island restrictions. If so, then one should be able to insert such an item, salvaging interpretability of the sentence at the cost of a syntactic violation. This is exactly what one finds:

He's the guy who I don't know whether he will come....

That these inserted items are indeed discourse entities is substantiated by the fact that resumptive anaphoric NPs also occur in wh-island violation positions, as Kroch points out:

The men that we didn't even know why the guys were in jail.

---

1. A sentence without a lexical Subject such as this one violates what [Chomsky 1981], [Kayne 1981], and others have dubbed the Empty Category Principle (ECP): if a sentence has a non-lexical or "phonetically "empty" categories -- such as in Who did you kiss [$_{NP}$empty]? -- then these categories must be bound in a "local" domain, usually the nearest sentential clause. In the case at hand, an empty category in the position after "whether" could not be locally bound.

In sum, we conclude that a computationally bounded machine of the sort McDonald proposes can actually _predict_ certain aspects of human language processing -- the best one could hope for from any theory, computational or not.

By now I hope that I have convinced you that it is precisely this emphasis on _process_ that gives these theories their special personality and flair. Webber aims to tell us how to _map_ from a logical form representation to discourse entity descriptions, Sidner how focus _moves_. Kaplan and Allen model how a hearer's beliefs about a speaker are _constructed_, McDonald, how language is _produced_. In every case the focus is on _how_ something gets done -- as befits the term _computational_ model. Having surveyed the territory and left behind some tourguide tips, I will leave it to the reader to judge how well they succeed in their respective theories of _how_.

CHAPTER 2

Recognizing Intentions From Natural Language Utterances

James Allen

2.1 Introduction

In order to design good question answering systems we need to build in some of
the characteristics of human conversation. In particular, they should be able to
provide responses that specify more information than strictly required by the
question. They should not, however, provide too much information or provide
information that is of no use to the person who made the query (cf. [Grice 1975]).
For example, consider the following exchange at an information booth in a train
station.

(1.1)	patron:	When does the Montreal train leave?
(1.2)	clerk:	3:15 at gate 7.

Although the departure location was not explicitly requested, the clerk provided it
in his answer. (All the examples given in this paper are taken from transcripts of
dialogues collected at the information booth in Union Station, Toronto [Horrigan
1977].)

Other examples of this kind of helpful behavior, however, do not involve
language. For example, if the patron approached a closed door in the station
carrying a large bag of groceries in each arm, the clerk might very well open the
door for him. This may occur without any communication occurring between
them. We claim that the motivation for the clerk's behavior in both these
examples is the same; the clerk wants to assist the patron in furthering his goals.

This paper concerns the modeling of such helpful behavior and, in particular,
it investigates how such a model can be used to explain several aspects of linguistic
behavior. We make the following assumptions:

> People are rational agents who are capable of
> forming and executing plans to achieve their
> goals

- They are often capable of inferring the plans of other agents from observing that agent perform some action

- They are capable of detecting *obstacles* in another agent's plans.

Let us define <u>obstacles</u> to be situations which inhibit the goal achieving process of an agent. In this paper, all obstacles will be in the form of subgoals that the agent cannot achieve without assistance.

The major claim of this paper is that many instances of helpful behavior arise because the observing agent recognizes an obstacle in the other agent's plan, and acts to remove the obstacle. In particular, we are most interested in the obstacles that can be removed by the use of language.

To model this, we view the use of language itself as goal-oriented behavior. Utterances are produced by actions (<u>speech</u> <u>acts</u>) that are executed in order to have some effect on the hearer. This effect typically involves modifying the hearer's beliefs or goals. A speech act, like any other action, may be observed by the hearer and may allow the hearer to infer what the speaker's plan is. Often a speech act may explicitly describe an obstacle (i.e., a subgoal) to the hearer. For example, utterance (1.1) conveys to the hearer that the speaker needs to know the departure time of the train. But there may be other obstacles in the plan that were not explicitly conveyed (e.g. the speaker may also need to know the departure location). The helpful response will attempt to overcome these obstacles as well as the explicitly mentioned ones.

Our viewpoint provides the basis for explaining some aspects of helpful behavior in dialogue, including:

- the generation of responses that provide more information than required (as in the above example)

- the generation of responses to sentence fragments

- the analysis of *indirect speech acts*.

Let us consider each of these aspects in turn, and see how the model proposed above applies to each.

It is fairly simple to see how the model could explain the providing of more information than explicitly requested. In the train domain, the clerk expects that the patron has goals such as boarding or meeting trains. A query (e.g. (1.1)) about a train departure time, as opposed to one about a train arrival, indicates that it is likely that the patron's plan is to board the train. In addition, assuming that the clerk believes that the patron does not already know the departure location, he believes that not knowing the location is also an obstacle in the plan. Thus he generates a response that overcomes both obstacles (i.e., (1.2)).

This same model can explain how sentence fragments can be understood when the context is sufficiently defined. For instance, the following exchange occurred at the train station:

> (2.1)   patron: The 3:15 train to Windsor?
> (2.2)   clerk: Gate 10

Neither the syntactic form of the query nor the meaning of its words indicate what the response should be. However, given our viewpoint above, it is quite conceivable that the information in the fragment is sufficient to allow the hearer to infer what the speaker's plan is. Hence he can produce a reasonable response based on what the obstacles in the plan are. In the above example, (2.1). is sufficient to identify the speaker's goal to board the 3:15 train to Windsor. An obstacle in this plan is knowing the departure location, hence the response (2.2). Other sentences in the dialogues are not treated at face value. For instance,

> (3.1)   patron: Do you know when the Windsor train leaves?

Syntactically, this is a yes/no question about the hearer's knowledge. However, an answer of "yes" in the given setting would be quite inappropriate. In other surroundings, however, it could be intended literally. For instance, a parent seeing a child off at the station and wanting to make sure that everything is arranged might say (3.1) intending to receive a yes/no answer. Sentences such as this that appear to mean one thing yet are treated as though they mean something else are termed indirect speech acts [Searle 1975]. These forms can also be explained using the viewpoint above. Simply stated, the solution lies in the realization that the speaker knows that the hearer will perform such helpful behavior, and hence may say something intending that the hearer infer the indirect goal.

This paper describes the plan inference and obstacle detection processes and shows how they can be applied to explain helpful responses and the understanding of sentence fragments. The model is then extended to provide a general theory of indirect speech acts. Section 2 provides an overview of the entire approach, and then Section 3 provides details of the plan inference and obstacle detection processes. Section 4 applies these techniques to language analysis. It considers two examples of responses that provide more information than explicitly asked for. Section 5 re-examines the definition of speech acts and introduces the notion of shared knowledge between the speaker and the hearer. The plan inference mechanism is then extended to handle indirect speech acts. Using the extended system, Section 6 describes an analysis technique for sentence fragments.

A system based on the work in this paper has been implemented and tested in the train domain described above [Allen 1979]. While the dialogues in this domain are somewhat restricted in subject matter, they provide a wide range of linguistic behavior that has not previously been explained.

2.2 An Overview of the Model

Let us start with an informal description of what we think occurs when one agent A asks a question of another agent B which B then answers. A has some goal; s/he creates a plan (plan construction) that involves asking B a question whose answer will provide some information needed in order to achieve the goal. A then executes this plan, asking B the question. B interprets the question, and attempts to infer what A's goals could be (plan inference). The inferred goals may include the original goal that A is pursuing, as well as many subgoals. Some of these may not be achievable without B's assistance and so represent obstacles. Being helpful, B may plan to remove some of the obstacles. This plan should include the response to A's original query.

This section outlines the mechanisms that are needed to specify this model a bit more precisely. The first part of it considers the issues of representing knowledge about the world, goals, actions and speech acts. The succeeding sections describe the plan construction, plan inference, and obstacle detection processes, respectively.

2.2.1 Actions, Plans and Speech Acts

We need to be able to represent our intuitive notions of plan, goal, and action and relate them to language. These problems have already received much attention, both as problems in the philosophy of language and from the point of view of artificial intelligence.

Our formulation of actions and plans is taken from some existing work in problem solving [Ernst and Newell 1969; Fikes and Nilsson 1971]. In these systems, the world is modeled as a set of propositions that represent what is known about its static characteristics. This world is changed by actions, which can be viewed as parameterized procedures. Actions are described by preconditions, conditions that must hold before the action can execute, and by effects, the changes that the action will make to the world. Given an initial world state W and a goal state G, a plan is a sequence of actions that transforms W into G.

Austin [Austin 1962] suggested that every utterance is the result of several actions or speech acts. We are particularly interested in the class of speech acts that includes requesting, warning, asserting, informing, and promising. These speech acts are appropriate only in certain circumstances. In particular, they may require the speaker and the hearer to have certain beliefs and intentions. For example, to sincerely *INFORM* you that I am tired, I must believe that I am tired and I must intend to get you to believe that I am tired. Both these conditions can be modeled as preconditions on the INFORM act. A simple version of this act could have the effect that you now believe that I am tired.

Cohen [Cohen 1978] demonstrated that speech acts such as requesting and informing can be modeled successfully as actions in a planning system. He showed how speech acts may be planned in order to achieve specific (typically non-linguistic) goals.

2.2.2 Plan Construction

Given a goal state, two major tasks need to be done to produce a plan to achieve that goal. One is to find a sequence of actions that will accomplish the transformation from the initial world state to the goal state. The other concerns specifying the bindings for the parameters of the actions in the constructed plan.

A typical method of constructing a plan is backwards chaining: given a goal G, find an action A that has G as one of its effects. Then evaluate the preconditions of A. If some of these conditions are not satisfied in the initial state, they become subgoals and the plan construction process repeats.

Another dimension of plan construction involves planning at different levels of abstraction (see [Sacerdoti 1973]). For example, in a domain where a robot has to plan a route through many rooms, the plan would first be developed in terms of "go to room x" and "open door y." Only after such a plan was constructed would one consider planning actions such as "rotate n degrees," "propel forwards," "twist arm," etc. To incorporate this, many actions must have the capability of being "broken down" into sequences of more specific actions.

We are, for the most part, interested in reasoning about the planning behavior of other agents. In order to facilitate this reasoning about the planning process, we characterize it as a set of planning rules and a control strategy. Since this paper is mainly concerned with plan inference, we will not consider control strategies for planning explicitly. However, many of the control issues for plan inference are directly applicable to planning as well. The crucial point here is that these planning rules will be used to derive a similar description of the plan inference process in the next section.

The planning rules are all of the form "If agent A wants to achieve X, then he may want to achieve Y." A simple rule is:

> (C.1) *If an agent wants to achieve a goal E, and ACT is an action that has E as an effect, then the agent may want to execute ACT (i.e., achieve the execution of ACT).*

One other rule of interest concerns reasoning about knowledge necessary to execute an action.

> (C.2) *If an agent wants to achieve P and does not know whether P is true, then that agent may want to achieve "agent knows whether P is true."*

These ideas will be made more precise in Section 3.

2.2.3 Plan Inference

Plan inferencing concerns the attempted (re)construction of some other agent's plan based on actions that that agent was observed performing. This process depends on both the observer's knowledge of what constitutes a rational plan and on his or her original beliefs about what goals the other agent is likely to have.

Possible candidates for the other agent's plan can be synthesized in two manners. Starting from the expected goals, the observer could simulate the other agent's planning process, searching for a plan that includes the observed action. Obviously, most of the time such an approach is impractical. The alternative is to construct a plan from the observed action, by applying the plan construction rules in reverse. The method we propose depends mainly on the latter approach, but does use the former when circumstances permit. People probably use much more specialized knowledge to infer the plans of other agents, thereby bypassing many of the inferences we will suggest here. Our approach so far, however, has been to specify a minimal set of reasoning tools that can account for the behavior observed. Given these tools, we then hope to precisely define and explain the more complex and specialized mechanisms by deriving them from the simple set.

As with the plan construction process, the plan inference process is specified as a set of inference rules and a control strategy. Rules are all of the form "If agent S believes agent A has a goal X, then agent S may infer that agent A has a goal Y." Examples of such rules, corresponding to the planning rules (C.1) and (C.2) are:

> (D.1) *If S believes A has a goal of executing action ACT, and ACT has an effect E, then S may believe that A has a goal of achieving E.*

> (D.2) *If S believes A has a goal of knowing whether a proposition P is true, then S may believe that A has a goal of achieving P.*

Of course, given the conditions in (D.2), S might alternately infer that A has a goal of achieving not P; this is treated as a separate rule. Which of these rules applies in a given setting is determined by control heuristics, as follows.

The plan inference process can be viewed as a search through a set of partial plans. Each partial plan consists of two parts: one part is constructed using the plan inference rules from the observed action (and called an alternative), and the other is constructed using the plan construction rules on an expected goal (and called an expectation). When mutually exclusive rules can be applied to one of these partial plans, the plan is copied and one rule is applied in each copy. Each of these partial plans is then rated as to how probable it is to be the correct plan. The highest rated partial plan is always selected for further expansion using the inference rules. This rating is determined using a set of heuristics that fall into two classes: those that evaluate how well-formed the plan is in the given context and those that evaluate how well the plan fits the expectations. An example of a heuristic is:

> (H1) *Decrease the rating of a partial plan if it contains a goal that is already true in the present context.*

2.2.4 Obstacle Detection

We claim that many helpful responses arise because the hearer detects obstacles in the speaker's plan. The most obvious obstacles are those that the speaker specifically brings attention to by his or her utterance. These explicit obstacles are indicated by subgoals that are an essential part of the chain of inferences that the hearer makes when he or she infers the speaker's plan. For example, to infer the plan of the speaker from the utterance

(4.1)   When does the Windsor train leave?

the hearer must infer that the speaker has the goal of knowing when the train leaves. Since the speaker does not know this information, this is an explicit obstacle.

The hearer cannot, however, base the response solely on these explicit obstacles. For instance, if A, carrying an empty gas can, comes up to S on the street and asks

(5.1)   Where is the nearest gas station?

and S answers

(5.2)   On the next corner

knowing full well that the station is closed, then S has not been helpful. But S's response did address the explicitly mentioned obstacle, namely knowing where the nearest gas station is. S may want to notify A if there are other obstacles to A's plan, especially ones that A is not aware of. This behavior is expected; even when A and S are strangers, if A believes that S knew all along that the gas station was closed, then A has justification for being angry at S, for S has violated some basic assumptions about human cooperation.

In the dialogues we have studied, all obstacles are caused by a lack of some information required in order to be able to execute the plan. This is not the case in general, as we saw in the example where the clerk opens the door for the patron carrying the groceries. There the clerk responded to an obstacle which arose from the patron's inability to open the door,

2.2.5 Related Work

Although there has been some previous work on recognizing plans and generating helpful responses, to our knowledge, no one else has attempted to combine the two techniques. [Bruce 1980] outlines a general model of story comprehension based on recognizing the intentions of the characters in the story as well as the intentions of the author. Although a slightly different application, our work here agrees with his view. Bruce does not, however, describe any algorithm for actually recognizing the intentions in his stories.

Schmidt et al. [Schmidt 1979] discuss a plan recognition algorithm where physical actions are observed and their task is to discover what the agent is doing. But they allow an arbitrary number of acts to be observed before committing themselves to a particular plan. This technique is appropriate for analyzing sequences of actions. In our work, however, it is essential that we identify at least part of the speaker's plan from a single observed action (i.e., the initial utterance). Thus, as the dialogue continues, this plan becomes further specified.

Wilensky's system, PAM [Wilensky 1978], analyzes stories by constructing a plan for the participants and then answers questions about the story using the plan. However, it does not attempt to recognize the plan of the agent asking the questions or to do any plan based reasoning about language. PAM answers questions solely on the form of the question asked (see [Lehnert 1977a]).

Kaplan (this volume) discusses helpful responses to questions which are based on violated presuppositions conveyed by the question. This work fits well with the approach described here, as violated presuppositions should introduce discrepancies between what the system believes and what the system believes the speaker believes. These discrepancies could then be recognized as obstacles in the speaker's plan, and hence influence the response. Thus our paper, by dealing with helpful behavior in a more general form, provides a general framework in which it is useful to view Kaplan's work.

2.3 Plan Inference and Obstacle Detection

Some representation issues must be considered before the plan inference process can be described in detail. Section 2.3.1 discusses the representation of belief, knowledge and want, and Section 2.3.2 considers actions and plans. The description of plan inference is then broken into three parts: we consider the plan inference rules in Section 2.3.3, the rating heuristics in Section 2.3.4, and the control of the process in Section 2.3.5.

The final section considers how obstacles are detected in the plans that are inferred.

2.3.1 Belief, Knowledge, and Wants

Describing an adequate model of belief would take an entire paper by itself. We can just outline a few of the important issues here. Our treatment of belief is virtually identical to that of [Hintikka 1963]. The reader interested in the implementation should see [Cohen 1978].

Formalizations of belief exhibit a crucial property: what one agent S believes another agent A believes has no logical relation to what S believes. Thus, S may believe A believes the world is flat while personally believing that it is round.

Intuitively, the belief operator allows us to consider actions and plans from another agent's point of view. This can be approximated by the axiom schema

$$(\text{BELIEVE}(A, P \supset Q) \ \wedge \ \text{BELIEVE}(A, P)) \supset \text{BELIEVE}(A, Q)$$

Thus, one may infer that A inferred some proposition Q if it is believed that A believes that there is sufficient evidence to infer Q. We also need an axiom that states that conjunction can "pass through" the belief operator. Thus, if S believes that A believes P is true and that A believes Q is true, then S also believes that A believes P and Q are true, and visa versa. Written more formally:

$$\text{BELIEVE}(A, P) \ \wedge \ \text{BELIEVE}(A, Q) \equiv \text{BELIEVE}(A, P \wedge Q)$$

A similar axiom is *not* valid for disjunction.

Note that the operator BELIEVE also has to be indexed by the time when the belief was held. For the sake of simplicity, however, we will ignore time throughout this paper.

Some formulas involving beliefs occur commonly enough to warrant special mention. In particular, there are three constructs associated with the word "know" that arise very frequently.

The first involves representing that an agent S believes some A knows that P is true. This not only conveys the fact that S believes A believes P, but also that S believes P as well, i.e.,

$$\text{BELIEVE}(S, P \wedge \text{BELIEVE}(A, P))$$

As an abbreviation, we define

$$A \text{ KNOW } P = P \ \wedge \ \text{BELIEVE}(A, P).$$

In other words, if BELIEVE(S, A KNOW P), then S believes that S and A agree that P is true. This, of course, has no implication as to whether P is "actually" true.

The next structure involves uses of "know" as in "John knows whether P is true." This is the type of belief S would have to have if S believed that John was able to answer a question such as "Is P true?". It is represented as the disjunction

$$A \text{ KNOWIF } P = (P \land \text{BELIEVE}(A,P)) \lor$$
$$(\neg P \land \text{BELIEVE}(A, \neg P))$$

The final use of know is in the sense demonstrated by the sentence "John knows where the box is." This case is represented by quantifying over the BELIEVE operator:

$$A \text{ KNOWREF } D = (\exists y)(D=y) \land \text{BELIEVE}(A, D=y)$$

where D is a description. In the above example it would be "the x such that the location of the box is x." For further details on these representations of "know," see [Allen 1979].

Goals and plans of agents are indicated by using an operator WANT, i.e.,

$$WANT(A,P) = A \text{ has a goal to achieve P.}$$

By this, we mean that the agent A actually intends to achieve P, not simply that A would find P a desirable state of affairs. The concepts of "wanting," "intention," and "having a goal" are extremely hard to distinguish and analyze. In this paper, the distinctions are ignored for the WANT operator is used to capture all three simultaneously. The properties of the WANT operator will be specified only by the planning and plan inference rules.

2.3.2 Actions and Plans

As with the operators in STRIPS [Fikes and Nilsson 1971], actions can be grouped into families represented by action schemas. An action schema consists of a name, a set of parameters and (possibly null) sets of formulas in the following classes:

- *Preconditions*: Conditions that should be true if the action's execution is to succeed.

- *Effects*: Conditions that should become true after the successful execution of the action.

- *Body*: A specification of the action at a more detailed level. This may specify a sequence of actions to be performed, or may be a set of new goals that must be achieved.

Each action definition may also specify applicability conditions on the parameters: conditions that must be true for the action to be well defined. Every action has at least one parameter, namely the agent or instigator of the action. Note that we do not have a set of deletion conditions for our actions as found in STRIPS. In our system, a proposition is deleted by asserting its negation.

An action instance is a proposition constructed from an action schema name with a set of parameter instantiations and a time specification. The proposition is true only if the described action is (was or will be) executing at the specified time. For example,

ACT(S)⟨t⟩ - a predicate that is true only if the action ACT with agent S was/will be executed at time t.

We will say that an action is intentional if whenever the action was performed, the agent wanted it to occur at that time. Thus, if ACT is an intentional act, A any agent, t any time, then

ACT(A)⟨t⟩ ⊃ WANT(A, ACT(A)⟨t⟩).

Thus, in a loose sense, there is a "precondition" on every intentional action that the agent must want to perform the action. We will sometimes refer to this condition as the want precondition of the act.

In general, the time specification will be omitted. If an action is within the immediate scope of the BELIEVE operator, it is assumed to have a time specification in the past. If it is within the immediate scope of a WANT operator, it is assumed to have a time specification in the future.

Actions are not only reasoned about, sometimes they are executed. The execution of an action is specified either as primitive or by its body. If the body is a sequence of other actions, this sequence may be recursively executed. If the body is a set of new goals, plan construction must be initiated on the goals and then the resultant plan executed.

It will often be convenient to refer to an action and its associated preconditions, effects and body as a single unit. Such action clusters are action schemas with instantiated parameters.

A speech act is an intentional action that has as parameters a speaker (i.e., the agent), a hearer, and a propositional content, and whose execution leads to the production of an utterance. Its preconditions and effects are defined in terms of the beliefs and wants of the speaker and hearer. For the present, we will assume that the speech act intended by the speaker can be readily identified from the syntactic form of the utterance. This assumption, which is obviously incorrect, will be removed in the later sections of the paper concerning indirect speech acts and sentence fragments.

In its final form, a plan is a linear sequence of action instances that will map an initial world state into a goal state. But as Sacerdoti [Sacerdoti 1975] points out, plans cannot easily be constructed in linear form. He uses a representation that imposes only a partial ordering on the actions, where the orderings are imposed only when necessary. We use a similar representation.

A plan can be represented as a directed graph with propositions (goals and actions) as nodes and labeled arcs indicating their interrelationships. These arcs implicitly specify a partial ordering on the actions. The *enable* arc links a proposition that is a precondition of an action to that action. Likewise, an *effect* arc links an action to a proposition that is its effect. The *know* arc links a KNOWIF or KNOWREF proposition to a proposition in a plan whose truth values cannot be determined unless the "know" proposition is true. For example, the planner cannot achieve the goal

"planner at the location of n"

unless

"planner KNOWREF the location of n."

To permit plans to be represented at varying levels of detail, a plan structure itself can be a node in a plan. These "plan" nodes represent the bodies of actions. The body arc links an action to a plan node that contains its body.

2.3.3 The Plan Inference Rules

The plan inference process starts with an incomplete plan, usually containing a single observed action and an expected goal and attempts to fill in the plan. The possible additions that can be made are described in this section as a set of plausible inference rules. They are presented without any consideration of whether the inference is reasonable in a given setting, for whether or not a rule is applied depends on the likelihood that the new plan specification it produces is the actual plan. This is evaluated using the heuristics described in the next section.

The notation

$$SBAW(X) \supset_i SBAW(Y)$$

indicates that if S believes A has a goal of X, then S may infer that A has a goal of Y. The "i" in the rule indicates that it is a plan inference rule, as opposed to a plan construction rule, which will be indicated by using a "c". Note that

"SBAW(X)"

is simply an abbreviation for

"BELIEVE(S,BELIEVE(A,WANT(A,X)))."

Note that all goals are propositions. If the proposition is associated with an action, then we will describe having such a goal by saying that A wants the action to occur. Otherwise, we will describe having a goal by saying that A wants to achieve the condition signified by the proposition.

The possible rules can be divided into three broad categories: those that concern actions, those that concern knowledge, and those that concern planning by others. All these rules are summarized in Tables 1 and 2 at the end of this section.

The Rules Concerning Actions

These rules arise from the model of how plans are constructed. Throughout this section, S refers to the agent that is inferring the plan of another agent A.

> *Precondition-Action Rule*
> $SBAW(P) \supset_i SBAW(ACT)$ -- if P is a precondition of action ACT.
> Thus, if A has a goal of P, then A may want an

action ACT enabled by P to occur.

Body-Action Rule

   SBAW(B) $\supset_i$ SBAW(ACT) -- if B is part of the
   body of ACT.
   Thus, if A wants an action B to occur, that is
   part of the execution of another action ACT, A
   may want ACT to occur.

Action-Effect Rule

   SBAW(ACT) $\supset_i$ SBAW(E) - if E is an effect of
   ACT.
   Simply, this says that if A wants an action ACT
   to occur, then A may want the effects of ACT to
   be achieved.

Want-Action Rule

   SBAW(WANT(n,ACT)) $\supset_i$ SBAW(ACT) - if n
   is the agent of the intentional action ACT.
   This rule is based on the want precondition for
   intentional actions.
   Intuitively, this says that if A wants n to want to
   do some action ACT, then A may want n to do
   ACT.

The Rules Concerning Knowledge

These inference rules indicate how goals of acquiring knowledge relate to goals
and actions that use that knowledge. The first two rules reflect the fact that if A
wants to know whether a proposition P is true, then it is possible that A wants to
achieve a goal that requires P to be true (or requires P to be false). The third one
indicates that A wants to know whether P is true in order to establish the identity
of one of the terms in P. For example, one might ask, "Does the RAPIDO leave at
3?" in order to establish a departure time of 3 o'clock.

   Know-positive Rule
      SBAW(A KNOWIF P) $\supset_i$ SBAW(P)

   Know-negative Rule
      SBAW(A KNOWIF P) $\supset_i$ SBAW($\neg$P)

Know-value Rule
SBAW(A KNOWIF P(a)) $\supset_i$
SBAW(A KNOWREF the x : P(x)).

Of course, in any plan alternative, at most one of the first two rules can be correct. The decision as to which of these is correct, or that none of these is correct, is the responsibility of the heuristic evaluation of the plans produced by applying the rules.

One special case is of interest here. If A indicates that he or she has a goal

A KNOWIF P

and it is known between S and A that A already knows whether P, then the path that agrees with A's knowledge is taken. For example, if S is playing with a dime in front of A, and A asks

"Do you have a dime,"

only the know-positive inference to the goal "S have a dime" would be produced.

The final inference rule about knowledge concerns goals, of finding the referents of descriptions. It suggests that such a goal indicates that A has another goal that involves the referent.

Know-term Rule
SBAW(A KNOWREF the x:D(x)) $\supset_i$
SBAW(P(the x:D(x)))
where P(the x:D(x)) is a goal or action involving
the the description (or its referent).

Because of the vagueness in the resulting goal, this rule does not produce reasonable plans unless a specific goal or action of form P(D) already exists in the expectations.

The Rules Concerning Planning by Others

The plan construction process can be described in the same manner as the plan inference process; as a set of rules that describe possible constructions, and a set of heuristics to evaluate the resulting plans. The plan construction rules are simply the inverses of the plan inference rules. Some examples are given below. X is the name of the agent doing the plan construction, and "XW(Y)" is an abbreviation for "BELIEVE(X,WANT(X,Y))." For these rules we use the notation "$\supset_c$" to indicate a plan construction rule.

> *Action-Precondition Rule*
> $XW(ACT) \supset_c XW(P)$ if P is a precondition of
> ACT.

Thus if X wants to execute ACT, X may want to ensure that its preconditions are true.

> *Action-Body Rule*
> $XW(ACT) \supset_c XW(B)$ if B is part of the body of
> ACT.

> *Effect-Action Rule*
> $XW(E) \supset_c XW(ACT)$ if E is an effect of ACT.

Of course, if E can be achieved by many actions, each one of them could be introduced by this rule. As with plan inference, the plans constructed using this rule would then have to be evaluated by a set of evaluation heuristics.

> *Know-Rule*
> $XW(P) \supset_c XW(X \ KNOWIF \ P)$

Thus, if X wants to achieve P but doesn't know whether P is true, X must find out whether P is true.

When X constructs a plan involving the cooperation of another agent Y, X may depend on Y to do some plan construction as well. Thus, X might get Y to perform some action ACT by getting Y to have the goal of achieving ACT's effects. For example, assume that X wants to have a surprise birthday party for his roommate Y and needs to get Y out of the house. X says

"We need some beer"

expecting Y to assume the goal of getting beer, and then construct a plan to get some. This involves leaving the house, the goal X had all along. Thus X has reasoned about Y's planning process. Crudely, this new planning inference rule can be described as

$$XW(WANT(Y,\text{"leave house"})) \supset_c XW(WANT(Y,\text{"get beer"}))$$

since X believes

$$WANT(Y,"get\ beer") \supset_c WANT(Y,"leave\ house")$$

Thus, if X wants Y to want to do ACT, he may achieve this by getting Y to want to achieve E, where Y's planning process will infer ACT as a way of achieving E. In general, we have the set of plan construction rules

Nested-Planning Rule
$$XW(WANT(Y,P)) \supset_c XW(WANT(Y,Q))$$
$$if\ XB(WANT(Y,Q) \supset_c WANT(Y,P))$$

This rule schemata is of interest when it is assumed that there is no deceit between the agents, and both realize that the planning by the hearer was intended. Thus, a king might say

"It's cold in here"

to a servant, expecting the servant to plan to make the room warmer.

Action-Precondition	$XW(ACT) \supset_c XW(P)$	P a precondition of ACT
Action-Body	$XW(ACT) \supset_c XW(B)$	B is part of body of ACT
Effect-Action	$XW(\exists) \supset_c XW(ACT)$	E an effect of ACT
Know-Rule	$XW(P) \supset_c$ $XW(X\ KNOWIF\ P)$	
Nested Planning	$XW(WANT\ (Y,P)) \supset_c$ $XW(WANT(Y,Q)$	if X believes $WANT(Y,Q) \supset_c$ $WANT(Y,P)$

Table 1 The plan construction rules.

But for the servant to understand the king's intention in the above example, he must recognize that the king's plan included planning by the servant. We can characterize inferences that construct these new plans as follows (reverting back to

S as recognizer, A as the observed agent):

The Recognizing Nested-Planning Rule
$$SBAW(WANT(S,P)) \supset_i SBAW(WANT(S,Q))$$
$$\text{if } SBAB(WANT(S,P) \supset_c WANT(S,Q))$$

This rule can be paraphrased as follows: If A has a goal of S wanting to achieve P, then A may also have a goal of S wanting to achieve Q, given that A believes S would plan to achieve Q in order to achieve P.

One of the most common ways in which an agent A can get S to want some condition is to get S to believe A wants the condition and then depend on S's cooperation. Thus, A is getting S to decide to accept the goal. This introduces the last inference:

Decide Inference
$$SBAW(SBAW(P)) \supset_i SBAW(WANT(S,P))$$

Unfortunately, the conditions under which an agent decides to accept a goal are extremely difficult to describe. In this paper, we take the naive view that an agent will decide to adopt a goal unless he explicitly is known not to want the conditions it implies. This condition is enforced by the rating heuristics in the next section.

Precondition-Action	SBAW(P) $\supset_i$ SBAW(ACT)	P a precondition of ACT
Body-Action	SBAW(B) $\supset_i$ SBAW(ACT)	B a part of the body of ACT
Action-Effect	SBAW(ACT) $\supset_i$ SBAW(E)	E is an effect of ACT
Want-Action	SBAW(WANT(n,ACT)) $\supset_i$ SBAW(ACT)	n is the agent of ACT
Know-Positive	SBAW(A KNOWIF P) $\supset_i$ SBAW(P)	
Know-Negative	SBAW(A KNOWIF P) $\supset_i$ SBAW(not P)	
Know-Value	SBAW (A KNOWIF P(a)) $\supset_i$ SBAW (A KNOWREF the x : P(x)))	
Know-Term	SBAW (A KNOWREF D) $\supset_i$ SBAW (P (D))	
Recognition of Nesting Planning Rule	SBAW(WANT(S,P)) $\supset_i$ SBAW(WANT(S,Q))	if SBAB(WANT(S,P) $\supset_c$ WANT(S,Q)))
Decide Inference	SBAW(SBAW(P)) $\supset_i$ SBAW(WANT(S,P))	

Table 2 The plan inference rules.

2.3.4 Rating Heuristics

As mentioned above, plan inferencing is accomplished by a search through a set of specifications of <u>partial plans</u> that consist of two parts. One part is constructed bottom-up using the plan inference rules from the observed action (and called the <u>alternative</u>), and the other is constructed top-down using the plan construction rules from an expected goal (and called the <u>expectation</u>). (In the implementation, partial plans may contain many expectations sharing one common alternative.)

Each partial plan is assigned a rating, which is determined using heuristics described in this section, that reflects how likely it is to be part of the "correct" plan. These heuristics are based solely on domain-independent relations between actions, their bodies, preconditions and effects. The initial partial plans are given a rating of 1. The heuristics are expressed here only in terms of increasing and decreasing the ratings. The actual formulas are very simple and given in Table 3 at the end of the section. This is organized in this way to emphasize the fact that while rating changes in the indicated direction are essential to our model, we feel that some variation is possible in the actual figures.

Finally, before we give the heuristics, we must make the distinction between actions that are currently in execution, those awaiting execution (pending), and those that have been executed. In particular, the observed action is considered to be currently in execution, and any action which contains an action currently in execution in its body is also considered to be currently in execution.

Action Based Heuristics

Generally, one expects agents to construct plans that they believe they are able to execute, and they execute them only to achieve goals that are not presently true. This gives us two rules:

> (H1) *Decrease the rating of a partial plan if it contains an action whose preconditions are false at the time the action starts executing.*

> (H2) *Decrease the rating of a partial plan if it contains a pending or executing action whose effects are true at the time that the action commences.*

Heuristic H1 implies that, if the action is presently in execution, then the preconditions should not have been false when the action was initiated. It also implies that, if the action is pending, then its preconditions must be achieved within the plan or must be achievable by a simple plan. As a first approximation to a simple plan, we define it as a hypothesized plan consisting of a single action whose preconditions are already true.

Expectation-Based Heuristics

This heuristic favors those partial plans whose alternatives seem most likely to merge with their expectation.

> (H3) *Increase the rating of a partial plan if it contains descriptions of objects and relations in its alternative that are unifiable with objects and relations in its expectation.*

The term unifiable is used here in the sense of the unification algorithm found in resolution theorem provers (see [Nilsson 1971]). Thus, if an alternative involves a train description, those expectations that involve a (compatible) train will be favored. Similarly, if an expectation involves a relation such as arrival time, its alternative seems more favorable if it also involves an arrival time relation.

Search Based Heuristics

The remaining heuristics involve evaluating which partial plans should be considered next from a search efficiency point of view. These measure how specific the plan fragment is becoming. A couple of heuristics relate to events that produce important specializations to the plan, i.e., identifying referents of descriptions and identifying the speech act.

> (H4) *Increase the rating of a partial plan if the referent of one of its descriptions is uniquely identified. Decrease the rating if it contains a description that does not appear to have a possible referent.*

> (H5) *Increase the rating of a partial plan if an intersection is found between its alternative and expectation, i.e., they contain the same action or goal.*

The final heuristic favors alternatives that have produced inferences that are well rated enough to be applied.

> (H6) *Increase the rating of a partial plan each time an inference rule is applied.*

Finally, we end this section with a few implementation details. Each partial plan has a <u>weight</u> that is used to calculate its rating. Heuristic H3 adds a fixed factor of 5 for each similarity found. (The actual value 5 has no effect on the search except possibly for roundoff considerations in the rating calculation.) All other heuristics affect the weight by a multiplicative constant.

The total weight of all the partial plans is used in calculating each plan's rating. The rating of a plan P is simply the percentage of the total weight that plan P has. The actual values of the multiplicative factors are provided in Table 3.

Heuristic	Description	Factor
H1	Preconditions false	.5
H2	Effects true	.5
H4	Referent Identified	1.5
H4	Referent impossible	.2
H5	Intersection found	1.5
H6	Inference Rule applied	1.25

Table 3 The multiplicative factors for the heuristics.

2.3.5 The Control of Plan Inferencing

As mentioned previously, partial plans are modified and refined by a set of programs (tasks) that are attached to them. When a task is suggested, it is given a rating that is strongly dependent on the partial plan that it is to manipulate and is placed on a priority list according to this rating. The top rated task is always selected for execution and removed from the list. This section describes the various types of tasks.

It is important for search efficiency considerations that there be extensive interactions between the expectations and alternatives. The information in an expectation may specify constraints on an alternative that restrict what possible inferences could be made from it, and vice versa. For instance, if both an expectation and an alternative refer to a train, the trains are assumed to be identical (unless they are incompatible).

The initial set of partial plans consists of all pairings of an alternative containing only the observed action and one of the original expectations. To allow for the possibility of an utterance that does not fit an expectation, a partial plan is also constructed with a null expectation.

The actual tasks that perform the plan inferencing can be divided into three classes: those that specify the structure of the plans, those that identify objects on the plans, and those that control the search.

The Plan Specification Tasks

The plan specification tasks make additions to a plan hypothesis according to the inference rules discussed above. Alternatives are expanded using the plan inference rules and expectations are expanded using the planning rules. There are many occasions when mutually exclusive rules can be applied. In such cases, copies of the partial plan are made and one rule is applied in each. When such a split occurs, the rating of the partial plan is divided between its successors.

Plan specification is performed by two tasks: Infer and Expand. Infer examines a plan and suggests possible inference rules to apply. Expand actually applies these rules to modify the partial plan. The processing is divided to allow explicit control of the "fan-out" of the search: when an Expand is suggested from an Infer, its rating is determined by the rating of the partial plan it concerns, plus an estimate of the number of splits it will make. The greater the number of splits, the lower the rating (see Table 4). The relation between these two is set so that the copying (i.e., the splitting) will not be done until the newly created partial plans would be sufficiently well-rated to produce tasks that are competitive on the agenda.

The Identify Task

The plan being inferred will usually contain many descriptions of objects whose referents must be identified. Some of these descriptions were introduced by the utterance itself while others are introduced by the inferences. As an example of the latter, in applying the precondition-action rule, there may be a parameter in an action definition that is not part of its precondition. Thus, this parameter will not be specified when the action is introduced into the plan, although there may be constraints on its referent imposed in the action definition.

Likewise, existing descriptions may acquire additional constraints as the inferences are made. An action introduced into a hypothesis may specify constraints on one of the parameters in the plan that unified with one of its parameters.

Thus new descriptions may be introduced and old descriptions may be further specified as the inferences are made. Each time such a change occurs, an Identify task is suggested that will attempt to find a referent.

Note that since some agent S is inferring another agent A's plan, all evaluation of descriptions must be done with respect to what S believes A believes. In general, if S believes that there is only one object that A believes could fit the constraints, then it is the referent. This is in fact not a sufficient condition, but will suit our purposes here. [Perrault and Cohen 1981] examine reference problems in detail.

Identification of referents may require the use of domain specific inferences. For example, in the train domain, there is a need for an inference rule that says, "If a train is described without a time specification, then it is probably the next train that fits the description." Whether such a heuristic could be inferred from the general structure of plans, or whether it is truly domain specific, remains a problem. For example, if the train domain were extended to also allow telephone calls for information, this assumption would probably not be valid.

The Search Control Tasks

Most of the control mechanisms are built into the rating scheme and the plan inferencing monitor. For instance, every time an addition is made to an alternative, the expectations are examined for new similarities caused by the addition. This may cause a change in the ratings according to the expectation-based rating heuristics.

Some mechanism must terminate plan inferencing. This is done by the task Accept, which is suggested by the monitor whenever an intersection of alternative and an expectation seems possible because they contain unifiable specifications of a step (i.e., an action or goal) in the plan, or when the plan with the null expectation has twice as high a rating as any other partial plan. Accept must decide whether to terminate the plan inferencing or not. At present, the termination condition is fairly simple: if the plan under consideration has a rating twice as high as any other partial plan, it is accepted. This is implemented by suggesting a dummy task at half the present task's rating. This task will sit on the pending list until all better rated tasks have executed. When it comes to the top, if no other Accepts have been executed, the original alternative is identified as the speaker's plan and plan inference stops. If another Accept has executed, there is an ambiguity, which can be used to generate clarification subdialogues (see [Allen and Perrault 1980]).

Task	Rating Formula
Infer	.75 * R
Expand	.75 * R * f(n) where f(n) = 1.25/n, where n is the number of new partial plans to be created by the Expand
Identify	R
Accept	R

Table 4 The rating of tasks relative to the rating (R) of their partial plans.

2.3.6 Obstacle Detection

Once S has inferred the speaker's plan, the next step, in order to be helpful, is to identify the obstacles in that plan. Most obstacles that we are concerned about involve a lack of knowledge that is necessary in order to execute the plan. For example, if a proposition P is a goal in A's plan, and S believes that A does not know whether P holds, i.e., SB(A not KNOWIF P), then A KNOWIF P is an obstacle. Similarly, if the plan involves a description, say "the x:D(x)," that S believes A does not know the referent of, then "A KNOWREF the x:D(x)" is an obstacle. These obstacles can be derived by applying the knowledge-based plan construction rules to each step in the plan. This, of course, might not detect every obstacle in the speaker's plan, since the entire plan of the speaker may not be inferred. Only enough of the plan to link the observed utterance to an expectation is generated by the plan inference component.

Given a set of obstacles, there are a few techniques useful for deciding which to address. For instance, the obstacles can be partially ordered using the ordering constraints imposed by the plan. In such cases, any obstacles prior to a given obstacle O must be addressed if O is to be addressed. For example, if A is carrying groceries in his arms and needs to pass through two doors, it does no good for S to open the second door unless he also opens the first.

Another effective filter on the obstacles involves considering which obstacles the hearer intended to communicate. In particular, the goals that (S believes) A believes S can achieve are most likely to have been intended by A. For example, in the train station setting, the clerk not only does not sell tickets, but he also believes that the patrons know this. As a consequence, although not having a ticket may be an obstacle in a plan to board a train, the clerk does not expect the patron to ask him for a ticket (because he can't provide one).

The above are useful strategies if S believes that both S and A agree on what the obstacles in the plan are. However, if S and A disagree on some issue, special obstacles occur that must be addressed. For example, if A thinks that state X already holds and is depending on X in his plan, but S believes X does not hold, then S is obliged to mention this fact to A. Otherwise, A's plan will fail and S will be considered as uncooperative. In the reverse case, if A thinks state X is not true, but S believes it in fact already holds, then S should tell A, for A may not execute his (valid) plan because he thinks it will not succeed.

There is one class of obstacle that is truly difficult to detect but should be considered. If there are two goals in a plan and one is just a step towards achieving the second, then the heuristics above will indicate that the first is the only obstacle. However, in some cases, achieving the second eliminates the need to ever (Even temporarily) achieve the first. For example, if A and S are in a locked room and A asks S where the key to the door is, S might deduce the following goals:

"A know where key is" in order to "Get the door open."

If S opens the door himself, say by some means other than using the key, then the goal of knowing the key's location becomes irrelevant. However, detecting such situations is quite difficult and beyond the scope of the present work, for it may involve considering the speaker's plan to an arbitrary distance into the future with no well defined termination condition.

The algorithm used in the system involves testing every goal statement in the plan. Obstacles are selected using the following preferences:

1) those goals that S and A disagree about whether they hold or not;

2) those goals that are explicitly indicated as obstacles by the utterance, i.e., the inference path from the surface speech act to an expected goal includes the obstacle;

3) those obstacles that prohibit the performance of the actions that are partially enabled by the goals in class 2); and

4) those obstacles that are not "preceded" by other goals in the plan.

The algorithm returns the set of obstacles in the highest preference class that is not empty.

2.4 Examples of Helpful Responses

This section provides two examples of helpful responses that can be produced using the plan inference and obstacle detection processes. The first shows a simple response that provides more information than was explicitly requested. It is described in some detail to give an idea of the actual plan inference mechanisms in operation. The second example considers a yes/no question and shows why extra information should be provided if the answer is negative.

Before the examples are presented, the train domain is specified (Section 2.4.1) and definitions are given for the speech acts (Section 2.4.2).

2.4.1 The Train Domain

The setting for the examples is the train station information booth, S is the system playing the role of the information clerk, and A is a patron at the station. The non-linguistic actions relevant to the simple train domain are:

BOARD(agent,train,station)

applicability conditions: SOURCE(train,station),
DEPART.LOC(train,loc), DEPART.TIME(train,time)

precondition: AT(agent, loc, time)

effect: ONBOARD(agent,train)

MEET(agent, train, station)

    applicability conditions: DEST(train,station),
    ARRIVE.LOC(train,loc), ARRIVE.TIME(train,time)

    precondition: AT(agent, loc, time)

    effect: MET(agent,train)

S's expectations are the partially instantiated plans formed from the following action instantiations with their preconditions and effects:

    BOARD(A, ⟨train⟩, TORONTO)

    MEET(A, ⟨train⟩, TORONTO)

where the angle brackets (⟨...⟩) indicate unspecified parameters in the expectations. At the start of processing, there are three partial plans each with a null alternative and each containing one of the BOARD, MEET, or NULL expectations. The first example shows that the number of expectations could be increased without greatly affecting the combinatorics of the search.

2.4.2 The Speech Act Definitions

The speech act definitions provided here are very superficial. A more adequate account will be given in the discussion of indirect speech acts in Section 5. The INFORM speech act, which is typically realized as a declarative sentence, is defined as follows:

    INFORM(speaker, hearer, P)

    precondition: speaker KNOW P

    effect: hearer KNOW P

For an agent A to sincerely inform an agent H that P is true, A must believe that P is true (the precondition), and he must intend to get H to know that P is true (the effect of a successful inform). Since INFORM is an intentional act, we also have the axiom

INFORM(speaker,hearer,P) ⊃
    WANT(speaker,INFORM(speaker,hearer,P))

Note that this action cannot succeed without the cooperation of the hearer, for only the hearer can change his own beliefs.

In many cases, agents reason about inform acts to be performed (by others or themselves) where the information for the propositional content is not known at the time of planning. For example, A may plan for S to inform A whether P is true; A cannot plan for S to perform INFORM(S,A,P) since this assumes that P is true. Thus we need two other "views" of the INFORM act: INFORMIF and INFORMREF. (From now on, the "want-precondition" axioms will be omitted):

INFORMIF(speaker, hearer, P)

precondition: speaker KNOWIF P

effect: hearer KNOWIF P

and

INFORMREF(speaker, hearer, description)

precondition: speaker KNOWREF description

effect: hearer KNOWREF description

One further speech act that we need models one agent requesting another agent to do some action:

REQUEST(speaker, hearer, action)

effect: hearer WANT (hearer DO action)

The following examples show typical realizations of these speech acts in English.

> "The train leaves at 3" intended literally is an
> INFORM that the train leaves at 3.

> "Open the door" intended literally is a REQUEST that
> the hearer open the door.

"Does the train leave at 3" intended literally· is a REQUEST that the hearer inform (INFORMIF) the speaker whether the train leaves at 3.

For the time being, we will assume that all speech acts are realized in their literal form, and thus can be easily identified from the input utterance.

2.4.3 Example I: Providing More Information than Requested

This is a very simple example to give an idea of the plan inference process in operation. It has been modified from the way the actual system runs so it can be described in terms of the simple view of partial plans as one expectation and one alternative.

Let the observed action be:

REQUEST(A,S,INFORMREF(S,A,time1))

where

TIME(time1) $\wedge$ DEPART.TIME(train1,time1)

TRAIN(train1) $\wedge$ DEST(train1,WINDSOR).

Such an action could be constructed from an utterance such as

"When does the train to Windsor leave?"

This action specifies an action cluster consisting of a REQUEST to INFORMREF that is added to the plan alternative in each partial plan. The partial plans are then examined for similarities. Within the BOARD plan is the definition of an instance of the BOARD action, with its preconditions and effects. Therefore the objects A, the train to Windsor, and the DEPART.TIME relation are found in both the alternative and expectation (adding a weight of 20 to the plan to make a total of 25). The train descriptions in the alternative and expectation are merged to form a more complete description, i.e., both the source (TORONTO) and the destination (WINDSOR) are known. With the MEET plan, only A is found to be similar (giving it a total weight of 10). The train description in the MEET plan is found to be incompatible with the train description in the alternative. If there were other expectations, they would be rated similarly, but most would probably have little in common with the utterance, and so would start off poorly rated. The null expectation plan starts with its token weight of 5.

The initial ratings are calculated as follows. There is a total weight of 40 assigned to the three partial plans. The board plan, with a weight of 25, receives a rating of 62; the meet plan, with 10, receives 24; and the null plan receives 12. After this initial processing, the partial plans are as in Figures 1a and 1b.

The initial tasks suggested are:

1) Identify the train in the BOARD plan, rated 62.

2) Infer from the REQUEST act cluster in the BOARD
        plan, rated 46
                (i.e., .75 x 62).

3) Identify the trains in the MEET plan, rated 25.

4) Infer from the REQUEST act cluster in the MEET
        plan, rated 19.

5) Identify the train in the NULL plan, rated 12.

6) Infer from the REQUEST act cluster in the NULL
        plan, rated 9.

Identifying the Train in the BOARD Plan

Identifying the train in the BOARD plan succeeds, the assumption being made that the next train leaving is the one intended unless the speaker says otherwise. Thus train1 is identified with an entry in the schedule, say ENTRY-TRAIN17. This provides further evidence that the BOARD plan is the correct one, increasing the BOARD plan's rating to 71 (weight 37) at the expense of the other partial plan ratings.

The BOARD plan (rated 62):

The expectation:
BOARD(A,train1,TORONTO)

↑
| enable
|

AT(A,loc1,time1)

The alternative:
(1) REQUEST(A,S,INFORMREF(S,A,time1)):

|
| effect
↓

(2) S WANT INFORMREF(S,A,time1)

where
-- TRAIN(train1) ∧ SOURCE(train1,TORONTO) ∧
    DEST(train1,WINDSOR)
-- DEPART.TIME(train1,time1)
-- DEPART.LOC(train1,loc1)

Figure 1a The initial set of partial plans (initial part).

The Infer and Expand Cycle

The Infer task on the BOARD plan (now rated 53) is executed. Inferring from (2) in the BOARD plan, the effect of the REQUEST finds only the want-action rule applicable. An Expand task is suggested (rated 53), which immediately executes, since it is the best rated task, adding the action

(3) INFORMREF(S,A,time1)

Added in the action cluster with (3) is its effect

(4) A KNOWREF time1

The MEET plan (rated 25):

    The expectation:
    MEET(A,train2,TORONTO)

        ↑
      | enable
      |

    AT(A,loc2,time2)

    The alternative:
    (1) REQUEST(A,S,INFORMREF(S,A,time3)):

      | effect
      |
      ↓

    (2) S WANT INFORMREF(S,A,time3)

where

    -- TRAIN(train2) ∧ DEST(train2,TORONTO)
    -- ARRIVE.TIME(train2,time2)
    -- ARRIVE.LOC(train2,loc2)
    -- TRAIN(train3) ∧ DEST(train3,WINDSOR)
    -- DEPART.TIME(train3,time3)

The null plan (rated 12) contains only the alternative as described above in the MEET plan.

Figure 1b The initial set of partial plans (concluded).

and another Infer task is suggested from (4). Since an inference has been applied, the BOARD plan's rating is increased (heuristic H6) to 75 (weight 46). This Infer and Expand cycle is executed again. The know-term rule finds a link between (4) and the DEPART.TIME relation in the precondition to the BOARD action expectation. The monitor notices this intersection between the alternative and the expectation (and boosts the rating by heuristic H5, to 82 (weight 69)), and suggests an Accept task (rated 82). This task terminates the plan inference for there are no other well-rated hypotheses. The final plan is shown in Figure 2.

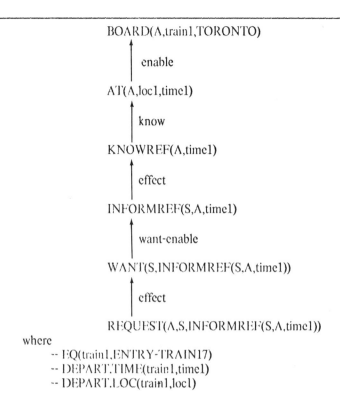

BOARD(A,train1,TORONTO)

↑ enable

AT(A,loc1,time1)

↑ know

KNOWREF(A,time1)

↑ effect

INFORMREF(S,A,time1)

↑ want-enable

WANT(S,INFORMREF(S,A,time1))

↑ effect

REQUEST(A,S,INFORMREF(S,A,time1))

where
-- EQ(train1,ENTRY-TRAIN17)
-- DEPART.TIME(train1,time1)
-- DEPART.LOC(train1,loc1)

Figure 2 The final plan fragment.

S now performs the next step to help A, namely, find the obstacles in A's plan and select from them some goals to achieve. One obstacle is straightforward. A has explicitly indicated the goal of knowing the departure time of the train. However, S examines the plan further and finds an implicit obstacle that A needs to know the departure location. S accepts these goals as his own and plans to achieve each goal simply with an inform. When this plan is executed, output is produced that corresponds to the English utterances:

"The train leaves at 1600"

"The train leaves from Gate 7"

An interesting problem remains as to how S could have planned to achieve both goals with a single utterance such as

"1600 at Gate 7"

How does one construct a plan to achieve multiple goals simultaneously? It may be possible that the specifications would be simply sent to a generation phase (see Chapter 4 of this volume) which could detect the similarities and collapse the two utterances into one.

2.4.4 Example II: A Yes/No Question Answered No

In this section we consider answering a question such as "Does the Windsor train leave at 4?". Assume that this utterance identifies the action

REQUEST(A,S.INFORMIF(S,A,DEPART.TIME(train1,1600)))

where

TRAIN(train1) $\wedge$ CITY-RELATION(train1,Windsor)

CITY-RELATION is a pattern that will match the predicate names DEST and SOURCE. The inferences from this action will eventually produce the goal (by applying the action-effect rule, the want action rule, and then the action-effect rule).

A KNOWIF LEAVE(train1,1600).

The possible knowledge-based rules suggest goals for A such as

"A wants the train to leave at 4" [know-positive]

"A wants the train not to leave at 4" [know-negative]

"A wants to know what train leaves at 4" [know-value]

"A wants to know when the train leaves" [know-value]

The first three of these possibilities do not lead to reasonable plans (i.e., they do not allow inferences that lead to a merge with an expectation). For example, none of the expectations involves a subgoal of knowing what train leaves at 4. The latter goal leads to a reasonable plan directly: applying the know-term rule from it produces a connection to the third argument of the precondition to the BOARD action, namely

AT(A,loc1,time1)

where

DEPART.LOC(train1,loc1)

DEPART.TIME(train1,time1).

Possible obstacles in this plan are found to be the explicitly mentioned goal of knowing whether the train leaves at 1600, plus the obstacles of knowing the departure time and location. For the sake of clarity, let us assume that the location is already known in this example. The obstacles remaining are

KNOWIF (A,DEPART.TIME(train1,1600))

KNOWREF (A,time1)

where DEPART.TIME(train1,time1).

If the answer to the original query were "yes," then both these goals would be accomplished by answering the query as a yes/no question. But if the answer is "no," only the first obstacle is achieved by the yes/no answer. The second obstacle accounts for the extra information.

This example reflects a general point. When a person asks about the truth of some proposition that happens to be false, s/he often is interested in a related, true proposition. The main problem is determining how to modify the original proposition to make it true. Our feeling is that, with respect to a given set of goals, the objects referred to by the terms in a proposition can usually be ordered by some criteria reflecting their importance in the plan. The more important the term, the less likely it is that it is what is wrong in the proposition. We suggest that a major indicator of a term's importance is how high up in the hierarchy of subgoals the term is first introduced.

In the example above, the train description was introduced in the top level goal of boarding the train, while the departure time was introduced (in terms of the train) in the subgoal created by the precondition of the boarding action. This approach seems to be quite general. As an example, consider a co-operative response cited by Kaplan (Chapter 3 of this volume).

(1a) Is John a senior?
(1b) No, he's a junior

It makes little sense to consider an answer out of context. For instance, if I am a professor needing a senior to do some project for me, a more appropriate response to my query (1a) would be

"No, but Sam is"

This is because my goal of finding a senior is a supergoal of the goal of finding out John's status. Thus the response that addresses the higher level goal is more appropriate. If, on the other hand, my goal were to find out more about John, then knowing John's status would be more important than knowing who is a senior, hence response (1b) would be appropriate.

2.5 Indirect Speech Acts

The indirect speech act problem is best introduced by an example. Consider the plan that must be inferred in order to answer (1) with (2):

(1) A: Do you know when the Windsor train leaves?
(2) S: Yes, at 3:15.

The goal inferred from the literal interpretation is that

(3) A KNOWIF (S KNOWREF "departure time").

Applying the know-positive rule, we obtain the goal

(4) S KNOWREF "departure time"

which enables P to perform the action (precondition-action rule)

(5) INFORMREF(S,A,"departure time")

to achieve the goal (action-effect rule)

(6) A KNOWREF "departure time"

S's response (2) indicates that he believed that both (3) and (6) were obstacles that S could overcome.

However, sentences such as (1) are often uttered in a context where the literal goal is not an obstacle. For instance, A might already know that S knows the departure time, yet still utter (1). In such cases, A's goals are the same as though he had uttered the request

(7) When does the Windsor train leave?

Hence, (1) is often referred to as an indirect speech act [Searle 1975].

Although the mechanisms already described are capable of answering such indirect acts correctly, they cannot distinguish between the two following cases:

(a) A said (1) merely expecting a yes/no answer, but S answered with the extra information in order to be helpful;

(b) A said (1) intending that S deduce his plan and realize that A really wants to know the departure time.

Theoretically, these are very different: (a) describes a yes/no question; while (b) describes an (indirect) request for the departure time. But the distinction is also important for practical reasons. For instance, assume S is not able to tell A the departure time for some reason. With interpretation (a), S can simply answer the question, whereas, with interpretation (b), S is obliged to give a reason for not answering with the departure time.

In this section we will reformulate our speech act definitions in order to handle such cases, as well as to bring our work in line with the philosophical views. We will introduce a new set of surface linguistic acts that correspond directly to the form of the utterance. For example, an imperative mood sentence will always be an instance of a surface request act (SURFACE.REQUEST) whether it is interpreted directly or not. Likewise, an indicative mood sentence will always be an instance of the SURFACE.INFORM act. These acts will be defined precisely in Section 2.5.3.

The speech acts will then be defined solely by intentions of the speaker and will correspond to the illocutionary acts in [Austin 1962]. These acts will usually be performed by executing some surface act. An essential condition for the performance of an illocutionary act will be that the speaker intended the hearer to recognize that the speaker intended to perform that act, as in [Searle 1969].

This recognition of intention condition can only be accomplished by introducing the notion of shared knowledge, or mutual belief, between the speaker and hearer. Mutual belief is the common set of beliefs between the speaker and hearer that each knows the other knows. Thus, each agent is aware of what inferences the other could make using this common knowledge. Since both agents are aware of the possible inferences that can be made from an utterance in a given context, the speaker should select his utterances so that only the desired inferences are made. The hearer, knowing this, may decide that the speaker intended him to make the inferences he made. In fact, at present, all inferences made in this context are considered to be intended by the speaker. As a result, some inconsequential conclusions may be assigned unwarranted significance. This has not led to trouble in the examples we have studied so far. To remove this problem will require considerable work on the nature of intentions.

Returning to the example above, we can now express the difference between the two interpretations of "Do you know when the Windsor train leaves?" with the aid of the following diagram (Figure 3):

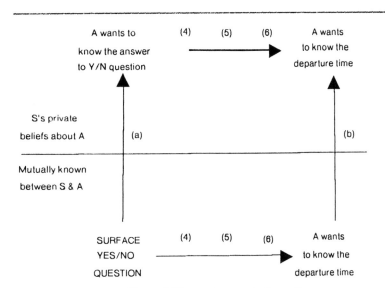

Figure 3 The two interpretations of
"do you know when the Windsor train leaves?"

Notes: The horizontal lines represent plan inferencing, the numbers referring to the steps in the initial discussion of this example. The vertical arrows represent the end of inferencing using shared knowledge, and hence determine the speech act interpretation.

In this figure, there are two paths from the shared knowledge that A asked a yes/no question (bottom left of Figure 3). to S's belief that A wants to know the departure time (top right of Figure 3). Both paths, identified as paths (a) and (b), involve the inferences through steps (4), (5), and (6). However, in path (a), S uses his private knowledge about A and hence believes that A intended only a yes/no question. In path (b), S made the same inferences using shared knowledge between them, and hence concluded that A intended S to recognize goal (b). Thus, path (a) represents the literal interpretation, and path (b) represents the indirect. Because of S's disposition towards helpful behavior, his response may be the same in both of these cases. However, as mentioned above, if S did know the departure time but was not allowed to tell A, then S's response would be different in each of the interpretations.

There is a fundamental assumption that determines which of these paths will be taken as the correct interpretation. This is that

> *the hearer will always attribute intention to the speaker if it is consistent to do so.*

In other words, the hearer will continue to use shared knowledge to make the inferences for as long as possible.

All of these issues will be discussed in detail in the following sections. In particular, Section 2.5.1 introduces the new speech act definitions and outlines the role of mutual belief; Section 2.5.2 defines the surface linguistic acts; Section 2.5.3 describes the extended plan inference system that can use the new speech act definitions; Section 2.5.4 presents some examples; and Section 2.5.5 discusses some remaining issues.

2.5.1 Speech Acts and Mutual Belief

It is important to the following discussion that it is clear at which level of abstraction we are attempting to define actions such as INFORM and REQUEST. The description we want is one where the acts are defined by the intentions of the speaker. Thus, saying "Close the door," "Can you close the door," or "the door," with the same intentions should all count as the same type of action, i.e., a REQUEST. Thus, these acts are not defined in terms of the linguistic forms that are used to attain them. The actual performance of a speech act consists of other actions that are performed with the correct beliefs and intentions. Thus we see that speech acts are not actions which are simply executed in plans, but are summaries of the beliefs and intentions of the speaker that allow an agent to describe the speaker's actions as constituting the speech act. The initial definition of the INFORM act in this paper suggests two of these conditions, namely that:

> -- the speaker must know that what he or she says is true (the precondition);

-- the speaker must intend that the hearer knows what
he or she says is true (intending the effect).

The weaknesses of the present definition have been well known to philosophers for some time. As mentioned above, [Grice 1975] suggested that communicative acts require that the speaker intends the hearer to recognize his intention to achieve the effects of the act. To see this, consider the situation where S believes P is true, and wants to get A to believe P as well. S walks up to another agent B and asks where A is for she wants to tell A that P. Unbeknownst to S, A overheard the question to B. Thus, the above two conditions hold, and S actually achieved her intended effect. Yet this does not seem to be a case of S sincerely informing A that P.

Thus we need to add a condition that the speaker intends to achieve the effect by means of the hearer recognizing the speaker's intention to achieve the effect. In our notation, this is the condition:

speaker WANT
  hearer BELIEVE
    speaker WANT
      hearer KNOW prop.

We are now quite close to the formulation of INFORM by [Searle 1969], except we have no conditions dealing with the production of the utterance.

Unfortunately, [Strawson 1971] points out that a single level of recognition of intention is not sufficient for a successful INFORM. [Schiffer 1972] then constructs a series of examples that show that no depth of recognition of intention is sufficient. These arguments could be discarded as not very relevant to our investigation, as the counter-examples are bizarre enough so that they should never arise in normal conversations. However, a solution close to Schiffer's is so simple that it will not hurt us to adopt it. He proposes that the speaker must intend that his intentions become mutually believed between the speaker and the hearer. This means that both the speaker and hearer know what the speaker intended, and each of them knows the other knows, etc. We can define a <u>mutual belief operator</u> as infinite conjunction as follows:

$$MB(S,A,P) = SB(P) \wedge$$
$$SBAB(P) \wedge$$
$$SBABSB(P) \wedge$$
$$...$$

[Cohen 1978] describes a finite representation of mutual belief using recursive belief structures.

Now we can rewrite the above condition as:

> speaker WANT
> MB(hearer, speaker,
>   speaker WANT
>   hearer KNOW P)

This replaces the previous condition, which now is the first conjunct in the infinite expansion of MB.

To summarize, whenever an agent H concludes the above three conditions about another agent S, basing at least part of the proof on the actions H observed S perform, then H will conclude that S informed him that P is true.

We can now modify our definition of INFORM by introducing this third condition. To allow the possibility of hierarchical planning, and to emphasize that the recognition of intention condition is the means by which the effect of the INFORM is accomplished, the recognition of intention condition is expressed as the body of the INFORM act. Thus we have:

> INFORM(speaker, hearer, prop)
>
> precondition: speaker KNOW prop
>
> body: MB(hearer, speaker,
>   speaker WANT
>   hearer KNOW prop)
>
> effect: hearer KNOW prop

Similarly, new definitions can be given for INFORMREF and INFORMIF by adding the extra recognition of intention condition. The new definition of REQUEST is

> REQUEST(speaker, hearer, action)
>
> body: MB(hearer, speaker,
>   speaker WANT
>   hearer DO action)
>
> effect: hearer WANT hearer DO action.

[Cohen 1978] suggests a precondition on REQUEST, namely that the speaker believes the hearer can do the action. This is a reasonable precondition, but is unnecessary in our formulation as the plan recognition process already effectively enforces the precondition by the rating heuristics, which consider plans involving requests to do undoable actions as unlikely.

We now have a better definition of when speech acts occur. However, we have divorced these definitions from the form of the utterances. This gap is filled in the next section, where a new set of actions is introduced that produce actual utterances. Speech acts can then be performed by executing one (or more) of these surface linguistic acts.

2.5.2 Surface Linguistic Acts

We now turn to the actions that allow us to reason about language itself. These will make the connection between the linguistic form of utterances and the intentions of the speaker producing these utterances. Obviously, there are many ways in which the form of an utterance influences what is perceived as being the speaker's intentions. We have selected only a few of the most obvious in this analysis. Surprisingly enough, the range of behavior analyzable with them is quite rich.

There is a basic assumption underlying the following analysis: speakers always mean what they literally say, and it is only by this literal meaning that any indirect meaning can be inferred. This is the position defended by [Searle 1975]. Given this assumption, the recognition of the literal meaning provides us with a set of intentions from which plan inferencing may proceed.

These initial intentions are summarized as surface linguistic acts. There are two of these acts of great relevance to our study which correspond to literal INFORMs and REQUESTs, and are defined as follows:

SURFACE-INFORM(speaker,hearer,prop)

effect: MB(hearer, speaker,
    speaker WANT
    hearer KNOW prop)

SURFACE-REQUEST(speaker,hearer,action)

effect: MB(hearer, speaker,
    speaker WANT
    hearer DO action)

These actions are indicated by a number of linguistic devices, most importantly the mood of the sentence and the use of certain "clue" words. For instance, an imperative sentence indicates a SURFACE-REQUEST, an indicative mood sentence indicates a SURFACE-INFORM, and an interrogative sentence indicates a SURFACE-REQUEST to inform (INFORMIF or INFORMREF) of the answer. Some examples of clue words are "please," which indicates a SURFACE-REQUEST, and words such as "when," "where," etc., which indicate a SURFACE-REQUEST to inform of a time, location, etc. The clue words play an especially important role in analyzing sentence fragments where the syntactic mood is not determined. This is discussed in Section 2.6.

The propositional content is derived using syntactic and semantic methods which can be found in most natural language understanding systems. The actual details of our algorithm are not important for this paper. Virtually any natural language analysis technique could be used, as long as it produces a representation of the literal meaning of the input (e.g. [Winograd 1972]; [Riesbeck 1975]; [Woods 1970]).

Notice that the effects of the SURFACE-INFORM act match the body of the INFORM act. This indicates that an indicative sentence is a common way of performing an INFORM. It is important, however, that it is not the only way. This same relationship also holds between the SURFACE-REQUEST and the REQUEST acts.

2.5.3 Extended Plan Inferencing

With the new action definitions given in the last two sections, it is not obvious that the plan inference rules can still apply. However, with the addition of one new inference rule, and two new control heuristics, the rest of the plan inference process can be used as is.

Before we introduce the new items, consider what the extended plan inference process should look like. The speaker speaks, thereby executing a surface linguistic act which is identifiable from the syntactic form of the utterance. The hearer believes the action was deliberate, so in fact the speaker intended to perform the surface act, and thus intended to achieve its effects (action-effect inference). Thus we have a belief of the form

```
hearer BELIEVE
   speaker WANT
      MB(hearer, speaker,
         speaker WANT X)
```

where X depends on the surface act. From this point, we want the hearer to be able to perform plan inferences based on what he believes is mutually believed. We can define this mode of reasoning in terms of the already existing plan inference rules as follows:

The Mutual Belief Rule
If

```
hearer BELIEVE
   speaker WANT
      MB(hearer,speaker,
         WANT(speaker,x))
```

and

```
hearer BELIEVE
   speaker BELIEVE
      MB(hearer,speaker,
         SBAW(x) ⊃_i SBAW(y))
```

then

```
hearer BELIEVE
   speaker WANT
      MB(hearer,speaker,
         WANT(speaker,y))
```

In other words, if the hearer believes the speaker wants it to be shared knowledge that the speaker intends X, and if the hearer believes the speaker believes it is shared knowledge that intending X infers intending Y, then the hearer may conclude the speaker wants it to be shared knowledge that the speaker intends Y.

Thus the hearer may infer various further intentions of the speaker using what he thinks the speaker believes is mutually believed between them. At some time (to be discussed below), the hearer ceases to infer new intentions and identifies a speech act via its body. The effect of the speech act produces an intention that the hearer privately believes the speaker has. From this, the hearer may infer other intentions of the speaker based on his private knowledge of the speaker.

Once this terminates, the plan can be inspected for obstacles as usual.

However, the hearer is obliged to address the obstacles that are mutually believed between the speaker and hearer. The obstacles based on the hearer's private beliefs may or may not be addressed, depending on how helpful the hearer feels.

The question remains as to how long the hearer continues using mutual beliefs. We have already mentioned that inferencing within mutual belief will continue as long as possible, i.e., that intention will be attributed if it can be. This is captured by the following rating heuristics.

The Level of Inferencing Rules

1. *Given a choice between an inference that continues using mutual belief, and an inference that does not, favor the one using mutual belief.*

2. *If there are multiple mutually exclusive inferences possible that continue to use mutual belief, then favor the inferences that do not use mutual belief.*

The second rule is important and is justified as follows: the inferences taken using mutual belief are taken to have been intended by the speaker. If, given the mutual knowledge, there are multiple paths that the hearer could take, then the hearer can no longer attribute intention to the speaker as he has no means of choosing which path the speaker intended. Thus it is the speaker's duty to ensure that the inference path to his intended goal is easily found by the hearer; otherwise the hearer will simply take the literal, or some intermediate interpretation.

The above might sound quite complicated to implement but, in fact, is not, if one views the plan inferences as based on the speaker's goals. In this scheme, there are two parameters to the inference process; the context in which goals are being inferred, and the context in which the inference rules are being evaluated. Thus, for basic plan recognition, the goal context is what the system believes the speaker wants (i.e., "SBAW(-)"), and the evaluation context is what the system believes the speaker believes (i.e., "SBAB(-)"). In the extended mode inferencing, the goal context is what the system believes the speaker wants to be mutually believed that the speaker wants (i.e., "SBAW(MB(S,A,AW(-)))"), and the evaluation context is what the system believes the speaker believes is mutually believed (i.e., "SBAB(MB(S,A,-))"). Given Cohen's representation of belief and mutual belief, these contexts are easily constructed and manipulated.

2.5.4 Examples of Indirect Acts

In the following examples we will abbreviate "SBAW(MB(S,A,·))" as "SHARED(-)." In each example, the correct inference path is shown and the major possible but not taken paths are discussed following the example. For some simple (and classic) examples, consider S and A sitting at a dinner table eating, where the salt is close to S. The relevant actions we will need are

> PASS(agent,beneficiary,object)
>
> precondition: HAVE(agent,object)
>
> effect: HAVE(beneficiary,object)
>
> REACH(agent,object)
>
> precondition: NEAR(agent,object)
>
> effect: HAVE(agent,object)

Example I: "*Pass the Salt*"

The utterance by A to S of "Pass the salt" causes the following inferences:

> (1.1) SBAW(SURFACE-REQUEST (A,S, Pass(S,A,Salt)))
>   [from observation]
> (1.2) SHARED(AW (Pass(S,A,Salt)))   [action-effect]
> (1.3) SBAW(Request (A,S,Pass(S,A,Salt)))   [body-action]

Hence, this is interpreted as a request to pass the salt. Note, according to the abbreviation described above, that (1.2) is actually the formula

> "SBAW(MB(S,A,AW (Pass(S,A,Salt))))."

Example II: "*Do You Have the Salt?*"

> (2.1) SBAW(SURFACE-REQUEST (A,S,INFORMIF
>   (S,A,Have(S,Salt))))
> (2.2) SHARED(AW (INFORMIF(S,A,Have(S,Salt))))
>   [action-effect]
> (2.3) SHARED(AW (A KNOWIF Have(S,Salt)))
>   [mutually believed action-effect]
> (2.4) SHARED(AW (Have(S,Salt)))
>   [mutually believed know-positive]
> (2.5) SHARED(AW (Pass(S,A,Salt)))
>   [mutually believed precondition action]
> (2.6) SBAW(REQUEST (A,S,Pass(S,A,Salt)))   [body-action]

This example involves plan inferences using mutual belief between steps (2.2) and (2.5).

The literal interpretation of this utterance would arise from identifying a speech act from step (2.2). The level of inferencing heuristic favors the indirect interpretation, however. Note that, even without the level of inferencing heuristic, the literal interpretation would be disfavored, for it involves A asking a question to which both S and A believe A already knows the answer. The know-negative inference is possible from step (2.3) (producing SHARED(AW(not Have(S,Salt)))). This path is disfavored since it is mutually believed that A knows that S has the salt. Note that it is still possible to describe this utterance as a yes/no question as well as a request to pass the salt. The utterance can in fact be both speech acts simultaneously. In general, however, the indirect interpretation is the more useful description of the speaker's intentions.

Another example, "Are you near the salt?", can be handled in a similar manner. Using shared knowledge, S would infer that being near the salt enables him to reach it which causes him to have the salt, which is a prerequisite to passing it, which is an expected goal for A in this context.

Example III: "*I Want to Have the Salt*"

This example requires S to recognize that A intended him to plan based on a goal inferred from A's utterance. Thus the example will use the nested planning rule in Section 3.3.

> (3.1) SBAW(SURFACE-INFORM(A,S,AW (Have(A,Salt))))
> (3.2)SHARED(AW(S KNOW(AW (Have(A,Salt)))))
>   [action-effect]
> (3.3) SHARED(AW(SW (Have(A,Salt))))
>   [mutually believed decide inference]

(3.4) SHARED(AW(SW (Pass(S,A,Salt))))
    [mutually believed,nested planning using effect-action rule]
(3.5) SHARED(AW (Pass(S,A,Salt)))
                  [mutually believed want-action]
(3.6) SBAW(REQUEST(A,S,Pass(S,A,Salt)))
                        [body-action]

In this example, S recognizes that A intends S to accept the goal of A having the salt (inference from 3.2 to 3.3), and then A intends S to plan to achieve the goal by passing the salt (3.4).

Example IV: Two Interpretations of "*Do You Know the Secret?*"

To emphasize the distinction between the levels of plan inferencing, let us consider two interpretations of the question "Do you know the secret?" In one, it is assumed to be intended at face value--however the hearer recognizes a motivating goal that the speaker really wants to know the secret, but does not want to ask. In the second, the hearer interprets it as an indirect request that he tell the secret. As we shall see, both plans involve the same inferences, only the level. at which they are made differs. Thus this example has the same structure as depicted in Figure 3 above. Details on representing a concept such as "the secret" are ignored as they are not relevant to the example.

The Literal Interpretation

(4.1) SBAW(SURFACE-REQUEST(A,S,INFORMIF
    (S,A,S KNOWREF "the secret")))
(4.2) SHARED(AW(INFORMIF
    (S,A,S KNOWREF "the secret")))   [action-effect]
(4.3) SBAW(REQUEST(A,S,INFORMIF
    (S,A,S KNOWREF "the secret")))   [body-action]
(4.4) SBAW(A KNOWIF (S KNOWREF "the secret"))
                        [action-effect]
(4.5) SBAW(S KNOWREF "the secret")   [know-positive]
(4.6) SBAW(INFORMREF(S,A, "the secret"))
                        [precondition-action]
(4.7) SBAW(A KNOWREF "the secret")   [action-effect]

The Indirect Interpretation

The first two steps are the same as in the above example.

>   (5.1) SBAW(SURFACE-REQUEST(A,S,INFORMIF
>   (S,A.S KNOWREF "the secret")))
>   (5.2) SHARED(AW(INFORMIF
>   (S,A.S KNOWREF "the secret")))
>   (5.3) SHARED(AW(A KNOWIF
>   (S,A.S KNOWREF "the secret")))
>   [mutually believed action-effect]
>   (5.4) SHARED(AW(S KNOWREF "the secret"))
>   [mutually believed know-positive]
>   (5.5) SHARED(AW(INFORMREF(S,A,"the secret")))
>   [mutually believed precondition-action]
>   (5.6) SBAW(REQUEST(A,S,INFORMREF
>   (S,A,"the secret")))
>   [body-action]
>   (5.7) SBAW(A KNOWREF "the secret")
>   [action-effect]

Note that the same chain of inferences are done except for the context. Step (4.4) corresponds to (5.3), (4.5) to (5.4), (4.6) to (5.5). In step (5.6) the indirect request is identified, whereas the literal interpretation was identified in (4.3). Steps (4.7) and (5.7) are identical. Hence S reaches the same conclusion in both cases. However, if S could not tell A the secret, in interpretation I he could simply answer "yes," while in interpretation II he would have to supply an excuse for not complying with A's request.

There are a few factors that affect which interpretation would be chosen by the system. For instance, if S believes that A believes that S knows the secret, then the literal interpretation is unlikely for it entails that A has a goal (4.5) that A believes already holds (see heuristic H2). This fact would also favor the indirect interpretation by eliminating an inference from step (5.3) to

SHARED(AW(¬S KNOWREF "the secret"))).

If on the other hand, S believes that A doesn't know whether S knows the secret, then the indirect interpretation is weakened by the uncertainty at step (5.3), and the literal interpretation is a reasonable plan. Thus the literal will tend to be favored.

2.5.5 Using General Knowledge

So far, the plan inference rules have solely concerned knowledge and action. These have allowed us to explain a wide range of utterances in a few domains. However, the inferencing about the speaker's goals can, in principle, draw on any fact that the hearer believes the speaker used in constructing his plan. In particular, general world knowledge is often depended upon in plans. For instance, if A believes that condition X causes condition Y, if A wants Y, A may attempt to achieve X. Thus we have new rules dealing with causality:

Causal Rules

If S believes that A believes X causes Y, then the following inferences are possible:

$$SBAW(Y) \supset_i SBAW(X); \text{ and}$$

$$SBAW(\neg X) \supset_i SBAW(\neg Y).$$

There is also general knowledge about the motivations of other agents. This knowledge can be used to infer new goals of agents. In particular, if an agent believed condition X holds, and that condition X is undesirable, then the agent may start to want notX. Thus we have a corresponding plan inference stating that if an agent wants another agent to be aware of some undesirable condition, then the agent probably wants the agent to eliminate that condition. This is summarized as:

Undesirability Condition

$$SBAW(SB(X)) \supset_i SBAW(SW(\neg X))$$
where S believes A believes X is undesirable.

These new rules dramatically increase the search space of possible plans, and, as yet, have not been implemented in a general manner. However, from a theoretical point of view, they allow one to investigate the adequacy of the proposed theory of speech acts. Using them, a wide range of complex language use can be explained. In particular, consider the classic example

(1) "It's cold in here"

issued by a king (A) to his servant (S). From (1), S may infer that the king is cold and, since being cold is undesirable, that the king does not want to be cold. Since, in this setting, the coldness is being caused by an open window, the servant may close the window. If the king intended this line of inference to occur, and intended the servant to recognize this intention, utterance (1) counts as a request to close the window. Thus, assuming the following general world knowledge:

(1) Cold(room) $\land$ IN(agent,room) $\supset$ Cold(agent)
(2) Undesirable (Cold(agent))
(3) Open(window) $\land$ Part-Of(window,room) $\supset$ Cold(room)

The plan can be summarized as:

(6.1) SBAW(SURFACE-INFORM (A,S,Cold(Room1)))
(6.2) SHARED(AW (S KNOW Cold(Room1)))   [action-effect]
(6.3) SHARED(AW (S KNOW Cold(A)))
                            [mutually believed Causal Inference]
(6.4) SHARED(AW(SW (notCold(A))))
                            [mutually believed undesirability condition]
(6.5) SHARED(AW(SW (notOpen(Window))))
                    [mutually believed, planning by S with Causal Inference]
(6.6) SHARED(AW(SW (Close(S,Window))))
                    [mutually believed, planning by S with effect-action]
(6.7) SHARED(AW (Close(S,Window)))
                            [mutually believed, want-action]
(6.8) SBAW(REQUEST (A,S,Close(S,Window))) [body-action]

2.5.6 Discussion

The above theory of speech acts is interesting in that it treats the direct and indirect forms uniformly and allows an utterance to be more than one speech act simultaneously. In addition, the range of indirect speech acts accounted for is considerably greater than with other approaches, such as [Gordon and Lakoff 1975] and [Brown 1980]). In cases where this work and the others overlap, this approach is more selective as it heavily uses the context in which the utterance is spoken, and de-emphasizes the actual form of the utterance. This, of course, is not done without some loss. For instance, the current theory cannot distinguish the subtle differences between

"Can you open the door?" and

"Are you able to open the door?".

The former sentence appears much more likely to be a request to open the door than the latter. Disregarding such subtleties, a large range of indirect uses can be explained. For example, in the train station domain, the following forms have been recognized in their indirect interpretations:

"I want to know when the Windsor train leaves?"

"I want you to tell me when ..."

"Can you tell me when ..."

"Do you know when ..."

"Will you tell me when ..."

In addition, more unusual analyses of sentences have been analyzed by hand. For instance, the mechanisms here explain how the sentence

"John told me to ask you to leave"

can be interpreted as

(1) a simple assertion of a fact that John did the action reported;

(2) an inform that John wants you to leave; and

(3) a request that you leave (giving a reason for the request).

This analysis can be found in [Allen 1979] and [Perrault and Allen 1980]).

2.6 Analyzing Sentence Fragments

As we have seen, plan knowledge is necessary to generate appropriate responses even to syntactically complete sentences. The mood of a sentence, given by the subject, auxiliaries, and main verb, is critical to speech act identification. With sentence fragments such as "the Montreal train," even the mood of the sentence may not be known, thus making even the surface speech act identification difficult. However, the plan inference process described so far is already powerful enough to handle many ambiguities of this type.

Even in sentence fragments, there remain syntactic clues to the surface speech act. Words such as "when", "what", "which", etc., signal a SURFACE-REQUEST to INFORMREF. The use of the word "please" in a sentence marks it as a request. Thus, an utterance such as "the door, please" could not be interpreted as an inform. Of course, there will often be cases where a mood ambiguity cannot be resolved at the syntactic level, and in these cases, the alternatives will be enumerated and each case will become a plan alternative. Since the number of surface speech acts is small, this approach is reasonable.

The less explicit the utterance, the more important the expectations become, for they provide the missing details of the speaker's actions and plans. Typically, a speaker has a specific speech act and propositional content that he wants to convey to the hearer. In addition, the speaker may have some idea of what the hearer expects him to say. Any fragment that singles out the correct expectation from the rest is acceptable to communicate the speech act and proposition. The fragment must also distinguish what particular subgoals in the expectation are being pursued. In restrictive domains, such as the train station, identifying the fundamental goal (i.e. boarding, meeting) is sufficient to identify the subgoals desired. In such settings, very brief fragments can be used successfully. For example,

> "The train to Windsor?"

successfully identifies the fundamental goal of boarding the train. Of the possible subgoals that are involved in this plan, only knowing the departure time and location are relevant (Expected), for this is what the information agent believes that the patron believes he can help achieve. Other subgoals required in order to board. the train such as having a ticket, are not relevant because (the information agent believes) the patron believes the information agent does not handle tickets.

2.6.1 An Example of a Sentence Fragment

As usual, the setting is the train station, A is a patron and S is the information agent.

> A: The train to Windsor ?

The syntactic analysis suggests two interpretations:

(5.1) SURFACE.REQUEST(A,S,INFORMREF(S,A,x)
where PROPERTY(train1,x) ∧ TO-PROPERTY(train1, Windsor)

(5.2) SURFACE.REQUEST(A,S,INFORMIF
(S,A,PROPERTY involving train1))
where TO-PROPERTY(train1,Windsor)

The use of TO-PROPERTY here is an attempt to encode some syntactic knowledge into the semantic representation; it stands for an arbitrary property (involving a train and a city in this case) that is realizable at the syntactic level using the preposition "to". The problem we are avoiding here is that the actual relation referred to here can only be obtained from the expectations, which are not considered until the sentence is parsed and the "literal" meaning constructed. It is not a simple matter to change this though, for arbitrarily many inferences may have to be made from the literal meaning before the correct relation can be identified. We have resorted to encoding such syntactic restrictions in special patterns that match the appropriate relation names.

This example will consider only the first interpretation. Details on how the second is eliminated can be found in [Allen 1979]. The described train is incompatible with the MEET expectation, leaving only the BOARD expectation as the reasonable interpretation. The inferences made from interpretation (5.1) lead to the goal:

A KNOWREF x

where PROPERTY(train1,x)

To identify the actual predicate indicated by the predicate pattern PROPERTY, the BOARD expectation is inspected for matches.

There are two relevant properties of trains, the DEPART.TIME and the DEPART.LOC. Assuming that S believes that A knows neither of the values for these relations, both can be considered obstacles and be used to form a response corresponding to

"It leaves at 3:15 from gate 7."

In another setting, S's response to the same fragment might be quite different. If the train station had only one platform, he would only respond with the departure time because he would believe that A knows the location already. To be completely different, if S were the ticket agent he would interpret the fragment as a request for a ticket (since this is what S expects, i.e. what S believes that A believes S is able to do), and might reply

"$10.50 please"

This approach covers a quite different range of sentence fragments than any other method described in the literature. The most common method, which could be called the "semantic approach," accepts fragments in the form of full syntactic units, such as noun phrases, and uses the fragments to build a partial "semantic" representation that is then matched into the representation of the previous utterance [Grosz 1977]; [Burton 1976]; [Hendrix 1977]. If this match is successful, the representation of the utterance is constructed out of the previous utterance's structure with the newly specified parts replacing the parts that they matched. This method is limited to those fragments that depend on the structure of the previous utterance for their interpretation. As shown in the train dialogues, there are many fragments used where this is not the case.

Our approach is suited for cases where the mere mention of a concept or phrase is suggestive enough to convey a thought/wish. These instances typically have little syntactic relation to previous utterances, and in fact can occur when there is no previous utterance. In many ways, the matching techniques are similar to the "semantic approach," but the goals are very different. The goal of the semantic approach is to find a structural similarity with the previous utterance. The goal of this work is to identify the plan and goals of the speaker. A syntactically complete utterance is never considered or constructed for it has no effect on the understanding of the utterance.

2.7 Conclusions

We have argued that a plan-based model of the language comprehension process can explain a wide range of linguistic behavior that has been problematic to previous approaches. In particular, we have addressed the problems of:

>   - generating responses that convey more
> information than was explicitly requested;

>   - generating responses based on indirect
> interpretations of the utterances;

- generating appropriate responses to utterances that consist solely of a sentence fragment;

The common thread through the solutions to these problems is the ability of the hearer to infer the speaker's plans and to then detect obstacles in these plans.

We have explicitly indicated the role that context plays in language understanding: only those plans that are reasonable in the current context (as determined by the rating heuristics) are potential analyses of the intention of the speaker. A large part of the context is the hearer's model of the speaker's beliefs and goals. If the context is sufficiently restrictive to uniquely determine the speaker's plan, then appropriate responses can be generated for a wide range of utterances often considered problematic.

The implementation based on this theory has supported the claim that such work can lead to more helpful, yet still practical, natural language understanding systems. Our current specification of the actual plan inference process, however, is not detailed enough to allow it to perform in more complex domains than the train station. Considerable work needs to be done to specify more control heuristics. Large domains probably require the introduction of domain specific inference rules. In this paper, we have begun to lay the groundwork by specifying characteristics that any plan inference mechanism would need in any domain.

In larger domains there will be a larger set of expectations, as well as more complex dialogues. In some ways, the growth of expectations may not seriously affect the system. This depends on the observation that at the beginning of a dialogue, people are often quite specific about their goals. In other words, they explicitly identify an expectation. If this goal is a task-oriented goal, then [Grosz 1977] has shown that much of the remaining dialogue will follow the structure of the plan to achieve that goal. This, however, will not help in dialogues where the topic may shift considerably. Possibly work along the lines of Sidner (Chapter 5 of this volume) and [Reichman 1978] can be used in conjunction with a plan-based model of the speaker's intentions to provide a full analysis of these dialogues.

Perhaps the most difficult remaining problems lie in the specification of the relation between the syntactic processing and the rest of the system. We saw in the section on sentence fragments a case where the syntactic information concerning the preposition "to" could not be used until the advanced stages of the plan inference process. Thus the parser may not be able to complete its job until the plan inference process has been running. However, the plan inference process depends on the output of the parser in order to begin inferring the speaker's intention.

One final concern is with the fundamental tools of our approach: our logics of belief, want and action are only minimally adequate. This has been acceptable so far, for our emphasis has been on demonstrating the usefulness of such notions in a model of language. Now that we have a better idea of how these tools can be used, it is time to return to them and attempt a better formulation.

Acknowledgments

This paper is the result of multiple papers and drafts written over the last two years. It represents my final attempt to clean up and present the work from my thesis. Much of the original work was done in conjunction with Ray Perrault and Philip Cohen while at the University of Toronto. They also have provided helpful comments on many drafts in the last few years. I would also like to thank Jerry Kaplan, David McDonald, Candy Sidner, and Bonnie Webber for their detailed reading and commenting on the final draft. All these people have greatly improved the quality of this document.

CHAPTER 3

Cooperative Responses From a Portable Natural Language Database Query System

S. Jerrold Kaplan

3.1 Introduction

Cooperation is an essential aspect of human conversation. Speakers cooperate for a variety of purposes: to perform tasks, solve problems, communicate needed information, etc. Indeed, for a conversation to occur at all implies some minimal level of cooperation. One way in which human conversants cooperate is by observing a variety of rules, conventions, postulates, etc., that allow the communication of intentions and beliefs in addition to the literal meaning of their utterances. This promotes smooth and effective communication. Consequently, syntax and semantics alone are not adequate to characterize a cooperative conversation: a knowledge of the conventions of use and expectations of a native speaker is required. The study of these conversational effects falls under the rubric of <u>pragmatics</u>: those aspects of linguistic communication that arise from the fact of utterance or the context of use.

Considering non-human conversational partners, Natural Language (NL) Data Base (DB) query systems sometimes engage in behavior that would be regarded as uncooperative or inappropriate in a human partner. Although this behavior is sometimes due to a lack of world knowledge, much of it can be attributed to a failure to deal in a systematic way with pragmatic issues. Consider the following exchange with a hypothetical NL DB query system:

    User: Which students got a grade of F in CS105 in
            Spring 1980?
    System: Nil. [the empty set]

    User: Did anyone fail CS105 in Spring 1980?
    System: No.

    User: How many people passed CS105 in Spring 1980?
    System: Zero.

    User: Was CS105 given in Spring 1980?
    System: No.

A cooperative system should be able to detect that the initial query in the dialog incorrectly presumed that CS105 was offered in Spring 1980, and respond appropriately. This ability is essential to a NL system that will function in a practical environment, because the fact that NL is used in the interaction will imply to the users that the normal cooperative conventions followed in a human dialog will be observed by the machine. While each response in the dialog is a correct, direct answer to the corresponding question, the overall effect is uncooperative - the system appears to "stonewall".[1]

A similar conversation with a cooperative human respondent might have gone as follows:

> Q: Which students got a grade of F in CS105 in
>   Spring 1980?
>
> R: CS105 was not given in Spring 1980.

A cooperative human speaker can infer from the (pragmatic) fact that the question was posed (and an assumption that the questioner believes the question to be appropriate in the context) that the questioner does not know that CS105 was not given in Spring 1980, and so s/he informs the questioner accordingly rather than answering the question directly. Notice that the appropriate response is not a direct answer to the question at all, but rather is an indirect response correcting the questioner's misimpression about the domain of discourse.

NL DB query systems that are capable only of direct answers to questions will necessarily give inappropriate or meaningless responses in this and similar contexts. Surprisingly, the conditions under which such indirect responses are considered more appropriate than direct answers can be formally defined, and a limited but non-trivial class of appropriate indirect responses can be incorporated into a computational question answering system using only a lexicon and the DB itself as sources of domain specific knowledge. This is possible in part because speakers naturally encode directly in the lexical and syntactic structure of their utterances a great deal of information about their intentions and beliefs beyond the literal content of their utterances.[2]

---

1. Stonewalling is a term used for uncooperative (and often misleading) yet technically correct responses to questions. It was popularized during the Senate Watergate Hearings to describe the behavior of several White House witnesses. For an example, see the interchange between Senator Ervin and H.R. Haldeman on P.586 of [New York Times 1973].
2. No claim is made here that all such information is encoded in this way, but rather that substantive conversational cues are recoverable at this level.

This chapter explores several aspects of the pragmatics of cooperative question answering, in the computational context of a NL DB query system. It is drawn from research originally reported in [Kaplan 1979]. The major contribution of this work is to demonstrate that:

> 1) Cooperative direct and indirect responses to a habitable class of NL questions concerned with data retrieval can be produced in a practical fashion from a reasonably portable NL DB query system.

> 2) The domain specific knowledge needed to interpret and respond cooperatively to a class of simple NL questions can be derived from the information already present in a DB system, if augmented by a suitably encoded lexicon. The inferences used to produce cooperative responses can be driven by the form chosen by the user to express his or her question. This decomposition of knowledge results in a portable (to new DBs) query system.

> 3) Maintaining the lexical and syntactic integrity of the original question throughout the interpretation process provides a means for explaining failures, errors, and responses in terms that the user is likely to understand. The use of an intermediate representation that captures relevant linguistic considerations without reflecting arbitrary organizational details of the underlying DB is central to this approach.

To underscore these points, a NL DB query system, CO-OP, has been developed. The design, behavior, and experience gained from its implementation will be described. CO-OP is designed to provide several types of direct and indirect responses to questions that request the retrieval of data already present in the DB system. It will not effectively respond to questions about data; for example questions that require substantial inferences, calculations, comparisons, or transformations of the data (such as "When can the JFK aircraft carrier rendezvous with the destroyer Lexington?"), or query the structure of the data (such as "Can a user have more than one account on the same project?").

The basic design of CO-OP is to regard each part of a question as making reference to some aspect of the DB. The meaning of these references are encoded at the lexical level by associating a non-procedural program schemata (in a simple formalism) with the entries for individual words in the lexicon. Through a series of translations, using knowledge of the domain inferred from the DB schema, the NL question is transformed into a suitable DB query by combining the program schemata associated with the words used in the question. At all stages in this process, it is possible to map failures, errors, and unexpected intermediate results back into the particular words or phrases of the original question, providing a basis for user comprehensible explanations, and indirect responses. Facilities for negation, disjunction, conjunction, and limited quantification are provided. The system is interfaced to a commercially available CODASYL

DB system (the SEED system [Gerritsen 1978]). In the current implementation, the syntactic coverage is rather limited. Only WH-questions (questions beginning with words such as what, which, who, etc.) can be processed. The program does not handle ellipsis or anaphoric references. An annotated sample of questions and responses produced by CO-OP is presented in section 4. The results of transporting the system to another DB is reproduced in section 5.

Projecting the more general problem of cooperation in unrestricted discourse onto the domain of a limited DB query system provides a method of both sharpening certain linguistic intuitions and reducing the problem to a tractable form without trivializing the problem or rendering the solutions ad hoc. The mechanisms described here, while motivated by the domain, provide an approach that could be applicable in some form to a significantly wider class of NL processing problems. On the practical side, the NL DB query domain provides a focus for the development and evaluation of engineering techniques for the processing of NL. The implementation of a query system serves as a testbed for new strategies and programming concepts.

This paper will focus primarily on motivating point 1 above. Points 2 and 3 are concerned mainly with the implementation constraints imposed by practical NL systems, and are dealt with in greater depth in [Kaplan 1979].

3.2 Computational pragmatics

Casual users of NL computer systems are typically inexpert not only with regard to the technical details of the underlying programs, but often with regard to the structure and/or content of the domain of discourse. Consequently, NL systems must be designed to respond appropriately when they can detect a misconception on the part of the user. Several conventions exist in cooperative conversation that allow speakers to encode their intentions and beliefs about the domain into their utterances. Questions 1A-1C below illustrate the encoding of goals and intentions by the different responses that they will reasonably admit.

    1A: Did John borrow my coffee cup?
    1B: Was it John that borrowed my coffee cup?
    1C: Was it my coffee cup that John borrowed?

1D: No, it was Bill.
1E: No, it was your sugar.

Superficially, all three questions appear to convey the same request for information. A closer examination reveals that although 1D and 1E are both appropriate responses to 1A, 1B favors 1D while 1C favors 1E. 1B indicates that the questioner is interested in who borrowed the coffee cup, while 1C indicates that the questioner is interested in what John borrowed.[1]

The form of the questions (how information is requested) conveys useful information, as well as content (what information is being requested). Such pragmatic cues can be recovered during the parsing and translation process to significantly enhance the performance of a NL system.

While a theory of syntax and semantics may be sufficient for the analysis of sentences in the abstract, the role of sentences in discourse (where they are realized as utterances) requires further knowledge. (The study of speech acts in Philosophy of Language deals with this distinction. For instance, see [Searle 1969] and [Cole and Morgan 1975].) To appropriately process NL utterances it is necessary to consider what Austin called their perlocutionary force [Austin 1962], or the effect on the hearer of an utterance.[2]

Though this term is often used to refer to the emotional reactions of the hearer, it could be construed to include the inferences drawn by the hearer beyond the literal propositional content of the utterance, particularly regarding the state of mind of the speaker. Producing cooperative responses from a NL query system requires at least a partial theory of language use. Aspects of such a theory will be presented here: specifically, the generation of indirect responses to "loaded" questions. The study of language use in a setting where computational effectiveness is important could be called computational pragmatics.

NL questions allow (in fact, often require) a cooperative respondent to address a questioner's intentions and beliefs beyond a literal, direct response. To be effective, NL computer systems must do the same. One problem, then, is to

---

1. Sentences 1B and 1C are it-clefts. They are used in discourse to focus certain aspects of the domain via fronting.

2. Austin's concept of perlocutionary force deals with the intentional or unintentional effects of an utterance on the hearer, that is, the consequences of hearing an utterance. This is distinguished from the force of saying (the locutionary force) and the force of doing something in saying (the illocutionary force). For example, in the context of a submerged submarine attempting to evade an enemy destroyer by being silent, a crew member might yell "If we don't get out of here we'll all be killed!" This exclamation may break the silence with its locutionary force, issue a warning with its illocutionary force, and frighten the rest of the crew with its perlocutionary force. These concepts correspond roughly to the event, the intention of the speaker, and the consequences on the hearer, respectively.

provide practical computational tools which will determine both when an indirect response is required, and what that response should be, without requiring that significant amounts of domain dependent world knowledge be encoded in special formalisms. This work will take the position that distinguishing language driven inferences from domain driven inferences provides a framework for a solution to this problem in the DB query domain.[1]

3.2.1 What is a loaded question?

A loaded question is one that indicates that the questioner presumes something to be true about the domain of discourse that is actually false. Question 2A presumes 2B. A cooperative speaker must find 2B assumable (i.e. not believe it to be false[2] in order to appropriately utter 2A in a cooperative conversation, intend it literally, and expect a correct, direct response.

> 2A: What day does John go to his weekly piano lesson?
> 2B: John takes weekly piano lessons.
> 2C: Tuesday.

Similarly, 3A presumes 3B:

> 3A: How many Bloody Marys did Bill down at the banquet?
> 3B: Hard liquor was available at the banquet.
> 3C: Zero.

If the questioner believed 3B to be false, there would be no point in asking 3A - s/he would already know that the correct answer had to be "Zero." (3C). Therefore s/he must find 3B assumable to appropriately pose the question.

Both examples 2 and 3 can be explained by a convention of conversational cooperation, proposed here:

A questioner should leave a respondent a choice of direct answers.

That is, from the questioner's viewpoint upon asking a question, more than one direct answer must be possible.

---

1. It will not be argued that this distinction is fundamental or even very clear cut, but rather that it is a fruitful way of viewing this problem.
2. See [Prince 1978] for a discussion of the different uses of "assumed" and "assumable" knowledge.

It follows, then, that if a question presupposes something about the domain of discourse, as 2A does, that a questioner cannot felicitously utter the question and believe the presupposition to be false. This is a result of the fact that each direct answer to a question entails the question's presuppositions. (More formally, if question Q presupposes proposition P, then the propositional content of each question-direct answer pair (Q, Ai) entails P, as developed in [Hull 1974].)[1]

Therefore, if a questioner believes a presupposition to be false, s/he leaves no options for a correct, direct response - violating the convention. Conversely, a respondent can infer in a cooperative conversation from the pragmatic fact that a question has been asked, that the questioner finds its presuppositions assumable. (In the terms of [Keenan 1971], the logical presupposition is pragmatically presupposed.) A substantial literature exists on the study of presupposition in NL, and no survey will be attempted here. A representative example of a linguistic approach can be found in [Karttunen 1977]; see [Joshi and Weischedel 1977] for a more computational approach.

Surprisingly, a more general semantic relationship than presupposition exists that still allows a respondent to infer a questioner's beliefs. Consider the situation where a proposition is entailed by all but one of a question's direct answers. (Such a proposition will be called a presumption of the question.) By a similar argument, it follows that if a questioner believes that proposition to be false, s/he can infer the direct, correct answer to the question - it is the answer that does not entail the proposition. Once again, to ask such a question leaves the respondent no choice of (potentially) correct answers, violating the conversational convention. More importantly, upon being asked such a question, the respondent can infer what the questioner presumes about the context.

Question 3A above presumes 3B, but does not presuppose it: 3B is not entailed by the direct answer 3C. Nonetheless, a questioner must find 3B assumable to felicitously ask 3A in a cooperative conversation - to do otherwise would violate the cooperative convention. Similarly, 4B below is a presumption but not a presupposition of 4A (it is not entailed by 4C).

4A: Did Sandy pass the Bar exam?

---

1. This entailment condition is a necessary but not sufficient condition for presupposition. The concept of presupposition normally includes a condition that the negation of a proposition (in this case, the negation of the proposition expressed by a question-direct answer pair) should also entail its presuppositions. Consequently, the truth of a presupposition of a question is normally considered a prerequisite for an answer to be either true or false (for a more detailed discussion see [Keenan and Hull 1973]). These subtleties of the concept of presupposition are irrelevant to this discussion, because false responses to questions are considered a-priori to be uncooperative.

4B: Sandy took the Bar exam.
4C: No.

If a questioner believes in the falsehood of a presupposition of a question, the
question is inappropriate because s/he must believe that no direct answer can be
correct; similarly, if a questioner believes in the falsehood of a presumption, the
question is inappropriate because the questioner must know the answer to the
question - it is the direct answer that does not entail the presumption. *In short, the
failure of a presupposition renders a question infelicitous because it leaves no options
for a direct response; the failure of a presumption renders a question infelicitous
because it leaves at most one option for a direct response.* (Note that the definition
of presumption subsumes the definition of presupposition in this context.)

3.2.2 Corrective indirect responses

In a cooperative conversation, if a respondent detects that a questioner incorrectly
presumes something about the domain of discourse, s/he is required to correct
that misimpression. A failure to do so will implicitly confirm the questioner's false
presumption. Consequently, it is not always the case that a correct, direct answer
is the most cooperative response. When an incorrect presumption is detected, it is
more cooperative to correct the presumption than to give a direct response. Such a
response can be called a <u>Corrective</u> <u>Indirect</u> <u>Response</u>. For example, imagine
question 5A uttered in a cooperative conversation when the respondent knows
that no departments sell knives.

5A: Which departments that sell knives also sell blade
     sharpeners?
5B: None.
5C: No departments sell knives.

Although 5B is a direct, correct response in this context, it is less cooperative than
5C. This effect is explained by the fact that 5A presumes that some departments
sell knives. To be cooperative, the respondent should correct the questioner's
misimpression with an indirect response, informing the questioner that no
departments sell knives (5C). (The direct, correct response 5B will reinforce the
questioner's mistaken presumption in a cooperative conversation through its
failure to state otherwise; 5B also appears to violates Grice's Conversational

Maxim of Quantity [Grice 1975])[1]

A failure to produce corrective indirect responses is inappropriate in a cooperative conversation.

3.2.3 Relevance to database queries

Many NL query systems stonewall, in part because they are not capable of producing corrective indirect responses. To some degree, this inability results from a view of NL as a very high level formal query language. NL questions admit a wider range of responses than formal queries do, and provide cues for selecting among these responses that are generally absent from formal query languages [Kaplan 1978]. The appropriateness of indirect responses is an important difference between NL questions and formal language queries. *A NL system that is only capable of direct responses will necessarily produce meaningless responses to failed presuppositions, and stonewall on failed presumptions.* Unfortunately, the domain of most realistic DBs are sufficiently complex that the user of a NL query facility (most likely a naive user) will make incorrect presumptions in his or her queries.

While the definition of presumption given above may be of interest from a linguistic standpoint, it leaves much to be desired for a computational theory. Although it provides a descriptive model of certain aspects of conversational behavior, it does not provide an adequate basis for computing the presumptions of a given question in a reasonable way. By limiting the domain of application to the area of data retrieval, where typical questions are purely extensional, the linguistic structure of questions encodes considerable information about the questioner's presumptions. This structure can be exploited to compute a significant class of presumptions and provide appropriate corrective indirect responses. A technique for computing such responses in cases where questions can be assumed to be purely extensional is the main thrust of this work.

---

1. Specifically, "Make your contribution as informative as is required (for the purposes of the current exchange)."

3.2.4 Language driven and domain driven inference

A long standing observation in AI research is that knowledge about the world is required in order to understand NL.[1] Consequently, a great deal of study has gone into determining just what type of knowledge is required, and how that knowledge is to be represented, organized, accessed, and used. One practical problem with evaluating systems that use a specialized knowledge representation is that it is sometimes difficult to determine if a particular failure is due to an inadequacy in the formalism or simply an insufficient base of knowledge. (Systems that clearly specify semantics and inference rules, such as PHLIQA1 [Bronnenberg et. al. 1980], do not encounter this problem.) In addition, the collection and encoding of the appropriate knowledge can be a painstaking and time consuming task. Many NL systems that could be said to use specialized knowledge representations (such as [Lehnert 1977] or Allen's work described in Chapter 2 of this volume) share a common approach: they decompose the input into a suitable "semantic" representation, and rely on various deduction and/or reasoning mechanisms to provide the intelligence required to draw the necessary inferences. Inferences made in this way can be called domain[2] driven inferences, because they are motivated by the domain[3] itself.

While domain driven inferences are surely essential to an understanding of NL (and will be a required part of any comprehensive cognitive model of human intelligence), the lexical and syntactic forms chosen by a speaker directly encode a great deal of information that might otherwise be derived from domain knowledge. Many of the variations and options available to a speaker in phrasing his or her utterances, while leaving the literal meaning unchanged, convey secondary information about the speakers beliefs and domain. This additional information can drive the inferencing procedures to detect a speaker's misconceptions and other conversational characteristics (such as focus, as in example 1 above), without the need for domain driven inference. Inferences driven from the particular phrasing of inputs can be called language driven inferences.

Language driven inferences have several useful properties in a computational

---

1. For example, to understand the statement "I bought a briefcase yesterday, and today the handle broke off." it is necessary to know that briefcases typically have handles.

2. "Domain" here is meant to include general world knowledge, knowledge about the specific context, and inferential rules of a general and/or specific nature about that knowledge.

3. Of course, these inferences are actually made on the basis of descriptions of the domain (the internal meaning representation) and not the domain itself. What is to be evaluated in such systems is the sufficiency of that description in representing the domain.

framework. First, being based on general knowledge about the language, they do not require an infusion of knowledge to operate in differing domains. As a result they tend to be transportable to new domains (new DBs, in the case of NL DB query systems). Second, they do not appear to be as subject to runaway inferencing [Rosenschein 1976], i.e. the inferencing is driven (and hence controlled) by the phrasing of the input. Third, they can often achieve results approximating that of domain driven inference techniques with substantially less computational machinery and execution time.

As a simple example, consider the case of factive verbs. The sentence "John doesn't know that the Beatles broke up." carries the inference that the Beatles broke up. Treated as a domain driven inference, this result might typically be achieved as follows. The sentence could be parsed into a representation indicating John's lack of knowledge of the Beatles' breakup. Either immediately or at some suitable later time, a procedure might be invoked that encodes the knowledge "For someone to not know something, that something has to be the case." The inferential procedures can then update the knowledge base accordingly. As a language driven inference, this inference can be regarded as a lexical property, i.e. that factive verbs presuppose their complements, and the complement immediately asserted, namely, that the Beatles broke up (as in [Weischedel 1975]). (Note that this process cannot be reasonably said to "understand" the utterance, but achieves the same results.) Effectively, certain inference rules have been encoded directly into the lexical and syntactic structure of the language - facilitating the drawing of the inference without resorting to general reasoning processes.

The CO-OP system, described below, demonstrates that a language driven inference approach to computational systems can to a considerable extent produce appropriate NL behavior in practical domains without the overhead of a detailed and comprehensive world model, other than a standard DB. By limiting the domain of discourse to DB queries, the lexical and syntactic structure of the questions encodes sufficient information about the user's beliefs that a significant class of presumptions can be computed on a purely language driven basis.

3.3 CO-OP: a cooperative query system

This section will summarize the design of the CO-OP NL DB query system. CO-OP is intended to provide cooperative responses to simple questions requesting data retrieval. It operates with a typical CODASYL DB. In addition to direct answers, CO-OP is capable of producing a variety of indirect responses, including corrective indirect responses. The design of the system is based on two hypotheses:

> 1) To a large extent, language driven inferences are sufficient to drive procedures that detect the need for an indirect response and select an appropriate one.

> 2) The domain specific knowledge required to process a significant class of NL DB queries is already present in standard ways in DB systems, if that information is augmented by a suitably encoded lexicon.

Consequently, the inferencing mechanisms required to produce the cooperative responses are <u>domain transparent</u>, in the sense that they will produce appropriate behavior without modification from any suitable DB. Transporting CO-OP to a new DB mainly requires the recoding of the lexicon. The results of transporting the system to a new DB is presented is section 5.

Central to providing cooperative responses in a domain transparent fashion is the design of an intermediate representation for NL queries that captures useful linguistic characteristics without assuming a particular structuring of the underlying DB. The representation adopted in CO-OP (called the <u>Meta Query Language</u>, or MQL) facilitates language driven inferences and provides a basis for composing useful direct and indirect responses. Inputs are parsed directly into the MQL, relying on the DB schema as a source of world knowledge. The inferencing required to produce cooperative responses is accomplished mainly by manipulating the MQL. Paraphrases and indirect responses are generated directly from it, and direct responses are organized in accordance with its structure. This section will focus on the MQL representation, and its role in the production of indirect responses.

3.3.1 The Meta Query Language

A significant class of DB queries can be viewed as requesting the selection of a subset (the response set) from a presented set of entities (this analysis follows [Belnap and Steel 1976]). Normally, the presented set is put through a series of restrictions, each of which produces a subset, until the response set is found. This view is captured and extended in the procedures that manipulate the MQL.

The MQL is a graph structure, where the nodes represent <u>sets</u> (in the mathematical, not the CODASYL sense [CODASYL 1971]) "presented" by the user, and the edges represent <u>binary relations</u> defined on those sets, derived from the lexical and syntactic structure of the input query. Conceptually, the direct response to a query is an N-place relation realized by obtaining the referent of the sets in the DB, and composing them according to the binary relations. Each composition will have the effect of selecting a subset of the current sets. The subsets will contain the elements that survive (participate) in the relation. (Actually, the responses are realized in a much more efficient fashion - this is simply a convenient view.)

As an example, consider the query "Which students got Fs in Linguistics courses?" as diagrammed in Figure 1.

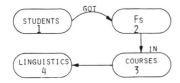

Figure 1 MQL representation of: Which students got Fs in linguistics courses?"

This query would be parsed as presenting 4 sets: "students", "Fs", "Linguistics", and "courses". (The sets "Linguistics" and "Fs" may appear counterintuitive, but should be viewed as singleton entities assumed by the user to exist somewhere in the DB.) The direct answer to the query would be a 4 place relation consisting of a column of students, grades (all Fs), departments (all Linguistics), and courses. For convenience, the columns containing singleton sets (grades and departments) would be removed, and the remaining list of students and associated courses presented to the user.

Executing the query (to compute its direct answer) consists of passing the MQL representation of the query to an interpretive component that produces a query suitable for execution on a CODASYL DB. The specific knowledge required to perform this translation is encoded in the lexicon, (by associating it with the entries for the words that label the nodes and edges of the MQL), or is inferred from the DB schema.

The MQL, by encoding some of the syntactic relationships present in the NL query, can hardly be said to capture the meaning of the question: it is merely a convenient representation formalizing certain linguistic characteristics of the query. The procedures that manipulate this representation to generate inferences are based on observations of a general nature regarding these syntactic relationships. Consequently, these inferences are language driven inferences. While the MQL, as implemented in CO-OP has its advantages and disadvantages, it has several characteristics that ought to be present in any representation used for similar purposes.

First, it reflects closely the surface structure of the input (indeed, it is little more than a modified parse tree), and so facilitates the capturing of surface syntactic features. For example, the representation of corresponding passives and actives is not the same. This has an important bearing the organization of the responses.

Second, it provides a level of description useful for providing explanations that a user is certain to understand. This occurs mainly because each part of an MQL expression is labeled with a lexical item or phrase that the user just used (with minor exceptions). Failures at lower levels of the system can always be localized to the processing of some subset of the MQL, and the offending subset can be explained to the user in his or her own terms.

Third, the MQL representation of a query is invariant under differing organizations of the underlying DB. Many of the organizational options available to a DB designer have no bearing on either the range of questions that can be appropriately posed to the DB or on the content of the responses - they affect only the efficiency of retrieval. Consequently, the options chosen by the DB designer ought to be transparent to the user. In CO-OP, the organization of the response is a function solely of the MQL, and so is not affected by variations in the organization of the DB.

Fourth, the complexity of the MQL structure is roughly proportional to the complexity of the input. This occurs mainly because the MQL corresponds closely to the surface syntactic structure.

3.3.2 Computing corrective indirect responses

The crucial observation required to produce a reasonable set of corrective indirect responses is that the <u>MQL query presumes the non-emptiness of its connected subgraphs</u>. Each connected subgraph corresponds to a presumption the user has made about the domain of discourse. If the user believed any connected subgraph to represent an empty response, s/he would also have to believe that the answer to the entire query was empty. Hence s/he would know a priori the answer to the question, violating the convention that a questioner should leave a respondent a choice of direct responses. The user must therefore find the non-emptiness of each connected subgraph assumable, i.e. not believe it to be empty. Consequently, should the initial query return a null response, the control structure can check the user's presumptions by passing each connected subgraph to the interpretive component to check its non-emptiness. Notice that each connected subgraph itself constitutes a well formed query. Should a presumption prove false, an appropriate indirect response can be generated, rather than a meaningless or misleading direct response of "None."

For example, in the query of Figure 1, the connected subgraphs and their corresponding corrective indirect responses are (the numbers represent the sets the subgraphs consist of):

1)	"I don't know of any students."
2)	"I don't know of any Fs."
3)	"I don't know of any courses."
4)	"I don't know of any Linguistics."
1,2)	"I don't know of any students that got Fs."
2,3)	"I don't know of any Fs in courses."
3,4)	"I don't know of any Linguistics courses."
1,2,3)	"I don't know of any students that got Fs in courses."
2,3,4)	"I don't know of any Fs in linguistics courses."

Suppose that there are no linguistics courses in the DB. Rather than presenting the direct, correct answer of "None.", the control structure will pass each connected subgraph in turn to be executed against the DB. It will discover that no linguistics courses exist in the DB, and so will respond with "I don't know of any linguistics courses." This corrective indirect response (and all responses generated through this method) will entail the direct answer, since they will entail the emptiness of the direct response set.

Several aspects of this procedure are worthy of note. First, although the selection of the response is dependent on knowledge of the domain (as encoded in the DB system - not as separate theorems, structures, or programs), the computation of the presumptions is totally independent of domain specific knowledge. Because these inferences are driven by the MQL, the procedures that determine the presumptions (by computing subgraphs) require no knowledge of the domain. Consequently, producing corrective indirect responses from another DB, or even another DB system, requires no changes to the inferencing procedures. Secondly, the mechanism for selecting the indirect response is identical to the procedure for executing a query. No additional computational machinery need be invoked to select the appropriate indirect response. Thirdly, the computational overhead involved in checking and correcting the users presumptions is not incurred unless it has been determined that an indirect response may be required. Should the query succeed initially, no penalty in execution time will be paid for the ability to produce the indirect responses. In addition, the only increase in space overhead is a small control program to produce the connected subgraphs. The linguistic generation of the indirect response is essentially free - it is a small addition to the paraphrase component already used in error detection.

The MQL also provides a means of selecting the most appropriate set of corrective responses when more than one is applicable. The presumptions of a question can be partially ordered according to an entailment relationship: the failure of some presumptions entail the failure of others. For example, if there are no courses, then there are no Fs in courses, which in turn entails that there are no Fs in Linguistics courses, etc. It is often the case that several presumptions of a question fail simultaneously, in part because of this partial ordering. In such cases, the most appropriate response is to correct the least failing set of presumptions in this ordering.[1]

In the MQL, this ordering manifests itself as a subgraph relation among the subgraphs of the MQL: some subgraphs are subgraphs of others. By checking the non-emptiness of the subgraphs in a suitable order, the most appropriate response can be formulated. Thus, in the example, it is possible for the system to produce a response such as "I don't know of any Fs, and I don't know of any Linguistics courses.", without producing the additional irrelevant facts that there are no Fs in courses, no students got Fs, etc.

Corrective indirect responses, produced in this fashion, are language driven inferences, because they are derived directly from the structure of the query as represented by the MQL. If the query were phrased differently, a different set of presumptions would be computed. (This is not a drawback, as it might seem at first - it insures that the response will be in terms that the user understands, since the terms used in the explanation are those presented in the original query.) For these reasons, corrective indirect responses, made possible by a careful choice of representations and associated algorithms, are produced in a domain transparent fashion with minimal system overhead using knowledge already available in the DB.

---

1. This is more an empirical observation than a provable fact. This set of failed presumptions provides the most perspicuous way of communicating the nature of the problem to the questioner, following the Maxims of [Grice 1975].

It is important to note that the success of this technique is strongly dependent on the extensional nature of most DB queries. The method assumes that each sub-part of the original query is making reference to some (possibly empty) identifiable set of items in the database. Similarly, it assumes that the meaning of the entire query is a well defined (through composition of relations) combination of these references. In areas of application where non-extensional NL expressions are common, different computational techniques for producing corrective indirect responses would be required.

In addition to facilitating corrective indirect responses, the MQL provides a convenient representation for producing other types of cooperative responses.

3.3.3 Focus and suggestive indirect responses

In NL contexts where conversational initiative can be shared, it is appropriate for a respondent to suggest relevant information that is likely to be requested in a follow-up question. Consider the following exchange:

> 1Q: Is there a mailbox on this block?
> 1R: No, but there's one down the street.

Responses such as this that anticipate a questioner's needs can be called Suggestive Indirect Responses, because they elaborate on the literal response by suggesting some (hopefully relevant) additional information. The key observation for computing suggestive indirect responses is that the response is usually an answer to a slightly modified question. Specifically, the original question is modified by varying or eliminating its focus. Roughly speaking, focus is that aspect of the question that is most likely to shift in a follow-up question.[1] In dialog 2 below, the focus is the particular location of available seats, while in dialog 3 it is the departure times of the trains.

---

1. This characterization of focus is a (perhaps oversimplified) projection of the more complex linguistic concept onto the DB retrieval domain. For a treatment of this issue in more richly structured (but still quite restricted) domains see [Grosz 1977] and [Lehnert 1977].

2Q: Are there any seats available in the orchestra for tonight's Rolling Stones' concert?
R: No.
Q: Are there any in the balcony?
R: Yes.

3Q: How many more trains leave for N.Y. this evening?
R: Zero.
Q: How many trains leave for N.Y. tomorrow morning?
R: 3.

Corresponding suggestive indirect responses to these questions could be:

4Q: Are there any seats available in the orchestra for tonight's Rolling Stones' concert?
4R: No, but there are some in the balcony.

5Q: How many more trains leave for N.Y. this evening?
5R: None, but there are 3 tomorrow morning.

In a computational setting, some means of detecting the need for a suggestive indirect response and determining the focus of the current question is required.

In human dialog, there appears to be a conversational convention that speakers should phrase their questions to avoid negative or trivial responses. A trivial response is one that denotes an empty set ("None."), or the result of a simple predicate, such as COUNT, on an empty set ("Zero."). By adopting this as a principle of cooperation in discourse, it is possible for speakers to communicate their expectations along with their questions. If a respondent is asked a question to which the response is negative or trivial, s/he is justified in assuming that some (perhaps rather weak) expectation the speaker had has been violated, and that the conversation has temporarily reached a dead end. It is then appropriate to produce a suggestive indirect response. That many questions carry this expectation can be illustrated by observing that a response of "Your assumption is correct." is not a meaningless retort to the following:

6: The A&P is open on Sunday, isn't it?
7: The A&P isn't open on Sunday, is it?

8: Is John a senior?
9: Is John an underclassman?

A related effect occurs with questions other than yes/no questions. Question 10 carries an expectation that some Friday classes are taken by students that live in the main quad dormitory - the answer "None." indicates a violation of this expectation. Similarly, 11 expects that some B-52s have logged over 1000 hours downtime - an answer of "Zero." indicates a violation.

> 10: Which Friday classes are taken by students that live in the main quad dormitory?

> 11: How many B-52s have logged over 1000 hours downtime?

These negative and trivial responses admit suggestive indirect responses. For example, 8 might be followed with "No, he's a junior."; 10 with "None, but here are the classes taken by students that live in any dormitory..."; and 11 with "Zero, but there are 25 B-52s that have logged over 900 hours downtime." The appropriateness of the various responses depends on the determination of the focus of the questions. It should be noted that it is (perhaps equally) often appropriate to elaborate on questions with positive responses. In addition, it is occasionally true that an elaboration after a negative response appears to be superfluous, for example in "Have any B-52s logged over 1000 hours downtime?". What is of interest here is that the negative responses can serve as a conversational cue for suggestive indirect responses.

Consequently, the CO-OP control structure attempts to produce a suggestive indirect response when the direct answer to a question is negative or trivial. Once a question has been parsed into the MQL,

> 1) it is translated to a formal query that will produce a direct response, and an attempt is made to execute this against the DB;

> 2) should the result be an empty set (a null answer), the presumptions of the question are checked in the hope of producing a corrective indirect response, as described above;

> 3) should no computable presumptions fail, a suggestive indirect response is attempted. This is done by eliminating one of the sets in the MQL (the set designated as the focus during the parsing phase) and executing this modified query.

This modified query will correspond to a question in which the focus has been changed, i.e. a likely follow-up question.

The success of this type of response is heavily dependent on the correct determination of the focus. Unfortunately, this is a difficult and subtle problem. To some degree, determining the focus of a question can be regarded as a special case of plan recognition. An understanding of the intentions of a questioner will lead to a very effective strategy for determining focus. (In a sense, a complete enough understanding would allow a respondent to ignore a questioner's utterances altogether!) Such information is rarely available to DB query systems, and quite simply is not available to CO-OP. Since CO-OP does not maintain an explicit user model, some simpler cues were sought for focus determination.

An alternative method of finding focus is to examine a sequence of questions, when possible, to explicitly determine what the likely focus is by finding what has shifted and what has remained constant in the immediately preceding dialog. This method could correctly locate the focus of the questions presented in dialogs 2 and 3 above. A simplification of this approach is to compare the MQL representation of the current question with that of the previous one. The focus can then be selected from the presented sets that differ between the two questions.

Should this technique still leave a number of choices for the focus, the problem can be resolved further through some syntactic cues. Questions are often phrased so that (in unmarked cases[1]) the focus is presented as "new" information, and consequently appears late in the question, as far as possible (syntactically) from the subject (This assumes that there is a tendency for new information in questions to be placed toward the end of a sentence). For example, the foci in dialogs 1 and 3 both occur at the end of the questions. (For a system that uses this observation to produce suggestive indirect responses, though they do not use this terminology, see [Steedman and Johnson-Laird 1976].) In the MQL, this distance through the syntactic parse tree tends to manifest itself as graphical distance from the presented set corresponding to the subject noun phrase. This occurs because of the close relationship between the structure of an MQL expression and the syntactic structure of a parse tree. Relations in the MQL tend to map one-to-one with phrases and clauses in the question. A simple graph search algorithm can therefore be used to locate or chose among likely candidates for the true focus.

An error in the selection of the focus does not produce disastrous results; it may, however, be an inconvenience for a user to be confronted with unwanted or irrelevant information.

Experience with the CO-OP implementation has uncovered a more serious problem with generating suggestive indirect responses. Once the focus has been chosen, it is important to vary it in a meaningful way. Generating a more general

---

1. Cases not overridden by contextual considerations.

question by simply eliminating the focus can result in uninteresting and excessively lengthy responses (such as "I don't know of any programmers in division 3, but you might be interested in any programmers in any divisions..."). Ideally, an intelligent selection of an alternative focus should be made, as in example 3 above, where "this evening" has been changed to "tomorrow morning". Often there are many dimensions along which the focus can be varied. Currently, CO-OP simply eliminates the focus and responds to the resulting query. Though the system's behavior may be of theoretical interest, a more sophisticated approach would be required for suggestive indirect responses to be of value in a practical NL DB query system.

In contrast to this approach, the work of Allen (described elsewhere in this volume) is in principle capable of producing more appropriate and sophisticated suggestive indirect responses. By maintaining an explicit model of the beliefs and goals of the speaker (as well as explicit knowledge about the domain) in a form that facilitates formal reasoning, responses attuned to the particular setting, speakers, and context can be generated. This more intelligent behavior is obtained at the cost of additional inferencing and the encoding of domain-specific and situation-specific knowledge.

These factors would tend to limit the transportability (to new situations and domains) of a NL DB query system, and so are not very practical given current implementation techniques, though Allen's work is of obvious theoretical importance. By contrast, the limited class of responses in CO-OP's cooperative repertoire are achieved on a more surface linguistic basis - without a special encoding of domain knowledge - and so were more appropriate for the goals of this work.

3.3.4 Vagueness and supportive indirect responses

A common problem in NL query systems is the production of unacceptably terse answers. Consider a response of 12R to 12Q, and 13R to 13Q.

12Q: What grades did students get in CSE110?
12R: A,B,B,A,C,...

13Q: What are the phone numbers of managers in
Marketing?
13R: 293-4958, 584-7945, 293-7754...

Obviously, both the grades and the phone numbers are likely to be useless without the associated names. The deeper problem here is that NL questions often do not explicitly indicate what information should be incorporated into the response; the language is designed to share this burden with the respondent. These questions require Supportive Indirect Responses - responses that provide the supporting information necessary to interpret the answer. (Both REL [Thompson et. al. 1969] and LUNAR [Woods et. al. 1972] can provide limited responses of this type.)

To insure that the appropriate supporting information is present, the query system could dump the entire contents of the DB in response to any question, since this would be likely to contain all information relevant to the questioner's needs. Obviously, this would be a less than optimal approach. The problem then is to make an intelligent selection of relevant information from the DB. Conveniently, the phrasing of the question provides excellent guidance in this selection. Questioners tend to explicitly mention in their questions those aspects of the domain that are relevant to their needs. Conversely, they tend to be vague with respect to irrelevant aspects of the domain. Vagueness is the deletion of information that may be relevant (but not essential given the context) to the selection of a response.[1]

Consider the difference between questions 14 and 15.

14: Which students passed CS105?

15: Which students got a passing grade in CS105?

While both questions appear to make the same request, 15 mentions grades while 14 does not. (That is, 14 is vague with respect to grades.) As a result, it is more appropriate to include the grades along with the students in a response to 15 than to 14. The use of vagueness serves as a cue indicating which aspects of the domain are relevant to the user's needs, and hence may be appropriately incorporated into a response in the absence of other contextual cues to the contrary.

This function of vagueness is used in forming the responses produced by CO-OP. The system assumes that if a user explicitly mentioned some aspect of the domain in his or her question, then that aspect may appear in the response.

---

1. Vagueness should be distinguished from ambiguity, where multiple interpretations can be assigned to the same question. As with focus, this characterization is a broad simplification of more subtle linguistic phenomena. As defined here, vagueness covers ellipsis, hedging, and a variety of other phenomena - all of which reduce in this domain to a lack of detail useful for selecting a response.

(Conversely, aspects not mentioned do not appear.) This is achieved by observing that each aspect mentioned will result in a corresponding presented set in the MQL. The strategy is then simply to provide information on each presented set that is not a singleton. Thus 14 above would produce a response containing only students (CS105 is a singleton), while 15 would produce a table of student - grade pairs. Similarly, a question such as "What are the phone numbers of managers in the marketing division?" would produce a response of not just phone numbers, but also the corresponding manager's names (assuming that this information is available in the DB).

Each lexical item that may define a set has in the CO-OP lexicon an associated list of fields that are to be printed to designate the individuals in the set. Thus, "students" above might result in the printing of both their names and social security numbers - but only if students were mentioned in the question.

Since the selection of relevant information to be incorporated into a supportive response is determined by the phrasing of the question, the technique is a language driven inference. The system is able to exploit the user's linguistic competence to drive its inferencing procedures.

3.4 CO-OP sample queries

CO-OP was implemented on a DEC KL-10 under TOPS-10 at the Wharton Computational Facility in RUTGERS-UCI-LISP and FORTRAN. The domain for these examples is a DB from the National Center for Atmospheric Research (NCAR) in Boulder, Colorado. One of the functions of NCAR is to provide computational resources to researchers across the country working on government grants, mainly in meteorology. The DB tracks the use of these resources. It contains information on users, programmers (users that work for the computing facility), divisions (which are organized further into superdivisions), accounts, projects, sponsors, and project advisors, to name a few. To understand the responses, it is important to note that users can be in many divisions, and work on many projects, but the projects are not considered to be in particular divisions. The projects, however, are organized into areas of interest, according to a set of area codes.

An annotated sample of questions and answers illustrating the salient features of the current implementation follows. In addition to demonstrating the types of cooperative responses discussed above, the examples cover other functional capabilities of the system such as limited quantification, issues of portability and domain transparency, graceful error recovery, and strategies for dealing with implausible semantic interpretations. Though these features are required for a realistic NL system, they are of lesser theoretical interest and are not described in detail in the text. (An extended discussion can be found in [Kaplan 1979].)

In the examples, names have been altered in the interest of privacy. "Q" (below) stands for question, "P" for paraphrase, and "R" for response. (The paraphrases are presented to the user for approval prior to execution of the query.) Commentary is in square brackets ([ ]). (Some irrelevant paraphrases and responses are deleted in the interest of brevity.)

> Q: *Who advises projects in area 36?*
> P: Assuming that there are projects that are in area #36,
>   who advises those projects?

[The system incorporates a powerful paraphraser,[1] that performs two types of disambiguation: lexical - it will explain its chosen interpretation for vague or ambiguous terms; and syntactic - it explains the clausal dependencies determined by the parser. It is also used for indirect responses, as illustrated below. This component has access solely to the MQL (parser output), and so requires no modification on new domains.]

> R: I don't know of any area #36.

[This is an example of a corrective indirect response. Rather than giving a misleading direct answer of "No one.", the system produces the appropriate indirect response, using the techniques described above. Note that the system carefully hedges its response with respect to its state of knowledge, rather than assuming either a closed or open world DB [Reiter 1978].[2]

> Q: *Which programmers from the ASD group are in*
>   *superdivision 5000?*

[The programmers are organized into groups, identified by group IDs.]

> P: (I am assuming that "ASD" is a GROUP ID.)
>   Which programmers are in superdivision #5000?

---

1. Designed and implemented mainly by Kathy McKeown [McKeown 1979].

2. A closed world DB is one in which the absence of a fact implies the truth of its negation. For example, if a DB does not contain information that John Smith is a manager, then it can be assumed that John Smith is not a manager, under the closed world assumption. In an open world DB, this assumption does not hold - if John Smith is not listed in the phone book, it cannot be inferred that he doesn't have a phone number.

Look for programmers that are from ASD group.

[This paraphrase illustrates both types of disambiguation, although the lexical disambiguation is probably unnecessary in this example.]

> R: I don't know of any ASD group. I don't know of any
> programmers that are in superdivision #5000.

[This corrective indirect response has two components. Rather than simply correcting all subgraphs of the MQL that denote empty referents in the DB, the system explains only the appropriate ones. For example, since there is no ASD group, it is obvious that there are no programmers in the ASD group. This parsimony, a reflection of Grice's "Maxim of Quantity" [Grice 1975], is achieved by noting that the presumptions (subgraphs) of the MQL are partially ordered according to a "subgraph" relation, i.e. some subgraphs are subgraphs of others. The emptiness of a lesser subgraph in the ordering will necessarily entail the emptiness of all greater subgraphs. CO-OP computes and corrects only the least failing subgraphs in this ordering. Note that this technique is entirely domain transparent: no additional domain driven inference is required.]

> Q: *Which projects in oceanography does Nasa Headquarters sponsor?*
> P: (I am assuming that "Nasa Headquarters" is a SPONSOR NAME.)
>   (I am assuming that "oceanography" is a AREA OF INTEREST.)
> Which projects does Nasa Headquarters sponsor?
> Look for projects that are in oceanography.

[Note that "Nasa Headquarters" and "oceanography" appear only as values in the DB - not as explicit entries in the lexicon. A set of heuristics are used to infer the appropriate fields in the DB in which these unknown terms are likely to occur [Kaplan, Mays, and Joshi 1979]. This allows the lexicon to remain current even though the DB may be subject to updates. (This problem is handled as a special case of word sense disambiguation.)]

> R: I don't know of any projects in oceanography that Nasa
> Headquarters sponsors. But you might be interested in
> any projects that Nasa Headquarters sponsors...

(PROJECT/ACCT #)   (PROJECT TITLE)

| 35071040 | NON-EQUILIB. OF ELECTRONS IN SOL |
| 35071048 | OUTER ATMOSPHERES OF DWARF STARS |

[This is an example of a suggestive indirect response. After discovering an empty referent in the DB for the entire query, the system attempts to find a corrective response. Since this query is well formed with respect to the DB (i.e. no presumptions fail), it attempts to locate a focus in the query which it can eliminate to produce a hopefully relevant and helpful response. On a syntactic basis, "oceanography" is designated as the focus, and a new query is formed for the indirect response by eliminating this from the query. Specifically, this focus is a modifying clause syntactically "furthest" from the subject (Nasa Headquarters). This new query is then executed and displayed.]

> Q: *Which projects advised by Thomas Wirth does Nasa*
>   *Goddard Space Center sponsor?*

[This question receives a direct response, and is designed to set up a context for the following question.]

> Q: *Which projects sponsored by NSF does Thomas Wirth*
>   *advise?*
> R: I don't know of any projects that were sponsored by NSF
>   that Thomas Wirth advises. But you might be interested
>   in any projects that Thomas Wirth advises, namely:

(PROJECT/ACCT #)   (PROJECT TITLE)   (ADVISOR TITLE)

| 35081027 | SATELLT-SLAR ABSORBTN | PROFESSOR... |

[This suggestive response was generated by designating the sponsor as the focus of the original query. Here the focus was determined contextually, by comparing the current query with the previous one to see what has changed. Syntactic cues, such as in the previous example, are used only when no contextual cue can be derived from the previous query.]

> Q: *Who sponsors projects not in oceanography?*

R: FAILURE.
Sorry, but I didn't understand you fully-
I have a very limited knowledge of English.
My best guess as to what you meant is:
  Who sponsors projects?
Could you please rephrase your question and try again...

[This is an example of failure in the system. In principle, the only kind of failure is parse failure - the interpretive components can process any legal output of the parser. (In addition, the parser will reach an interpretation of any syntactically valid input, regardless of its semantic well-formedness.) Consequently, the only type of failure diagnostics that are required are in the parse. During the parse, a current hypothesis regarding the input is maintained at all times. In the event of a parse failure, the best guess (largest hypothesis) encountered is displayed for the user, in the hope that this will aid the user in localizing the nature of the problem. This approach, to try to explain what went right with the parse rather than what went wrong, is motivated by the fact that the point at which the error actually occurred is often considerably before the point at which the error is detected - English is more than locally ambiguous. Any attempt to diagnose the error at the point of failure is more likely to mystify the user than to help him or her re-phrase the question. In this case, the system is unable to process a negation preceding a prepositional phrase.]

Q: *Who doesn't sponsor projects in the oceanography area?*

[Here the user has re-phrased the question.]

P: (I am assuming that "oceanography" is an AREA OF INTEREST.) Assuming that there are projects that are in the oceanography area, who doesn't sponsor those projects?

R:

(SPONSOR NAME)

CTR NATL DE LA RECHERCHE SCIEN
ERDA/WASHINGTON
NASA/MARSHALL SPACE FLT. CNTR
OFFICE OF NAVAL RESEARCH/ARL.
U.S. NUCLEAR REGULATORY COM.

[This example illustrates two points. First, that the system can process negation. This is handled by the quantification routines, essentially by counting the number of projects in oceanography sponsored by each sponsor and selecting those that sponsor exactly zero. This is a special case of quantification. Second, the system must decide in such cases just what the set "Who" should appropriately refer to. If it took the set of all people in the DB (i.e. users, advisors, programmers, sponsors, etc.) the response would include a great deal of extraneous information. CO-OP selects as the referent those individuals that could reasonably participate in the unnegated relationship. The resolution of vague referring expressions is made solely on the basis of the lexicon and DB schema.]

Q: *Which programmers are in division 4111 and 4361?*

[The scoping of conjunction is a subtle problem that must be handled in any serious NL query system. Here the parser is faced with essentially three syntactically valid scopes: conjoining the numbers, the divisions (division 4111 and division 4361), or conjoining the programmers (programmers in division 4111 and programmers in division 4361). The system chooses the narrowest scoping that could result in a non-empty response set based on an inspection of the DB schema. The basic structure of the CODASYL formalism is the functional relationship (in-or-above in the DB schema diagram), in this case revealing that divisions can have only one number. On this basis, the narrowest scope is ruled out. However, the schema does admit the possibility of programmers being in two divisions (a many-to-many relationship), and so this interpretation is chosen. The paraphrase makes this choice clear to the user.]

P: Which programmers are in division #4361 and division #4111?

[By contrast, the following question is given a wide scope interpretation, although it is syntactically identical. Areas, like divisions, can have only one number, but in this case, projects can be in only one area.]

Q: *Which projects are in area 6 and 27?*

P: To simplify matters, I'm going to split your question into several parts. I understand your question to mean:

Which projects are in area #27? Which projects are in area #6?

[Mainly for its own convenience, the system interprets wide scoped conjunctions as presenting multiple questions. Notice that the effect of the "and" in this case is rather like that of an "or". The system then answers each question in turn.]

> Q: *Which users work on projects in area 3 that are in division 200?*
>
> P: Assuming that there are projects that are in area #3, which users work on those projects? Look for users that are in division #200.

[Relative clause and prepositional phrase attachment is another difficult problem that involves the use of semantic tests in the parsing process. Once again, the DB schema provides sufficient information for disambiguation. Syntactically, it is unclear whether the relative clause "that are in division 200" modifies users or projects. The system decides that users is the most likely referent, by scoring the potential referents on three dimensions. The first is the semantic relatedness of the subject and object of the resulting MQL relation, in this case (users, divisions) and (projects, divisions). The semantic relatedness is measured by the distance through the schema between the records denoting those items. In the schema, DIST(USER,DIVIS) = 2, while DIST(PROJT,DIVIS) = 4 (recall that projects are not organized into divisions). Second, the distance back in the question from the clause to the potential referent is measured, on the assumption that the modifier is most likely to be near its referent. Third, a prediction is made on the basis of the information content of the lexical items designating the relation (in this case, the word "in" contains little predictive value, and does not affect the decision). This is done by associating with each preposition and verb in the lexicon a (possibly empty) list of probable subjects and objects. For example, a verb like "sponsor" in this domain predicts a sponsor as a subject and a project as an object.]

> Q: *What are the advisor's phone numbers?*
>
> R:

(ADVISOR NAME)	(ADVISOR TITLE)	(ADVISOR PHONE #)
MOYER, ROSCOE	PROFESSOR	312-753-2184
OBRIEN, JOANNE	PROFESSOR	713-845-0365
ORSZAG, VANCE	PROFESSOR	804-924-8675...

[This is an example of a response containing supportive indirect components. Although the question literally asks only for phone numbers, the response includes the additional relevant information of the advisor's names and titles, as discussed in section 3.4. The basic strategy here is to incorporate into the response information on each class of items explicitly mentioned in the question that is not restricted to a singleton.]

Q: *What are the groups?*

[The programmers work in programming groups. Unfortunately, the DB designer never considered the possibility of a user querying the DB with respect to the groups directly, and so simply made group a field of the programmer record. In keeping with a design goal of making the responses invariant under differing DB organizations, CO-OP performs an inversion on the "group" field to present the response in the form in which the data was requested. The response, therefore, is purely a function of the input and the contents of the DB, not the DB organization.]

R:

(GROUP ID)

AQM
HAO
SYS
UL

Q: *Which programmers work in groups?*

R:

(USER #)	(PERSON NAME)	(GROUP ID)
8002	TAKAMINE, GARY	UL
8056	AITKEN, JOYCE	HAO
8061	VALENT, JO	AQM
8063	WALSH, MARIE	HAO
8067	WORKING, MARIE	SYS

[This question illustrates how the system organizes the responses according to the way the information is presented by the question. This can be contrasted with the following question, which requests the same information in a different form.]

Q: *Which groups do programmers work in?*

R:

(GROUP ID)	(USER #)	(PERSON NAME)
AQM	8061	VALENT, JO
HAO	8056	AITKEN, JOYCE
	8063	WALSH, MARIE
SYS	8067	WORKING, MARIE
UL	8002	TAKAMINE, GARY

Q: *Who sponsors more than 3 projects?*

P: Who sponsors 4 or more projects?

R:

(SPONSOR NAME)
NASA GODDARD SPACE CENTER
NATIONAL SCIENCE FOUNDATION

[Quantification in CO-OP is done by a counting mechanism. While the handling of quantification in this system is a very partial solution to a difficult problem, it is sufficient for handling simple existentials, universals, negations, and counts. Scoping of nested quantifiers is simply taken left to right in the question.]

Q: *Which users work on every project in area 55?*

P: Assuming that there is at least one project that is in area #55, which users work on every such project?

R:

(USER)   (PERSON NAME)

8000   PENNEYS, JEANNE
8002   TAKAMINE, GARY
8067   WORKING, MARIE

[Universal quantification (all, every, etc.) requires executing more than one query against the DB. First, a query is executed to determine the size of the universally quantified set (in this case, the number of projects in area of interest 55). This value is substituted into a second query to produce the appropriate response. Note that the paraphrase in the above example reflects the fact that in English, universally quantified expressions are normally assumed to be non-empty.]

> Q: *Which programmers work in division 3513 or project 43610008?*

R:

(USER #) (PERSON NAME)   (DVSN NAME)   (PROJECT TITLE)

8005   TAKAMINE, JOYCE   *****   PRO DVLPMNT
8061   VALENT, JO   U. OF HAWAII   *****
8068   WONG, THOMAS   *****   PRO DVLPMNT...

[Disjunction is handled quite differently than conjunction. The resulting report is normalized to a tabular form with asterisks substituted for missing values.]

> Q: *What are the specialties of the HAO group?*

[This question, while quite natural for English speakers to interpret, contains a form of indirect reference. "HAO group" here does not actually refer to the group itself, but rather to its members. If the system were very literal minded, it would find this question semantically ill-formed, since groups don't have specialties. However, because the question has been posed, CO-OP assumes that the user must have meant something, no matter how poorly expressed. This pragmatic effect is reflected in the system's ability to reach a most reasonable interpretation of virtually any syntactically valid input, regardless of its literal implausibility. In this case CO-OP discovers that the simplest path in the schema from specialties to groups is through the programmers, and so it responds as follows.]

    R:

(PERSON NAME)	(SPECIALTIES)
AITKEN, JOYCE	LINEAR ALGEBRA
WALSH, MARIE	GRAPHICS, FRONT ENDS...

[Perhaps a more interesting example of this phenomenon is the system's response to the following.]

    Q: *What is knowledge?*

    P: Display knowledge.

    R:

(USER #)	(PERSON NAME)	(SPECIALTIES)
8002	TAKAMINE, GARY	PLIB MAINTENANCE
8056	AITKEN, JOYCE	LINEAR ALGEBRA
8061	VALENT, JO	LIBRARY MAINTENANCE...

3.5 Portability

Much work in AI has focused on methods for organizing and representing large amounts of world knowledge. Motivating this research is an assumption that the more knowledge that can be incorporated into a system, the more intelligent its behavior will be. While this assertion is almost certainly valid, it is equally interesting to explore the question of how little knowledge may be necessary to perform particular tasks, and how that knowledge may be partitioned into "general" and "specific" components.

For this reason, a design limitation was placed on CO-OP that all domain specific knowledge be encoded at the lexical level. Only the information coded in the lexicon or already available in the DB system could be used as sources of knowledge about the domain. All other aspects of the system, including the generation of cooperative responses, had to be totally free of any DB specific knowledge. (That is, the programs had to be completely <u>domain transparent</u>.) Though this limited the type of questions that could be handled to simple extensional requests for the retrieval of existing data, it provided a means of separating the general knowledge required for this task from the domain specific knowledge, and for discovering what, if any, additional knowledge sources were required.

A by-product of this limitation was that the system could be transported to new domains simply by changing the DB and lexicon. This portability provided a rigorous test of the programs. To verify the claims of domain transparency and portability, CO-OP was moved from the NCAR DB to the ONRODA DB, a collection of military information on ships, aircraft, submarines, etc., created as part of the Operational Decision Aids Program of the Office of Naval Research at the University of Pennsylvania.[1]

The move was quite successful: the CO-OP programs continued to produce cooperative responses without modification. This section reports on the results.

3.5.1 Domain specific structures

Several data structures required recoding to affect the changeover. They are as follows:

> 1) The lexicon. Some of the domain specific words available to the users must be encoded explicitly in the lexicon, along with their definitions in terms of the DB.

> 2) The DB schema. This has to be put in a special form to facilitate path finding. This task can be performed automatically if the schema is a tree structure (i.e. if no ambiguous paths exist), and so a program could be written that inputs a standard CODASYL Data Definition Language and outputs the needed structure. In the case of a graph structured schema, a selection of preferred paths is required.

> 3) The DB itself. Obviously, the new DB must be supplied.

> 4) The item print names. A special list (ITEMPRNAME in the program) associating a print name with each field in the DB is required for labeling the output and providing lexical disambiguation in the paraphrase.

---

1. Under contract N00014-75-C-0440 with the assistance of CTEC, Inc., of McLean, Va.

5) The DB name and password. These are needed to open the DB.

3.5.2 Effort required and extent of new domain

Since the translation of the DB schema could be done automatically (it was not in this instance), with the exception of resolving ambiguous paths, the time required to encode it by hand is not particularly relevant here.[1]

Similarly, no significant effort was expended to acquire the DB, or supply the DB name and password. The remaining time was occupied by the preparation, keypunching and verification of the lexicon and list of print names: this required about 5 hours. Several caveats should be observed in extrapolating this experience, however.

Only a subset of the ONRODA DB was used. A selection of 18 records and 22 sets was made, containing a total of about 58 fields. The basic lexicon contained about 110 entries, not including morphological variants or nouns and numbers occurring only as DB values. Estimating the true extent of the lexicon is difficult because of the system's ability to handle unknown terms. However, given the current contents of the DB as a starting point, the system has an effective relevant vocabulary of about 750-1000 words. This proved more than adequate to formulate a wide variety of non-trivial queries.

3.5.3 Results and examples

Immediately upon completion of the ONRODA lexicon, the system was able to produce the same types of responses to the same classes of questions as with the NCAR DB. No further tuning or modification of the programs of any kind was required. In fact, the ONRODA DB proved to be a richer domain than the NCAR DB, and consequently provided a wider range of interesting questions with which to test the system. (As a result, several new bugs were discovered in addition to those already revealed by the NCAR DB.) However, the bulk of these additional problems could be easily corrected (but were not), and none of them seriously affected the performance of the system, as illustrated below. Response times were comparable to those observed with the NCAR DB.

---

1. By hand, it took about 5 hours.

The ONRODA DB was operational under the SEED CODASYL DB system on a DEC KL-10. It consists of records on ships, aircraft, submarines, guns, torpedoes, radar, and bombs, with a significant variety of data on each. The sets generally indicate which and how many of the latter four exist on the first three. The data has been falsified, and so does not accurately reflect the real world. No modifications of any kind were made to either the DB, DB schema, or the DB system.

An annotated sample of questions and responses is listed below. As before, "Q" means question, "P" means paraphrase, "R" means response, and comments are enclosed in square brackets ([ ]). (Irrelevant paraphrases and responses are deleted for brevity.) The programs that produced this output are the same ones that produced the transcript in section 4: absolutely no changes were made.

Q: *What is the maximum ceiling of aircraft that carry MK-84 bombs?*

R:

(ARCRFT MAX CEIL (FT))	(ARCRFT NAME)
41500	A-7
44000	A-6
50000	AV-8A
58000	F-5

[This query gives a flavor of the type of data in the ONRODA DB. Notice that the system has produced the information for each aircraft - it is currently incapable of selecting only the greatest of these.]

Q: *What is the fire rate of the M-61?*

P: (I am assuming that "M-61" is a GUN NAME.) Display the fire rate of the M-61.

R: (GUN FIRE RATE)

3000

[M-61 appears only as a value in the DB system. CO-OP has to infer which field it is likely to occur in. Here it has correctly identified it as a gun name. The same domain transparent procedures that resolved these references in the NCAR DB apply equally well here.]

Q: *Which ships have strut curve radar that carry M-61 guns?*

["Strut curve" is a type of radar.]

> P: (I am assuming that "strut curve" is a RADAR NAME.)
> (I am assuming that "M-61" is a GUN NAME.) Which ships
> have strut curve radar? Look for ships that carry M-61 guns.

[This question is syntactically ambiguous. To determine whether the relative clause "that carry M-61 guns" modifies "ships" or "radar" it is necessary to make a semantic judgment. The system correctly chooses "ships", as the paraphrase indicates.]

> Q: *Which guns are on aircraft and ships?*

[This is a case of simple conjunction. Note the organization of the answer.]

> R:

(GUN NAME)   (SHIP NAME)   (ARCRFT NAME)

MK 12	TARAWA	A-4
NR-30	DODRY	SU-7B
	OSA	SU-7B...

> Q: *Which subs with radar don't carry MK-44 torpedoes?*
>
> R: I don't know of any subs with radar. I don't know of any
> subs that carry MK-44 torpedoes.

[This is an example of a corrective response. Notice that the latter correction entails that all subs don't carry MK-44 torpedoes. Here the negated presumption does not entail an empty set, but rather the entire set, indicating that the restriction was irrelevant.]

> Q: *What is the detection range of ships with torpedoes?*

R:

(RADAR RANGE)	(SHIP NAME)	(TRPDO NAME)
100 NMI	AGERHOLM	MK-46
	FISKE	MK-46
140 NMI	COCHRANE	MK-46
200 NMI	GRIDLEY	MK-48

[This response contains supportive indirect components. In addition to the detection range, which was the only information literally requested, it supplies the ship name and torpedo names as well.]

Q: *Which aircraft that carry MK-46 torpedoes have refuel capability?*

R: I don't know of any aircraft that carry MK-46 torpedoes that have refuel capability. But you might be interested in any aircraft that carry any torpedoes that have refuel capability...

(ARCRFT NAME)

CH-53D
P-3
S-3

[Here, the system produces a suggestive indirect response. It has designated the torpedo type as the most likely focus, and consequently answers the more general question, as indicated.]

Q: *What are the classes of ships?*

R:

(SHIP CLASS)	(SHIP NAME)
BLUEBIRD	VIREO
KNOX	DOWNES
	TRUETT
SKORY	STEPANNY

[This question requires the system to perform an inversion on the ship class field to present the data in a form consistent with the request. Although the user has presented the classes as entities, they are represented in the DB as attributes of the ships. Responses in CO-OP are a function of the phrasing of the query and the information in the DB, but not the particular organization for the data chosen by the DB designer.]

Q: *What is the fire rate of ships with SPS-40 radar?*

R:

(GUN FIRE RATE)	(SHIP NAME)
18	GARCIA
	OWENS
40	HIGBEE
	TARAWA...

[To interpret this question, it is necessary for the system to recognize that an indirect reference has been made. In the DB, ships don't have fire rates; guns do. Rather than reject the question as semantically ill-formed, CO-OP concludes that the user is probably referring to the fire rate of the guns on the ships, and responds accordingly. The response could be improved by including the gun names. A minor change to the lexicon would achieve this.]

3.6 Conclusion

In practical environments, the acceptance of NL DB query systems will be decided in part by the degree to which they adopt the pragmatic discourse conventions normally observed by human speakers. In human conversation, a variety of conventions, postulates, rules, etc. facilitate smooth and effective communication. The use of NL by a query system will imply to the users that these conversational principles will be observed. Pragmatic conversational effects, particularly those that relate to cooperation, will be essential to the behavioral repertoire of successful NL systems.

However, it is not the case that those effects are desirable for all users that wish to query a DB. For some users, NL is not an appropriate means for interacting with a DB system. Some thoughts on the types of users most likely to benefit by NL query systems are included here.

Users with high-level or vague needs: If a user is unclear about what information s/he wants or is unsure of what information is present in the DB, the ability of NL to express vague questions and the appropriateness of indirect responses to NL questions can aid the user in locating relevant information. NL is an appropriate vehicle for browsing through a DB. By contrast, users with specific or detailed needs may find NL too imprecise for expressing their queries: various ambiguities, such as the interpretation of nested quantifiers, may hinder rather than help in communicating with a DB system. If a particular form and content is desired for the responses, a formal query language may be more effective.

Occasional or casual users: For these users, the investment of time and effort to learn a formal query language may exceed the potential value of the information retrieved. For the user with a single question, the fact that the syntax and semantics of NL are already known may be a major advantage to its use. Frequent users, however, may be better off with a terse, special-purpose language: unrestricted NL may be too verbose and unstructured for their needs. The relative cost of becoming familiar with a particular query language falls off rapidly as frequency of use increases.

Naive users: Naive users are unfamiliar with the details of the DB structure, and have no desire to learn how the information in the DB is organized in order to appropriately phrase their queries. While most formal query languages require some knowledge of how the DB is normalized, NL questions do not. NL provides a measure of data independence that most formal query languages lack, facilitating access to data by naive users. On the other hand, users knowledgeable in the structuring of a DB may find this independence a hindrance - they cannot help but conceive their queries with respect to their understanding of the details of the DB. The additional effort required to map their view of the data onto a NL question, and hope that the system performs the inverse mapping properly, may simply be an annoyance.

In summary, a NL DB query system is likely to be of most use to users who conceive of the system as an expert in its own structure and content, and are willing to share the task of formulating queries and selecting the form and content of the responses with the system itself. Users who regard the system as a tool, and wish to exert maximum control over its operation, are likely to find a NL DB query system of limited value.

This work has examined the feasibility of providing cooperative responses from a portable NL DB query system. Beginning with a study of some of the more obvious pragmatic aspects of cooperation in human discourse, a few principles have been projected onto the DB query domain, where computational approaches have been explored. To assess the effectiveness of the techniques developed, a NL DB query system, CO-OP, has been implemented and the results described. While it leaves open many questions, the design of CO-OP suggests several concepts of potential linguistic and computational interest:

1) The communicative effect (perlocutionary force) of questions includes considerable information as to the intentions and beliefs of the questioner. A significant class of propositions that a questioner must find <u>assumable</u> in order to appropriately pose a question and intend it literally are derivable from the pragmatic fact that the question was asked, and a conversational convention that the questioner not know the answer to the question. These propositions, called <u>presumptions</u>, subsume the more widely studied class of logical presuppositions, and are central to the production of cooperative responses.

2) A variety of presumptions are encoded by human speakers directly in the lexical and syntactic structure of their questions, and can be recovered in a computationally efficient fashion via <u>language driven inference</u> techniques.

3) By making the assumption that all aspects of a question are making reference to something in the DB, various types of indirect responses, most notably <u>corrective indirect responses</u>, can be produced in a domain transparent fashion from a NL DB query system.

4) Maintaining the lexical and syntactic integrity of the original question throughout the interpretation process provides a means for explaining failures, errors, and responses in terms that the user is likely to understand. The use of an <u>intermediate representation that captures relevant linguistic considerations without reflecting arbitrary organizational details of the underlying DB</u> is central to this approach. Given such a representation, the organization of data in the responses can and should be independent of the organization of data in the DB.

5) The domain specific knowledge required to answer simple NL questions requesting only retrieval of existing information from a DB can be effectively <u>decomposed to the lexical level</u>, if it is augmented by the knowledge already present in the DB system.

6) As experience with CO-OP indicates, relegating all domain specific knowledge to the lexicon and DB system provides a high degree of portability to new DB domains.

3.7 Acknowledgements

This work was partially supported by NSF grant MCS 76-19466 and ARPA contract MDA 903-77-C-0322.

CHAPTER 4

Natural Language Generation as a Computational Problem: an Introduction

David D. McDonald

4.1. Introduction

Research into the process of goal-directed natural language generation by computers is in its infancy. Until recently there has been no pragmatic pressure to go beyond the simplest ad-hoc generation facilities because the communications needs of the programs that would use the facilities has not required it. Theoretical accounts of generation have lagged accordingly since sophisticated theories of language use cannot be developed apart from equally sophisticated models of language users. Now however, the advent of expert programs in medicine, command-and-control, computer-aided-instruction, and similar language-intensive fields has made deep theories of language generation a necessity if these programs are to have an adequate ability to explain their conclusions and reasoning in a continually changing task environment.

The meager amount of computational research on language generation to date requires us to begin with simple questions with the goal of developing a general organizing theory. Without answers to the most basic questions about the process, analyses of specific phenomena of the sort that the other papers of this volume address in the context of language understanding cannot yet be profitably addressed in generation; rather we must first determine: What does language generation start with? What kinds of decisions are made and how are they controlled? What sorts of intermediate representations are needed? Modern theories of linguistic competence, though cast in a "generative" framework, are not suited to the job of goal-directed generation because their formal structure does not permit them to address the central problem, i.e. *how specific utterances arise from specific communicative goals in a specific discourse context.*

This paper is extracted from a much larger work, [McDonald 1980], which elaborates and argues for my computational theory of natural language generation. Since there is relatively little experience with natural language generation in the literature, we will begin with an exposition of some of the results that have been achieved using this theory with several artificial speakers, elaborating the linguistic and rhetorical problems that have been dealt with. This discussion will give the reader an idea of the kinds of problems that this research has concentrated on and where the focus of the theory lies. Following that we will consider what it means to have a computational model of generation and sketch the limitations that have been imposed on it. The main points of the model will then be presented, including a walk-through of one of the example outputs. Finally the model will be contrasted briefly with earlier generation techniques and the utility of the present computer program discussed.

4.2. Results for Test Speakers

It is a truism in artificial intelligence research that one cannot study thinking except by studying thinking *about* something in particular. This is true in the study of language generation: there is no such thing as generation in the abstract; one must study the generation of specific, well-developed artificial speakers performing in specific discourse contexts. The most fluent goal-directed generators of the past have all been based on a conceptually well-developed "speaker" program, e.g. the tic-tac-toe model of [Davey 1974] or the psychoanalytic patient of [Clippinger 1978], since it is only when the conceptual basis for the decision-making is well-grounded that stylistic linguistic decisions can be made on a sound basis.

The present research takes this one step further by generalizing the "linguistic component" of the generator to deal with more than one conceptual input representation. The question of "what do you start from" in generation has always been a vexing one: When studying language understanding, the input representation to the process (i.e. English text) is agreed upon by everyone and its details can be specified to whatever degree one likes. The psycholinguistically correct source for language generation on the other hand is utterly unknown and likely to remain so for some time; furthermore any variation in the details of the input representation will have considerable repercussions within the generation process (cf. [McDonald 1980] chapter four). Faced with this situation, I have (1) deliberately separated the conceptual and the linguistic phases of decision-making in generation into two modules connected by an explicit interface, thereby making the dependencies between them clear; and (2) tested the linguistic module with six different conceptual modules ("speakers"), four completed, two in progress, employing five different styles of conceptual representation.

Research on a separable linguistic component within the generation process is based on the hypothesis that linguistic decisions and representations within the process can be legitimately and profitably distinguished from conceptual ones. For this separation to be sensible, it must be the case (1) that the interactions between the "linguistic component" and the rest of the process can be specified precisely, and (2) that the extent of their shared assumptions about representations and contingencies is small (otherwise the linguistic component would have to be largely rewritten for each new speaker).

The relationship between the linguistic component and the larger system is sketched in figure 1.

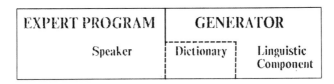

Figure 1 A Coarse View of the Total System

The *expert program* is what human users really think they are talking with; the generator is just part of a "natural language interface". The expert is grounded in a particular *conceptual domain* such as internal medicine or petroleum geology. It is expected to have no linguistic knowledge of its own; instead, any domain-dependent knowledge about how to answer questions, what information to include, what to leave out as obvious, knowledge about how to give explanations at the appropriate level of abstraction, or comparable discourse abilities is located in a *speaker component* which may or may not be a physically independent part of the expert program. The speaker assembles a *message* for input to the linguistic component, describing the goals it wishes to achieve with its utterance using whatever representation is convenient to it and the expert program. Messages are decoded by a *dictionary* compiled specially for each new representation; the dictionary is where the knowledge of what natural language phrases could be used to realize the components of the messages is stored.

The *generator* consists of a *dictionary* that is specialized to the expert program's speaker, and the "linguistic component": the speaker deciding roughly "what to say" and the linguistic component deciding "how to say it" and orchestrating the actual production. A distinction like this is common to nearly every generator that has been developed. (See for example, [Simmons and Slocum 1972; Goldman 1974 ; Davey 1974; Moore 1981], but compare [Shapiro 1975].) For existing expert systems, the notion of a separable "speaker component" is only a convenient fiction, the knowledge of the speaker having been incorporated *ad hoc* into the expert proper; nevertheless, if future experts are to have the fluency and versatility they will require, then this special kind of conceptual knowledge that I am attributing here to a "speaker" will have to be incorporated in a theoretically sound way. In any event, it will be convenient to think in terms of the speaker as the part of the expert system that makes all the decisions about what to say, providing the input to the linguistic component.

4.2.1. The Different Input Representations

In this section we will go briefly through the six input representations that have been explored and then look at a sample of the results that have been achieved, giving examples of generated texts and discussing the linguistic phenomena involved in their construction.

The speakers/expert-programs have been by necessity artificial and minimal: The burden of this research was intended to be on the linguistic problems of generation rather than the conceptual ones, and the expert programs in existence at the time this research was begun were not sufficiently sophisticated to motivate the linguistically interesting constructions of English and thus could not be used. (Relevant English constructions include: embedded clauses, ellipsis, pronominal and non-pronominal subsequent reference, arbitrarily embedded wh-movement, and thematic relations such as focus and given/new.) Consequently each speaker had to be built from scratch, and was elaborated only as far as was needed to motivate the English it was intended to illustrate. In the completed speakers, not much more than the examples shown was ever actually developed. Below is a summary of the speaker programs used according to the type of conceptual representation they employed; a detailed description of the first two will follow.

Predicate Calculus   Well-formed formulas in the predicate calculus, in isolation and in natural deduction proofs, were supplied directly as the linguistic component's input, e.g. from $\forall(x)\ man(x) \supset mortal(x)$ the component produced: *"All men are mortal"*. This domain presented an opportunity to study the decoding of message-level conventions such as expressing quantifiers as determiners or type predicates as class nouns, as well as discourse coherency and the symbolic analysis of possible realizations.

Assertions in PLANNER-style Data-bases   A description of a semantic net was supplied to the generator as a set of simple relational assertions about the nets component parts. One net corresponded a multi-paragraph text, one paragraph per node, ordered according to a depth-first scan. This domain provided an opportunity to produce large texts without developing an elaborate expert program, and provided a study of stylistic variation, the use of the thematic relations focus and given/new, and of the use of ellipsis and indefinite anaphora including the automatic collapsing of conjoined predicates at the message-level.

OWL The language OWL, developed by William Martin [Hawkinson 1975], is a compositional representation specifically designed as the target output formalism of a natural language understanding system (and therefore able to represent naturally the kinds of underspecification, ambiguity, quantification, etc. found in natural languages). The work on this domain was done by a beginning MIT graduate student, Ken Church, part-time during the fall of 1978. The inputs to the program were literal procedures taken from DIG, the digitalis therapy advisor developed originally by Silverman [Silverman 1975] and reimplemented for explanations by Swartout using OWL [Swartout 1981]. The resulting texts from Church's work (which will not be shown) were comparable to, though not quite as smooth as, the texts originally obtained by Swartout. Church's work demonstrated what had been suspected earlier, namely that because its one-pass control structure is biased to expect rhetorically pre-planned input, this linguistic component is not a good place to stage large-scale reanalyzes of a domain's conceptual structure.

FRL FRL, "Frame-oriented, Representation Language" was developed by Goldstein and Roberts [Goldstein and Roberts 1974] as an experimental implementation of "frame" ideas of Minsky [Minsky 1974]. It was used by Winston as the representation for his program for making and evaluating analogies [Winston 1980]. A dictionary was compiled for Winston's database on the play "Macbeth", from which texts were directly produced describing the actors and major scenes. Winston imposed a rigid "case-frame" discipline on the fields of his FRL frames, making them very easy to translate into English. This made it possible to concentrate instead on the coherency of the text (as in the semantic net domain), and to develop a battery of general linguistic transformations to deal with propositional attitudes, subordinate clauses, sentence-level adjunction, and thematic focus, and to study explicitly planned cataphor and subordination (as in *"Because Lady Macbeth persuaded him to do it, Macbeth murdered Duncan."*).

KL-ONE KL-ONE is a highly structured semantic net formalism under development at BBN [Brachman 1978; Woods 1979]. The work on this representation is still very much underway and has been initially reported in [McDonald 1980]. In their primary generation application KL-ONE nets are used as the knowledge base of a tic-tac-toe program, modeled after the work of Anthony Davey [Davey 1974], that gives fluent commentaries of games of tic-tac-toe that it has either played or read. It provides an opportunity to experiment with discourse-level planning, and to study how rhetorical intentions can control descriptions (e.g. whether to say *"the corner opposite the one you just took"* or just *"a corner"*). A second project using the KL-ONE representation has the task of producing paragraph-length English descriptions of natural scenes starting from the output of an A.I. scene-understanding system. This work focuses on the problem of high-level planning of paragraph length text, particularly how the choice of spatial description may be constrained by grammatical context.

Next we will look at some example input and output from the first two test domains and consider the linguistic problems that had to be faced in order to produce them. After this section, we will discuss the principles behind the linguistic component and follow through an example in detail.

4.2.2. The LOGIC Domain

In any study of language generation, it is important that the message-level representation with which the process starts be credible. It would be questionable, for example, whether a program that started from a dictionary of fragments of English sentences could be said to have solved any significant·problems. The predicate calculus, on the other hand, is a very credible message representation: it is an accepted, comfortable "internal representation" for the programs of a large part of the artificial intelligence community; it has a universally agreed upon interpretation; and it is sufficiently unlike natural language in form that demonstrations of the "value added" of the linguistic component are readily available.

The *logic domain* consists of a representation for well-formed formulas in predicate logic, routines for translating formulas typed by a user into this representation and storing them, and a dictionary with fixed entries for the logical connectives and inference rules and a set of conventions for new entries that the user may write for particular predicates, constants, and typed variables. There is no speaker or expert program *per se*, all of the interpretation of conventions and application of discourse heuristics that a "speaker" would do being embedded directly in the entries of the dictionary.

The original work with the logic domain consisted simply of presenting the program with a single well-formed formula ("wff") and having it produce an English rendering. For example

$\forall$(block)$\forall$(surface)
   space-for(surface,block) $\leftrightarrow$ (table(surface) $\lor$ cleartop(surface))

was rendered as:

> *"There is space on a surface for a block if and only if that surface is the table or it has a clear top."*

Different conventional interpretations of formulas were experimented with, originally under explicit control of the designer and later under program control using both lookahead at the linguistic decisions and simple tests of the logical structure of the expressions to determine whether an interpretation would go through. The same formula, say: **"∀(x)   man(x) ⊃ mortal(x)"**, can be understood conventionally and rendered as: *"All men are mortal"*, or understood literally and rendered as: *"For any thing, if that thing is a man, then it is mortal"*.

It does not take long, however, to exhaust the linguistic insights to be gained from looking at single formulas in isolation. A predicate calculus formula is underdetermined with respect to the more sophisticated forms of reference and quantification supported by natural languages, and its connectives and predicates can usually be given many equally plausible renderings. When formulas appear in isolation, there is no motivation for using one rendering or one interpretation of a quantifier over another.

One way to provide the needed motivation is to look at formulas in the context of a proof. Figure 2 shows a natural deduction proof followed by the text that the logic domain's dictionary selected for it. (The first line is a statement of the "barber paradox" created by Bertrand Russell as a popular rendering of the set of all sets paradox.)

The lines of the proof are passed to the program in sequence; the English text selected for earlier lines provides a discourse context to narrow the choices available to later ones, directly controlling subsequent references to constants, variables interpreted as generic references, and predicates and formulas used as descriptions. Further motivation for text choice is provided by the labels that are attached to certain lines to reflect their role in the structure of the proof (e.g. *"the assumption"* or *"a contradiction"*), and by the logical inference rules that derived the lines: a large part of the rendering of the proof must be an explanation, guided by the inference rules, of how each line follows from the earlier ones.

```
line1:   premise
         ∃x (barber(x) ∧ ∀y(shaves(x,y) ↔ ¬shaves(y,y)))
line2:   existential instantiation (1)
         barber(g) ∧ ∀y(shaves(g,y) ↔ ¬shaves(y,y))
line3:   tautology (2)
         ∀y shaves(g,y) ↔ ¬shaves(y,y)
line4:   universal instantiation (3)
         shaves(g,g) ↔ ¬shaves(g,g)
line5:   tautology (4)
         shaves(g,g) ∧ ¬shaves(g,g)
line6:   conditionalization (5,1)
         ∃x (barber(x) ∧ ∀y(shaves(x,y) ↔ ¬shaves(y,y)))
              ⊃ (shaves(g,g) ∧ ¬shaves(g,g))
line7:   reductio-ad-absurdum (6)
         ¬∃x (barber(x) ∧ ∀y(shaves(x,y) ↔ ¬shaves(y,y)))
```

Assume that there is some barber who shaves everyone who doesn't shave himself (and no one else). Call him Giuseppe. Now, anyone who doesn't shave himself would be shaved by Giuseppe. This would include Giuseppe himself. That is, he would shave himself, if and only if he did not shave himself, which is a contradiction. This means that the assumption leads to a contradiction. Therefore, it is false, there is no such barber.

Figure 2 The Barber Proof

The proofs that were used in the logic domain were selected from a set of proofs that had been used by Daniel Chester [Chester 1976] in virtually the same task. The choice was made deliberately to permit a direct comparison of the output of the two systems on the same material—something that is rare in studies of language generation. Chester's version of the "barber proof" is as follows:[1]

Suppose that there is some barber such that for every person the barber shaves the person iff the person does not shave himself. Let A denote such a barber. Now he shaves himself iff he does not shave himself, therefore a contradiction follows. Therefore if there is some barber such that for every

---

1. My source for Chester's results is a personal communication with him in November of 1975; the major effort on the logic domain was completed in December of 1977.

person the barber shaves the person iff the person does not shave himself then a contradiction follows. Thus there is no barber such that for every person the barber shaves the person iff the person does not shave himself.

Chester's program belongs to the "direct translation" school of natural language generation systems (see [Mann et al. to appear]). It produced the paragraph above by recursively replacing the formulas of the proof with English text (after editing it for production), entirely on the basis of local properties of the formulas. The lack of contextual input to the program's realization decisions is reflected in its minimal treatment of subsequent reference and the occasional abruptness of transition from line to line.

At this point, I will use the example of the barber proof to point out some of the accomplishments that are embodied in the current version of my generation program.

The ability to go beyond the literal content   The program processes a proof by realizing its formulas and subformulas one at a time in top down order (i.e. the construction axioms of the predicate calculus are followed). The formulas are not translated mechanically, but rather at each step along the way, a context-sensitive decision is made as to how (or whether) the major logical connective (or inference rule) is to be realized. and which (if any) of the subelements of the formula are to be involved in that realization. Line three of the proof, for example, has no corresponding sentence in the text because we can assume that such a step in the proof would be made automatically by the audience. (This is an implicit, conventional assumption: there is no simulation model of the user.) Line four, on the other hand, has been expanded into three sentences because the logical substitution of a second instance of the same constant is assumed to be liable to confuse the audience. The three sentence subargument is constructed by putting a special rhetorical twist on the formula of line three (to define the set), adding a new formula based on the variable being substituted (sentence four), and concluding with the formula from line four.

The logical conjunction in line one is interpreted as a conventional way of defining the type of the variable **"x"**. Similarly the two quantifiers in that line are realized in the determiners of their variables (*"some barber"*, *"everyone"*) rather than as *"for"* phrases.

Subsequent reference   Knowing when *not* to use a pronoun is very important in the production of understandable texts. Thus while the barber is identified and given a name in first two sentences, he is not pronominalized in the third and fourth because those sentences are part of a new new discourse structure (the "subargument" composed to ease the transition to line 4) where the discourse focus is on the universally quantified variable **"y"** rather than on the barber *"Giuseppe"*. When the focus shifts to him in sentence five as a result of the use of the intensifying reflexive (*"Giuseppe himself"*), he can then be pronominalized in the four instances in sentence six. (N.b. the name *"Giuseppe"* was picked arbitrarily.)

Descriptions may be "pronominalized" as well as references. At the end of sentence one, the original description of **"y"** (i.e. *"everyone who doesn't shave himself"*) is recapitulated in the description of the complement set as: *"no one else"*. Then in the final sentence, the original complex description of the barber is reduced to just the adjective *"such"*.

Functional labels   The premise functions in the proof as *"an assumption"* that is to be shown to be false because it leads to a contradiction. Since this role is known to the audience (we began by saying *"Assume that... ."*), we can use the label later (sentence seven) as a succinct reference to the entire first line. The logical schema **"A ∧ ¬A"** is similarly labeled as *"a contradiction"*. Part of the concept of a label is the ability to include a literal rendering of the labeled expression as an appositive (final sentence). In the logic domain's dictionary, appositives are triggered if the last literal rendering was not in the same paragraph or, as in this case, if the line is the conclusion of an argument.

Context sensitive realizations   Part of the linguistic context that is produced to guide later decisions is a rhetorical description of the discourse structure. The different terms of this structure will guide decisions at syntactic and morphological levels: in sentences one and three a contraction is used (*"doesn't shave"*) while the same logical structure in the *formal* context created by the *conclusian* sentence of the subargument is not contracted (*formal* being an experimental rhetorical feature in the grammar). Similarly the connective ↔ is spelled out in a formal context (sentence five), but in an unmarked, informal context, it is understood as a restriction on a variable and expressed as a relative clause. In another case, the same quantified variable (**"y"**) is realized in the unmarked context of sentence one as *"everyone"*, but when marked in sentence three as identifying a set it is realized as *"anyone"*.

Part of the discourse context is the distance between phrases. When a contradiction is deduced from the immediately previous line, as in line five, the identification of that deduction is given in the most direct way possible by adjoining a relative clause to the last sentence; when the dependency line is much earlier (as in line six), the formula from the line is repeated and the phrase *"leads to"* is used.

Attempts to avoid ambiguity   In sentence one, the interpretation of "↔" as a restriction on a variable's range must include some phrase to indicate that the entire range has been specified and not just a part of it. Consequently the "iff-entry" is designed to say "<restriction> *and* <complement of restriction>". (An equivalent technique would have been to replace the word *"everyone"* with *"all and only those men who... "*.) Because the presentation of this combined restriction should be done carefully, a special monitoring routine is activated in an attempt to avoid introducing scope ambiguities in the conjunction. On the basis of the point where the conjunction is attached (i.e. as the direct object of *"some barber who shaves X"*), the projected contents of the second arm of the conjunction (a noun phrase), and the fact that the first arm has ended with a direct object, the monitor decides that it is possible that the second arm will be misinterpreted as conjoining with the more immediate, lower direct object rather than with the intended one. It causes the parentheses to be added around the second arm as one way available to it in this case to try and forestall misinterpretation.

4.2.3. PLANNER-style Assertions

The source data structure in this domain was a KL-ONE network reimplemented as a set of binary relations expressed as PLANNER-style assertions. A KL-ONE net consists of a set of named objects of various types (only "concept" and "role" will be shown here), linked together by the relations: "subconcept", "has-role", "value-restriction", and others not shown. This domain took the network as input and produced an English description of its literal contents; that is, rather than interpret the net as a representation of certain facts (e.g. *"every phrase has a head, a modifier, and an interpretation... "*), it is interpreted at its literal level as a collection of KL-ONE objects (e.g. *"The concept <u>phrase</u> is the top of the net, it has a <u>head</u> role that..."*).

Figure 3 shows the first paragraphs of the text constructed for one of the development networks in use at Bolt Beranek and Newman Inc. ("BBN") during the spring of 1979. (It represents a first pass at a conceptualization of an English grammar.) The text was created by scanning the net depth-first following its "subconcept" links, devoting one paragraph to each concept. Each paragraph mentions (or assumes—see below) three facts about about its concept: (1) the name of the concept(s) it is a subconcept of, (2) the names of its "roles" and the

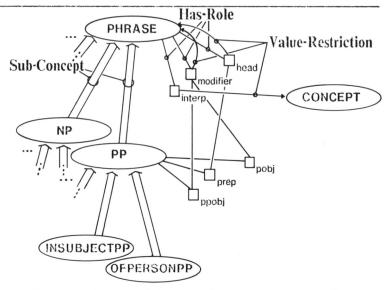

Phrase is the top of the net. Its *interp* role must be a *concept*, and its *modifier* role and its *head* role must be *phrases*. Its subconcepts are *pp*, *np*, *adjunct*, *indobjclause*, and *word*.

Pp has the roles: *pobj*, *prep*, *interp*, and *ppobj*. *Pobj* must be a *np*, *prep* a *prep*, *interp* a *relation*, and *ppobj* a *pp*. *Pp's* subconcepts are *ofpersonpp*, *insubjectpp*, *locationpp*, and *aboutsubjectpp*.

Ofpersonpp has a *pobj* role which must be a *humanp*, and a *prep* role which must be an *of*.

Insubjectpp's pobj role must be a *subjectnp*, its *preprole* an *in*, and its *interp* role a *subject*.

...[[further paragraphs for the rest of pp's subconcepts]]

Np is another subconcept of phrase...

...[[further paragraphs for the rest of phrase's subconcepts and the subconcepts of each of those in turn]]

Figure 3   Describing a Semantic Net

"value-restrictions" they are subject to, and (3) the names of its own subconcepts if any. (The fact that each paragraph will present a new concept is taken to be already known to the audience, and as a consequence, the information that, e.g., *"phrase is a concept"* is omitted as already given.)

Varying the paragraph structure   The few paragraphs shown in the figure are sufficient to illustrate the stylistic heuristics that the dictionary for this domain incorporates. (Like the logic domain, this domain had no speaker as such; its messages were comprised directly of KL-ONE nets or coherent subnetworks.) In each of the first three paragraphs, the presentation of the concept's roles and their value-restrictions is given in a different style. It is done by varying the rhetorical pattern of the description according to the number of roles the concept has. In the first paragraph, "phrase" has three roles and the style chosen puts each role in a separate sentence: "<role> *must be* <value-restriction>". The second paragraph's concept has more than three roles, leading to the use of a summarizing sentence to identify them as its roles before giving their value-restrictions. The third paragraph, with only two roles, uses sentences based on the "has-role" relation, with each value-restriction embedded as a relative clause.

Omitting "given" information   Note that the second, third, and fourth paragraphs do not start with a sentence about what their concept is a subconcept of. This is because that information appears in the text already (in the last sentence of each previous paragraph) and the dictionary entry that would make the decision to include that information decides that it will be still remembered and thus would be redundant if included. Similarly in the second paragraph where there is a summary sentence listing roles of the concept pp's, the "has-role" facts have been left off of the later sentences since to leave them in would have led to an unacceptably redundant text.

Varying descriptions with context   The noun phrases constructed to describe roles vary along the same lines as paragraphs, i.e. they include facts or leave them out depending on what facts have already appeared in their paragraph and what remain to be given. Thus we go from using just a name to introduce a role (paragraph three) to giving the concept that owns it, its name, and the fact that it is a *"role"* (in paragraph four).

Using ellipsis   Throughout the example text, grammatically-driven ellipsis is applied to reduce redundant verbs (paragraph two), and to merge relations with common arguments (paragraph one). These are general purpose transformations, triggered by the syntactic and lexical properties of the texts, independently of the content of the relations involved.

4.3. A Computational Model

The ability to speak is as natural to us as the ability to see or to use our hands to grasp objects. We are fast, we are accurate, and we are unaware of the mechanics of how we do it.[1] As easy as it is for us to speak, we know from linguistic and ethnomethodological analysis that the process is complex. Even if we leave aside the question of how we arrive at the thoughts behind our words and look just at the "linguistic" part of the process—selecting words and constructions, applying grammatical rules, and producing the words in sequence—it is clear that very sophisticated rules are being followed. Somehow we select one lexical/syntactic combination from the many possible alternatives, managing to attend simultaneously to the potentials of the different constructions, our multiple goals, and the constraints arbitrarily imposed by our grammar. We follow conventions of direct utility only to our audiences and actively maintain elaborate coherency relations across large stretches of discourse.

Our ability to do all this with such facility needs to be explained. For this, a static description of the rules being followed will not be sufficient: we must explain what it is about the way these rules are represented and manipulated that insures that the process of language production is tractable and gives the process the character that it has. In short, we must develop a computational model: a simulacrum whose processing steps and representational devices when viewed from the intended level of abstraction we take to be isomorphic with those operating in the human mind.

It is important to appreciate that by "computational model", we do not simply mean a program whose input/output behavior matches that of people (though that in itself would be a considerable accomplishment). The internal structure of the program—the reasons *why* its input/output behavior is what it is—is critical to its value as a model. This is comparable to the requirement for "strong" rather than "weak" equivalence in constructing a grammar for a natural language. If the model is to be truly successful (and ultimately to be a source of testable predictions), its behavior must follow inescapably from its structure rather than from stipulated rules; it will stand as an explanation of the behavior because any device with comparable structure would be incapable of behaving otherwise. If

---

1. The normal speaking rate for English is approximately four syllables per second or 160 words per minute. (The Guiness Book of Records speed record for reading English is 400 words per minute.) A study by Labov [Labov 1966] has shown that 75% of everyday speech is grammatical by any criterion. If general rules for ellipsis and self-editing are added, this figure rises to 90% for non-academic speakers talking about everyday experience. Introspective reports of production appear to go no deeper than mentally "hearing" full phrases (or alternative words) at a time. We appear to have no conscious access to any of the actual assembly processes such as the sequencing of the words or their morphological specialization.

one can then independently show that the human language faculty is structured in the same way as the model (perhaps by comparing the kinds of errors that the two systems make), then one will have explained why people have the modeled behavior. Consequently, if our model is to be compelling, we must limit its computational power very carefully. A computational model that permitted the use of arbitrary procedures (e.g. a Turing machine) would not be interesting as the basis of a theory because all that it would explain would be that language production was computable: something we already believe. We must look instead for the weakest model that can do the work: a model from whose computational properties the characteristics of human language production would inexorably follow. By doing this, by restricting the kinds of behavior that our model is capable of, we can extract non-trivial predictions from it and make it subject to empirical tests.[1]

4.3.1. Characterizing the Problem

What computational problem is the mind solving when we talk? "Talking" is of course a loose term used to cover many kinds of activities, each likely to have its own requirements in processing time, necessary memory, possibilities for editing, or conscious involvement. We know intuitively that there is an enormous difference in behavior between, say, writing a careful essay and holding a fuzzy conversation over breakfast; so much so that there is little reason to believe *a priori* that they pose identical problems to the human speaker. In the present research, I have focused on *immediate speech*, spoken (or written) without rehearsal and with only a rough conscious knowledge of what will be said next. There is introspective evidence to suggest that this mode of speech is primary since even in deliberate writing where there is ample opportunity for editing and planning, it is the common experience that phrases and even multiple sentences "spring to mind" as immediate percepts without any conscious effort having been made to form them from their constituent parts.

Given this restriction on the mode of speech to be considered, I take the core of the "problem" for the mind to be the re-expression of a delimited, deliberately selected "packet" of information (including references, propositions, descriptions, and probably specific rhetorical instructions) from its original form in the mind's

---

1. Neither of which I intend to do in this paper. As will be clear, the model already meets a number of "obvious" psychological criteria such as sequential production and indelibility (see also [McDonald 1980]). Its first non-obvious application is expected to be in a theory of the mechanisms behind certain naturally occurring "speech errors", particularly exchange errors and blends. (See [Garrett 1980] for an extensive description of speech-errors.) This work, however, is still in progress.

internal representation into a constrained, fixed-format language (e.g. English) according to a fixed, context-free, conventional mapping.

4.3.2. Language Generation as Decision-making

What are to be the primitive operations of the model—at what "grain size" will it characterize the generation process? Following the lead of systemic grammarians such as Halliday [Halliday 1966] and Winograd [Winograd 1972], I view the output of the process—the natural language text—as the result of a series of decisions, the set of possible consistent decisions being determined by the language's grammar. The most relevant aspects of a generator will then be how it goes about making those decisions, which is what the theory is to determine. In particular: (1) what kinds of decisions are to be made, what prompts them and what is the nature of their output; (2) what kinds of information the decisions require and how that information will vary in its accessibility and form according to the state of the process; (3) what dependencies there are between decisions and how they influence the overall control structure (e.g. are decisions made nondeterministically or are they necessarily ordered?); (4) to what extent the results of previous decisions and the foreknowledge of planned decisions are a part of the generator's state, i.e. is this kind of information explicitly represented and accessible to current decision-makers?

4.3.3. Restrictions on the Model

Given the problem of translating a packet of expressions/instructions into a highly constrained, fixed format language given a context-free mapping (i.e. the translation dictionary), there are many known ways we could use to solve it: Approaches have ranged from nondeterministic optimizers that worked on whole paragraph-sized texts at once [Moore 1981], to programs that have attempted to model stream-of-consciousness and were liable to interrupt themselves with new plans or constraints at every phrase [Clippinger 1978]. All approaches have in common the notion that the input packet or "message" will be decomposed into its component elements; that the elements will be looked up in the dictionary and a context-sensitive decision made as to how they can be realized in the target language; and that these realizations, subject to the constraints of the grammar and the overall goals of the message, are pieced together into the utterance. The approaches differ in nearly every other aspect, e.g. how large an utterance to construct at once, how to control the process and order the decisions, or how to represent the grammar and implement its constraints.

In the interests of narrowing the field of candidates, and because I believe that the resulting model is both more perspicuous to the engineer and more interesting to the psychologist, the following additional computational limitations have been stipulated in my theory.

On-line Operation   The input message is viewed by the linguistic component as a stream of elements, the specific order and chunking of the "message elements" being dictated by the dictionary entries designed for that particular domain. The component may be conceptually (though not literally) decomposed into *two transducers* cascaded together, the first taking the next element of the message stream and converting it into a surface structure phrase attached to the tree at the point where the message element was, and the second then traversing that phrase and producing the text from it (see section 4.1 below). The two transducers are constrained to operate "on-line", that is, the output from the first transducer must be completely consumed by the second before the first transducer moves on the next message element at the same level.

Indelibility   The decisions of the first, "realizing" transducer are exhaustively represented in the surface structure phrases that it produces. The actions of the second, "tree-walking" transducer are then completely dictated by the structure and annotation of those phrases. *Surface structure is indelible*, i.e. once a phrase has been constructed and incorporated into the ongoing surface structure tree, it can not be removed or edited (though it may be augmented). As a consequence of indelibility and the fact that the surface structure is organized as a strict tree without loops, the process will not backup—it is impossible to retraverse earlier sections of the tree once the realizing transducer has past through them. (This same stipulation has been applied to the recognition of phrases by a parser [Marcus 1980] with intriguing results.)

Locality   Decisions may only make reference to contextual information that is local to them at the position within the tree where they occur. There is no mechanism available in the model that would allow a decision to scan the tree for information; all potentially relevant information must be expressly recognized as such and specific provisions made in the grammar to make it available to decision-makers via locally defined and updated variables. The effect of this stipulation is to restrict the information available for a decision to no more than would be available to a parser using an LL(0) grammar.

Real-time   The overall process must perform its computations in *quasi-real time*; that is, the number of operations that take place between the consumption of any one message element in the stream and the next or between the output of two successive words must be no greater than some fixed maximum unrelated to the size of the input or output streams. This is a stronger time bound that the usual one of linear time, and reflects the intuition that the process always proceeds at a constant rate.

4.4. The Relationship Between the Speaker and the Linguistics Component

4.4.1. 'Messages'

If the linguistic component was used with only one speaker/expert program, then there would be no need for an elaborate interface between the two: all of the speaker's conventions and the linguistic component's conventions could be integrated and the responsibility for obeying them distributed evenly in a seamless merger of the two decision-makers. Explicit messages (and thus conventions for representing messages) would be needed only when it was necessary to represent goals that referred to the message itself (such as "don't be long-winded" or "don't use technical vocabulary"). But of course the opposite is true: there are many qualitatively different expert programs to be linked with a common generator; consequently, the linguistic component is a distinct module computationally as well as conceptually, and a uniform interface is required to smooth over the differences between domains.

Functionally, the linguistic component lies on the path between the speaker and its audience. The speaker decides what it wants to say, constructs a representation of its goals and references—a *message*—and passes it to the linguistic component. This transfer of an explicit expression is required simply because the linguistic component is not telepathic: it does not automatically know what a speaker will want to say, nor, since it works with many speakers, can it even have *a priori* assumptions about the kind of things that are going to be said or how they will be represented internally in the speaker/expert program. These must instead be spelled out (1) in the *dictionary*, which holds the information on how to interpret the expert's representation element by element to determine its linguistic correspondences and relevant substructure, and (2) in a set of *interface functions*, which know (a) how to link up an individual element of a message to the appropriate dictionary entry, and (b) how to answer certain idiosyncratic linguistic questions for the message elements such as their "person and number" or whether they act as references or descriptions.

Both the dictionary and the interface functions must be specifically designed for each new speaker/expert program; they are the repository of all the information required to adapt the linguistic component to such new domains. Given this modularity, especially the functional interface, we can be flexible about the choice of formal representation for a message; we can use whatever representation is convenient for the speaker's planning, typically the representation used in the expert program (e.g. as described in section 1.1).

There is no presumption that messages should result in texts of any fixed size. With the present test speakers, single messages have produced texts ranging from single exclamations to multi-paragraph discourses. Neither do messages have to be equated with turns in a conversation since the linguistic state of the component is preserved between activations and a text can be "picked up where it left off".

Structurally, messages have fallen into two broad classes. The simplest just consist of pre-existing expressions taken directly from the expert's data base. (All of the completed test speakers fell into this class.) The data base expressions become "instructions for what to say" through the interpretation provided by their dictionary entries, and the result is a fairly literal rendering of the expression, the structure of the output text following the compositional structure of the input expression. Figure 4 below shows an example expression from Winston's data base of Shakespearian plays (given in FRL) followed by the text that the linguistic program generates for it using the dictionary for that domain.

In a simple "direct translation" message such as this, the linguistic component has some ability to simplify and smooth the text by following default rules keyed by the local linguistic structure as the text is built; however, all of the choices of ordering and level of detail are fixed by the internal structure of the data base expression. Since the structure of the data base is determined by whatever is convenient for the expert's internal computations rather than by considerations of text planning, messages of this sort are necessarily limited in the applicability. (See [Swartout 1981] for an extensive discussion of this problem.)

```
(ma (ako (story))
    (part (macbeth)
          (lady-macbeth)
          (duncan)
          (macduff))
    (subpart (heath-scene)
             (murder-scene)
             (battle-scene))))
```

"'Macbeth' is a story. It has four characters: Macbeth, Lady Macbeth, Duncan, and MacDuff, and three scenes: the heath scene, the murder scene, and the battle scene."

Figure 4   A Simple Message and Its Output

The second class of messages are those that are deliberately planned by the speaker and involve relations among the expert's expressions that are specific to that speech event and may involve special rhetorical relations (instructions to the linguistic component) that have no counterpart elsewhere in the expert. The formal structure of these messages will again be whatever is convenient computationally for the designer of the speaker component, typically an extension of the representation already in use in the expert, with the interface functions adapted to match. Figure 5 shows a handcrafted example of a planned message in Winston's domain. The development of planning programs that can take advantage of the abstract planning vocabulary that a linguistic component such as this one can support (e.g. instructions like "focus", "sequence", or "constrast"; note for example that the sentence structure of the output text was determined dynamically by the linguistic component rather than given in the message) is the subject of on-going research by the author and others, especially [Cohen 1978; McKeown 1980]. Experimental messages such as the one in Figure 5 are aimed at determining what degree of rhetorical abstraction is plausible and how much foreknowledge of the linguistic properties of expert's expressions is required in planning at this level. That a planner can in fact be designed at this level of modularity that will produce indelibly realizable messages is a hypothesis that underides most of the work on this linguistics component.

```
(message1
  (sequence
    (macbeth (murder (duncan)))   ;"murder-ma"
    (macbeth (become (king)))   ;"ma-become-king"
    (lady-macbeth
      (persuade (macbeth (action murder-ma))))   ;"persuade-ma"
    (lady-macbeth (hq (ambitious))))   ;"ambitious-lm"
  (time-frame (before-time-of-speech))
  (focus (macbeth))
  (ancillary-facts
    ((murder-ma (motive (ma-become-king)))
     (persuade-ma (purpose (cause (murder-ma)))))))))
```

"Macbeth murdered Duncan in order to become king. He was persuaded to do it by Lady Macbeth who was ambitious."

Figure 5 A Planned Message

In summary, what matters about a message is not the notation that is used but what it specifies and what it leaves to default. The structure of the message (as interpreted by the dictionary) directly determines the order in which the linguistics component will break it down and realize its elements; in simple speaking situations, literal expressions from the expert's data base may be the best messages—implicitly wrapped in the directive "describe these objects and relations"; however, as the situations become more complex and less predictable, a full-scale, rhetorically knowledgeable planner will be needed to compose messages as the speaker's goals and discourse context demand.

4.4.2. Run-time Relationships

From the point of view of the speaker/expert program, the linguistics component is a *subroutine*, a subprocess that the speaker explicitly activates to realize an individual message. It is only activatable by the speaker, i.e. it has no independent existence as a parallel process (though the history of the discourse is contiguous across activations), and once activated runs to completion independently of the rest of the system. Its internal state is a black-box, not designed to be monitored, interrupted, or edited (though it could be "shut-off" and completely restarted).

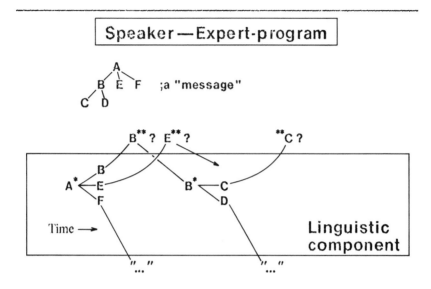

Figure 6 A Sketch of the Run-time Relationships

Though independently controlled, the linguistic component is not cut off from the speaker while it is processing. Figure 6 shows diagrammatically how the component may at any point ask the speaker questions about a specific message element in order to determine facts that are only important linguistically (for example "person" and "number") or to apply domain-based tests to some element, in effect extending the message. In the figure, the message is reduced to its essentials: a composite relation over objects selected by the speaker/expert program (i.e. A(B(C,D), E, F)). We see it broken down within the linguistic component layer by layer starting with the root relation A. B and E have been referred back to the speaker for further elaboration, while F and then D were realized directly in English (indicated as "..." in the figure). The speaker is accessible continuously, but the timing and the computational context in which it is actually consulted are dictated entirely by the linguistic component.

The speaker has no control over the actions of the linguistic component beyond supplying it with messages; whether the speaker continues to be active while the component is operating is not important to the theory. Whether it should have the ability to interrupt the linguistic component and restart it, perhaps in reaction to what it hears while "listening" to the component's output, is a question we will leave open. There are some eventualities (such as structural ambiguities) that are difficult to foresee when realizing a message via a linguistic component of this design, and there are also potential divisions of effort within the speaker's planning process which might benefit from a "feedback" design of this sort. Before developing such a design, however, it is critical to have a clear understanding of the kinds of linguistic information that are naturally available at different stages in the production process and of how they relate to the vocabulary of the speaker's planning process—one of the prime concerns of my research. (Clippinger and Brown [Clippinger 1975, 1978 ; R.Brown 1973] developed a model of the production of psychoanalytic discourse that made critical use of such a feedback design, with the result that it was able to produce very natural hesitations and restarts in its monologue.)

4.5. The Internal Structure of the Linguistic Component

4.5.1. A cascade of two transducers

As an automaton, the linguistic component is best described as *two cascaded transducers folded together under the command of a single, data-directed controller.* The first transducer goes from the message to a surface structure level linguistic representation of the utterance to be produced—the "working" data structure of the linguistic component—and the second goes from the surface structure produced by the first to English text. (See the sketch in figure 7.)

The "decisions", whose dispositions are so important to this theory, are made almost exclusively by the first transducer; they are the decisions that realize the individual elements of the message through the selection of particular surface structure phrases (or refine existing ones). The second transducer in effect "executes" the decisions of the first by interpreting the surface structure as a program of linguistic actions: printing words, annotating the grammatical context, recording the history of the process, and propagating grammatical constraints.

The bulk of my theory of language production is contained in the characteristics of the surface structure representation and the transducer that produces utterances from it. The transducer from the message to surface structure—conceptually an extension of the speaker—will be less rigorously developed: it is defined chiefly by its relationship to the first transducer—*the controller*—which gates its activities and imposes filters and constraints on its decisions. A complete definition of the first transducer has been developed for use in the computer program and is discussed in detail in [McDonald 1980], however, only certain of its details are critical and the others are expected to be refined and modified as the program is used with real speaker-level planners.

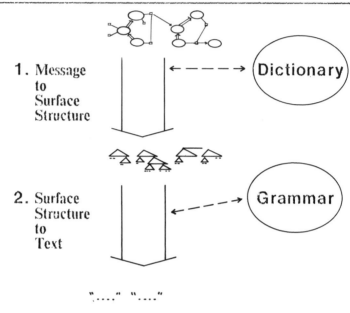

1. Message
to
Surface
Structure

Dictionary

2. Surface
Structure
to
Text

Grammar

"...." "...."

Figure 7 Two Transducers

As inputs to the transducers, both the message and the surface structure are treated as totally ordered sequential streams of data; tokens from the streams are processed one at a time, and are processed only once (i.e. the streams never reverse or loop). The two streams are processed "on-line", which means that the output from the first transducer for one token is completely consumed by the second transducer before the first moves on to its next token. The transducers *per se* are only *interpreters*. They have the ability to follow their input streams and to bind certain predefined variables but little else; their transducing powers derive from two bodies of permanent information, the "dictionary" and the "grammar", to which the transducers will dispatch according to what they find in their input streams. The dictionary associates elements from the message with potential realizing phrases, using a linguistic vocabulary defined by the grammar; the grammar interprets this vocabulary and enforces the constraints and conventional details it specifies. The procedures and schemata in these two "libraries" do all of the real work of the linguistic component; the transducers are responsible for controlling when the libraries are used and for maintaining the linguistic context to which they refer. (The dictionary and grammar consist of a large number of small procedures that are associated with individual tokens that can appear in the data streams (specific message elements, names of grammatical categories, etc.). When a transducer sees one of these tokens, it "dispatches to" the associated procedure (i.e. calls it as a subroutine) and waits until that procedure has finished its execution before going on to the next token.)

The special property of this cascade is that the two transducers have been folded into a single process: the traversal of the surface structure. This procedure can be summarized as follows: The message starts out as the sole constituent of the root node of the surface structure tree; the first transducer then decides which English phrase should realize its dominant element and that phrase, which incorporates at its fringe the next level of message subelements, *replaces* the message in that constituent position. A tree-traversal controller (the second transducer) now takes charge of the process and proceeds to traverse this newly constructed surface structure ("*the tree*") following its normal top-down, left-to-right order. As the controller passes over it, the linguistic annotation on the tree triggers dispatches to the procedurally represented grammar and to the dictionary for the realization of the embedded message elements. (The dictionary thus constitutes the real content of the first transducer.) If a fringe constituent is a word, it is printed out as part of the text; if it is a message element, it is realized, replaced in the tree by the new phrase, and the new phrase then traversed as an extension of the surface structure.

The two transducers can be reliably folded together because of a well-formedness condition I have imposed on the structure of messages, the "*constraint-precedes*" stipulation, which dictates that the enumeration order of a message—the position of message elements within the input stream—must be such that any message element that makes reference to other elements in the message must be realized before any of those elements are.

This condition is required because of the stipulation that the generation process must be *indelible* (cf. section 2.3). The theory insures indelibility by designing the tree-walking controller so that it is unable to retrace any part of the surface structure tree after it has passed through it once. When coupled with the locality stipulation, this means that the first transducer is prohibited from arbitrarily scanning the message in search of potentially relevant subelements that denote constraints but must "wait" until those elements are reached in their normal order in the message stream. Consequently if a message includes elements that should be interpreted as constraints on the realization of other elements (for example they might specify discourse focus or pick out attributes that are to be specially contrasted), then those constraining elements should be dealt with first so that their implications can be noted and incorporated into the context of the later decisions. If the process had not been stipulated to be indelible, then we might imagine ordering constraints haphazardly within the message and editing affected parts of the output text by backing up the generator and restarting once a constraint was noticed. Allowing even bounded backup however (as for example with the equivalent of a well-formed substring table) would remove the process from the realm of real-time and would make the "on-line" stipulation impossible to maintain, not to mention requiring a considerably increased memory in order to retain all potentially reopenable states of the process. The "constrain-precedes" condition and the stipulations of section 2.3 are thus effectively working hypotheses that claim that the appropriate processing trade-off within generation is to supply heavily planned conceptual messages to a relatively unsophisticated but quick and clean linguistic generator, rather than the other way round.

4.5.2. Representing linguistic context — the tree

In order to understand the two transducers we must understand the data structure that binds them together: the surface structure representation of the utterance under construction known for short as *the tree*. We first describe its format and its relationship to the grammar and the dictionary. We then move on to a sketch of the controller, showing how it traverses the tree and how the tree is used to indicate the proper routines to dispatch to within the grammar and dictionary.

Figure 8 is a diagram illustrating the representation used for the tree. (It is not a snapshot of the tree itself; we will not see one of those until the main example.) Two kinds of structures are indicated: *constituent structure*: defining positions within the tree, how they are connected and how the controller is to traverse them; and *grammatical labels*: defining the properties those positions are intended to have.

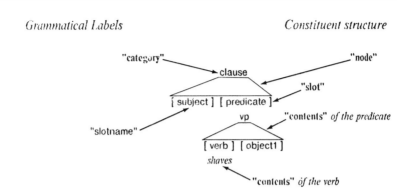

Figure 8 Representing Consitutent Structure: Positions and Labels

The constituent structure is indicated graphically by the pattern of trapezoids and brackets: the trapezoids indicate the "nodes" in the tree, and the brackets indicate the positions of possible constituents within the nodes and are referred to as "slots" or "constituent slots". The actual constituents themselves are the slots' "contents": for example the node labeled "vp" is the "predicate constituent" (abbreviated "[predicate]") of the "clause node". Besides a node, the contents of a slot may be a word, or a message element, or they may be empty. A subtree from a given node to the fringe of the tree will be referred to as a *phrase*. (Since the tree is always growing through the action of the first transducer replacing message elements with phrases, the notion of the "fringe" of the tree is a dynamic one, constantly changing as the generation process proceeds.) Grammatical labels either label nodes, in which case they may be referred to as "categories" and printed just above the trapezoid; or else they label constituent slots, in which case they are called "slot-names" and printed inside the brackets. A node or slot may have more than one label.

This constituent structure representation is different from most others in the linguistic literature because it explicitly labels the constituent positions rather than just defining them in terms of the relative position of nodes. (This explicit naming of constituents is also done in so-called "relational grammar" [Perlmutter and Postal to appear] and was used in some early phrase structure systems, see [Postal 1963].) The "subject" constituent, for example, could alternatively be defined as the noun phrase node directly under a clause node. Slot-names cannot be dispensed with in the present theory, however, because they are used to carry the grammatical properties of the constituent positions they label. Attempting to use a relative position scheme here would lead either to combinatorially increasing decoding computations as the tree grew in depth or to an undue multiplication of category names; consequently, in this theory the use of explicit slotnames leads to a more natural treatment of grammatical functions.

The constituent structure is only really used by the controller. It defines the path it will take through the tree: a standard, depth-first search pattern as shown in figure 9.

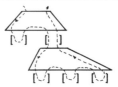

Figure 9 Controller Path Through Completed Constituent Structure

The importance of this path is in the sequence of grammatical labels that it defines and in the contents of the slots at the tree's fringe. Each label is associated in the grammar with a set of procedures, either of its own or procedures of other labels that are contingent on it; these procedures are referred to as *grammar-routines.* The slotname "subject", for example, has grammar routines of its own (i.e. triggered by the controller when the [subject] is reached, see below) that handle such things as the inversion of subject and verb in questions and the insertion of the function word *"it"* in extraposed clauses such as *"it's easy to be confused by all the terminology".* The constituent labeled "subject" is looked for specifically by the grammar-routine that performs subject-verb agreement in tensed clauses, and by the morphology routine when it needs to determine whether a pronoun should be in the nominative case.

4.5.3. The Controller

The algorithm for the controller is the heart of this theory of generation: it *is* the second transducer, interpreting the tree position by position and thereby dictating the order of events within the process, the contextual information available to routines in the dictionary or grammar (i.e. what parts of the tree they can access), and the potential scope of the decisions made by those routines. The algorithm itself is quite simple since all the controller must do is traverse the tree and dispatch to library routines according to the labels on the positions and the contents of the slots. It is diagrammed in figures 10, 11, and 12.

The import of the algorithm lies not in its flowchart which is simple enough, but in the constraints it imposes implicitly on the designer of the grammar and dictionary. *No action can be taken by the linguistic component unless it is specifically selected by this controller at the time and place that the controller dictates.* Thus all actions are local to the controller's position and subject to contextual control. No part of the tree is "visible" to the grammar or dictionary except for those parts specifically picked out by the controller's pointers and prearranged pointers positioned by the grammar routines above and behind the controller's position; this means that hierarchical constructions such as embedded clauses or rules with left to right dependencies such as pronominalization or ellipsis can be treated naturally while phenomena with opposite dependencies must be explicitly planned for or they will be missed. Similarly, since only a single position in the tree is seen at a time (in contrast with the multi-position buffers of natural language parsing systems such as [Marcus 1980]), phenomena that can only be seen by processes with a distributed view of a constituent structure—such as structural ambiguities—cannot be easily appreciated by this system and will typically go uncorrected. This controller is thus the embodiment of the hypothesis that only hierarchical and sequential dependencies can be appreciated during immediate speech; all others being either expressly anticipated and planned for ahead of time or left to a *post hoc* monitor to detect and compensate for later.

Initialization   When a new message is passed to the linguistic component, it becomes the contents of the constant slot "root-constituent". If at that time the component has finished processing any earlier messages then it will have returned to that position at the top of the tree and the message's processing will start immediately; alternatively should an earlier message still be in progress it will not be disrupted and nothing will happen to the new one until the old one is finished and the controller completed its traversal back to the root. The initial state of the controller is shown in Figure 10.

MUMBLE (message)

argument: a message
return value: none

The initial tree: **root-node**

[root-constituent]

START

Initialize the environment:

> **current-grammatical-filters** < = **'empty**
> **discourse-history** < = **'empty**
> **⟨all grammatical-variables⟩** < = **'undefined**

Initialize Controller Variables:

> **current-node** < = **'root-node**
> **current-slot** < = **'root-constituent**
> **current-contents** < = **(Make-elmt-instance message)**

A   Start the Controller at
"Dispatch on current-contents"

Figure 10 The Controller: Initialization

The Block-level Organization of The Controller   The controller decomposes
into three recursive procedures named *Process-node*, *Process-slot*, and *Dispatch*,
whose definitions are given in the next two figures. They are threaded in that
same order: Process-node calls Process-slot on each of its immediate constituents,
and Process-slot in turn calls Dispatch on the content of the slot presently being
processed. The recursive structure of the tree is matched in the controller
algorithm by the recursive call to Process-node from within Dispatch.

The algorithm differs from the standard recursive descent algorithm for
traversing a tree only in its "realize and replace" step within Dispatch: This step

has the effect of dynamically extending the tree even while the controller is traversing it. The extension stops when a phrase is selected that has no further message elements embedded at its fringe. The dynamic extension of the tree as is the key to the *progressive refinement* technique that characterizes this theory: the embedded message elements in effect constitute "delayed decisions" that are not taken up until all of the prior decisions that might effect them have been made and their constraints established (all such dependencies being, by hypothesis, associated with positions in the surface structure above and behind the embedded element). This technique is akin to the technique of *delayed binding* that is used in the processing of some programming languages.

Dispatch (current-contents)

argument type: either 'empty, a word-instance, a node, or an elmt-instance
return value: none

Depending on the type of **Current-contents** do:

'empty
       RETURN

a WORD-INSTANCE
       (Morphology-routine current-contents)
         ;modify the word's print name as needed and "say" it
         〉
       RETURN

a NODE
       (Process-node current-contents)
         〉
       RETURN

an ELMT-INSTANCE
       current-contents <= (Realize current-contents)
         〉
       After-Realization
       (Foreach feature of current-slot
         do (evaluate (get-grammar-routine
                                'after-realization feature)))
         〉
       (Dispatch current-contents)
         〉
       RETURN

ERROR

Figure 11 The Controller: Dispatching on the Contents of a Slot

---

Gating the First Transducer   The first transducer is taken up exclusively in the dispatch to the function named "realize". This function contains the procedures and heuristics that are common to all realization decisions: i.e. criteria for pronominalization, alternate subsequent reference forms such as *"one"* or *"such"*, and "gap-creation" for WH-movement; if none of these apply, it dispatches to the message element's dictionary entry and the standard entry interpreter sketched later in the paper (for a complete specification of the realization process, see [McDonald 1980]).

Every message element that is embedded in the tree must eventually pass through this step of the controller, and then and only then will its English realization be decided on. On return from the function Realize, the selected node, word, or subelement is knit into the tree in place of the original element, at which point the controller loops around and repeats the dispatch on the new contents of the slot.

A Last-stage, Morphological Process   When an English word is found as the contents of a slot, it is passed to a procedure named the *Morphology routine* for any required specialization and from there to the output stream. The Morphology routine does not have much work to do in English: it is responsible for the case of pronouns, for plural forms, verb conjugation, contractions, and the possessive. It bases its decisions on properties it associates with the slot-names of the slot that contains the word (e.g. "subject" is understood as forcing the nominative case) and on inherited attachments to the constituent structure marking such "extra-constituent" information as tense, aspect, and negation. It is the routine within the generator with the clearest representation of the notion "next word", and as a result is responsible for grammatical phenomena dependent on successive linear position such as the verbal auxiliary.

Process-node (current-node)

argument: a node
return value: none

Enter-node:
(Foreach feature of current-node
    do (evaluate (get-grammar-routine 'enter-node feature)))

(Foreach slot in (constituents current-node)
    do (process-slot slot))

Leave-node:
(Foreach feature of current-node
    do (evaluate (get-grammar-routine 'leave-node feature)))

RETURN

Process-slot (current-slot)

argument: a slot
return value: none

current-contents <= (contents current-slot)

Enter-slot:
(Foreach feature of current-slot
    do (evaluate (get-grammar-routine 'enter-slot feature)))

(Dispatch current-contents)   **A**

Leave-slot:
(Foreach feature of current-slot
    do (evaluate (get-grammar-routine 'leave-slot feature)))

RETURN

Figure 12. The Controller: Processing Nodes and Slots

Associating Grammar-routines With Constituent Structure Labels   The   two procedures Process-node and Process-slot are the primary place where the library of active procedures that constitutes the active aspect of the grammar is used. These procedures are referred to as *grammar-routines* and are associated with specific grammatical labels (also referred to as *features*). Grammar-routines are further specified by the point in the controller's algorithm where they are to be executed, marked in the flowcharts in **bold** type. there are five generic events in the traversal of a tree All of the active parts of the generator's English grammar are associated with the labels attached to the nodes and slots of the surface structure. These points correspond to five generic "events" in the traversal of the tree: entering or leaving a node. entering or leaving a slot, and just after a message element has been realized but before the realizing phrase has been knit into the tree. As indicated in figure 12, when one of these events is reached, each of the labels associated with the current node or slot is checked for a grammar-routine of that event type, which if found is immediately executed.

Grammar-routines may perform any of the following actions:

(1) Add function words directly into the output text stream;

(2) Set or reset reference pointers ("grammar variables") to immediately accessible parts of the tree for the maintainance of grammatical context (see below);

(3) Make specifically constrained "edits" to the constituent structure they immediately dominate so as to implement locally triggered phenomena such as heavy phrase shift or conjunction reduction;

(4) Make local "grammatical decisions" that are not required by the speaker's message but are necessary grammatically such as the selection of complementizers.

The current context   The rules of grammar embedded within the grammar routines are couched in a vocabulary that is always interpreted with respect to the current position of the controller in the tree. This position is defined in terms of the values of three variables: *current-node, current-slot,* and *current-contents,* which are set and reset as the controller moves. Grammatically important facts about the tree—the vocabulary of the grammar rules—are represented in terms of a set of variables that are bound locally in the tree but have their values set and reset by of specific grammar-routines. The three variables above are referred to as *controller-variables,* and a second, open-ended set are termed *grammar-variables.* In addition to these variables, the controller maintains a *discourse history,* consisting of records of all important events that have occurred, including the realization of every message element instance, every selected choice, and every decision brought about by the grammar.

In summary, the current context of the linguistic component can be viewed as a four dimensional array consisting of (1) the name of the controller event or subroutine presently being executed, (2) the values of the three controller-variables, (3) the values of the grammar-variables, and (4) the records of the discourse history. This representation of the context will be used in the diagrams of the main example.

4.6. An Example

This example should serve two purposes: first, to put flesh on the apparatus of the linguistic component just discussed by showing how it acts as a system; and second, to illustrate some of the sorts of linguistic analysis that one is lead to as a scientist working in terms of this theory of language generation. From the point of view of conventional, competence-based linguistics some of the analyses that will be sketched may seem unusual or even bizzare; this is perhaps to be expected since the need to smoothly interact with an independent, non-linguistically based process (the speaker/expert program) has imposed its own mark on the analyses everywhere from the timing of decisions to the details of the surface constituent structure.

This example is drawn from the logic domain described in section 1.2. We will look at the generation of the last part of the "barber proof": initially in considerable detail in order to demonstrate how the controller interacts with the selected surface structure, and then at a coarser level of detail so as to concentrate on the analyses and the motives behind them. The example will actually be only the last two lines of the proof, but we will put those lines in context first by sketching the events up to that point.

Generation in the logic domain is an example of "direct translation". There is no planning component; instead, messages are constituted directly from the regular data structures of the domain, the lines of the proof. This is the characteristic pattern of direct translation systems (for example [Swartout 1977; Shortliffe 1976]), and it the source of their convenience—side-stepping an elaborate planner by taking advantage of the organization already in the domain's native data structures, as well as of their limitations—they lock the generator into a single level of abstraction and invariably leave many conceptual connections implicit. By translating first into a linguistic representation and then applying general grammatical rules and usage heuristics, we are able to generate a smoother, more natural text than earlier generators that translated directly into word strings; however, the overall form and content of the text remain in the mold set by the input proof. It is safe to say that the direct translation technique is pushed here to the limits of its fluency; further improvements will only come with the addition of a planner with a knowledge-base of rhetorical heuristics.

The "message" that started the generator off was the seven lines of the proof in sequence. Figure 13 is a snapshot of the tree just after this message was received and distributed into the slots of a simple paragraph; note that the order of the lines has been preserved in the left-to-right sequence of the slots. The formulas have been abbreviated to just the names of their lines.

---

line1: premise
$\exists x\ (barber(x) \wedge \forall y(shaves(x,y) \leftrightarrow \neg shaves(y,y)))$

line2: existential instantiation (1)
$barber(g) \wedge \forall y(shaves(g,y) \leftrightarrow \neg shaves(y,y))$

line3: tautology (2)
$\forall y\ shaves(g,y) \leftrightarrow \neg shaves(y,y)$

line4: universal instantiation (3)
$shaves(g,g) \leftrightarrow \neg shaves(g,g)$

line5: tautology (4)
$shaves(g,g) \wedge \neg shaves(g,g)$

line6: conditionalization (5,1)
$\exists x\ (barber(x) \wedge \forall y(shaves(x,y) \leftrightarrow \neg shaves(y,y)))$
$— (shaves(g,g) \wedge \neg shaves(g,g))$

line7: reductio-ad-absurdum (6)
$\neg \exists x\ (barber(x) \wedge \forall y(shaves(x,y) \leftrightarrow \neg shaves(y,y)))$

Becomes:

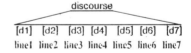

Figure 13 Message and Initial Snapshot

The fixed traversal pattern of the controller dictates that the text will be produced incrementally following the sequence of the lines. This guaranteed conventional sequence provides the basis for a chronological discourse context: The text for the first line will have been selected and produced before that of the second line is begun, the second before the third, and so on. On this basis, a model of what the listener will have heard can be inferred, and, coupled with a (very simple) model of what inferences the listener will make or can be lead through, will give us some justification for extending the context-free interpretation of the lines of the proof to an interpretation in terms of the roles the lines play in a conventional proof technique. Thus while there are seven lines in the proof and seven sentences in the text, there is by no means a one-to-one mapping: The first line of the proof, the premise, is rendered as an imperative to the listener, setting the form of the argument as a proof by contradiction. The second line instantiates the variable. Logically its formula is a restatement of the body of the existential formula from line one with a constant substituted for the body. It is realized in the text however only in terms of its role in the proof, *"Call him Giuseppe"*, the formula itself being appreciated as redundant.

Assume that there is some barber who shaves everyone who doesn't shave himself (and no one else). Call him Giuseppe. Now, anyone who doesn't shave himself would be shaved by Giuseppe. This would include Giuseppe himself. That is, he would shave himself, if and only if he did not shave himself, which is a contradiction. This means that the assumption leads to a contradiction. Therefore, it is false, there is no such barber.

Figure 14 The 'Barber' Proof

The third line does not appear in the text *per se* at all since it is an obvious conclusion from what was known so far. The fourth line, on the other hand, has been expanded into a three sentence "mini-argument" because of its importance to the proof and because its logic may not be obvious. The fifth line, the derivation of the contradiction, is interpreted for its conventional role, i.e. announcing the derivation of the contradiction. In the text it is adjoined to the previous sentence as a relative clause—a kind of "renaming" speech-act.

We see the changes that these realization decisions have made in the tree in figure 15. Only the top nodes of the sentences are shown. The controller is now positioned at slot "d6", and the two final lines of the proof remain. In looking at the generation of those lines, we will be begin with very cursory descriptions of the first few lines to establish the basic pattern, then move to very detailed snapshots of the controller and the tree for several decisions that involve straight-forward analyses, and then back away from the detail during the last line to highlight the special kind of reasoning that generation can entail. For further examples and a thorough discussion of the analyses, see [McDonald 1980].

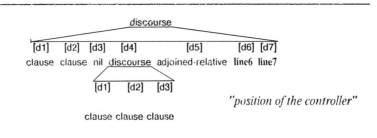

Figure 15 The Tree after Line 5

4.6.1. Recursive Descent Through the Formula

The logical decomposition of line6 begins with the relation between the inference rule "conditionalization" and the formula it derives (abbreviated "formula89 — conj101"); thus the generator must do the same. The dictionary entry for conditionalization must select a phrase that will convey how the formula is related to the rest of the proof before it, and then the formula will be realized in the context of that phrase. By default, we have the inference rule realized as a bridging phrase stating the connection, *"this means that..."*, which embeds the formula as a complement. The knowledge-base of the domain would not motivate anything more elaborate without appeal to a richly annotated, self-conscious theorem-prover, and one was not available. The controller traverses this fixed phrase "saying" the subject and verb. The complementizer *"that"* is produced by a grammar-routine associated with the label "complement" rather than from its own slot in the tree because of a design hypothesis that says that slots should be reserved for items derived directly from the message; function words are by hypothesis a part of the linguistic background just like the annotation on the tree.

The next step in the descent is the major connective of the formula, the implication. Implications can take many forms in English, but the most direct is the subject-predicate relation selected here. The verb *"leads to"* is specific to this conventional use of the contradiction. The snapshot in Figure 16 shows the tree from [d6] down at the point after the clause realizing the implication has been put in place. The four parts of the controller's state are given explicitly.

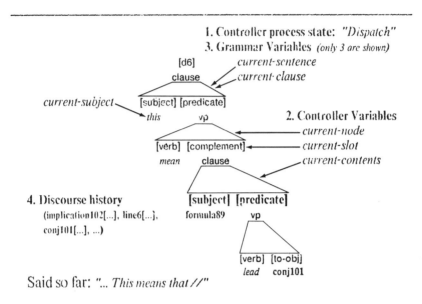

1. Controller process state: *"Dispatch"*

3. Grammar Variables *(only 3 are shown)*

[d6]   *current-sentence*
clause   *current-clause*

current-subject   [subject] [predicate]
                      this   vp

2. Controller Variables
                      current-node
[verb] [complement]   *current-slot*
mean   clause   *current-contents*

4. Discourse history   [subject] [predicate]
(implication102[...], line6[...],   formula89   vp
conj101[...], ...)

[verb] [to-obj]
lead   conj101

Said so far: *"... This means that //"*

Figure 16 Snapshot of the Controller's State

4.6.2. Stepping The Controller Through the Tree

With the controller in its "Dispatch" state, the next step from the position of the snapshot is a recursive call to Process-node (refer to the earlier flowcharts). The controller variable "current-node" is reassigned to the new node labeled "clause", and we execute any grammar-routines associated with the label "clause" and the controller-event "enter-node". There are presently two of these: one for assigning the current-sentence, which no longer applies, and one that recursively reassigns the grammar-variable "current-clause", which does. From here the controller moves to Process-slot, reassigning "current-slot" to the first of the clause's constituent slots, the "subject", and "current-contents" to formula89. One grammar-routine applies here to assign the grammar variable "current-subject" to the current-contents. (Working in recursive environments such as this clause requires care in the timing of assignments. By "delaying" the updating of the pointer to the subject until now, we have retained access to the higher subject where it was needed, e.g., for potential applications of equivalent-np-deletion or conjunction-reduction at the level of the clause.)

From Process-slot, the controller calls Dispatch and selects the "msg-elmt" case. The function Realize will now control the selection of a realizing phrase for formula89 which will then become the current-contents and the controller will loop through Dispatch again. The realization of formula89 involves appreciating its redescription as an object with a special role in the proof, i.e. *"the assumption"*. Its dictionary entry is considerably more involved than average; consequently rather than look at the interpretation of that entry, we will digress here to consider a more "normal" entry and how it fits into Realize. The redescription technique itself will be described later.

4.6.3. The Realization Process

Figure 17 is a high-level flowchart of the function Realize: It divides into two paths depending on whether this is the first instance of the message element to appear in the tree, in which case we go directly to its dictionary entry, or whether this is a subsequent reference (as with formula89), in which case we apply various heuristics to determine if it should be realized as a pronoun or some other form of "subsequent reference". (Summarizing an entire formula with the phrase *"the assumption"* is a form of subsequent reference.)

Every entry has a "matrix" decision, the one that determines what category of phrase will be used, e.g. noun phrase or clause, and may have an arbitrary number of other "refining" decisions that can add additional features to the phrase or add optional constituents.

A dictionary entry consists of a set of possible "choices" and a set of "decision-rules" to pick between them: A *choice* is a symbolic specification of phrases, words, or subelements of the element being realized; A *decision-rule* has two parts: one, a list of predicates that may examine both the linguistic context and the context of the speaker, and two, the choice that should be selected if those predicates are true. The bulk of the realization process consists of interpreting the decision-rules to select a choice, then possibly going through further sets of decision-rules to see if the grammatical or rhetorical context dictates that the choice should be transformed. Extensions to the tree occur when the selected choice specifies a phrase.

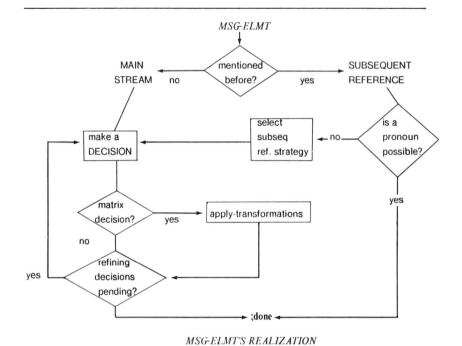

MSG-ELMT'S REALIZATION

Figure 17 flowchart of the realization procedure

The vocabulary of the specification comes from the permanent knowledge base in the grammar, part of which is a listing of all of the legitimate categories in the language and for each category, of the legitimate sequences of slotnames that it can dominate. These listings are organized in terms of "constituent schemas". ("Schemas" in the sense that they will be used as templates for the construction of "instances" of those category configurations in the tree.) Every choice has (at least) three parts: (1) a "phrase-schema" that defines a tree of constituent-schemas possibly augmented by additional labels and by specific words from the English vocabulary; (2) a list of formal parameters that will be used to pick out subelements of the message element being realized; and (3) a mapping from parameters to slots at the fringe of the specified phrase.

Figure 18 lists the entry, choice, and grammar that are required to realize the logical predicate *shaves*.

Message Element   shaves(x,y)

Dictionary Entry   (define-entry shaves-entry (shaver shavee)
          (matrix
              default (clause-direct-object shaver "shave" shavee)))

the Choice   (define-choice clause direct-object
        parameters (subj verb object)
        phrase (basic-clause ()
                predicate (vp-obj1 ()))
        map ((subj . (subject))
            (verb . (predicate verb))
            (object . (predicate object1))))

Constituent-   (define-schema basic-clause   (define-schema vp-obj1
schemas   categories (clause)   categories (vp)
        slots (subject predicate))   slots (verb object1))

WHICH PRODUCE:

Figure 18 Entry, Choice, and grammar for the relation 'shaves'

The dictionary entry *shaves-entry* will be the one to perform the realization. It decomposes the original message element into two subelements, the variables **X** and **Y** plus the verb *"shave"*, and binds them to three local variables for ease of manipulation. Shaves-entry has only one choice, which it has marked as its default. As it includes no decision-rules, this default choice will always be taken. The choice, *clause-direct-object* (named for the kind of constituent structure it builds), is given in the figure just below the entry. It uses two constituent schema, *basic-clause* and *vp-obj1*, to define a two-level phrase-schema (shown instantiated at the bottom of the figure) whose *verb* constituent has been filled in but other constituents left vacant in anticipation of being filled by message elements selected by the entries that select clause-direct-object. Because this choice will inevitably be used with many different entries, its mapping is given in terms of its own formal parameters (i.e. *subj, verb,* and *object*), which are then bound to the values of the local variables of the entry when the choice is taken. To produce new constituent structure from the choice, its phrase-schema must be instantiated and the mapping applied to fill its leaves with the message elements the entry has selected.

4.6.4. Continuing through the tree

Once the phrase for formula89 has been instantiated and knit into the tree, the controller as before recurses on Process-node and begins to traverse the new noun phrase. Nothing new happens within the phrase, so we will move on to the next snapshot, taken after the controller has finished with the subject and moved down and through the slot "to-obj" to the object constituent.

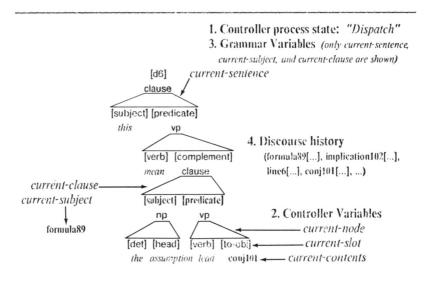

1. Controller process state: *"Dispatch"*
3. Grammar Variables *(only current-sentence, current-subject, and current-clause are shown)*

[d6]   *current-sentence*
clause

[subject] [predicate]
this   vp

[verb] [complement]   **4. Discourse history**
mean   clause   (formula89[...], implication102[...],
                              line6[...], conj101[...], ...)
current-clause
current-subject   [subject] [predicate]
                       np   vp   **2. Controller Variables**
formula89   ———— *current-node*
              [det] [head]   [verb] [to-obj] ◄——— *current-slot*
              the assumption leads   conj101 ◄— *current-contents*

Said so far: *"This means that the assumption leads to//"*

Figure 19 Snapshot after producing the verb

Notice that we have not replaced the verb with its third person singular form even though that is the form that appears in the output stream. By design, we have decided that the level of representation exhibited in the tree should be the level needed by the library routines that reference it; we will not gratuitously "update" its contents or add labels if they are not going to do further work in the grammar. The correct morphological form of the verb was needed only for the output text and so was not constructed until the morphology routine was passed the word on its way to the text stream. Later grammatical references to the verb are going to be concerned with its grammatical properties rather than its morphological ones (for example whether it can take complements, and if so whether they are subject or object controlled) and these properties are by convention associated with the root form of the verb which is the one in place in the verb slot. The preposition *"to"* was introduced by a grammar-routine attached to the label "to-obj" rather than having its own slot for the same reason: we expect no other part of the generator, dictionary or grammar, to need to know about the presence of that preposition so we make our expectation concrete by having the preposition completely "invisible" within a grammar routine rather than occupying a slot where it could be noticed.

Redescription according to function   The last significant operation before moving on to line7 is the realization of conj101, the formula **shaves(g,g)** ∧ **¬shaves(g,g)**, as the English phrase *"a contradiction"*. This is of course not a literal rendering of the formula; that would have been *"He shaves himself and he doesn't shave himself"*. Instead it is a rendering of the *conventional role* that the formula played in the proof at that point, i.e. an indication that a contradiction had been derived. This ability to realize expressions in terms of their functional redescriptions was also used in the realization of formula89 as *"the assumption"* at the beginning of the sentence.

Redescription is a way of seeing the same concept or operation at multiple levels simultaneously depending on one's intent, and has become an important part of the representational "repertoire" of modern expert systems, where it is used in plan recognition and in defining levels of abstraction (see particularly [Mark 1981]). Intuitively, redescription is associated with particular turns of phrase in English such as appositives (as in the last sentence of this example) or some noun-noun combinations (e.g. *"the role pobj"*); consequently, it is useful to make specific arrangements for it within the linguistics component.

Ordinarily, redescription would be an operation at a conceptual level rather than a linguistic one, and we would expect it to be explicitly indicated in the message; however, since the present microspeaker has no real conceptual knowledge of logic and starts with only the bare formulas of the proof, we must compensate by performing the redescription locally within the dictionary. The relevant parts of the dictionary are the entries for the inference rules, these being where the microspeaker's tacit knowledge about the structure of proofs resides. The redescriptions of the individual formulas are deduced as the entries are interpreted and stored within the linguistics component on a special association list: the entry for a Premise, for example, notes that the formula on its line serves the function of being the assumption of the proof; and the entry for tautologies (which is actually a clearing-house for an entire set of logical manipulations) notes that any derived line of the form **A ∧ ¬A** is serving to mark the derivation of a contradiction at that point in the proof.

The access function that associates formulas with their entries includes a special check for redescriptions and passes every redescribed formula to a common *meta-entry* for its realization. (A meta-entry chooses between other entries rather than between English constructions.) This entry knows how to use the special redescription phrases, and has access both to the literal renderings and to the functional-level renderings. which it combines according to the context (see discussion below in conjunction with the realization of neg103).

4.6.5. Delaying Decisions

One problem that can arise with the direct-translation technique is that while the formal structure of the data used in a message (here the predicate calculus) may be convenient within the domain, it can be at odds with what would be convenient for the generator. Negation103, the last line of the proof, is a case in point.

$$\neg \exists x\,(barber(x) \wedge \forall y(shaves(x,y) \leftrightarrow \neg shaves(y,y)))$$

Linguistically, the principle contribution to the content of any text created from negation103 will come from the "shaves" relations, yet these are the most deeply embedded in the formula. If we follow the formula's natural decomposition order, five logical operators will have to be passed through before these content relations are reached. Given the indelibility stipulation, the realization decisions for those operators must be made "on the way down" as it were, but how can this be done if those decisions are contingent on linguistic details of how the content relations can be realized—details that will not be determined until those relations are actually reached by the controller.

This problem is solved by delaying the affected decisions. We postpone them until the information on which they depend has been determined, implementing only those decisions that can be made independently and attaching annotations to the tree indicating that the remaining decisions are still pending. Consider the first two realization decisions in line7: The inference rule, *reductio-ad-absurdum*, is realized like the previous conditionalization rule by picking a bridging adverb that will convey the fact that the line is the conclusion (e.g. *"therefore"*) and then embedding the line's formula in that linguistic context. However, because this is a proof by contradiction, we know by convention that this final formula will be a copy of the premise but with opposite polarity. We should somehow emphasize this polarity in the text, but from this vantage point in the process we do not yet know what linguistic mechanism should be used (e.g. an explicit "do" or an emphatic "not"). We must thus delay the decision until we know more, which means that we add an annotation to the formula we embed, expecting the annotation to be recognized by later routines that will be active when the needed information is known.

As it happens, the dictionary entry of the very next operator in the decomposition, the negation, has an alternative among its choices that we have determined in designing the grammar will serve to emphasize negative polarity, i.e. "<body of the negation> is false". The negation entry is allowed to select this choice if the body of the negation, the premise line formula89, can be expressed as a simple noun phrase (nominalized clauses are disallowed); that is the case here, since formula89 was just referred to in the last sentence as "the assumption" and that nominal form will carry over. If only a clausal realization had been possible, then the negation decision would have been delayed as well.

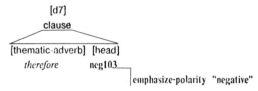

Becomes:

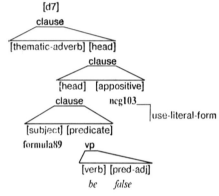

Said so far: *"... Therefore//"*

```
(define-entry  negation-entry  (neg)
      variables  ((body (body neg)))
      (matrix
            ((equal (get-annotation neg emphasize-polarity) 'negative)   ;decision-rule
            (will-be body 'np)
            (X-is-false body))   ;choice to select

            ((will-be body 'np)   ;i.e. do it whenever possible because it's more fluent
            (X-is-false body))

            default (Mark-X-negative body)))
```

Figure 20 Delayed Decisions

Expressions like *"The assumption is false"* lend themselves to appositive phrases that expand on what was summarized in the subject. This is a fact of the grammar that can be implemented in a generator in terms of a transformation that we associate with this expression. The transformation acts independently once triggered by the use of the expression and examines the subject to see if an appositive would be appropriate. The heuristic used here is a very simple and arbitrary one: redescriptions such as *"an assumption"* or *"a contradiction"* will draw appositives if their long forms have not been mentioned within three sentences. The same heuristic applies to pronominalization decisions and is intended to reflect when a reference has faded in memory—research on discourse structure should lead to a more principled criterion. The fact that the appositive has been planned at the level of the clause inhibits it from appearing redundantly with the noun phrase; that is, the local decision that would have produced *"The assumption that there is no such barber is false, there is no such barber"* is filtered out by the presence of the higher appositive in the tree.

4.6.6. Interaction Between Decisions

Traversing the tree below the clause that realized the first instance of negation103 is a simple matter. The embedded formula in the subject is pronominalized because of its proximity to its last instance and the fact that both instances were in subject position (in effect a "poor man's" rule of discourse focus). The pronoun, verb, and adjective are then passed to the output stream as the controller moves through their constituent positions.

At the position of the appositive, the negation entry this time passes its decision down to a later process since its body has been specially annotated because of its appositive function so as to block the redescription of formula89 as a noun phrase. We go then to the next level of neg103, the existential quantifier, where we have two choices: either to pass the realization of the quantifier down to appear as the determiner in the realization of the variable (as in *"Someone shaves everyone who doesn't shave himself"*) or to use the special existential construction *"There is"*. As one might imagine, this decision is designed to be sensitive to the pending decision on the negation, and we select the special construction since the negation would preempt the determiner and make the other alternative ineffective.

In English, clauses with the existential *"there"* are grammatically unusual because the verb agrees in number with the object rather than the subject. This is handled here via the same mechanism as presently used in transformational grammars: The word *"there"* is taken to be a lexically filled "trace" pointing to the logical subject of the clause, such that when the grammar routine that implements "subject-verb" agreement refers to the variable "current-subject" it is passed transparently to the object instead. (The reference is not actually to the "object"—it cannot be, since the position of the object has not yet been reached by the controller and thus its contents cannot be known. Instead the trace points to the message element that would have been the subject if *"there"* had not been used, and the transformation that introduced the word *"there"* redirected that element to the object position.)

4.6.7. Realizing Message Elements in terms of their Roles

The conjunction that is now the object constituent of the *"there"* clause is yet another conventional expression within the proof.

$$\text{barber}(x) \;\wedge\; \forall y(\text{shaves}(x,y) \leftrightarrow \neg\text{shaves}(y,y))$$

The predication "barber(x)" is a restriction on the variable **X**, which, in other logical notations, would have appeared in other places in the expression. The actual "content" of the conjunct is just the universally quantified formula. If we knew nothing else about this conjunction, we would be forced to realize it literally, as in *"Someone is a barber and he shaves everyone who doesn't shave himself"*. However, if we make the conventional structure of the conjunction apparent to the linguistic component, we can be much more fluent. By labeling the predication as a "description" and the formula as a "proposition", both predictable on the variable **X**, we can take advantage of a general purpose dictionary entry for that combination.

As shown in figure 21, a description and a proposition can be combined in several ways according to what is needed (i.e. which of the two elements is more important, which order is more important, etc.). In this case since the conjunction is acting as an object, the combination where the two are set up as modifiers in a noun phrase denoting the variable is the most appropriate, and that is the phrase that is built and replaces conj88 in the tree.

Combinations of a description and a proposition
predicated of the same object.

proposition[object¬]
 ⌐description
  Someone who is a barber shaves everyone who doesn't shave himself.

description[object¬] ˙
 ⌐proposition
  Someone who shaves everyone who doesn't shave himself is a barber.

[np object¬]
 ⌐modifier
 ⌐proposition
  A barber who shaves everyone who doesn't shave himself.

Figure 21

This particular conjunction has of course appeared before in the first line of the proof. We are therefore dealing with a subsequent reference and the heuristics in that section of the Realize function apply. Because of the distance of the original instance from the present position, the conjunction should not be pronominalized, however there are of course "intermediate" subsequent reference strategies. One of these, particularly appropriate to the style of a mathematical proof, is the word *"such"*; this word can "pronominalized" the modifying phrases of the reference, leaving its head and determiner.

4.7. Contributions and Limitations

4.7.1. Specific Contributions of This Research

The computer program developed in this research (see [McDonald 1981]) is the most linguistically competent natural language production program that has been reported to date. This is due primarily to the advances in the computational theory of production reported here and in [McDonald 1980] which have simplified the process of representing linguistic rules and usage-heuristics. In particular:

(1) This is the first theory to be specifically designed for use with source programs that use different representational systems.[1]

(2) This is the first theory to be grounded on psycholinguistically plausible hypotheses embodied in a processor of limited computational power; relevant hypotheses include: the left to right refinement and production of text,[2] linguistically motivated limitations on the examinable buffer, indelible decisions, and a structural distinction in the treatment of function words versus content words.

(3) Production is driven directly by the message to be expressed, not by the hierarchical structure of the grammar. This is more efficient, and facilitates the conceptualization of messages as descriptions of goals to be achieved by the text.

(4) The linguistic structure of the text being produced is explicitly represented.[3] Grammatical rules can be implemented directly as manipulations of linguistic descriptions, thereby gaining generality and perspicuity. Details of the structure of produced and planned text may be referenced directly and used as the basis of usage decisions.

(5) The possible realizations of each element of a message are explicitly represented and are available for inspection or special-case manipulation.

4.7.2. Relation to previous A.I. work on natural language generation

Virtually all of the earlier work on language generation by people in A.I. including that of this author and most of that done by psychologists shares a common view of the process: an expert-program/speaker with no linguistic knowledge or motivations begins the process by deciding—in its own terms—what will be talked about. The differences between the various proposals concern the kind of device that is to take such a "message" and to produce a natural language text from it through application of grammatical knowledge (encoded in some form) and the use of some kind of "dictionary" to interpret the speaker's message.

---

1. The ATN-based generator originally developed by Simmons and Slochum [Simmons and Slocum 1972] and later adopted by Goldman [Goldman 1974] has been used with many different programs: [Reisbeck 1974; Lehnert 1977 ; Yale A.I. Group 1976; Meehan 1976]; however, all of these employed the same representational system: conceptual dependency [Schank 1976].
2. Gerard Kempen [Kempen 1977] writes that production should be incremental and left to right, however, his program as described in [Kempen and Hoenkamp 1980] while realizing clauses sequentially, refines the constituents of each clause in parallel.
3. This was true also of the German-to-English translation program of Gretchen Brown [Brown 1972], and locally true in the systemic grammar used by Anthony Davey [Davey 1974].

Two other perspectives have been taken (see [Mann et al. to appear]): one school can be termed *grammar-controlled linearization and translation* [Simmons and Slocum 1972; Goldman 1974; Shapiro 1975]; another, larger though less linguistically sophisticated school can be termed *production directly from program data* [Swartout 1977; Chester 1976]. (Two other important systems, [Clippinger 1978] and [Davey 1974], fall into neither of these categories as they both employ extensive grammars and vest control with non-grammatical processes; unfortunately. neither has been further developed.)

The *grammar-controlled* school vests total control of the process in a topdown generative grammar, typically given as an augmented transition net ("ATN"). This grammar hypothesizes a way in which the message might be realized, and then tests the message to see if that way is feasible. It constructs the hypothesized text if the test succeeds; otherwise it backs up and considers the next grammatically possible realization. Texts are produced as a side-effect of traversing the ATN. Compared with using the message decomposition itself to control the process, this technique is inefficient at best, and at worst, allows the possibility of producing totally confused text should the ATN ever backup over an arc-path that produced words (i.e. it would start repeating itself without regard for context). Historically it is the case that none of these systems has ever had occasion to backup; we conjecture that the reason for this is that the space of possible message configurations dealt with by these systems is relatively small, making it possible to directly encode the space on the arcs of the ATN grammar as tests for all of the possible contingencies. We predict that when the contingencies become too diverse to anticipate when the grammar is written, that grammar-controlled systems will metamorphose into a more message-controlled style.

The *direct production* school is much closer to the philosophy underlying the present work. Their approach is to start with a data structure from the expert program (their "message") and to evaluate it with a special "text generation" evaluator just as in other circumstances they might evaluate it with, e.g., the normal LISP evaluator in order to execute some function. The structure of the message governs what generation processes are run and in what sequence (invariably a strict depth-first sequence. translating arguments before functions and using the internal LISP stack to record what to do next and what to do with "subtexts" as they are constructed). The "generation functions" for individual kinds of program objects assemble texts by embedding the texts produced for their argument objects within a matrix text; conceptually, generation functions play exactly the same role as dictionary entries in the model presented here. We suggest that the difficulties these systems face—almost complete ignorance of grammar, and an inability to produce text that is not absolutely isomorphic in structure to its message—could be overcome if they were to adopt an intermediate, *linguistically motivated* representation. Such a linguistically motivated representation would, suitably interpreted, serve as a ready description of context and a mechanism for the automatic (i.e. not expressly requested in the message) application of general rules, a policy which, not coincidentally, is the central theme of the present theory.

4.7.3. When is this linguistic component appropriate?

The utility of an independent linguistic component is that it can be incorporated whole into a new system, relieving its users of the need to develop their own version of this level of the generation process. This utility is not without its price however, since preparing an interface between a new expert program and this component is not a trivial undertaking: creating an adequate dictionary will require the new user to provide explicit representations for relations that are often left implicit in expert programs; and thought must be given to the mechanics of message construction and to the practical exigencies of dealing with another independent computer program. If all that a person wanted to do was to take already highly sugared expressions directly from his or her program's data structures and produce "linearizations" of them, then it is questionable whether they should go to the effort of using this component since the already established "direct-translation" technology should be able to do the job with considerably less overhead.

From an engineering point of view the strength of this component is its ability to combine disparate internal data structures on the basis of their linguistic descriptions to produce cohesive, context-sensitive texts. If, to choose an extreme example, all of the remarks that an expert program were ever going to have to make could be anticipated at the time the program was written, then this component would be entirely superfluous since the texts could be included at the time the program was written. If on the other hand the expert program is continually entering into new discourse situations, learning about new objects and relations, and forced to dynamically configure its remarks to the audience and situation, then using this component (or something like it) is a necessity.

To be specific, a program that needs to produce texts with any of the following characteristics should benefit by using this linguistic component for its generation. These linguistic properties of a text are controlled by a complex set of rules of little interest to the nonlinguist, yet are crucial if the texts are to be natural English. With these rules incorporated once and for all into a shareable component, the system designer is freed to move on to other problems.

Embedded clauses: Any internal relation that is used as part of a description or is modified by or is an argument to another relation, for example the propositional arguments of modal predicates such as "believe" or "possible", will appear as some form of embedded clause when rendered in English. The grammar of these constructions involves complex syntactic rules to coordinate adjustments to the text of the relation and to the matrix text it is embedded in.

Coherence relations in multi-sentence texts: Text that is part of a larger discourse must obey certain linguistic conventions that have no counterparts in the purely conceptual structure of the information being conveyed, e.g. the use of pronouns or definite noun phrases for subsequent references to the same objects, the ellipsis of predictable phrases, segmentation into sentences and paragraphs, the subordination or focusing of individual items, or the deliberate use of explicit relational connectives and ordering to present complex relations sequentially.

Context sensitive realizations: Within a program it is often possible (even desirable) to be vague about whether an expression denotes an object, a relation, or a predicate. The corresponding linguistic choice (e.g. noun phrase, clause, or verb phrase) then depends on how the expression is being used in a given instance, as determined by its context in the message or by the linguistic context into which it is introduced. The choice of realization must be postponed until the context is clear.

Describing objects from their properties: When a program is continually creating or being told about new objects, pre-stored texts for object descriptions must be abandoned in favor of algorithms that will construct descriptions from properties. For general algorithms, linguistic descriptions of the properties are required to insure that only grammatical phrases are built. Planning is required to judge how thorough a description must be, and the nature of the description selected will effect how it can be realized linguistically. For example deciding between the two texts: *"(I put an X on) the adjacent corner"* versus *"...the corner adjacent to the one you just took"*, the choice between using the prenominal adjective versus using the postnominal adjective phrase depends on the prior choice of how much detail of the position must be given for the audience to recognize it.

4.7.4. What This Model Cannot Do

Efficiency has its price. Because of its design, there are certain kinds of potentially useful operations that this linguistic component is intrinsically incapable of. This is not taken as a failing, but as the necessary result of a deliberate distribution of tasks according to the components that are architecturally most suited to performing them; that is, I claim (but will not justify here) that the bulk of what this linguistic component cannot do can be done better by other the components that it will interact with. Specifically:

Creative expression—fitting old words to new situations: This linguistic component does not know what words mean. By inverting its dictionary it could compute in what circumstances a word could be used, but it has no means of its own for interpreting these "circumstances" and generalizing them. (How could it if it is able to be used with expert programs with different conceptualizations?) A dictionary entry selects words reflexively according to its precomputed possibilities; in particular, it does not use any sort of pattern-matching on "semantic features", both because of the computational expense and because features that capture useful generalizations are unlikely to be refined enough to pickout specific words.

Monitoring itself: It is generally easier to anticipate and forestall problems by planning than to monitor for them and then have to edit an ongoing procedure. This linguistic component capitalizes on this rule of thumb by omitting from its process architecture the expensive state history that would make editing through backup possible. The kinds of unwanted effects that are difficult to avoid through planning (because they would require essentially full simulation) are coincidental structural or lexical ambiguities; these require a multi-constituent buffer to detect (the sort which is natural to parsers) and are thus better noticed by "listening to oneself" and interrupting the generator with new instructions when needed, rather then burdening that process with a large buffer which will otherwise go unused.

Recognizing when a message will unavoidably lead to awkward or ungrammatical text: Again, given the present design this possibility cannot be foreseen at the linguistic-level without a complete simulation (i.e. rehearsing to oneself). Either the speaker's message-building heuristics will be such that these problems just will not occur (this is almost inevitable when messages are planned and motivated in detail in accordance with the "constraint-precedes" stipulation), or, by planning the message in terms of rhetorical predicates such as "modifies" or "focus", potentially awkward phrasings will be foreseen at the linguistic level and planned around by general rules.

Reasoning about trade-offs caused by limited expressibility: It can happen that the inability to simultaneously express, say, both modality and subordination will not become apparent until the realization of the message is already begun. To be able to reassess the relative importance of the message elements that prompted those choices, this linguistic component would (1) need a common vocabulary with the speaker in which to express the problem (since what should be done is ultimately the speaker's decision), and (2) need to be aware of the potential problem early enough to be able to plan alternatives. Without such a vocabulary, the component must rely on the tacit specification of relative-importance provided in the ordering of the message and the speaker must be prepared for its messages to sometimes not be realized completely.

Planning by backwards chaining from desired linguistic effects: One cannot give a specific grammatical relation as a high-level goal in a message and expect this linguistic component to perform the means-ends analysis required to bring it about; e.g. one cannot give it instructions such as: "the subject of what I say next should be the same as the direct object that I just said". Such reasoning can require exponential time to carry out and a high processing overhead. The effects of such instructions can sometimes be achieved "off-line" however, by having the designer precompute the decision-space that the deliberation would entail and then incorporate it into the component's library as what would in effect be an extension of the rules of the grammar. (The above instruction, for example, is roughly equivalent to the existing focus heuristic.)

CHAPTER 5

Focusing in the Comprehension of Definite Anaphora

Candace L. Sidner

5.1 Introduction: Interpretation of Definite Anaphora

In spoken and written discourse, people use certain words to "point back" in the discourse context to the people, places, objects, times, events and ideas mentioned there. The use of such a pointing back device is called <u>anaphora</u>, and I will refer to words or phrases used in this way as <u>anaphors</u>; in particular, <u>definite anaphora</u> include the personal pronouns, certain uses of definite noun phrases, and noun phrases containing *this* and *that*. Traditionally, researchers have defined the problem of anaphor comprehension as one of determining <u>the antecedent</u> of an anaphoric expression, that is, determining to which word or phrase an anaphoric expression refers or "points". Recent studies in both artificial intelligence and linguistics have demonstrated the need for a theory for anaphor comprehension which accounts for the role of syntactic and semantic effects, as well as inferential knowledge in explaining how anaphors are understood. In this chapter a new theory, based on the concept of focusing in the discourse, will be introduced to explain the interpretation of definite anaphors.

Before a theory can be given, and before even the difficulties in interpreting anaphors can be discussed, we must first re-consider what an antecedent is. The traditional definition encounters difficulty right from the start; it is founded on the notion that one word in a sentence refers or points back to another word in the (same or another) sentence. But words don't refer back to other <u>words</u> [Morgan 1978]; people use words to refer to objects. In particular people use anaphors to refer to objects which have already been mentioned in a discourse. Since an anaphoric phrase does not refer to an antecedent, one might want to claim that both the antecedent and the anaphor co-refer to some object. This definition is adequate for sentence (1) below,

> (1) I think <u>green apples</u> taste best and *they* make the best cooking apples too.

though not for discourse D1, where there is no antecedent word in the discourse which co-refers with the pronoun *they*.

D1-1 My neighbor has a monster Harley 1200,
    2 They are really huge but gas-efficient bikes.

As an alternative to viewing antecedence as co-reference, one might propose
that antecedence is a kind of cognitive pointing, the kind of pointing that causes
they and *green apples* to point to the same class of objects in one's mind (in some
unknown way). This proposal is problematic for same reason that co-reference is:
people use anaphora when there is no other noun phrase in the discourse which
points to the right mental object. In D1, *they* refers to bikes which are Harley
1200s as a group, while the speaker's use of the noun phrase *a monster Harley
1200* only serves to mention some particular Harley 1200. *They* seems to be able
to refer to Harley 1200s as a group when used with the previously mentioned
phrase *a monster Harley 1200* without the two phrases either co-referring or
co-pointing.

If an anaphor does not refer to an antecedent phrase, and if it need not always
co-refer with its apparent antecedent (as in D1), then anaphor interpretation is not
simply finding the antecedent. Nevertheless the concept of antecedence as a kind
of pointing back does seem to capture some aspect of the comprehension of
anaphora, for when certain antecedent words are missing from a discourse, people
often fail to understand what is being said.

Let us define the problem of interpreting and understanding an anaphor in the
following way. The phrase *apples* in (1), when syntactically and semantically
interpreted, will be said to specify a cognitive element in the hearer's mind. In the
computational model of that process, this element is a database item, which might
be represented by the schema below:

> Phrase76:
> string: "green apples"
> context: speaker1 think * tastes best
> specifies: Apples2
>
> Apples2:
> super-concept: apples
> color: green
> used-for: cooking

The speaker uses the information in a cognitive representation like Apples2
above to choose the phrase *green apples* in (1). The hearer then uses the phrase
green apples plus the syntactic and semantic interpretation of rest of the sentence
to locate a similar cognitive element in his own mind; it may be slightly different
because the hearer may not associate use in cooking with green apples. A
cognitive element, such as Apples2, is called the *specification* of *green apples*.

These elements, present in the memories of speaker and hearer, are of course related to other cognitive elements in their memories.

What is the relation of specifications to the real world? One might like to claim that a reference relation exists between specified cognitive elements and objects in the world, but since referring is what people do with words, this relation is problematic for cognitive elements. Instead, specifications will be said to represent the objects referred to, that is, they bear a well-structured correspondence to objects in the world. Apples2, the specification of *green apples*, represents the objects that are green apples. For phrases such as *Santa Claus*, where there is no real world object to represent, a specification represents the properties normally associated with this imaginary person.

The phrase *they* in (1) also specifies a cognitive element, namely the same one that *green apples* does. Since the two bear the same relation to the representation Apples2, they will be said to *co-specify* that memory element, or alternatively, that the interpretation of *green apples* in (1) is the *co-specifier* of the interpretation of *they*. Co-specification, unlike co-reference, allows one to construct abstract representations and define relationships between them which can be studied in a computational framework. With co-reference no such use is possible, since the object referred to exists in the world and is not available for examination by computational processes.

Even if a noun phrase and a pronoun do not co-specify, the specification of a noun phrase may be used to generate the specification of a pronoun. For example, in D1 *they* does not co-specify with the apparent antecedent phrase *a monster Harley 1200*. Here the anaphor *they* refers to the class of Harley 1200s of which the apparent antecedent (the neighbor's monster Harley 1200) is an instance. Thus anaphor interpretation is not simply a matter of finding the corresponding cognitive element which serves as the specification of the anaphor; some additional process must generate a specification for the anaphor from the related phrase *a monster Harley 1200*.

The concepts of specification and co-specification capture the "pointing back" quality of antecedence, and also permit us to formulate an explanation of anaphor interpretation which avoids the pitfalls of the concept of antecedence. Anaphor interpretation can be studied as a computational process that uses the already existing specification of a noun phrase to find the specification for an anaphor. The process uses a representation of the discourse preceding the anaphor which encodes the syntactic and semantic relationships in each sentence as well as co-specification relationships between phrases.[1]

These definitions in themselves do not constitute a theory of anaphor interpretation. They do, however, make possible a succinct statement of the problem: how does one determine the specification of a anaphor? Also since we suspect that the specification of an apparent antecedent phrase plays some role in choosing an anaphor's specification, we may ask, just what is this role? We hope for a direct answer to these questions, but before one can be given, let us consider how a theory of interpretation ought to address these questions. A brief look at the difficulties of finding co-specifiers will suggest which issues our theory should cover.

Determining the co-specifier of an anaphor is difficult because there are a multitude of possible co-specifiers in a given discourse, and there is no simple way to choose the correct one. Yet human hearers and readers generally do recover the correct co-specifying phrase intended by the speaker. Human readers and hearers also fail to recover the co-specifying phrase in certain situations; this behavior is just as valuable an observation as garden path phenomena for theories of parsing. A theory of interpretation must predict the pattern of the hearer's and reader's correct and incorrect choices, as well as failures to understand, by a rule-governed account. In addition, a taxonomy of the cases in which specifications are used to generate other specifications must be given, as well as a means of predicting their distribution; Webber [Chapter 6 of this volume] provides additional treatment of some aspects of these phenomena.

5.1.1 Research on Anaphora

Before exploring the use of specification and co-specification for anaphor interpretation, we must consider other aspects of human communication and knowledge which bear on anaphor interpretation; two significant characteristics are the context of discussion and the inferences people make.

People use the context surrounding an anaphor in understanding it. If a theory of anaphor interpretation is to capture understanding, it must include a means of encoding discourse context and whatever structure it has; the context

---

1. In the rest of this chapter, I will speak of a phrase co-specifying (or specifying) with another phrase, when what I really mean is that the relation is between representations of phrases that have been interpreted by some parsing process, which indicates the sentence syntactic relations, and by a semantic interpretation process, which computes semantic relations among words of the sentence. The kind of processes I envision are rather like running "in reverse" the realization procedure that McDonald describes in this volume.

must be distilled into a form that preserves its richness without adding overwhelming complexity to the interpretation process. In addition, researchers have discovered that anaphor interpretation involves making inferences, some of which can be complex, each of which must be chosen from a large base of knowledge about objects, people and things. The practical deployment of inferential capabilities for any task requires control: knowing what to infer when, and knowing when to stop. Since the general control problem is poorly understood, solutions to the more specific problem of controlling inference in anaphor interpretation must be provided by a theory of anaphor interpretation.

The role of context and inference, as well as syntax and semantics on anaphor interpretation have been explored extensively. A brief look at these explorations will indicate the necessity of a new approach. Research on anaphora falls into four broad categories:

General heuristics for finding antecedents
([Winograd 1972])

Syntactic and semantic constraints on anaphora
([Katz and Fodor 1963], [Woods et al. 1972],
[Chomsky 1976], [Lasnik 1976],
[Reinhart 1976], [Walker 1976]).

Use of inference to find antecedents
([Charniak 1972], [Rieger 1974].
[Hobbs 1976])

Analysis of objects in a discourse context
([Grosz 1977], [Lockman 1978],
[Reichman 1978], [Webber 1978a],
[Hobbs 1979])

Rather than review each approach, I will point out the contributions of each category to a theory of anaphor interpretation.

General heuristics, as a means of choosing antecedents, predict reliably in a large number of typical examples. However, no simple characterization fits the wide variety of cases where they fail (see [Winograd 1972] and [Hobbs 1977]); furthermore, the heuristic approach is not theoretically grounded and cannot offer a unified approach to the phenomena.

Semantic selectional restrictions, based on the Katz-Fodor theory of semantic markers, and used by many computational linguists, can reduce the space of possible antecedents, but they cannot be used to eliminate all possibilities, as the example below illustrates:

(2) Take the mud pack off your face. Notice how soft it feels.

Syntactic restrictions, stated in logical form ([Chomsky 1976]) and in constituent structure ([Lasnik 1976] and [Reinhart 1976]), stipulate conditions in which a pronoun and a noun phrase must have disjoint references.

(3) * Near Dan, he saw a snake.

(4) * The man whose house he bought went gold digging in Alaska.

These rules, however, do not stipulate the interpretation of an anaphor; in a general theory they act as filters on the class of possible co-specifiers. Furthermore, these rules are not yet theoretically complete as linguists are still studying the disjoint reference conditions on reflexive anaphora.

Work by artificial intelligence researchers on inference has led to methods for forward and backward chaining of inferences to "bind" the anaphor, represented as a free variable, with some piece of knowledge; with this approach the anaphor's interpretation was whatever value became bound to the free variable. This approach revealed that inferences about world knowledge are often needed to interpret anaphors. However, the methods tried failed to control the inference process sufficiently. Charniak, attempting to resolve this problem, proposed demons that would "wake up" in the appropriate situation (that is, processes which could notice themselves when they were to begin processing). But a large cache of demons would be required, and no assurance could be given that demons would exist in every situation. Most significantly, his proposal said nothing about the situation where two or more demons might apply (who gets control? how are the decisions made?). Finally all of the inference based approaches to pronoun interpretation fail to offer any theoretical approach because they rely on a simple mechanism, (simple variable binding between pronoun and some other phrase) which does not apply in many uses of anaphora, such as D1.

Discourse approaches to anaphora have included a technique similar to the inference method; one identified sentence pairs and examined them for the coherence relations of similarity, contrast, parallel structure; the pronouns were interpreted by variable binding between items of the sentence pairs ([Hobbs 1979]). A different approach, used by Webber (see Chapter 6 of this volume, or [Webber 1978a]) relies on identifying representational constraints which will restrict what discourse phrases and associated discourse entities may be used in coherent discourse. She presents a form of restricted quantification which provides such constraints. I will consider the role of Webber's formalism in focusing later in this chapter.

Grosz [Grosz 1977, 1978, 1981] defined a focus space as that subset of the speaker's total knowledge which is relevant to a discourse segment. Elements in the space are highlighted via focusing, a process which reflects what a speaker says and the nature of the knowledge in the space. Several such spaces, dubbed "focus spaces," may be relevant at a time although only one is centered on for processing at any given time. Grosz presented a procedure for interpreting non-pronominal noun phrases using the focusing and focus space notions. Reichman [Reichman 1978] has expanded this paradigm by describing "context spaces" which are delineated by their topics. Within a context space, entities receive various focus levels; only phrases that are in high focus may be pronominalized. Reichman's work leaves open important questions: what is the recognition procedure for determining a context space, how does one identify its topic, and how does the hearer determine the interpretation of a anaphor, that is, how does a hearer decide which highly focused phrases act as the co-specifier of a anaphor?

To summarize, current research on anaphor interpretation suggests that control of inferring and constraints on representation of discourse are necessary aspects of a theory of anaphor interpretation. Grosz' approach indicates that one must also consider what the speaker is talking about; Reichman's analysis shows that certain phrases in the conversation play a special role in interpretation, while Webber indicates how the representation of quantifiers affects the interpretation of anaphor. All these approaches support the view that since hearers do not have privileged access to a speaker's mind, other than through what a speaker says, imposing structure on the speaker's discourse will provide a framework for establishing the interpretation of anaphors.

5.1.2 The Focusing Approach to Anaphora

One of the basic units of language communication is the discourse. Informally and intuitively, a discourse is a connected piece of text or spoken language of more than one sentence spoken by one or more speakers. If such an informal definition is to be helpful at all, some notion of what it means to be "connected" is needed. While there are many different properties which contribute to discourse connectedness, in this chapter I want to consider only one: the speaker or speakers talk about something, one thing at a time.

In a discourse speakers center their attention on a particular discourse element, one which I will call the focus. It is the element which is elaborated by a portion of the discourse. Sometimes speakers' discourses can be quite different; their discourses are incoherent or at least hard to follow because:

1a) they talk about several elements without relating
them or

1b) they talk about several elements without informing
the hearer that several elements will be
discussed at once or

2) they do not choose a central element for the
discourse.

In a nutshell, discourses with these properties are not connected, that is, they lack
an element which is focused on. The focus is then one of the connecting threads
that makes a text or a set of utterances a discourse.

Focusing is a discourse phenomenon rather than one of single sentences.
When a speaker uses several sentences about one focus, one would expect that it
would need to be re-introduced in each sentence. However, re-introduction is a
redundant and thus inefficient process; in fact, speakers do not use it.   If
re-introduction is not used, and still hearers claim to know what is being talked
about, there must be some means by which the discourse remains connected. In
fact, there are two ways. First, special words indicate to the hearer "that I am still
talking about the thing I talked about in the previous sentence;" traditionally
these signals are called anaphoric expressions. Second, speakers rely on assumed
shared knowledge in discourses; the speaker assumes that some connections
between the focus and some other elements are already shared with the hearer so
that she or he need not explicitly state what they are. Of course, there is a risk that
the connections are no longer obvious, resulting in a set of sentences which simply
confuse the hearer.

Now a possible line of investigation becomes clear. The focus and the
assumed shared knowledge can be used as one of the chief constraints on the
choice of the co-specification of anaphoric expressions.   Rules governing an
anaphor interpreter can be discovered which use these two sources of constraints.
In these rules the focus will play a central role as a source of co-specification. The
focus and the structure of assumed shared knowledge are significant to rules
governing the choice of anaphors because they capture the effects of what has
been talked about previously and what the speaker has assumed is knowledge that
is shared with the hearer.

This view of focusing and anaphora rests on four assumptions about the nature
of communication, each of which is true in most situations. First, the speaker is
assumed to be communicating about something. This assumption implies that the
speaker is not speaking gibberish, that the utterance contains referring expressions

and communicates some intention. The something which the communication is about will be called the <u>focus</u> of the discourse. Second, the speaker assumes that the hearer can identify the focus of the discourse. The speaker wants to communicate about something, and for the communication to occur, the hearer must be able to distinguish what the speaker is communicating about. Third, the speaker is not trying to confuse or deceive the hearer. The speaker uses referring expressions with the intention of referring to someone or something, or with the intention of describing something or some event. In Gricean ([Grice 1975]) terms, the byword is "Be perspicuous." Finally the speaker assumes the hearer has certain knowledge about the real world which can be used to reason about referring expressions during the communication process. Recent research ([Perrault and Cohen 1981], Allen (Chapter 2 of this volume) [Clark and Marshall 1978]), and the well known work of Searle [Searle 1969] and Austin [Austin 1962], describe models of the speaker's knowledge of what the hearer believes. In this chapter, the weakest form of such a model is assumed: the speaker assumes the hearer has enough real-world knowledge in common with the speaker to know about the entities in the real world which the speaker refers to and to know about the cognitive elements of the discourse which the speaker mentions; Webber (Chapter 6 of this volume) speaks of this assumption as that of shared knowledge between speaker and hearer. The speaker draws on that knowledge in constructing a message for a hearer. These four assumptions will play an important part in the discussion of co-specification interpretation which follows.

By viewing focusing as a process that chooses a focus as one of the elements of discourse structure, a new tool for interpreting anaphors becomes available. The focus of the discourse will act as an index to the specifications of referring expressions. For definite anaphora the focus is the locus of the specification information. Either the focus is the co-specifying phrase for an anaphor, when it meets certain syntactic, semantic and inferential knowledge restrictions, or else the the discourse representation of the phrase in focus can be used to generate the specification of the definite anaphor. Because representations and knowledge are essential to how an anaphor is interpreted, an explanation of focus is incomplete without some consideration of the way in which it is represented, and how it is related to other concepts people know about and other items mentioned in the discourse. The use of focus also requires another type of computational machinery, an inferring process, which is used to infer from general knowledge and other suppositions that a certain proposition is consistent with what else is known.

An example to illustrate the concept of focus will be helpful here. In the discourse below, the focus of discussion is the meeting of D2-1.

D2-1 I want to schedule a meeting with Ira.
    2 It should be at 3 p.m.
    3 We can get together in his office.
    4 Invite John to come, too.

All four sentences give information about the focused element. While D2-3 and 4 make no direct reference to the meeting of D2-1, as human hearers, we assume that these sentences are related to the rest of D2 because they can be interpreted as giving information about the focus *meeting*. D2-3 names the location of the meeting while D2-4 introduces an additional participant by use of *invite*, and by taking advantage of knowledge that people are invited to meetings.

If we assume that speakers know that meetings have associated places, times, participants, and purposes, then when a new instance of meeting is evoked, this knowledge can be used to understand what the speaker is communicating to the hearer about meetings. It also makes possible an explanation for how the hearer understands the role the pronouns play in the discourse; the pronouns co-specify the element in focus.

Of course, the co-specifier of a pronoun must be proposed by some process, a process which can interpret rules which restrict what might be the co-specifier and then test proposed co-specifiers. Thus in D2-2, once the focus is proposed as the co-specifier of *it*, this interpretation process must assure that meetings can occur at a particular time. To provide confirmation, an inferring process uses knowledge of the world to determine that meetings have times. This being so, the proposal of meeting as the co-specifier of *it* is accepted.

The explanation of the role of focus cannot be quite so simple because the focus of a discourse can change to a new element of the discourse. A means of recognizing this change is required in the model of the focusing process. For example, in D3 the focus begins on meeting, but the *it* in D3-3 has *my office* as its co-specifier, not the meeting. Detecting this co-specifier requires a means of noticing a movement of focus to *my office* and using the inferring mechanism to confirm the choice of the new focus as co-specifier.

D3-1 I want to schedule a meeting with George, Jim, Steve and Mike.
    2 We can meet in my office.
    3 It's kind of small,
    4 but we'll only need it for about an hour.

In addition to the comprehension of pronouns such as *it*, focusing will be shown to provide an explanation for the definite anaphora of *this* and *that*, as used in the discourses below. Since these definite anaphors have received little treatment in any literature, an explanation of their behavior as part of focusing will offer new insights about how language is understood.

D4-1 The axon may run for a long distance, sending off several
    sidebranches along the way,
2 before it terminates in an even finer network of filaments, the
    terminal arbor.
3 Man's longest axon runs for several feet, from the spinal column
    to muscles that control movements of the toes.
4 In spite of its great length, this axon, like all nerve fibers, is a part
    of a single cell.
5 It is living matter.
D5-1 I'm having a party tomorrow night;
2 it will be like the one I had last week.
3 That party was a big success
4 because everyone danced.
5 This one will have better food.
6 I've asked everyone to bring something special.
7 Want to come?

If focusing is to be viewed as part of anaphor comprehension, some process must choose, in a reliable way, what I have described loosely as the focus of the discourse. The process will be required to make use of representations of elements of a sentence that are linked to other memory elements because people seem to use just such information themselves. In addition, an interpreter will make use of the focus, as well as as syntactic, semantic, and-general knowledge restrictions, in determining the co-specifier of the anaphoric expressions. This brief description of a focus, the focusing process and the anaphor interpreter raises some questions which must be answered. What is the focus of the discourse, and how is it determined? What kinds of assumptions about the structure of the knowledge must be made in order to use a focus for definite anaphor disambiguation? What inferences are used in the prediction of co-specifiers? How does an anaphoric interpreter use the focus to interpret personal and *this/that* pronouns?

The answers to these questions will be provided in the new few sections. As the theory unfolds, I will also support the following claims about definite anaphora.

1. The role of focus in co-specification
   Focus and a knowledge network together determine the relationships among elements of the discourse. These relationships indicate ways in which co-specification with the focus can be accomplished.

2. Focused inferring
   Focusing controls the inference mechanism needed to determine a specification relationship between a focus and an anaphoric noun

phrase because inferring is used to confirm a hypothesized link between an anaphor and a focus.

3. Distinguishing and disambiguating definite anaphora

Focus, used with the representation of knowledge in (1), with Webber's representation (see Chapter 6) and with information describing sentence syntactic constraints, such as c-command, and semantic selectional restrictions, can distinguish those definite anaphora governed by discourse effects. It can be used to disambiguate their specifications as well.

The theory of focusing makes certain testable predictions, ones which are produced by the processes and interpreters that are to be described in this chapter. They will predict which representations are the specifications of anaphors and what decisions are made to find the representations. Since the theory relies on representations of knowledge, it also makes predictions and suggests constraints on both the structure and the content of these representations. In discussing all these predictions, I will illustrate the advances of the focusing theory over earlier work as well as explain the limitations of the theory for interpreting one class of definite anaphora.

5.2 The Definition of Focus

5.2.1 A Sketch of the Process Model of Focusing

A process model of focusing consists of three distinct processes, which function in a cycle for each sentence of a discourse. The first process chooses foci based on what the speaker initially says. Then an interpreter uses these foci and a set of rules of anaphor interpretation to interpret the anaphoric expressions in the discourse. This interpreter, like a human hearer, must "keep in mind" whatever other newly mentioned elements the speaker has introduced, since sometimes an anaphor may co-specify with one of these instead of the elements in focus. A third process updates the foci using the anaphoric interpretations chosen by the interpreter. During this last phase, the updating process will move one of the foci to a new element of the discourse, if the phrase previously in focus is no longer part of the information conveyed by the sentence. The three processes taken together sketch a simple process model of focus tracking; the model behaves like its human counterpart in the way it interprets anaphors and in the instances in which it fails to "understand."

The three process cycle can be illustrated with the example below.

D6-1 Last week there were some nice strawberries in the refrigerator.
  2 They came from our food co-op and were unusually fresh.
  3 I went to use them for dinner, but someone had eaten them all.
  4 Later I discovered it was Mark who had eaten them.
  5 Mark has a hollow leg, and it's impossible to keep food around
    when his stomach needs filling.

Suppose the first focusing process initially guesses that strawberries are the focus in D6-1. Next a pronoun interpreter would apply a rule that says "A pronoun that can be replaced by the focus phrase, with the resulting sentence remaining syntactically acceptable, co-specifies with the focus, unless some pragmatic knowledge rules out that co-specifier." to determine that strawberries can replace *they* in D6-2 with no syntactic failure. An inference process, governed by the pronoun interpreter, could confirm that strawberries can come from food co-ops and can be fresh; that is, no contradiction in general knowledge results. Finally, the third process can confirm strawberries as the focus since it has been re-mentioned and because other objects mentioned in D6-1, the refrigerator and the previous week, were not discussed in D6-2.

The focusing mechanism will be a useful theoretical tool only if it is coherent to talk about some element of the discourse as being in focus. While our intuitions as speakers and hearers led us to believe that there is something we talk about, the intuition is problematic because there appear to be many phenomena which function in distinguishing what it is that someone is talking about. One such phenomenon for marking focus are syntactic constructions, such as there-insertion sentences as (5) and cleft sentences as (6).

  (5) There once was a wise old king who lived on a mountain.

  (6) It was the butler who kidnapped the heiress.

Another phenomenon which marks focus is speech stress and prosodics: it appears that these mark what the speaker is most interested in talking about. In (7) if contrastive stress is put on Jeremy, the hearer might expect that the next sentence will say more about him.

  (7) I want one of JEREMY'S pictures.

In an upcoming section these and similar phenomena will be presented and analyzed in detail for their role in determining focus. In the theory that will be presented, the focus will be defined as that discourse element selected by the computational process; the process will be defined so that it takes into account all the phenomena. Hence, the definition of focus will be a function of the theory rather than an independently defined object.

5.2.2 The Representation of Focus

In the focusing theory, the element of the discourse in focus will be modeled as a data structure. Each of the phrases in a sentence, evoke such structures, which correspond to structures in the mental models of speakers and hearers; that is, each phrase specifies a piece of a mental database, which is represented in some way. In Webber's terms, these structures are "discourse entities" and the whole collection is a "discourse model." I will use the terms "cognitive elements" or "discourse elements" when discussing these structures because they are meant to be analogous to the structures in the mental models of speakers and hearers.

Since the cognitive elements are specifications, they bear a representational correspondence to objects in the speaker's world, and one must consider how these elements are represented. I will assume that each element is represented as a piece of a network of elements. The network contains many elements, but the focus is the element selected as primary among them for a given part of a discourse.

What kind of data structure is required for representing the focus? First of all, it is associative; that is, certain special associations are marked between elements of the network. The associations are special in the sense that an element has direct links to certain other elements but not to all elements. For example, **meeting** has built-in associations for a **time**, a **place**, a set of **participants**, and a **topic** of discussion, but it has no associations to color, cost or age. Each phrase in a discourse is encoded as an instance of the generic element specified by that phrase. Thus *a meeting* is encoded as an instance of the generic network element of **meeting** (existing prior to the discourse). With a hierarchical net, instances of generalized templates can be created, as in Figure 1.

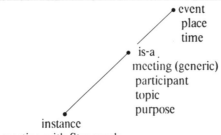

Figure 1 Instances of a general meeting element.

The data structure must also support two kinds of hierarchical links with the ability to inherit on both. One link expresses the is-a kind of relation; it allows properties from the network description of one element to be inherited by another. Thus the generic **meeting** is a conceptual element which is-a kind of **event**, and it inherits the associations of place and time from the is-a relation. The second relation with inheritance captures the notion of an instance type. This relation occurs between a conceptual element like **meeting** and a particular meeting like **meeting-with-Stanoczyk**. This element is a particular copy or instance of its parent node. Elements that are generics represent abstract kinds while instances represent objects in the world. Both may serve as the specification of a phrase in discourse.

The data structure needed must have other properties. It must also allow for the embedding of structure within structures, because these represent other discourse elements subject to discussion and re-mention. If we are told that John is eating an ice cream cone, the representation must show that the act of eating includes two sub-structures, one representing John and the other the ice cream cone. Finally the data structure must allow for a natural representation of scope of quantifiers; their representation is considered by Webber in this volume, and a discussion of how that representation may be used is given later in this chapter. These data structure characteristics are necessary for anaphor comprehension because loss of any characteristic has important effects on what anaphors can be comprehended, as we will see in the examples in this chapter.

The properties of a net structure expressed here are sometimes part of Artificial Intelligence representation languages (see KL-ONE, [Brachman 1978], OWL, [Hawkinson 1978], KRL [Bobrow and Winograd 1977] among others). These properties will be necessary in the discussions of focusing and anaphor interpretation that follow, so whichever representation language is used, it must have the features mentioned for the focusing theory.

The illustration of focus in figure 1 is slightly misleading because it suggests that the focus is only the computational encoding of the specification of a particular noun phrase. In fact, the process which establishes the specification of a noun phrase in focus must have access to the syntactic and semantic forms of the phrase. If they are left out, some anaphors will appear ambiguous, when in fact they are not. Unnecessary ambiguity can be illustrated using D7 below.

D7-1 The first man on the moon became a national hero.
   2 Due to his status, he rode in ticker tape parades, met public
      officials and was chased by autograph hunters.

The focus of this example is *the first man on the moon*. Suppose that the specification of that phrase is the focus as depicted below, without benefit of the referring definite noun phrase.

Database representation of:

FOCUS:

NEIL ARMSTRONG
Rank: colonel in U.S. Army
Father: 3 children
Achievement: first moon walker

The specification of *his status* will be ambiguous because Neil Armstrong has several roles in which he has status, those of father, colonel and moon walker. But *his status* in D7-2 is not ambiguous for human speakers. To avoid unnecessary ambiguity, the expression with its syntax and semantics must be included as part of the focusing process. Hereafter, focus will be spoken of as being on a particular noun phrase. This is an informal means of referring to the encoding of focus by the focusing process, that is, focus is encoded as a representation built by syntactic and semantic constructs of the noun phrase which points to another representation. its specification.

In addition to the focus, focusing must take into account the actors of the discourse. An actor focus is a discourse item which is predicated as the agent in some event. It is distinct from the main focus, which will be called the discourse focus. Actors can become the discourse focus only when no other item is available for focusing. Actors must be specified separately because (1) the focus of the discourse often is distinguished from the actor (see the example below), and (2) actors can be spoken of anaphorically at the same time that the discourse focus is pronominalized. As a result, different rules for governing mention of actors are needed.

A typical example of an actor focus can be found in D8.

D8-1 Jerome took his pigeon out on a leash.
2 Since he was trying to train it,
3 he hollered "heel" and "run" at it,
4 as they sauntered along.

The actor focus is just whoever is currently the agent in the sentence. When the agent of the next sentence is a pronoun, the actor focus is usually chosen for co-specifier. Jerome is the actor focus in the first sentence of D8. Using this actor focus, the co-specifier of *he* can be established as Jerome. At the same time, the discourse focus is on Jerome's pigeon. It is needed as well because the pigeon is re-mentioned using *it*, and since *they* in D8-4 co-specifies both Jerome and his pigeon. Bringing the the actor focus and discourse focus together is quite common, as shown below, where the discourse focus is needed to establish who actually went to the movies from among the three actors. Rules for anaphors co-specifying with actors will be discussed later.

D9-1 I wanted to go to the movies on Saturday.
2 John said he'd come too, but Bill decided to stay home and study.
3 So we went and afterwards had a beer. (*we = John, the speaker*)

5.2.3 Finding The Discourse Focus

For the focusing process to proceed, an initial discourse focus must be found as early as possible in the discourse. The focus recognition algorithm I will propose can be viewed as part of a bootstrapping operation. The focusing algorithm depends upon the selection of an initial focus, but on the basis of one sentence, it is not always possible to predict what the focus will be. To choose a focus, an initial prediction after the first sentence will be made, and then this selection, called the expected focus, will either be confirmed or rejected by the basic focusing algorithm on the basis of the anaphors in the discourse.

The expected focus algorithm can select an expected focus that is not the discourse focus. Luckily speakers talk in such a way that incorrect predictions are easily recognized, and better choices can be easily computed. Hence the basic focusing algorithm is designed to confirm the expected focus, and if it cannot, to choose an alternate phrase to be the focus. This method provides an effective algorithm because once a false prediction is recognized, an alternative phrase is always available.

Before I review the reliable focus indicators and the defaults, I want to point out how I judged which phrase was the discourse focus. In each example, I used the pronouns which occur in the second sentence of the discourse (if there are any) as a signal of discourse focus. Since pronouns contain little lexical information, they reflect what the speaker has focused on in the previous sentence, so that the focus is that phrase which co-specifies with the pronoun (I am assuming that co-specifiers can be reliably chosen on an intuitive basis by native speakers of English).

There are a few indicators of focus that are highly reliable means of marking focus. When these indicators are not present, the only criteria that remain permit a noun phrase or verb phrase to be selected on the basis of preferences for focus locations. One criterion which will not be discussed here is stress and prosodics. While it appears to affect anaphor comprehension in discourse, not enough is known about stress and prosodics to discuss these behaviors in computational terms. When they are better understood, perhaps new algorithms can be revised to incorporate their role.

There are a few sentence syntactic types that make recognition of focus easy since these sentence types have the purpose of singling out one discourse element from the others. These types are cleft, pseudo-cleft and *there*-insertion sentences as shown below:

(9) (pseudo-cleft agent) The one who ate the rutabagas was Henrietta.

(10) (pseudo-cleft object) What Henrietta ate was the rutabagas.

(11) (cleft agent) It was Henrietta who ate the rutabagas.

(12) (cleft object) It was the rutabagas that Henrietta ate.

(13) (agent) There once was a prince who was changed into a frog.

(14) (object) There was a tree which Sanchez had planted.

As the introductory sentence of a discourse, sentences (13) and (14) provide a means of introducing a new object or agent for further discussion. Sentences (9)-(12) rarely occur as initial sentences in a discourse since they assume there is some object already under discussion about which they provide new information; for example, (9) tells who ate the rutabagas, the rutabagas already being known about. As I will show in depth later on, sentences like those of (9)-(12) move the focus from one element to a new one. These examples suggest that *there*-insertion sentences mark an initial expected focus.

When an expected focus is chosen on the basis of semantic categories of a verb, the most reliable default is in the verb position of the theme.[1] In the two examples below the expected focus is indicated in parentheses.

D10-1 Mary took a nickel from her toy bank yesterday.

2 She put it on the table near Bob. (the nickel)

D11-1 Sandy walked her dog near a bull one day.

2 He walked quietly along. (Sandy's dog)

In D10, *it* co-specifies with a nickel. While it is inferentially acceptable for *it* to co-specify Mary's toy bank (since toy banks can be put on tables), on first reading, people understand the nickel to be the antecedent of *it*. A similar behavior occurs with D11. In these cases the noun phrase in a prepositional phrase following the theme cannot be the focus of the discourse unless the expected focus is explicitly overridden by a full definite noun phrase co-specifying with some other phrase of

---

1. This is Gruber's [Gruber 1976] term for the notion of the object case of a verb. His theory extends verb semantics to include verbs such as the ones below where the theme is located inside a prepositional phrase.

(15) We waited out the thunderstorm in a rundown old shack.

(16) Please focus on the star of India in the case on the left.

If the concept of theme is used as the default choice for expected focus, these examples fit naturally within the framework.

the initial sentence. For example, in D10-2, if *the bank* were used in place of *it*, the expected focus would be overridden in favor of bank.

In a sentence without a theme, that is, where only non-theme prepositional phrases are present, there does not appear to be a preference for expected focus. Most other thematic positions (instrument, goal and locatives) do not offer a strong preference for focus although some weak preferences sometimes appear. These weak preferences are for goal and any position in which an indefinite occurs. However, it is difficult to know how reliable these preferences are without some means of determining the role of stress and prosodics in these cases. Therefore, no claims will be made about preference for expected focus for these positions. Instead the algorithm for computing expected focus below will rely on a simple scheme of sentence surface order for these thematic positions.

One thematic position that is not preferred for discourse focus is the agent. When a pronoun occurs in a non-agent position, and in the preceding sentence, both an agent and a phrase in another thematic position can be its co-specifiers, the agent is not preferred, as is illustrated in the example below. Hence in the choice of expected focus, the agent is ordered last among possible noun phrase choices.

D12-1 A group at HXN developed a high speed technical chip packer.

2 The press gave it rave reviews.

Two sentence forms affecting focus do not depend on thematic position. One, is-a verbs, take the subject of the sentence as expected focus.

D13-1 The Personal Assistant group$_i$ is a research group that is designing pieces of a personal assistant program$_j$.

2 (a) Several graduate students and research faculty are members of it$_i$.

(b) * Several graduate students and research faculty are members of it$_j$.

While the predicate nominative is being associated with the subject in *is-a* sentences, it does not co-specify with the subject. Instead the subject is being described as having some particular properties, and hence is fundamental to the discussion. [1]

---

1. There are to-be nominal forms which do not contain the focus in subject position:

(17) A woman with great ideas is Amelia Michels. She is inspiring and works incredibly hard.

As far as I can tell, these forms are a kind of topicalization that is well marked (to the point of being grammatically odd for some speakers). In these cases, the subject is inverted from predicate nominal position and hence the focus is in nominal position instead of in the subject.

In the other non-thematic sentence form, the verb phrase can be expected focus as is evidenced by the use of *do-so* and *do-it* anaphora, as well as the sentential *it* anaphora shown below.

D14-1 Last week, we went out to the lake near my cottage.

2 It was a lot of fun.

Sentential anaphora seem to co-specify with an element representing the whole predication of the sentence while do-anaphora co-specify with the verb phrase. The verb phrase will be used in the list for expected focus, and the anaphor interpreter must determine whether just the verb or the whole sentence was the focus. Sentential *it* anaphora examples show that both theme and agent are preferred before the verb phrase. Examples such as D15 indicate that sentential *it* anaphora are not preferred as focus when a theme is present since the two uses of *it* co-specify bear, and not the capturing.

D15-1 Mike captured a bear.

2 Everyone said it made a lot of noise,

3 but I was asleep and didn't hear it.

The agent is preferred over sentential *it* as well. In D16, *it* co-specifies the bear although D16-2 is semantically neutral[1] between bear and the entire first sentence.

D16-1 One of the black bears got loose in the park the other night.

2 It frightened all the campers and generally caused panic.

To summarize, the choice of expected focus has been shown to depend upon the grammatical relations in a sentence, although a few sentence types can be judged on the basis of syntactic properties. This means of choosing is an alternative to the approach of [Baranovsky 1973] who used a list of discourse "topics" ordered by recency. The algorithm below chooses an expected focus on the basis of the preceding analysis of syntactic and semantic preferences; included in the algorithms are comments about the data structures and sentence information required for the decisions in the algorithm.

---

1. By "semantically neutral," I mean that the selectional restrictions on the thematic position in question do not rule out the use of either bear or the event of getting loose.

The Expected Focus Algorithm:

Choose an expected focus as:

1. The subject of a sentence if the sentence is an *is-a* or a *there*-insertion sentence.

    This step presumes information from a parse tree about what the subject, and verb are and about whether the sentence is there-insertion.

2. The first member of the default expected focus list (DEF list), computed from the thematic relations of the verb, as follows:

    Order the set of phrases in the sentence using the following preference schema:

    - theme unless the theme is a verb complement in which case the theme from the complement is used.
    - all other thematic positions with the agent last
    - the verb phrase

    This step requires a list of the surface order of the noun phrases, and a data structure which indicates which noun phrases fill which thematic slots in the verb. Such a data structure must be computed by a case frame mechanism such as the one reported in [Marcus 1980].

The expected focus algorithm is used to choose the discourse focus. An analogous algorithm to choose the actor focus can be defined. This algorithm would choose John as the expected actor in the sentence below.

(18) John rode his pony to the big meadow at the edge of the farm.

Were that sentence to be followed by a sentence with a pronoun in agent position, as below, the pronoun would confirm the expected actor focus as the actor focus.

(19) He liked to sing as he rode.

Later I will discuss the interaction between the actor and discourse foci.

5.2.4 Rejecting the Expected Focus

While the expected focus algorithm can always choose an expected focus, its choice may have to be rejected because the default position is overridden by other factors. Typically, this occurs when a pronoun, which does not co-specify with the expected focus, is used in the second sentence of the discourse, and no anaphor is used to co-specify with the expected focus. In the sample D17, the expected focus is the graduation party, but in the following sentence the use of *it* to co-specify with Cathy's house indicates that the focus is on the house.

D17-1 Cathy wants to have a big graduation party at her house.

2 She cleaned it up

3 so that there would be room for everyone.

Two questions come to mind: How can one recognize that the expected focus is not the focus? How can an alternative noun phrase be chosen as the focus? Recognition and selection both depend on the use of inferences about general knowledge. For example, in D17 the choice of party for *it* can be rejected since having cleaned up an event would be rejected as incompatible with other knowledge about cleaning. Following the rejection of the expected focus, a correct co-specifier can be selected because it is available in the previous sentence. To find it, each alternate default focus must be considered in turn, until one is found which is not rejected on the basis of general knowledge. When the focusing process runs again after all the anaphors are interpreted, the proper focus can be chosen.

The default expected focus can be rejected only when the inference mechanism clearly indicates that the predicted co-specifier is unacceptable. That is, the inference must contradict given knowledge from the discourse or be incompatible with other general knowledge. The fact that a noun phrase besides the expected focus might be acceptable as a co-specifier is irrelevant as long as the expected focus is acceptable. For example, in D11, repeated below, while the bull might be an acceptable co-specifier for *he*, it is not considered since the expected focus is acceptable.

D11-1 Sandy walked her dog near a bull one day.
    2 He trotted quietly along.

A matter which is related to the problem of rejecting a focus is how speakers recover from co-specification failures. Consider the following variation on D11:

D18-1 Sandy walked her dog near a bull.
    2 She saw how he threw back his great menacing horns.
    3 He certainly was an unusual looking dog and the name "Little
    Bull" fit him well.

After D18-2 the co-specifier of *he* seems to be the bull mentioned in D18-1. After the third sentence, the reader is likely to have discovered that the dog has been the focus all along and that this discourse is a bit bizarre. Virginia Woolf [Woolf 1957] points out that literature is interesting for the ways in which authors break rules. This chapter will only point out what rules can be violated. Why those rules are violated, and how native speakers recover from violations of those rules remains to be explained.

In summary, the expected focus can be rejected in favor of another phrase in the discourse. Rejection is possible only when the predicted co-specification between a definite anaphor and the expected focus is unacceptable. The rejected phrase must be retained for possible re-introduction later in the discourse.

5.2.5 Inferring and Focusing

Confirming the expected focus often requires inferring some truths and can be quite complex. [Winograd 1972] cites the sentence "The city council refused the demonstrators a permit because they feared violence," and he describes some of the knowledge needed to determine the antecedent of *they*. [Charniak 1972] presents numerous examples of general knowledge, and [Isner 1975] presents one approach to handling inference for Winograd's sentences. The crucial difference between these theories and the one presented here is that the focusing process predicts an anaphor's co-specifier and then an inferring process confirms the prediction. A contradiction may be reached, which indicates that the expected focus must be rejected. The inferring may be trivial: for D18, *he* as co-specifying Sandy's dog is rejected because dogs do not have horns. When inferring is complex, focusing is advantageous.

Focusing simplifies the inference process because it delimits the beginning and end propositions that the inferring process uses, and it governs which inference can be taken back if a contradiction results. Schemes such as Isner's depend upon unification to bind the pronoun *they* to a "constant" noun phrase. While [Rieger 1974] never stated how pronouns are to be resolved for his system, his methodology for inference suggests using unification in a manner similar to Isner. By contrast, focus techniques "bind" the pronoun to the specification of the focus and then look for an inference chain that supports the resulting sentence.

For Winograd's sentence and its dual, both given below, the use of actor focus rules predicts that *they* co-specifies the city council in both sentences (actor focus rules are pertinent because *they* is an actor in the sentence "they feared violence".).

> D19-1 (a) The city council refused to give the women a permit because
> they feared violence.
> (b) The city council refused to give the women a permit
> because they advocated revolution.

For D19-1a, the inference chain from "city council fears violence" to "city council refuses to give the permit" would be established by reasoning of the following form:

Form of reasoning:
- Find chain of inference from (CC fears violence) to (CC refuses (CC gives Permit Women)).
- If (X refuse (X gives Y Z)) is defined as caused by either:
   X is-Selfish or
   (X wants Y) or
   (X Dislikes Z) or

there is event (W) and (W is-undesirable-to X) and ((Z have Y) --> Occur W)

- Then the chain of inference must be found between (CC fears violence) and one of the above.

The first three disjuncts cannot be proven, so a chain must be found between (CC fears violence) and some event, which is undesirable to the council and which will occur if the women have a permit. If violence is taken as the event W, then one can easily deduce the second conjunct from: (CC fears violence) --> (Not (CC wants Violence)), and (Not (CC wants Violence)) --> (Violence is-undesirable-to CC). The third conjunct, that is, (W have Permit) --> (occur violence), cannot be established as true, although it is consistent with other information (no contradiction is reached). For focusing, consistency between the two ends of the inference chain is sufficient, while for traditional schemes, establishing of the third conjunct is necessary. Furthermore, for traditional schemes, the simple chain of inference above would not occur, because it is not known when the inferring process begins that it is the city council who fears violence.

For D19-1b, focusing predicts incorrectly that *they* co-specifies with the city council. Since a traditional scheme might also choose this co-specifier on its way to the correct solution, the significance of focusing follows from the control which occurs in inferring. This claim can be illustrated by the details of the inferring process. During the process of chaining from the city council advocating revolution to the council refusing to give a permit, a contradiction would be reached about the event of revolution being both advocated by the council (from the choice of co-specifier) and undesirable to the council (from the fourth conjunct of the definition of refusing above and general knowledge that city councils usually find revolution undesirable). Traditional schemes might search for another event W to infer about, while for focusing, the contradiction reached follows from the co-specifier choice. This choice is then retracted in favor of another focus choice, that is, the women advocating revolution. Hence the search is considerably reduced. Once the choice of women for *they* is made, inferring is also simplified just was it was for D19-1a.

A comment about finding contradictions in databases. Some research on truth maintenance systems ([Doyle 1978] and [McAllester 1978]) has experimented with constraint checking and developed algorithms for efficiently finding and undoing contradictions; these techniques have been developed as a means of reasoning mechanically in ways typical of the problem solving often needed by people. However, for a large scale problem, finding contradictions may still be impractical. One solution might be to choose a database that is a subsection of the whole database with the discourse elements or even the focus as the database core. As yet, no one has considered how to explore only certain "sub-sections" of a database for contradictions.

One might wish to argue against the use of inferring with focus on the grounds that for D19-1b there may be some other inference path chain between the city council advocating violence and the city council refusing to give out a permit; such a path would indicate consistency in the hearer's general knowledge of the world and would permit *they* to co-specify with the city council. If indeed such a path existed, the unlikely co-specifier would go through. But this choice would depend on a hearer thinking that city councils advocate violence, a very unlikely belief to hold. What hearers take to be the co-specifiers of anaphors does depend on what they believe, and were they to have such beliefs about city councils, we would expect them to produce such anaphoric interpretations.

Sometimes there is no other focus choice. If no other groups have been discussed before (20) is uttered, the focusing process would respond just as hearers do: reject the only available choice for the co-specifier of *they*.

(20) The council refused a permit because they advocated revolution.

On the focusing theory, the only possible co-specifier for *they* is the council, which would be rejected by the inferring process. Since no other choice is available, the focusing process will fail to find a choice, and the theory will predict that such sentences are odd. Conceivably, the speaker intended to say such an odd thing, or the speaker did not mean to say what was actually said. In either case, focusing does not eliminate the need for making inferences; it offers a constraint on how they are made. The complexity of the inferring process is constrained to asking for confirmation of the sentence predication, thereby eliminating combinatorial search for free variable bindings and non-terminating inferring.

5.2.6 An Algorithm For Focusing

I will now state the focusing algorithm which confirms or rejects the expected focus (found by the expected focus algorithm applied to the first sentence in the discourse), and in the case of rejection, determines which phrase is to move into focus; it is used for all sentences of a discourse except the first, where the expected focus algorithm applies. The algorithm makes use of several data structures: the current focus (CF), the alternate focus list (ALFL), which is initialized to either the default expected focus list (DEFL) or the potential focus list (PFL); and the focus stack; the latter two structures have not yet been introduced, and their purpose, as well as the condition given in steps 2 and 9, will be discussed below.[1] In the algorithm, the term "discourse initial" applies to the algorithm's first operation, which is on the second sentence of a discourse, while "in progress" applies to any of the later sentences.

The Focusing Algorithm

NOTE: The focus stack is initially empty when this algorithm is used.

NOTE: Before this algorithm runs, the current focus (CF) is set to either the default expected focus found from the expected focus algorithm or the discourse focus when discourse is in progress.

To confirm the current focus as focus or to reject the current focus for another focus in the next sentence of the discourse:

0. INITIALIZATION: Make note of the existence of do-anaphora, anaphors co-specifying the CF and ALFL, implicit specifications, anaphors which specify elements not in the discourse or the lack of an anaphor use.

1. DO-ANAPHORA: If the sentence contains do-anaphora, take the last member of the ALFL as the focus. Stack the current focus in the focus stack and halt.

2. FOCUS SET COLLECTION: When the discourse is in progress, if focus sets are being collected, and no anaphora occur in the current sentence, continue the collection. If some anaphor appears in the current sentence, use its co-specifier as the focus. Halt.

---

1. Steps 2 and 9 make use of focus sets. These will be discussed latter in the chapter. Step 7 of the algorithm makes use of implicit specification, a concept which will be not discussed here; the step is included to assure completeness of the algorithm. Implicit specification is important when considering the interpretation of full definite noun phrases, a topic not included in this chapter. For a discussion, see [Sidner 1979].

3. CHOOSING BETWEEN CF and ALFL: If there is an anaphor co-specifying the CF and another co-specifying some member of the ALFL, retain the CF as focus if the anaphor is not in agent position. If it is, take the member of the ALFL as focus. If both are non-agents, retain the CF as focus unless only the ALFL member is mentioned by a pronoun. In that case, move the focus to the ALFL member (Focus is moved by stacking the CF, setting the CF to the co-specifier of the anaphoric term, and then stacking any flagged implicit specifications as long as that specification is not the specification to which focus moves.). Halt.

4. RETAINING THE CF as FOCUS: If there are anaphors which co-specify only the CF, retain the CF as focus. Halt.

5. ALFL as FOCUS: If the anaphors only co-specify a member of ALFL, move the focus to it. If several members of the ALFL are co-specified, choose the focus in the manner suggested by the expected focus algorithm. Halt.

6. FOCUS STACK USE: If the anaphors only co-specify a member of the focus stack, move the focus to the stack member by popping the stack. Halt.

7. IMPLICIT SPECIFICATION: If a definite noun phrase implicitly specifies an element associated with the focus, retain the CF and flag the definite noun phrase as implicit specification. If specification is associated with member of ALFL, move focus to that member and flag the definite noun phrase as implicit specification. Halt.

8. LACK OF ANAPHORA: If there are no anaphors co-specifying any of CF, ALFL or focus

stack, but the CF can fill a non-obligatory case[1] in the sentence or if the verb phrase is related to the CF by nominalization, retain the CF and halt.

9. FOCUS SET INITIALIZATION: If there are no foci mentioned and the sentence is discourse initial, collect focus sets.

10. NO FOCUS USED: Otherwise if there are no foci mentioned, retain the CF as focus. For any unspecified pronouns, the missing co-specifier condition holds.[2]

To illustrate the focusing algorithm in action, its behavior will be traced during the recognition of the initial focus of D6, which is repeated below:

D20-1 Last week there were some nice strawberries in the refrigerator.
2 They came from our food co-op and were unusually fresh.
3 I went to use them for dinner, but someone had eaten them all.
4 Later I discovered it was Mark who had eaten them.
5 Mark has a hollow leg, and it's impossible to keep food around when his stomach needs filling.

D20-1 is a there-insertion sentence, so step 1 of the expected focus algorithm indicates that the expected focus is the subject of the sentence, that is, *some strawberries*. The focusing algorithm contains a note that the current focus is set to the expected focus, and the ALFL be set to the other phrases in D20-1, that is, *last week* and *the refrigerator* and the verb phrase. The state of the entire focusing process at the point in which D20-2 is encountered, is illustrated in Figure 2.

---

1. Obligatory relations are cases of a verb that must be filled or the sentence is odd as in "John sold." Non-obligatory cases need not be filled; in "John sold a book," one non-obligatory case is the person to whom the book was sold.
2. See section 4.4 of this chapter for a discussion of missing co-specifier uses.

CF: *some strawberries* --specifies--> database representation of strawberries

ALFL: *last week, the refrigerator,* verb phrase of D20-1

Sentence: D20-2

Anaphors: *they* co-specifies with CF

Processor: skips through steps 0-3 of the Focusing Algorithm
At step 4: CF is taken as focus

Figure 2 Action of focusing process for the start of D20-2.

The focusing algorithm causes step 4 to be applied to retain the CF of *some strawberries* as focus, because there are no do-anaphora, no focus sets and no anaphors co-specifying with members of the ALFL.

In the example above rules to be formulated later governing the choice of anaphors given a focus (in this case an expected focus) determine that *they* co-specifies the CF. Definite noun phrase interpretation, of which *our food co-op* is an example, will not be discussed here although it is treated fully in [Sidner 1979]. Now that the algorithm has been demonstrated on discourse initial sentences, we turn to the use of the algorithm for a discourse in progress where focus movement, the focus stack, and the alternate focus list play a role.

5.2.7 Focus Movement

Since speakers do not always talk about just one thing, the focusing process must provide for the focus of the discourse to change. In D6, the strawberries are discussed for a few sentences, and then the discussion moves to the person who ate them. Accounting for this movement is necessary for anaphor interpretation because the new discourse element may be co-specified in later sentences. This process of moving the focus will be called focus movement. The discourse below illustrates focus movement from *meeting* to *office* (in D21-3) and back to *meeting* (in D21-4).

    D21-1 I want to schedule a meeting$_j$ with Harry, Willie and Edwina.

        2 We can use my office$_i$.

        3 It's$_i$ kind of small,

        4 but the meeting$_j$ won't last long anyway.

How can one tell if focus movement has occurred? Judging from D21, one might guess that focus moves whenever a new term is introduced. A counterexample to this rule is the alternate form of D21 below.

D22-1 I want to schedule a meeting$_j$ with Harry, Willie and Edwina.

    2 We can use my office$_i$.

    3 It won't take very long,

    4 so we could have it in the conference room.

In D22-3, there is no focus movement. If the focus were moved to office and back to meeting, the moves would be unnecessary since all the sentences are about the meeting.

Focus movement is recognized in a manner which is akin to initial focus recognition. Any new term in the discourse is a potential focus. The sentence following its introduction may contain either an anaphor which can be confirmed as co-specifying with the potential focus or an anaphor which co-specifies with the element already in focus. If the anaphor co-specifies with the potential focus, the co-specification causes the potential focus to become the discourse focus.

With the above description there is no focus movement following D22-2 because no expression co-specifies with *my office*. For the original version, D21-2, the focus does moves because *it* can be taken to co-specify with the speaker's office,[1] and nothing co-specifies with meeting.

The two versions of D21 indicate the basic point of focus movement: when the sentence following a potential focus contains no co-specification with the potential focus, then focus movement does not occur. Since a potential focus does not always become the discourse focus, focus movement is like expected focus recognition; if one tried to predict a focus movement before the anaphor occurred, the prediction could be wrong, just as predictions of expected focus can be. Rather than consider focus movement a matter of prediction, it is best to think of it as a matter of recognition based on the anaphoric terms that follow in the discourse.

Potential foci have a short lifetime. If a potential focus does not become the focus after the interpretation of the sentence following the one in which the potential is seen, it is dropped as a potential focus. For example, at D22-3 *my office* is dropped. Hereafter if *office* is discussed, it cannot be referred to using *it* until some sentence re-introduces *my office* as a potential focus.

Since any new term in a sentence can be a potential focus, when several terms

---

1. Note that *it* cannot co-specify with the meeting because the tense of the sentence rules out the co-specification.

occur in one sentence, some means of choosing a potential focus is needed. Syntactic cleft constructions, as I have noted, indicate focus movement. In addition, one would expect that the theme should be the preferred position for a potential focus. In fact the same order used for default expected foci can be used for potential foci, except that the phrase which confirms the focus is not included in the list because it cannot be a potential focus. In English sentences, phrases which mention new information tend to occur towards the end of the sentence, while old information occurs at the beginning; this method of choosing potential focus captures that behavior.

In summary, the algorithm for determining the potential focus list (PFL) is:

> 1. If a cleft or pseudocleft sentence is used, the potential focus is the cleft item if and only if the element in non-clefting position co-specifies the focus. When it does not, the sentence is incoherent.

> 2. Otherwise order a potential focus list of all the noun phrases filling a thematic relation in the sentence, excluding a noun phrase in agent position and the noun phrase which co-specifies the focus if one exists. The last member of the PFL is the verb phrase of the sentence.

How strong is the focus/potential focus expectation? An indication of the strength of focus is given in the example below.

D23-1 Expert: Take off the bolts.
    2 Apprentice: I am loosening them with the pliers that used to be in one of the tool boxes. Where are they?

The use of *they* in the last sentence is difficult to understand. The expected focus is bolts and is confirmed by the use of *them* in the apprentice's first statement. The apprentice also introduces the pliers as a potential focus, but *they* cannot co-specify to either the pliers or the bolts (because, as the inferring process must determine, the apprentice knows where they are in order to do the task). Hence the use of *they* is strange. Some informants say that *they* could co-specify the tool boxes but that such a choice is forced upon them only as a last resort to find something that makes sense. Such odd readings are captured by the failure to use the focus or potential focus as the co-specifier of a pronoun.

In general, focus movement occurs only when there are definite anaphora that are used to co-specify something besides the focus; these anaphora signal the movement. However, there is one condition which does not follow this general rule. When two different anaphors co-specify with the focus and a potential focus respectively, and only one of the anaphors is a pronoun, there is no certainty about which will be focused on in the next sentence. Yet, there seems to be a preference for the focus to be marked by the pronoun use. In other words, pronouns seem to support a focus more strongly than anaphoric definite noun phrases do. Consider the case below:

D24-1 I got a new hat,

    2 and I decorated it with a big red bow.

    3 (a) I think the bow will brighten it up a lot. (*it* = the hat)

      (b) I think it will brighten up the hat a lot. (*it* = the bow)

    4 If not, I think I'll still use it.

After D24-2, the focus is the hat, co-specified by *it*, and the potential focus list includes *a big red bow*. Either form of D24-3 uses anaphors which co-specify the hat and the bow. D24-4 is syntactically and semantically neutral on the choice of hat or bow as antecedent of *it*. However, if the sequence D24-3a and D24-4 occurs, the *it* co-specifies hat, while if D24-3b is used, the bow is slightly preferred. This example suggests that unlike the general case, the element co-specified by the pronoun should become the focus. The second condition for focusing is: Whenever both the current focus and a potential focus are co-specified but only one of them is co-specified by a pronoun, the focus is determined by the pronoun co-specifier. This condition appears in the focusing algorithm as step 3.

Steps 2 and 9 of the focusing algorithm distinguish a feature unique to focus confirmation. The focus set initialization steps in the focusing algorithm are designed to recognize a discourse situation illustrated in D25.

D25-1 John and Mary sat on the sofa and played cards.

    2 Henry read a book.

    3 At 10 p.m. they went to Joey's Bar to hear a new rock group.

After D25-1 and 2, the focus of this discourse is not *sofa, cards* or *book*. It appears that D25 is about John, Mary and Henry and what they did for an evening. In other words, the focus in D25 is collected over several sentences. The expected focus algorithm will choose *sofa* as expected focus, while the focusing algorithm without step 9 would confirm the expected focus since no anaphors occur in D25-2. To capture the focus collection and to prevent confirmation when no anaphors occur in the initial part of a discourse, focus set collection is used. In collecting focus sets, discourse items in the same thematic position in each sentence are collected as one set. For D25, this method makes sets of (1) cards and book, (2) John, Mary and Henry, and (3) sitting, playing and reading actions. When D25-3 is processed through the focusing algorithm, *they* co-specifies with John, Mary and Henry, and so the three will be chosen as discourse focus.

The informal description of focus movement given here illustrates that focus confirmation and focus movement are similar behaviors. So similar are these behaviors that they can be formally described by one algorithm. That algorithm provides a statement of control flow and the details of the conditions for confirming or rejecting a focus.

The significance of a single algorithm for both processes must not be overlooked; the one algorithm provides a uniform treatment of two phenomena which at first glance appear unrelated, namely, expected focus confirmation and focus movement. Furthermore, the one algorithm indicates just how the two processes are similar. The similarity in expected focus confirmation and focus movement can be extended beyond the parallel between default expected foci and potential foci since there are syntactic structures which mark focus movement just as there are syntactic forms which mark initial focus. More importantly, the focusing algorithm shows that expected focus confirmation and focus movement are both processes which require additional mention of the element in focus to confirm the choice.

5.2.8 Backwards Focus Movement

In discourse, discussion may be returned to a previous focus, that is, the focus may eventually shift back to a noun phrase previously in focus. This process is called focus popping. In D21-4 the phrase *the meeting* co-specifies with a meeting previously in focus.

> D21-1 I want to schedule a meeting$_j$ with Harry, Willie and Edwina.
>
> 2 We can use my office$_i$.
>
> 3 It's$_i$ kind of small,
>
> 4 but the meeting$_j$ won't last long anyway.

To retain previous foci, a stack is used. Generally whenever an expression mentions an element listed as a focus in the stack, called the stacked focus, the focus is popped, and the stacked focus becomes the focus again. In terms of the focus movement algorithm, a stacked focus is considered as a possible focus choice following the discourse focus and potential foci list.

To claim that focus popping is in fact a stack behavior requires criteria for explaining why other behaviors cannot and do not occur. The basis for such claims requires further investigation which has not been undertaken here. Focus popping is described as a stack behavior because discussions in dialogues do return back to a previous focus without concern for intervening foci, and because once a focus pop occurs, the intervening foci are not mentioned without focus movement similar to the regular focus movement.[1]

A sample discourse will indicate why a stack notion seems to be the right one. In the discourse below, the focus moves from Wilbur to the book, to quarks, and to elementary field theory. Then a pop back to the book occurs. Once the pop is made, Wilbur can be co-specified by *he* easily. A stack representing the foci at the time that D26-8 is processed is given in Figure 3.

D26-1 Wilbur is a fine scientist and a thoughtful guy.

2 He gave me a book a while back which I really liked.

3 It was on relativity theory,

4 and talks mostly about quarks.

5 They are hard to imagine,

6 because they indicate the need for elementary field theories of a complex nature.

7 These theories are absolutely essential to all relativity research.

8 Anyway, I got it while I was working on the initial part of my research.

9 He's really a helpful colleague to have thought of giving it to me.

FOCUS: elementary field theories

FOCUS STACK: quarks
                   book
                   Wilbur

Figure 3 Stack of foci at D26-8.

The discussion of focusing so far has been concerned with <u>localized</u> movements of focus from one discourse element to another, from a second to a third and possibly back to a first. Focus-popping, however, is a non-local behavior because the focus may move past several foci in the stack to some element that has not be mentioned for a long portion of the discourse. Typically, this non-local popping back to an old focus is accompanied by the use of a definite noun phrase to specify the old focus. The definite noun phrase is a clear signal of

---

1. Current implementations of the focusing process have been designed with a simple last-in first-out stack to pop foci until the proper focus is found, since this type of stack reflects the popping back in a discourse.

what is being talked about because of its distinguishing noun phrase head. Pronouns can be used as well, but their use is more restricted and governed by the interpreter rules, which prevent a pronoun from co-specifying a stack item if the discourse or actor foci are acceptable co-specifiers. The interpreter rules, in connection with the focus algorithm, impose a kind of stacked focus constraint that maintains localized focus movement. In D27 a pronoun may be used to pop back to an old focus. There the focus begins on career in law and moves to the friends of the speaker, with a potential focus of *their jobs*. The *it* in the last sentence co-specifies with a law career and re-establishes it as focus.

D27-1 A: Have you ever thought of a career in law?

    2 B: I have some friends who are lawyers, and I've talked with

        them about their jobs, but I don't think it's for me.

In contrast some readers find D26 difficult because the transition at D26-8 is too abrupt for a pronoun to be used, especially if *anyway* is deleted from the sentence; *the book* in place of *it* seems to be more acceptable. This suggests that the stacked focus constraint should be modified so that pronouns are not interpreted to co-specify with items more than one position back in the stack. Rather than propose such a modification, some additional evidence about discourse must first be considered.

There are circumstances where the stacked focus constraint, in its original form or modified as suggested above, fails to account adequately for some language behavior. In some discourses, a pop back to an old focus can occur with a pronoun even though the pronoun could co-specify with the discourse or actor focus, and even when many foci intervene. In these cases the non-local, popping back movement occurs not only because a pronoun was used, but also because the hearer is aware of other structures that help him or her to discern where to pop to. These structures make it possible to use a pronoun to move the focus back without confusion. In the example below, *it* co-specifies with the pump, not the ratchet wrench, which was under discussion when D28-9 occurred. It appears that in conversations, words such as *ok* in combination with a discourse that reflects the task structure defined by [Grosz 1977], make it possible for speakers to use pronouns to co-specify with a phrase from an earlier part of the discourse.

D28-1 A: Bolt the pump to the base plate. There are 4 bolts, 4 nuts and 4 washers. ⟨here follows an explanation of where to put the bolts and what tools to use.⟩

2 B: I would like to know if I can take off the back plate.

3 A: You shouldn't have to. Are you having trouble with the bolts?

4 B: Yes

5 A: ⟨Now follows a long discussion of the use of the ratchet wrench, the extension and the socket for the wrench. The discussion ends with:⟩ You will use the 2" extension and a 1/2" socket.

6 B: It is bolted. Now what should I do?

The type of popping back in discourse illustrated here indicates that the focusing algorithm and the anaphor interpreter might be joined with a mechanism which recognizes the task structure assumed by a speaker. Just such a mechanism has been proposed by [Grosz 1977], and another one, for informal conversations has been sketched by [Reichman 1978]; how the algorithm and such mechanisms might be joined remains to be discovered.

5.2.9 Using the Focusing Algorithm for Movement

To make clearer how the focusing algorithm is used for focus movement, let us trace the action of the algorithm on the following example discourse.

D29-1 Alfred and Zohar liked to play baseball.

2 They played it everyday after school before dinner.

3 After their game, Alfred and Zohar had ice cream cones.

4 They tasted really good.

5 Alfred always had the vanilla super scooper,

6 while Zohar tried the flavor of the day cone.

7 After the cones had been eaten,

8 the boys went home to study.

Using the expected focus algorithm, the expected focus for D29-1 is baseball (it is the theme of the verb complement). There are two pronouns in D29-2, but only one is considered by the discourse focusing algorithm because *they* is in agent position. As shown below, because *it* co-specifies with the expected focus, the expected focus is confirmed as focus.

CF: *baseball* --specifies--> database representation of baseball

ALFL: verb phrase   FOCUS STACK: empty

Sentence: D29-2: They played it everyday after school before dinner.

Anaphors: *it* co-specifies with *baseball*

Processor at Steps 1-2: Not applicable

        at Step 3: CF taken as discourse focus since
                    anaphor co-specifies with CF

D29-3 also mentions baseball, by means of the definite noun phrase *their game*. This use is a case of lexical generalization of focus, a common means of referring with an anaphoric definite noun phrase. D29-4 shows a movement of the focus.

CF: *baseball* --specifies--> database representation of baseball

ALFL: *ice cream cones*, verb phrase FOCUS STACK: empty

Sentence: D29-4: They tasted really good.

Anaphors: *they* co-specifies with *ice cream cones* in ALFL

Processor at Steps 1 - 4: Not applicable

        at Step 5: Since no anaphor co-specifies with CF, stack CF
                 and take CF as *ice cream cones* plus its
                 specification. Discourse focus is CF.

D29-4 contains the anaphor *they*. Since, on syntactic grounds, it does not co-specify with the focus, the ALFL (set to the PFL before the start of the focusing algorithm) contains *ice cream cones*, an acceptable co-specifier for *they*, so *ice cream cones* is confirmed as focus. The old focus of baseball is stacked in the focus stack. In just this way, focus moves. In the remaining two sentences each ice cream cone is spoken about separately using definite noun phrases; this phenomenon, called co-present foci, will be discussed later.

We have seen that a process model of focusing and focus tracking consists of three sub-processes. The first, the focus recognizer, chooses an expected focus based on what the speaker initially says. Then an interpreter applies its rules of interpretation, which make use of the focus to interpret the anaphoric expressions in the next sentence of the discourse. A third processor, the focusing algorithm, updates the focus using the anaphor interpretations to decide either to confirm an initial discourse phrase as expected focus, maintain an established discourse focus, move the focus to a new phrase in the discourse or shift the focus back to a phrase which was once in focus. The interpreter and the focusing algorithm cycle through the remaining discourse. Our understanding of anaphor interpretation would not be complete without an explanation of the anaphoric expression interpreter; to illustrate its behavior and to provide a theory of anaphor interpretation, the rules it uses for personal pronouns and for *this-that* anaphora will be presented and explained.

5.3 Focus for Pronoun Interpretation

In this section, I will show how the discourse, actor, potential and stacked foci can be used by a rule-governed interpreter for finding the co-specifications of pronouns. I will discuss the general form of the rules and some of the interaction problems between the actor and discourse foci that must be resolved. Then I will turn to how the stacked foci are used in these rules. Following this discussion, I will review a number of examples where the pronouns interpreter cannot function adequately unless a representation of scope and related matters are included in the representation of specifications. Using Webber's representation in this volume, I will discuss how these are treated. Then I will point out some uses of pronouns which remain unaccounted for in the focusing theory.

The focusing theory assumes that when interpretation rules for anaphora are "run" by the interpreter, there are several groups of discourse elements available as possible co-specifiers: the discourse focus and its associated potential and stacked foci, and the actor focus and its associated foci. The interpreter must choose among these possible elements using constraints from sentence structure and semantics, and the hearer's knowledge of the world. In this section an account of the interpretations of pronouns for examples which have appeared previously will be given.

The proposal made here contains two implicit processing assumptions, (1) serial processing, and (2) end-of-sentence processing. By "serial processing," I mean that the interpreter checks a focus as a candidate for the interpretation of a pronoun, and then if that focus is unacceptable, checks alternate candidates in turn. By "end-of-sentence processing," I mean that pronouns are not interpreted until the entire sentence has been syntactically and semantically interpreted. Both of these criteria can be given up without undermining the focusing theory. One could envision processing in parallel by checking the foci and alternates and then determining the pronoun's specification from an ordering of all those candidates that meet the criteria of choice; for interpretation of pronouns before the end of the sentence, conceivably the pronoun interpreter could choose a specification from available information and then review it as more of the sentence is processed. These two implicit processing assumptions have been made because they simplify the account of focusing and because they reflect an implemented version of a system with focusing. Further research will indicate whether these assumptions are too strong--if so, the focusing theory can be revised.

5.3.1 Using Focus for Pronoun Interpretation Rules

To begin the discussion, let us consider a pronoun interpretation rule that follows naturally from the discussion of focus and focus movement in the first half of this chapter. This rule is not adequate for reasons I will discuss below and will be revised over the course of the section.

> R1: If the pronoun under interpretation appears in a sentence thematic relation other than agent, choose the discourse focus as the co-specifier unless any of the syntactic, semantic and inferential knowledge constraints rule out the choice. If the pronoun appears in agent position, choose the actor focus as co-specifier in the same way.

Ruling out a co-specifier on the basis of syntactic and semantic constraints is accomplished by computing the various syntactic relationships and restrictions (such as Lasnik's disjoint reference rules) and by use of semantic selectional restrictions (such as those of Fodor and Katz discussed in the beginning of this chapter) on sentence thematic categories. For inferential knowledge, the inferring process discussed earlier is used.

When a suggested co-specifier for a pronoun must be given up, R1 does not suggest how to proceed in using either the actor or the discourse focus to find some other choice for a co-specifier. It is here the potential foci are used, as illustrated in the example below.

D29-1 Alfred and Zohar liked to play baseball.

2 They played it everyday after school before dinner.

3 After their game, Alfred and Zohar had ice cream cones.

4 The boys thought they tasted really good.

5 Alfred always had the vanilla super scooper,

6 while Zohar tried the flavor of the day cone.

7 After the cones had been eaten,

8 the boys went home to study.

Alfred and Zohar are the initial actor focus while baseball is the initial discourse focus. D29-2 contains two pronouns, *they* and *it* which, according to R1, co-specify respectively with Alfred and Zohar, and baseball. D29-3 uses *their,* which co-specifies with Alfred and Zohar, but is not accounted for by rule R1. Furthermore *they* in D29-4 does not co-specify with baseball but with ice cream cones. How does the interpreter conclude these facts?

R1 must be extended in a manner that takes advantage of the potential foci, discussed earlier, that are available to the focusing algorithm and the anaphor interpreter. The potential foci can be used whenever the current actor or discourse focus is ruled out by criteria from syntax, semantics or inferential knowledge. Thus since *they* in D29-4 cannot co-specify with baseball (on both syntactic[1] and semantic [2] grounds), a potential focus is chosen. Whether the potential focus becomes the actor or discourse focus depends on whether the pronoun is used as an agent. In D29-4, *they* is the theme, so the discourse potential foci are used. The first potential focus which meets all the constraints is chosen as the co-specifier; in D29-4, ice cream cones is the first acceptable potential focus which meets all the necessary constraints as a co-specifier for *they.*

Use of R1 modified in this way follows hand-in-hand with the focusing algorithm discussed previously. The algorithm updates its discourse model after each sentence by tracking pronoun use. When a pronoun is used to co-specify a new potential focus, either the discourse focus or actor focus moves to that potential focus; which focus moves depends on whether the pronoun fills the agent position in the verb frame, and in the case of multiple agents, whether the ongoing actor focus is re-mentioned. For example, after D29-4, the discourse focus changes to ice cream cones because *they* co-specifies with the ice cream cones; the boys remain the actor focus, since *they* is not an agent case for *taste* and since the boys were already the actor focus.

The pronoun interpretation rule takes into account the movement of focus and

---

1. *They* is a plural pronoun while baseball is singular.
2. The discourse items filling the object case of taste should be tastable items.

constraints on syntax, semantics and inferential knowledge. However, some additional pragmatic criteria need to be added to deal with the interactions between actor and discourse foci, because a pronoun in agent position may co-specify with the discourse focus rather than the actor focus! One such example of this observation is below.

D30-1 I haven't seen Jeff for several days.

2 Carl thinks he's studying for his exams.

3 but it's obvious to me that he went to the Cape with Linda.

Although Carl is the actor focus after D30-2, and *he* in D30-3 is an agent thematic relation in the embedded sentence, the proper choice for the co-specifier of *he* is Jeff. Rather than suggest that Carl is considered as the co-specifier and then is ruled out (which seems unlikely as there are no syntactic, semantic or knowledge constraints which eliminate it), one might ask whether Carl is ever even considered for processing. In D30 it appears not. The discussion is about Jeff, who is introduced first, while the actors seem relatively incidental. In general such cases are resolved because if the discourse focus is animate and is established earlier in the discourse than the actor focus, the discourse focus takes precedence even for pronouns in agent position. In essence this approach takes the discourse focus as primary, the discourse focus being what the speaker is talking about so far while the actor focus is the locus of information about actions in the discourse.

This precedence rule does not indicate what to do when the discourse focus and actor focus are both animate, have the same gender, number and person, and are both established during the same sentence of the discourse. Interestingly enough, people sometimes have difficulty choosing interpretations in such circumstances. In D31-2a below, *he* co-specifies with *John* (the actor focus) but if D31-2b followed D31-1, *he* may co-specify with either John or Mike (the expected discourse focus).

D31-1 John called up Mike yesterday.

2 a. He wanted to discuss his physics homework.

b. He was studying for his driver's test.

In these cases, native speakers report that the co-specifier for the pronoun is ambiguous. If the pronoun fills an agent relation, the actor focus is preferred, but this preference is not a strong one. It appears that in such cases the ambiguity may not be easily resolved unless additional information about the two foci is known that stipulates that the sentence is true of only one.

What about the interpretation of possessive pronouns such as *their* in D29-3?

The general rule for possessives[1] can be formulated as: if the discourse focus and actor focus were not established in the same sentence of the discourse, then the discourse focus is the co-specifier (if acceptable on the usual grounds); if the discourse focus was unacceptable, the actor focus is checked for acceptability and that failing, the potential discourse foci are considered; if both were established in the same sentence, the use will be ambiguous. As in the interpretation of personal pronouns, this rule shows that the discourse focus take precedence as the co-specifier. Unlike the case of personal pronouns, *their* is ambiguous between agents and other discourse elements; when the precedence of the discourse focus cannot be established, ambiguity occurs. Only when the discourse focus is not a possible co-specifier, can the actor focus be considered without ambiguity.

Another source of ambiguity occurs when an actor and one potential actor are both present in a previous sentence where the discourse focus is a non-animate element. An example is given below. Suppose that sentence (21) below followed each of (22), (23), (24) and (25).

(21) He knows a lot about high energy physics.
(22) Prof. Darby will tell Monty about the neutron experiment.
(23) Prof. Darby will lecture Monty on the neutron experiment.
(24) Prof. Darby will help Monty with the neutron experiment.
(25) Prof. Darby will teach Monty about the neutron experiment.

Some native speakers find all of these sentence pairs ambiguous, while some native speakers find only the pair (22) followed by (21) ambiguous. These examples are surprisingly similar to D31. How do some speakers decide that *he* co-specifies with Monty or Prof. Darby? It appears that they make a comparison and choose between the actor focus and the potential actor on the basis of evidence for their preferred interpretation. When that evidence is not forthcoming, informants are confused. Such a behavior suggests that the inferring process postulated thus far should be capable of a special judgment when given one actor and one potential actor; it must weigh its findings, and choose one of the two candidates as superior.

What kind of evidence can be used in such cases? The hearer knows that there is some person named Monty, who is probably male, that there is a professor named Darby, possibly male as well, that Darby is giving information to Monty about some physics experiment, the experiment being marked by the definite article as known to the hearer, as well as some criteria for determining who knows a lot about high energy physics in the context of teaching, helping, or lecturing.

---

1. Some special cases require a few additional rules that are discussed fully in [Sidner 1979].

A computational system that makes such judgments must have a very rich knowledge base (that is, to know that Monty is a male name, that professors can be male, that professors are experts, that neutron experiments are physics experiments) and be able to draw inferences from that base. None of this is surprising; however, a computational framework for carrying out such subtle judgments is still beyond the state of the art. The matter of weighing evidence to decide between two candidates is similar to the semantic choice mechanism postulated by [Marcus 1980] for parsing certain kinds of structures such as prepositional phrases. This device, when attaching prepositional phrases, asks the semantic processor about its preferences for making the attachment.

In summary, this kind of ambiguity can be generally handled with the following condition.

POTENTIAL ACTOR AMBIGUITY CONDITION:

Whenever a pronoun may co-specify with the actor focus, and a single potential actor exists, expect a possible ambiguity. To resolve it,

1. Look for evidence supporting the statement in which the pronoun occurs, evidence which is true of the actor focus as the co-specifier, but not of the potential actor. If this is found, the actor focus is the co-specifier.

2. Choose the potential actor when evidence exists for it but not for the actor focus.

3. However, if there is evidence true for both, choose the actor focus but indicate possible ambiguity.

A summary of a full set of rules for interpreting possessive and personal pronouns can be found in [Sidner 1979]. In this section we have considered their motivation and general form. These rules represent what can be said about pronoun interpretation in the absence of any additional information in knowledge representation beyond that suggested in the discussion of co-specification. To interpret certain pronouns, such as those where a co-specifying phrase does not precede the pronoun in the discourse, as in the previously given D1, we must consider how knowledge is structured and represented. It is to this matter that we now turn.

5.3.2 Focus and Knowledge Representation

[VanLehn 1978] presents extensive evidence for the view that people do not normally disambiguate the scope of certain ambiguous quantifiers when understanding sentences such as D32-1.[1]

    D32-1 Wendy gave each girl Bruce knows a crayon.

        2 She used it to draw a Christmas card for her mother.

He reviews the major theories of scoping phenomena and concludes that disambiguation of quantifier scope does not seem to take place during parsing or semantic interpretation of a sentence and that the determination of quantifier scope is the result of other linguistic processing.

To explain the comprehension of D32 above, some underlying semantic form representing scope is needed at some point in the processing of the discourse. In this volume, Webber argues why a representation of scope is needed and what the representation should be. What remains to be determined is when it is used. The pronoun interpreter requires such a representation, for example, to choose the proper co-specifiers of *she* and *it* in D32-2. The interpreter's behavior indicates that such a representation is needed, not in the initial determination of a focus, but in the process of determining the pronoun's co-specifier. This use of scope information is compatible with Van Lehn's findings because interpretations of scope are not considered until additional discourse material beyond the single sentence is presented.

A crayon in D32 may be used to specify objects which can be represented by the formal representations of Webber (Chapter 6 in this volume). Rather than list the actual formal notation, a paraphrase will be presented.

> The first representation (call it R1) expresses that there is a unique set of entities that are crayons and were evoked in D32-1. The members of the set are distributed so that each one was given by Wendy to some one of the girls Bruce knows. The representation leaves open whether all the crayons were given out, but makes explicit the fact that all the girls got crayons.

> The second representation (call it R2) represents *a crayon* as a unique singleton object that is a crayon and was evoked in D32-1. It was given by Wendy to a unique entity that is a girl and that is prototypic of the girls Bruce knows.

---

1. Some informants find this example unacceptable English because they cannot decide whether she in D32-2 is Wendy or someone else.

A third representation (R3) (which is a possible reading only for some speakers) can be derived from R1 by interpreting *a crayon* as a unique set having only one member. This corresponds to the reading that there was only one crayon given (in a collective way) to the set of girls Bruce knows.

Suppose now that D32-1 is vague, and no processing of it adjudicates the two readings (R1) and (R2) for *a crayon*. When the focus algorithm runs after D32-1 is processed, *a crayon* will become the discourse focus, but its representation either will not distinguish between (R1) and (R2) or will list both as possible representations.[1] When the pronoun interpreter uses its rules to choose a co-specifier for *it* in D32-2, both readings must be available. The set reading (R1) may be eliminated immediately because of syntactic constraints that rule out a co-specifier for *it* with that reading, so (R2) is left, forcing a reading for *each girl* as the prototypic girl. If however, a speaker accepts (R3) as an alternative reading, then D32 is ambiguous since both one crayon (R3) and a prototypic crayon (R2) are available to focusing.

To determine the actor focus specification for *she* in D32-2, the ambiguity between Wendy and *each girl* must be resolved since this is a case of potential actor ambiguity. Actually the interpretation is three ways ambiguous; there is Wendy, *each girl* interpreted as a set as in (R1) and (R3), or as a prototype as in (R2). The set reading may be eliminated immediately because *she* is singular. For the anaphor interpreter to choose between the remaining two, the inferring process must rule out one of the readings and find the other acceptable. Many hearers cannot choose between Wendy and the prototypic girl; in fact numerous native speakers find D32 odd, presumably because neither choice is particularly sensible for them. On the whole, the focusing rules suggest just what people do - they rule out several readings (all of which can apply after D32-1) and then they fail to choose given the discourse actor ambiguity.

Another case of semantic ambiguity, similar to the one in D32, is illustrated in D33 below.

D33-1 Sally wanted to buy a vegomatic.

2 She had seen it advertised on TV.

A vegomatic may be interpreted specifically, to mean there is one particular

---

1. Both [Martin 1979] and Webber [Chapter 6 of this volume] have asked whether a sentence which is ambiguous between several readings must be represented by several different structures, one for each reading. Martin proposes representations that preserve ambiguity until some processor demands a refinement. Whether this approach or an alternative representation listing all readings is best is still an open question.

vegomatic, or non-specifically[1] , to mean it is one of the many vegomatics. The focus does not distinguish between the two after D33-1 because, like D32-1, D33-1 is ambiguous, and neither interpretation can be chosen with certainty. When *it* is resolved for co-specification in D33-2, both readings can be considered, and the inferring process must determine that Sally saw a specific one on TV. Notice that the vegomatic Sally saw is not identical to the one she wanted to buy; in D33-2, *it* does not co-specify with Sally's vegomatic. Therefore the pronoun specification must be generated accordingly--a specific one seen by Sally on TV.

Suppose, for a moment, that D33-1 is interpreted so that a representation that maintains ambiguity is available. When the pronoun interpreter processes a subsequent sentence with a pronoun, it need only rule out readings if the the inference machine discounts as contradictory one of the readings (Sally didn't want to buy the very one she saw on TV). If no reading is ruled out, the co-specifier would remain ambiguous, so that both the indefinite phrase and the pronoun would have ambiguous co-specifications. As the next example shows, there is some evidence for this behavior.

Consider the case shown in D34.

D34-1 Sally bought a vegomatic that had a broken cutting blade.

2 She had seen it advertised on TV.

A vegomatic that had a broken cutting blade in the context of D34-1 usually means some particular vegomatic that Sally bought. However, *it* is ambiguous among the vegomatic Sally bought, some one vegomatic and a vegomatic that is an instance of the generic vegomatic; that is, "it" is ambiguous among three readings, Sally's vegomatic, and vegomatics taken as the specific and non-specific readings.

For D34-2, pronoun interpreter does not distinguish among the three readings since it accesses the one provided by the specification in D34-1, which is the specific reading. To find the specification of "it," the inferring process must discover that it is odd (1) for Sally to have seen the vegomatic with a broken blade which she bought being advertised on TV, and (2) for Sally to see any broken vegomatics on TV, and (3) for Sally to have seen the very one she bought on TV. Then if no other choices for co-specification are available, the specification of vegomatic from D34-1 must be used to generate an appropriate specification for "it". Since only unbroken ones not bought by Sally are appropriate, the

---

1. The terms 'non-specific" and "specific" are traditional semantic expressions which bear no relation to "specify" and "specification." A non-specific reading of *a dog* corresponds in computational terms to a representation of an instance of the generic dog, that is, what is represented is a dog which has the characteristics of the generic dog - that is, an animal with four legs, a tail, medium size, brown, friendly, barks, and the like.

specification of "it" must be generated using only part of the phrase from D34-1.

This example seems problematic because it places much weight on the inferring process to decide that certain readings are odd. However, this is likely to be just where the weight of the decision ought to be; many native speakers find D34 slightly bizarre because their first reading is that Sally had seen a vegomatic with the broken blade advertised on TV. In fact, it appears that when a specific indefinite noun phrase such as *a vegomatic* is introduced, the speaker can direct attention to the non-specific reading more readily with a plural pronoun, as shown below.

(26) She had seen them advertised on TV.

The plural non-specific reading as in (26) has been incorporated in the pronoun interpretation rules, but the generation of specifications for the singulars in more unusual cases, such as D34-2, has not; it is difficult to recognize that a specification should be generated when the inferring process rejects the two readings. However that people falter in such cases suggests that some additional, possibly general, problem solving behavior is relevant to the proper treatment of these cases.

Examples such as D34 are perplexing for another reason; they are examples of what I will call, following [Fahlman 1979], the "copy phenomenon". The ambiguity centers around the fact that there can be many copies of an abstract prototype. Automobiles, computer programs, airplane flights and money are other common cases of entities which exhibit the copy phenomenon. In D35, the interpretation of *it* depends on whether the speaker is referring to a particular flight or the normal Sunday flight, a copy of which occurred on *this Sunday*.

D35-1 TWA 384 was so bumpy this Sunday I almost got sick.

2 It usually is a very smooth flight.

Note that the *it* cannot co-specify with the particular flight on *this Sunday*. However, it is possible that the speaker intended TWA384 to refer to a particular flight; if this is so, the speaker mixed the specific and non-specific interpretations for the co-specifier of *it*, just as in D34-2.

Another characteristic use of anaphora is the bound variable case given by Partee [Partee 1972, 1978]. In D36 below, *him* co-specifies with Archibald, while if *himself* were used, it would constitute a reflexive use of *every man*.

D36-1 Archibald sat down on the floor.

2 Every man put a flower in front of him.

In linguistic theory, bound variables are assumed to be represented in sentence semantics; when used in conjunction with syntactic disjoint reference rules, pronouns within the scope of the quantifier can be distinguished from non-scoped ones. Since the pronoun interpreter takes account of these conditions, it can easily choose a proper co-specifier for *him* in D36 in terms of the focus, but for *himself* it will recognize the bound relation to *every man*. It is crucial to these cases that part of the representation of the interpretation of sentence phrases is some scope of quantification, especially when it is unambiguous.

5.3.3 Focus Restrictions on Co-specification

There are other restrictions on co-specification that result from the processing of the focusing algorithm. As discussed previously, the focusing algorithm can access a stack on which old foci are stored. In addition to co-specifying with current actor and discourse foci, a speaker may use a pronoun to co-specify a discourse element that was once in focus but is no longer; [Grosz 1978] described and illustrated this behavior for anaphoric noun phrases in task oriented dialogues. It can be captured in the pronoun interpretation rules by a rule which selects candidates from the focus stack. However, there is a constraint, called the stacked focus constraint, on this use due to the nature of the focusing algorithm. An anaphor which is intended to co-specify with a stacked focus must not be able to co-specify with either the focus or potential focus. An example from a literary text[1] where a pronoun co-specifies with a stacked focus is presented below.

> Was that old lady evil, the one Saul and I had seen sitting on the porch? I had dreamed about her. When the trolley car took me and Saul past her house again this morning, she was gone. Evil, it had a queer sound to it in English.

> {Here the narrative moves on to an incident in a school classroom. A discussion between the speaker and a male teacher ensues for five paragraphs. The succeeding paragraph begins:}

> She had worn an old brown coat and a green scarf over her head.

In this example, *she* co-specifies with the old lady discussed previously. If Potok had told of a discussion between the speaker and a female teacher, it would no longer be possible to tell that *she* was co-specifying with the old woman. The reading of *she* as teacher might be a bit surprising because what the teacher is wearing was not relevant to the previous conversation, but it certainly is not the

---

1. "In the Beginning" by Chaim Potok, page 212, chapter 4, Fawcett Publications, Inc. Conn, 1975.

case that an inferring process would decide that teachers do not wear old brown coats and so forth.

The stacked focus constraint is not stated directly within the focusing algorithm. Rather it is implicit in its function. The following situation is ruled out by the manner in which a focus is used: A pronoun cannot co-specify with a stacked focus when a current focus is an acceptable co-specifier, since that current focus will be taken as the interpretation, and the stacked focus will never come into consideration. The stacked focus constraint is a consequence of the movement of focus in the focus machinery.

The stacked focus constraint, however, may be overridden. An astonishing set of examples was identified by Grosz (see [Deutsch 1974], [Deutsch 1975]). One such example was given previously (D28), and another is shown below.

A: One of the bolts is stuck and I'm trying to use both the pliers and the wrench to get it unstuck.
E: Don't use the pliers. Show me what you are doing. Show me the 1/2" combination wrench.
A: Ok.
E: Show me the 1/2" box wrench.
A: I already got it loosened.

Generally readers understand this example without taking enough time to go back and test the intervening co-specifiers before choosing one of the bolts in this example.[1] Instead some other process is helping drive the understanding of what is meant. One explanation is that understanding depends on knowing that something being loosened completes the task that A originally indicated in the first sentence. The focus of A's first command indicates exactly what is bolted. Thus the focus could provide the co-specification for the object under discussion, but some other mechanism, which interprets completion of task goals, indicates where to pop back in the set of task environments under consideration. The focus relevant for that task environment is used to determine the co-specification of a pronoun.

How many such discourse interpretation mechanisms exist? While this chapter does not address this question directly, some speculation is possible due to research reported elsewhere (see [Grosz 1981], [Sidner 1979], [Robinson 1981]). In general, it appears that discourses permitting violations of the stacked focus constraint must contain an implicit structure of tasks pertinent to the conversation

---

1. This informal evidence needs to be tested out in a psychological laboratory. The author has not done so, but the results of such experimentation would be helpful.

or some other well specified structure which guides the hearer in understanding. Without this structure the hearer has no means for choosing something other than the current focus as co-specifier.

5.3.4 Pronouns Which Have No Co-specifiers

The previous discussion has assumed that a pronoun is always preceded by a co-specifying phrase. However, this is not always the case, and a complete theory of pronoun interpretation must address cases where the co-specifying phrase appears <u>after</u> the pronoun; and where <u>no co-specifying phrase exists</u> but one is implied by the discussion.

Pronouns which are used with their co-specifiers appearing after the occurrence of the pronoun have been called backward anaphora in the linguistic literature; I will refer to them as <u>forward co-specifiers</u>. Two such examples, (27) and (28) are given below.

(27) If <u>he</u> comes before the show, give <u>John</u> these tickets and send <u>him</u>
        to the theatre.

(28) Near <u>him</u>, <u>Dan</u> saw a snake.

In general the pronoun co-specifies with some noun phrase interpretation, but the phrase is placed forward in the discourse. The types of sentences in which this behavior can occur are limited. In general it seems to be permitted for fronted sentential prepositional phrases (as in (28)), for complement sentences fronted on another sentence (as in (27)), and for sentences containing co-ordinating conjunctions. Extensive research in linguistics on forward co-specifiers ([Solan 1978] contains a good review) gives reliable evidence that it is governed by structural constraints. In particular, syntactic rules can be stated that determine when forward co-specifiers are not permitted. The most recent formulation, by Solan, called the backward anaphora restriction, fails on certain sentences such as *In her room Mary saw a ghost*, so further research is still needed.

Whatever the best formulation of the syntactic rules for forward co-specifiers, they are preferable only in initial sentences of a discourse. For example, when a sentence such as (27) occurs in mid-discourse, if a speaker has been talking about Henry, and just begun mention of Charles, <u>he</u> will be taken (by native speakers) to co-specify with Henry, or with Charles, if Henry can be ruled out on basis of some special pragmatic knowledge. The focus rules can capture just this behavior when used in conjunction with the proper syntactic rules .

The pronoun interpreter acts on a condition that will be called the <u>missing co-specifier condition</u>. In the remainder of this section, I will define that condition. The pronoun interpretation rules include a rule for recognizing a missing co-specifier, and this recognition forms the basis of the condition to which the focusing algorithm responds.

There are many uses of pronouns where the pronoun has no co-specifier in the preceding discourse, where the pronoun is not used to co-specify forward, and where it is not used in conjunction with some action such as pointing. One such use, pronouns that specify a generic from a non-specific reading, has already been considered. However, such a case is distinguished from the ones given below because the pronoun is not used to specify a generic which is generated from the focused noun phrase; rather the pronouns below specify without a generating phrase. The examples given below are from several sources; the first three are from [Postal 1969], the fourth from [Chafe 1972], the fifth from dialogues collected for the PAL system ([Sidner 1978]), and the last was spoken by a lecturer at a presentation this author attended.

D37-1 I saw Mr. Smith the other day; you know, <u>she</u> died last year.

2 John is an orphan. He misses <u>them</u> very much.

3 Pro-Castro people don't believe <u>he</u> is a monster.

4 I went to a concert last night. <u>They</u> played Beethoven's ninth.

5 I want to meet with Bruce next week. Please arrange <u>it</u> for us.

6 I used to be quite a tennis player. Now when I get together
with the young guys to play, I can hardly get <u>it</u> over the net.

With the exception of D37-1, most hearers are able to say which is the intended specification of the pronoun in the cases above; D37-1 can be understood if the hearer is informed that Mr. Smith had a wife. However, some of these, especially 1 and 2, are so odd that most hearers read the sentence several times before comprehending. Hearers are divided on the acceptability of 3, and most hearers find 4 and 5 acceptable. Such examples, as far as I can tell, do not occur naturally in written samples.

While these uses of pronouns can be recognized by the rule interpreter, how they are understood remains a mystery. [Webber 1978a, 1978b] provides some additional constraints on their use. However, the focusing approach provides some basic structure that help to provide an explanation. In all the multi-sentence cases, the pronoun specifies something which is closely associated with the focus. More explanation is required since speakers do not understand those pronoun uses which seem to be related to the non-existence of an object (such as John's parents in light of John's orphanhood). Whatever the manner in which hearers recover specifications for such pronouns, some principles are needed that govern why some pronouns are acceptable and others are not.

5.3.5 The Problem of Parallelism

The pronoun interpretation rules give incorrect predictions for certain uses of pronouns, uses that are difficult to define. Intuitively, they may be characterized as instances of <u>parallel structure</u> between sentences of a discourse. To understand what is meant by parallel structure, two simple cases, one in which the rules do predict correctly, and another in which they fail, will be discussed. In D38, the pronoun co-specifies with the mud pack, as the pronoun interpretation rules would predict. The parallelism of these sentences is reflected in the semantics of *put on* and *pull off* as well as in the similarity of the syntactic structure of the two sentences, each containing an imperative mood main clause.

> D38-1 Put the mud pack on your face.
>   2 After 5 minutes, pull it off.

he pronoun interpretation rules predict the proper co-specifier in D38 because the thematic relations of the verb follow the similarity of structure. In D39, the pronoun *it* co-specifies with rose and not with the green Whitierleaf. The initial focus after the first sentence is Whitierleaf, but the parallel syntactic structure of the sentences seems to govern the choice of co-specifier. To summarize, between similarity of structure and the focus rules, similarity is preferred as a means of choosing the co-specifier, so when each gives a different prediction, similarity of structure must be used.

> D39-1 The green Whitierleaf is most commonly found near the wild
>   rose.
>   2 The wild violet is found near it too.

On first glance it appears that the pronoun interpretation rules could be "fixed" by simply observing that the initial focus is wrong and that a potential focus should be chosen. No such option is available, for such a "fix" requires that the inferring process reject the initial focus. To do so, the inferring process needs some knowledge about the world that indicates the unacceptability. For D39 no such knowledge could possibly be forthcoming since all the flora involved are found near one another. There is no knowledge to the effect that violets are found near wild roses and not near Whitierleafs.[1]

Another example of parallel structures is shown in D40. The parallel structures again are reflected in the similarity of the syntactic forms as well as the

---

[1]. In certain cases a special audience may have different responses to the parallelism above. For example, botanists who know what flowers are near others might behave differently. But even special audiences must sometimes use general techniques. Such is the case in the D39 example, because Whitierleafs are imaginary flora.

semantics of *most* and *mine*. After D40-1, the initial focus is the car radiator (that is, the prototypic car radiator). Using the focusing rules, *it* will be taken to co-specify with that radiator. But this prediction is incorrect; *it* co-specifies with the radiator of the speaker's car.[1]

D40-1 On most cars the radiator has a free bolt hook.

2 But on mine, it has a floating bolt hook.

The use of *it* here is similar to the instance of a generic for *it* in the example of the vegomatic with the broken cutting blade. What makes it different is that D40-2 has an underlying semantic form which is similar to D40-1. D40-1 specifies a universal set of cars and says something about one of the parts for those cars; D40-2 specifies a set of one thing, the speaker's car, and says something about a part of it; the speaker's car is related to the universal car by instantiation. Thus *it* in D40-2 is not pointing to some instance of the prototypic radiator; it co-specifies with the radiator of the speaker's car, but the co-specification seems to come about partly due to the representation of the *radiator* in D40-1. The similarity in the underlying semantics of D40-1 and D40-2 must be used in interpreting the pronoun.

One might wish to construct some special purpose mechanism that looks for similarities in structure between two sentences. This method is doomed for two reasons. First, parallelism exists in many aspects of language, and it happens at arbitrary levels of structure. Second, at any given level, the problem of recognition of parallelism has plagued computational models of language since such models were first suggested. For example, parsing of English sentences containing conjunction is as yet an unsolved problem. Methods tried for parsing conjunctions, such as those of [Woods 1973] in LUNAR, fail because of overgeneralization. Recognition of parallelism is still beyond computational theory.

The fact that interpretation of parallelism has failed for other aspects of computational models of language only indicates that the problem is a deep one. An extended example in [Sidner 1979], which will not be shown here, indicates that parallel constructions may be found between whole paragraphs in a discourse. Such constructions affect the interpretation which speakers and hearers choose for anaphors; hearers seem to take advantage of the parallel structure between two paragraphs of a discourse in deciding what was meant.

One possible consequence of these observations could be that the focus algorithm should be abandoned in favor of some as yet unspecified mechanism

---

1. The author thanks R.C. Moore for suggesting this example.

that is able to determine parallel relations among sets of sentences in a discourse. However, methods for interpreting pronouns from parallel sentences and paragraphs offer no constructive way of interpreting the pronouns in most of the examples presented in this chapter. Many cases of co-specification occur where there is no similarity of structure other than the common subject-verb-object pattern typical of English sentences. Since what is being talked about appears in many constituent positions in sentences of a discourse, the s-v-o pattern is too gross a level to specify similarity. Hence while parallelism is needed to deal with a certain set of cases for which the pronoun interpretation rules predict incorrectly, those rules are effective for many other cases of co-specification where parallelism would not be helpful. One may conclude that focus process accounts for one aspect of anaphor interpretation, and that some different mechanism is needed to encode similarities in structure which are used in discourse. The examples in this chapter provide some additional observations about the nature of parallelism in interpreting pronouns in natural languages and led us to conclude that further research is needed.

5.4 The Interpretation of *This* and *That*

5.4.1 Co-present Foci in Anaphor Disambiguation

In an earlier section, it was pointed out that sometimes speakers discuss several concepts at once without indicating that they are doing so. Generally this causes the discourse to be confusing enough to prevent the hearer from understanding. Sometimes however people discuss more than one thing without confusion. How is that possible? One such case has already been presented; in the last section, it was shown that an actor focus may be present in many discourses in addition to the discourse focus. It is also possible to have co-present discourse foci within the discourse.

In this section I will first describe in more detail the concept of co-present foci. Then I will illustrate how it can explain the use of *this* and *that* in discourse. Finally I will discuss the rules of interpretation for these anaphors and their relation to the focusing algorithm. I will show that, when used together in a discourse, *this* and *that* keep the focus on two objects at once, while when used separately, *this* generally moves the focus and *that* does not.

Just what is meant by co-present foci? When more than one element is introduced in a discourse and each is discussed relative to the other or relative to a class in which both occur, the discourse is said to be maintaining co-present foci. An example will be helpful for understanding how this behavior occurs.

D5-1 I'm having a party tomorrow night;
2 it will be like the one I had last week.
3 That party was a big success
4 because everyone danced.
5 This one will have better food.
6 I've asked everyone to bring something special.
7 Want to come?

Two different parties are talked about; that is, both of them are in focus. To indicate that the speaker wants to discuss both, *that* is introduced to co-specify with the one mentioned second. The second party is used as a means for comparison to the first; hence *this* indicates the main concern of the speaker while *that* a secondary concern.

5.4.2 Interpretation of Co-present *this* and *that*

The anaphoric use of *this* and *that* has been difficult to explain. Most previous explanations (for example, by [Halliday and Hasan 1976], [Fillmore 1971] and [Lakoff 1974]) require some concept of proximity. Linguists have observed that deictic (that is, physically pointing) uses of *this* and *that*[1] seem to involve proximity to the speaker. The sense of proximity for *this* is being near the speaker, while for *that*, it means "near you or not near either of us but at any rate not near me."[2] By analogy, they explain anaphoric *this* indicating either proximity in the time and space of the context or in the sense of experience or empathy with the speaker, while for *that*, there is less proximity or empathy. These explanations are vague enough for us to ask for a more concrete one.

With focusing a different explanation is possible. The speaker needs a way to talk about two objects of the same type (for example, *this letter* and *that one*), but cannot use a pronoun because it will co-specify with only one of them. To distinguish the two and yet allow both to be spoken about, *this* and *that* phrases are used. In the case where the speaker wants to indicate that one of the two is more important, it will be co-specified using *this*; when *this* is used to mark relative importance, it will be referred to as primary focus.

To consider how this is accomplished with the focusing algorithm, let us analyze D5 in detail for a summation of the focusing behavior. D5-1 and 2

---

1. In the sample case below, the speaker would be pointing at each painting as the sentence is uttered.
   (29) *This* painting is a Van Gogh; *that* one is a Renoir.
2. [Halliday and Hasan 1976], *op. cit.*, pages 58-59.

establish a focus on the party tomorrow night according to the focusing algorithm. Among the potential foci of D5-2 is *the one I had last week.* D5-3 indicates that the speaker wants to say more about the potential focus while maintaining the first focus; this is accomplished by means of using *that* instead of *the* to co-specify with the party last week. If *the* had been used, it would cause the hearer to suppose initially in processing that the speaker was talking about the upcoming party; then the hearer would need to reject the choice because of the tense of the verb. *That* is a much clearer means of telling the hearer which one is under discussion.

How is the first focus maintained in the focusing algorithm for D5? While two discourse foci could be introduced, a simpler choice is available; the first focus could be stacked at the top of the focus stack. When a noun phrase with *this* as determiner is encountered, the co-present focus from the stack could then be chosen as the co-specifier.

The kernel of the rule for *this* and *that* is:

> *this* is a determiner used for main focus, that is, *this* + <noun phrase> determines main focus, while *that* + <noun phrase> co-specifies with a potential or old focus. However, if the focus has been mentioned using *that*, then a *this* definite noun phrase must co-specify with an old focus.

D5 is a case where the primary focus (tomorrow night's party) is stacked, in favor of a discussion of a second element in the discourse, signalled by the use of *that*. It moves into focus, and when the first party is discussed again, *this* must be used. An example of the normal rule instantiation is given below in D41. First Hilda's plan is in focus and then the speaker's own plan. Thereafter Hilda's plan is talked about using *that*.

> D41-B: What are the plans for the banana raid?
>
> A: According to Hilda's plan, you and I stay here until everyone else is in position. I don't much like it because I think we'll miss all the action. I think I've got a better plan: we'll be the guide party, and Eloise and Hilda the search party. With this plan, we'll be in on the action. Well, what do you think, isn't it a better plan than that one?

The rule for *this* and *that* reflects the locus of the speaker's concern. In D5 the first thing introduced is the chief concern, while in D41, A indicates concern with her own plan rather than Hilda's. In general, when the speaker uses *that* as determiner for a definite anaphor that co-specifies with the focus, the speaker is indicating that chief concern lies with another element, one that has previously been in focus, but that has been "put on hold" until the speaker finishes with the element mentioned by the *that* phrase.

The above explanation is incomplete. Speaker concern functions slightly differently when the speaker and hearer are not focused on the same elements, and especially when *this* and *that* co-specify elements of different types. In D5 and D41, speaker and hearer are focused on what the speaker makes the focus of the discourse. However, in some dialogues, the speaker and hearer do not always share focused items. Consider D42 below.

D42-1 A: Let's flip a coin and see who calls it.
    2 B: Heads.
    3 A: That's what it is. (* This is what it is.)

The focus of this dialogue is the coin which is being flipped. B has a second focus which is the result of the toss. When A speaks of B's focus, A uses *that* to refer to it; *this* cannot be so used. When several examples are considered, the proper formulation of the rule becomes clear: when speaker and hearer (as a second speaker) have different focus, use *that* as the determiner of a definite noun phrase that co-specifies the hearer's focus, and use *this* for the speaker's focus.

That in D42 is used non-co-presently. Non-co-present uses of *this* and *that* are those where the anaphors specify discourse elements that represent two different types of objects and where there is only one focus per speaker. In non-co-presence, *this* co-specifies an element which becomes the focus while *that* co-specifies some other discourse element, which stays out of focus in spite of the anaphoric term. Since non-co-present uses concern focus movement, let us discover just how they behave in discourse.

5.4.3 *This* and *That* in Focus Movement

When considering the behavior of *this* in discourse, one may observe that a *this* definite noun phrase moves the focus to whatever is specified by the head noun of the definite noun phrase. As the rules in the discussion of pronouns indicate, usually the focus moves to the leading potential focus in the potential focus list. Yet sometimes the focus moves to the entire description given by the previous sentences; sometimes, surprisingly, the focus does not really move in the sense that a new element is co-specified; the same element is specified but from a different perspective.

This definite anaphora are used in four ways depending upon the type of noun phrase heads that they and the focus contain. The cases are enumerated below with sample illustrative texts.

1. The focus and *this* definite anaphor have the same head nouns: the co-specifier for the anaphor is a member of the potential focus list and can be chosen just as pronoun co-specifiers are; move the focus to co-specifier.[1]

> D4-1 The axon may run for a long distance, sending off several
> *sidebranches* along the way,
> 2 before it terminates in an even finer network of filaments, the
> *terminal arbor.* (FOCUS: the axon)
> 3 <u>Man's</u> <u>longest</u> <u>axon</u> runs for several feet, from the spinal column
> to muscles that control movements of the toes.
> 4 In spite of its great length, <u>this</u> <u>axon</u>, like all nerve fibers, is a part
> of a single cell. (NEW FOCUS: Man's longest axon)
> 5 It is living matter.

2. The focus and *this* definite anaphor have different head nouns: the focus should be considered as a co-specifier of the *this* definite anaphor before other potential foci. If the focus is an acceptable co-specifier, the focus does not move.

> D43-1 Consider the roomful of electronic equipment that makes up a
> modern, high-speed digital computer.
> 2 Rack after rack of transistors, diodes, magnetic core memories,
> magnetic film memories--
> 3 all laced together by an intricate system of wiring many miles in
> length.
> 4 Imagine <u>the</u> <u>room</u>, and everything in it, shrunk to about the size
> of a cigarette package. (FOCUS: the room)
> 5 Now suppose we give <u>this</u> <u>marvelous</u> <u>box</u> to a clever electrical
> engineer, a man working, however, not in our own midcentury,
> but about the year 1900.
> 6 We present our gift
> 7 and demonstrate a few of the remarkable feats it can perform:
> several hundred thousand additions in one second...
> 8 We leave <u>this</u> <u>tantalizing</u> <u>device</u> with the suggestion that he try
> to find out what's inside the cigarette package...

3. *This* definite anaphor has an empty head. Choose the co-specifier from the potential focus list, but order the verb phrase predication as first choice. Move the

---

1. This example and the next are from [Denes and Pinson 1973], *The Speech Chain: The Physics and Biology of Spoken Language.*, Anchor Press, Garden City, New York, pages 124, and 122, respectively.

focus to the co-specifier.[2]

> D44-1 Since however, the interpretation has been put forward as a
>   hypothesis,
>   2 some weight will be added to it
>   3 if it can be shown to have an antecedent probability. (FOCUS:
>   the interpretation)
>   4 This is what I shall endeavor to do in the remaining pages.
>   (NEW FOCUS: show that the interpretation has antecedent
>   probability)

4. A *this* definite anaphor occurs inside of a quantified phrase. The *this* definite anaphor takes its co-specifier from the quantified variable; such cases are similar to the bound variable pronouns discussed in earlier.[3] The focus does not move. (In the example[4] below, the quantified phrase and *this* anaphora are underlined.)

> D45-1 We can, therefore, associate with each point near the earth a
>   vector **g** which is the acceleration that a body would experience
>   if it were released at this point.
>   2 We call **g** the *gravitational field strength* at the point in question.

Why are *this* anaphora provided as a signalling behavior when *it* and definite anaphora using *the* are available? The cases cited above permit the conclusion that the speaker needs a way to signal focus movement where *it* and *the* anaphora would keep the focus on an existing discourse element. Sometimes the speaker also needs a way to signal a new view of the focus (case 2); in such cases *it* could not provide this signal, and *the* noun phrases are too easily taken to be new items in the discourse, rather than the focus from a different description. Only in quantified phrases can *this* anaphora be used without moving focus; as these cases are well marked by the quantifier, the hearer can distinguish them as a special case.

In contrast to *this*, *that* used non-co-presently singles out an element of the text for re-mention without causing a focus movement. The focus may move later, but another anaphor must cause the move.

There are two kinds of non-co-present *that*, which will be called new mention

---

2. This example is from Thomas A. Goudge. [Goudge 1969] *The Thought of C.S. Peirce.* Dover Publications, Inc., New York, page 326.

3. Quantified phrase patterns also use *that* in a similar way.

4. From Resnick, Robert and David Halliday [Resnik and Halliday 1966]. *Physics: Part I.* John Wiley and Sons, Inc. New York, page 405.

that and previous mention *that*. New mention *that* describes an element which has not been mentioned previously in the text. It signals a new discourse element and can be used without confusion as long as no other definite noun phrases with the same noun head as the *that* phrase exist in the discourse. Two examples of new mention *that* are given below.[1]

D46-1 This is a course in biology.
2 Biology studies those entities that are called organisms: men, worms, yeast cells, bacterial cells are organisms.
3 Some organisms are unicellular,
4 some are multi-cellular.

D47-1 In Marigold's garden, roses grow everywhere.
2 She likes roses of the Eastern gorge variety more than those of the Western shore,
3 so she has a lot of them in her collection.
4 They grow to prize winning shapes and sizes.

A previous mention *that* phrase takes as its co-specifier the interpretation of some phrase, mentioned previously in the discourse. An example[2] is given below.

D48-1 If MNMSD is referred to by D either as "the mayor of San Diego" or "D's neighbor,"
2 then node 'MNMSD' represents the individual referred to.
3 The problem is that only looking at that node provides no reflection of the differences in the two references to MNMSD,
4 even though the surface DEFNPs do express this difference.
5 Focus spaces provide a means of representing this difference.

In D48, *that node* co-specifies with the node of D48-2. If the rest of the discourse is ignored, D48-3 would have been equally acceptable using *this*. However, the author does not want to focus on *that node* since in the next sentence she uses *this difference* to focus.

The important question about previous mention *that* is why it exists at all in English. It is clear from D48 why *this* cannot be used, but what about *the* or *it*? In the examples I have found, *it* in place of *that* is ambiguous in indicating what object is being referred to. *The* in place of *that* seems to be possible, but has a certain effect. Suppose D48-3 were:

(30) The problem is that only looking at the node provides no reflection of the differences in the two references to MNMSD...

The use of *the* forces a movement of focus from the person to the node, when

---

1. The first example comes from Luria, S.E. [Luria 1975] *Thirty-Six Lectures in Biology*, Cambridge: MIT Press, 3. It also contains a use of deictic *this*.
2. From [Grosz 1977], page 82.

what the author actually wants to turn her attention to is the differences in the two references to the person. In other words, an intervening, and in this case unnecessary, focus movement occurs.[1] Hence *that* serves a useful function in the language; it allows the speaker re-mention discourse elements without them becoming the focus of the speaker's (and therefore the hearer's) attention.

5.4.4 Using the Focus Movement Algorithm

To conclude this section and illustrate how the anaphor interpreter and the focusing algorithm function for *this* and *that* anaphora, their behavior will be illustrated on an example which uses *this* and *that* non-co-presently.

> D49-1 One day Bill's father bought Bill a new softball.
> 2 Bill and his friends played with it daily.
> 3 Not long after Harry was given a hardball by his uncle.
> 4 This ball, allowing more speed and accuracy than Bill's, became the boys' choice for all their baseball games.
> 5 That bothered Bill's father
> 6 because he didn't like to see Bill neglect his toys.

The expected focus of D49 is *a softball*. It is confirmed by the use of *it* in D49-2. D49-3 introduces a hardball, which is a potential focus for the discourse. Since *this* definite anaphora must use the potential focus list as a source for co-specifiers (when no co-present *that* is present), and since the source passes syntactic, semantic, and inference criteria, *this ball* in D49-4 is chosen to co-specify with the potential focus of *a hardball*. When the focusing algorithm runs after D49-4, the focus must move because of the use of *this*. In the next sentence a noun phrase consisting only of *that* occurs. The potential focus list of the previous sentence contains *the boys' choice, their baseball games* and the predication expressed by the verb phrase. The rules for *that* predict that the last member of the potential focus list is the co-specifier of *that*, a predication, which is what, intuitively, *that* co-specifies with.

This section has introduced and developed the notion of co-presence in discourse, for understanding the use of *this* and *that* anaphora. Co-presence is a means for talking about two or more discourse elements that are related to each other. Because language is spoken in a linear dimension, and perhaps because

---

1. There is another reason for using *that*. The context which precedes the text of D48 makes reference to a figure in the text. *That node* doubles as a deictic phrase. This example suggests that there is an important relation between focusing and deixis, a matter demanding further research.

people have trouble paying close attention to two things at once, it is not really possible to focus on both elements simultaneously. Instead, two elements are set up for discussion and considered in turn using the normal focusing process. Co-presence cases are well signalled in language behavior, perhaps to prevent confusion for hearer. Since hearers are sometimes confused by single focus, it is not surprising that co-present foci must be signalled clearly enough so that some of the potential confusion is reduced. It may well be that the signalling is necessary for the speaker as well, to help keep track of what he or she is trying to say. This is mere speculation until focusing is applied to the generation of language, and a theory of its behavior is given. Some research in this direction is discussed by McDonald in this volume.

In contrast to co-present foci use of *this* and *that* noun phrases, non-co-present uses of them allow the speaker to indicate which of all the things she or he has mentioned is most important to the discussion. *This* and *that* used in non-co-presence allow the speaker to point at the relevant material with the least confusion. Hence the real difference in these uses is a difference in the speaker's plans for, and the hearer's means of deciding, what will be talked about.

5.5 Conclusions

In this chapter the concept of focus has been defined and the role of focusing in understanding discourse has been illustrated. To formalize and clarify this behavior, I have described algorithms for finding the focus and for moving the focus as the discourse progresses. Tracking the movement of the focus includes a means of distinguishing the presence of more than one focus in the discourse; the focusing algorithm tracks both the discourse focus, the chief element of discussion and the actor focus, the chief actor in a portion of the discourse.

Focusing provides the foundation for a theory of anaphor interpretation. The foci and aspects of the focusing algorithm together with linguistic rules for disjoint reference and selectional restrictions, and with representations of network relations and sentential scope information provide an account of the interpretation of many uses of definite anaphora. Both the rules and representations have been shown to be compatible with the process of focusing, and necessary to focusing in providing information relevant to determining the co-specifier of a pronoun. In most cases, the focus itself provides a co-specifier, and in some cases, a generator for the specification.

Focusing simplifies a crucial step of anaphor interpretation. In choosing a co-specification, inferences about knowledge of the everyday world are needed, and focusing has contributed a means of controlling the inferring process.

Because the pronoun interpreter predicts a co-specifier and then asks for confirmation or rejection based on the presence of contradictions in the inferring process, the inference process is controlled by the focus machinery. In previous AI natural language systems interpretation resulted from binding of free variables during inferring; however, many inferences had to be drawn and then "undone" due to incorrect binding choices. The focusing approach eliminates this kind of blind binding and unbinding as well as shortening the inference chain search.

In this chapter I have also illustrated the value of concept of co-presence for interpreting the use of *this* and *that*. Co-presence is the means by which a speaker can be focused on more than one thing in a conversation, and it has been shown that *this* and *that* used co-presently allow the maintenance of two foci, one of main concern and the other of secondary concern to the speaker. *This* and *that* used non-co-presently, that is, when only one of the two types of noun phrases is found, also indicate main concern (*this*), or secondary concern (*that*) relative to some other focus.

The focus "popping" cases described by Grosz, and the need for parallelism underscore the role of higher discourse structures in focus interpretation. The Grosz examples violate the stacked focus constraint, but are comprehensible because the speaker relies on knowledge of task structures. The parallelism examples show that some additional structure is also used in understanding discourses. While focus popping makes use of the focus algorithm, the parallel structure cases seem to rely on a mechanism which is different in kind.

This chapter further specifies the nature of focusing as it relates to a theory of definite anaphor interpretation. A focus-based theory with stipulations for syntax, semantics and inferential knowledge, provides a predictive and explanatory theory of anaphor interpretation. The theory is predictive because it stipulates legal and illegal pronoun uses as well as their interpretations; it is explanatory because it hinges on the focusing algorithm using anaphora as signals of what is being discussed, while the syntactic, semantic and inferential knowledge used in interpreting anaphora provide for changes in the foci of discourse, changes that are reflected in pronoun use.

Focusing seems to be a necessary part of the theory of the pragmatics of language. In his well known William James lectures, [Grice 1975] defined several maxims of conversation, one of which was the maxim of relevance. Grice[1] says about this maxim:

---

1. Grice, *op. cit.*, page 67.

> Under the category of *Relation* I place a single maxim, namely, "Be relevant." Though the maxim itself is terse, its formulation conceals a number of problems which exercise me a good deal; questions about what different kinds and foci of relevance there may be, how these shift in the course of a talk exchange, how to allow for the fact that subjects of conversation are legitimately changed, and so on.

As long as relevance is a part of a theory of pragmatics, focusing must be included in that theory, whether it is the theory which Grice has begun to unfold or some other one. Focusing and focus as they have been used here bear directly on Grice's concerns; for they suggest a means for carrying out the maxim of relevance. Namely, a speaker is speaking relevantly in a discourse if he or she introduces a focus, and proceeds to another one by mentioning it and re-mentioning it with definite anaphora. Old foci are re-invoked by a definite noun phrase which points out which old focus is co-specified or in one of the other, less direct, ways discussed in the previous chapters. Nothing less than the use of focus will suffice for relevance; for the moment the speaker fails to provide a focus for the hearer and to point back to it in successive utterances, the hearer has no means of knowing what is relevant in the discourse at hand. In some sense the discourse ceases to be a discourse.

Perhaps it is surprising that focusing should play such a central role in a theory of pragmatics. In particular, it is surprising that focusing one's attention on something and signalling one's focus is part of the criteria for speaking relevantly. One expects relevance to be a matter of what is said about some thing, rather than that the thing is mentioned consistently. But if we remember that focusing allows for the speaker to tell the hearer that the same thing is still under discussion and without needing to say explicitly what that thing is, then the role of focusing is not so surprising. Focusing must then be the first criterion for speaking relevantly, since it explains how a hearer decides what the speaker is talking about.

5.6 Acknowledgements

The research reported in this paper was supported in part by the Advanced Research Projects Agency under contract No. N0014-77-C-0378. Research reported here was also done at the Artificial Intelligence Laboratory of the Massachusetts Institute of Technology. Support for the laboratory's artificial intelligence research is provided in part by the Advanced Research Projects Agency of the Department of Defense under ONR contract N0014-75-0643.

CHAPTER 6

So What Can We Talk About Now?

Bonnie Lynn Webber

6.1 Introduction

I started my research on anaphoric reference in natural language when I was
struck by the following two examples:

    D1-1 John gave Mary five dollars.
        2 *It* was more than he gave Sue.
    D2-1 John gave Mary five dollars.
        2 One of *them* was counterfeit.

in which both *it* and *them* seem to follow from the same phrase, *five dollars.* This
seemed extraordinary: if definite pronouns like *it* and *they* referred anaphorically
to text strings, how could the same string of text justify both a singular and a
plural pronoun.

Moreover, neither of the natural language understanding (NLU) systems that I
had worked on up to the time - LUNAR [Woods et. al. 1972] and BBN's speech
understanding system [Woods 1976] - could handle both examples either. That is,
while these systems had rules for identifying what noun phrases made available
for subsequent definite anaphora,[1] for each type of noun phrase, there was only
one such rule. As a consequence, one could program the system to treat *five
dollars* as either an indefinite plural noun phrase (NP), later to be referenced as by
they, or as a mass NP - a singular quantity - later to be referenced as as *it*, but not
both.

Nor was this problem acknowledged, much less solved, by any of the anaphor
resolution heuristics coming from either artificial intelligence or psychology (i.e.,
heuristics for choosing the intended referent of a definite anaphor from among
possible alternatives). All these heuristics simply assumed that a text made things
available for later anaphora, and that the intended referent would always be
among the possible alternatives. Nor could standard linguistic theory at the time
account for the anaphoric behavior in both examples: definite pronoun anaphora

---

1. one of the functions served by definite pronouns like "it" and "they" and definite NPs.

was only of interest within the single sentence and even that, only with respect to lexical, syntactic and/or semantic constraints on what a pronoun could be associated with, *within that same sentence.*

Five dollars is clearly not an isolated example. One can quickly discover many instances where a single sentence admits a variety of things available for subsequent anaphora, based on what seems to be the same phrase. For example,

>The Rhodesian ridgeback down the block bit me yesterday. *It*'s really a vicious beast.

>- The Rhodesian ridgeback down the block bit me yesterday. *They*'re really vicious beasts.

>- Each girl in Mary's class marched up to the desk and took a brick. *She* then went back and sat quietly in her seat.

>- Each girl in Mary's class marched up to the desk and took a brick. *They* used them to build a mockup of the Great Wall of China.

>- John didn't marry a Swedish blonde. *She* was Danish.

>- John didn't marry a Swedish blonde. *She* had brown hair.

>- John didn't marry a Swedish blonde. *She*'s just living with him.

>- Wendy gave each boy a green T-shirt. She gave *one* to Sue as well.

>- Wendy gave each boy a green T-shirt. Sue, she gave a red *one*.

In beginning my research, my feeling was that whatever regularities were present in making things available to either definite pronoun or "one" anaphora, they could not be formulated purely in terms of text strings, parse trees or any of the then-current AI representations. While I shall not comment on the first two types of representations, the AI representations used within computer-based NLU systems fell roughly into three categories, none of which was motivated by understanding continuous discourse and the phenomena common to it.

    1. Several followed formalisms often borrowed from linguistics (e.g., LUNAR's syntactic parse tree, SHRDLU's systemic analysis [Winograd 1972], most "case" representations [Bruce 1975]) that were meant to map "paraphrases" (syntactic and/or lexical variants) into the same representation.

    2. Several were modifications of a logical formalism (e.g. the meaning representation languages used in LUNAR, PHLIQA [Bronnenberg et. al. 1980], etc.) that were meant to provide a well-understood single-sentence semantics.

    3. Several were meant to fill in for material often left unsaid in natural language utterances (Schank's frame-like conceptual dependency representation [Schank 1975]). Whatever procedures were used to handle instances of anaphora were ones that could be grafted onto these formalisms, *a posteriori*.

Surprisingly enough, such procedures were not complete failures, and even had modest success. LUNAR, for example, was able to make use of its logical meaning representation to deal with such non-obvious anaphoric references as

D3-1 Do any samples contain bismuth and ruthenium?
    2 YES
    3 Give me *their* overall analyses.

where it correctly interpreted "their" in D3-3 to refer to the set of samples which contain bismuth and ruthenium. In forming this set description -- i.e., "samples that contain bismuth and ruthenium" - LUNAR ignored its own answer to question D3-1. Thus in example D4, it would incorrectly propose "samples that contain bismuth and ruthenium" (rather than "samples") as the interpretation of "they".

D4-1 Do any samples contain bismuth and ruthenium?
    2 NO
    3 Then what do *they* contain?

So, to summarize the then-current situation in linguistics and AI natural language understanding, the former either weren't interested in discourse anaphora or tried to handle it by either string or structure matching - clearly inadequate - while the latter attempted to deal with it using whatever ad hoc methods could be grafted onto representations primarily designed for other purposes. What my research has been directed at then is (1) a definition of what a text makes available for anaphora that can accommodate the kinds of examples presented above and also be amenable to computational treatment and (2) within that computational treatment, a characterization of features of a representational formalism (or set of related formalisms) that would most efficiently support the procedures.[1] That is, I have attempted to articulate what a text makes available for anaphora in terms of the structure (as opposed to content) of its sentences, as they are represented in such a formalism. Like any other structure-based understanding strategy, this would have the advantage of being common to all users of a language, whether the content were completely understood or not.

As for the remainder of this paper, the first part is based on my thesis research [Webber 1978a], although it has profited from recent work with R. Bobrow on a natural language interface we call PSI-KLONE, for "Parsing and Semantic Interpretation in KL-ONE" [Bobrow and Webber 1980a, 1980b, 1981]. I have also changed my terminology somewhat, to emphasize the commonality of this work with the complementary set of issues discussed by Sidner (this volume). The second part of the paper contains an approach to "one" anaphora that differs substantially from that presented in [Webber 1978a]. This new approach has the attractive feature of reducing two separate difficult problems into the same (albeit still difficult) one.

6.2 Fundamental Assumptions

The approach I have adopted to identifying what a text makes available for the interpretation of definite pronoun and "one"-anaphora is based on the notion of a "discourse model".[2] The assumption is that one objective of discourse is to talk about some situation or state of the real or some hypothetical world. To do this, a speaker must have a mental model of that situation or state. The ensuing discourse is thus, at one level, an attempt by the speaker to direct the listener in synthesizing a similar "discourse model" and by that, acquire information about the speaker's situation or state. (In this sense, I am equating "understanding" with "synthesizing an appropriate model".)

---

1. As [Hankamer and Sag 1976] point out, both definite pronoun and "one" anaphora may be "controlled" by things other than the previous text. In particular, they demonstrate "control" by the spatio-temporal context that speaker and listener share. In this paper, I shall only be discussing what texts (and, to a limited extent, what inference) make available.

2. This is a notion that has been explored in cognitive psychology to explain the inferences that people draw in understanding text. See, for example, [Collins, Brown, and Larkin 1977].

Informally, a discourse model (DM) may be described as the set of entities "naturally evoked" (or in Sidner's terms, "specified") by a discourse, linked together by the relations they participate in. I have called these things "discourse entities", and Sidner has called them "cognitive elements". In linguistics, they harken back to what [Karttunen 1976] has called "discourse referents". The alternate terminologies that Sidner and I have adopted rest on wanting to keep "refer" a separate technical term. That is, "referring" is what people do with language. Evoking and accessing discourse entities are what texts/discourses do. A discourse entity inhabits a speaker's discourse model and represents something the speaker has referred to. A speaker *refers* to something by utterances that either *evoke* (if first reference) or *access* (if subsequent reference) its corresponding discourse entity.

To illustrate the notion of entities "naturally evoked" by a discourse, consider the following sentence.

D5-1 Each 3rd-grade girl brought a brick to Wendy's house.

Then consider each of the following continuations. In each case, I would label what is accessed by the definite pronoun an entity "naturally evoked" by sentence D5 -1.[1] As the reader can see, such entities may have descriptions appropriate to individuals, sets, stuff, events, activities, etc.

- She certainly was surprised.
  she ≡ Wendy

- They knew she would be surprised.
  they ≡ the set of 3rd-grade girls

- She piled them on the front lawn.
  them ≡ the set of bricks, each of which some 3rd-grade girl brought to Wendy's house

- She was surprised that they knew where it was.
  it ≡ Wendy's house

- Needless to say, it surprised her.
  it ≡ the brick-presenting event

---

1. The symbol ≡ in these continuations should be taken as indicating the same target for both expressions.

- Generally, Wendy can always find something to do with them.

them ≡ bricks, bricks people bring her

Notice moreover that texts identical at a conceptual level may not be identical vis-a-vis the discourse entities they naturally evoke, even though their phrasings differ only slightly. For example

D6-1 John traveled around France twice.

2 ??They were both wonderful.

D7-1 John took two trips around France.

2 They were both wonderful.

McDonald makes a similar point in [McDonald 1977], where he discusses the problem of generating subsequent "referring" expressions. He takes as his example conceptual level the first-order predicate logic and considers English renderings of the simple formula,

$$\forall x \; man(x) \Rightarrow mortal(x)$$

which include

1. For any thing, if that thing is a man, then it is mortal.

2. Being a man implies being mortal.

3. All men are mortal.

McDonald notes that only the first version gives the variable x a separate status, thereby making it something that can be specified again (e.g., "it is mortal). The second version gives the open formula "man(x)" separate status, making it in turn available for re-specification (e.g., "It also implies being subject to supply-side economics."). McDonald concludes

In short, it is not possible to predict which objects will be explicitly referred to and which not just on the basis of a formula in the internal representation language.

It is not just what the conceptual level information is, but how that information is realized that determines what types of discourse entities are available when.

Now a speaker is usually not able to communicate all at once the relevant properties and relations s/he may want to ascribe to the referent of a discourse entity. To do that, s/he may have to direct the listener's attention to that referent (via its corresponding discourse entity) several times in succession. When the speaker wants to re-access an entity already in his/her DM (or another one directly inferrable from it), s/he may do so with a definite anaphor (pronoun or NP). In so doing, the speaker assumes (1) that on the basis of the discourse thus far, a similar entity will be in (or "directly" inferrable from) the listener's growing DM and (2) that the listener will be able to re-access (or infer) that entity on the basis of the speaker's cues. (For example, pronouns are less of a cue than anaphoric NPs.) The problem then, at least for definite anaphora, is identifying what discourse entities a text naturally evokes.

What characterizes a discourse entity? My minimal view is that a discourse entity is a "conceptual coathook" (a term coined by William Woods) on which to hang descriptions of the entity's real world or hypothetical world correspondent. As soon as a discourse entity is evoked, it gets a description. Over the course of the text, the descriptions it receives are derived from both the content of the speaker's utterances and their position within the discourse, as well as whatever general or specific information about the discourse entity the listener can bring to bear. (For example, as the text conveys the passage of time, a description like "the 16-year old girl that..." might change to "the 20-year old girl that....") These descriptions provide part of the means by which a listener can decide the intended target of subsequent definite anaphora (the other being provided by focusing mechanisms, as discussed by [Grosz 1977] and Sidner in Chapter 5 of this volume). What I claim is a special status for the initial description (ID) that tags a newly evoked discourse entity. (Examples of such IDs follow the equivalence symbol ($\equiv$) in the continuations to example D5-1 above.)

In what way is a discourse entity's ID special? For one thing, it is the only information about an entity that can, from the first and without question, be assumed to be shared (though not necessarily believed) by both speaker and listener alike. Thus, at least initially, it is an inference that the speaker can assume the listener both capable of and likely to make. That the speaker needn't believe the description for it to be effective is discussed in [Perrault and Cohen 1981] -- that the listener needn't believe it either is discussed in [Webber 1978b]. The important thing is that it is *shared*, and hence useful.

Now this view of discourse understanding does not preclude discourse entities from being evoked by other things than the text. In fact, I will argue that certain types of discourse entities must be derived from other ones inferentially. In particular, I will argue that it is the simplest way of accounting for anaphoric access to "generic set" discourse entities. I will show that, from any discourse entity (except, in general, ones evoked by a proper noun phrase, name, title, etc.), the speaker can presume that a listener is capable of deriving a discourse entity corresponding to one of a limited number of generic sets to which the referent of the original discourse entity belongs.

The problems I set out to solve - identifying what a text makes available for definite pronoun anaphora (and, it turns out, for "one" anaphora as well) and developing computationally feasible ways for making them available in an NLU system - were thus transformed into (1) identifying the discourse entities a text evokes and (2) ascribing to them appropriate IDs. What I discovered was that these things depend heavily on *combinatoric* features of a sentence.[1] Moreover, these features can be captured in the *structure* of a representational formalism (as opposed to its lexical content), and can be the basis for procedures which identify the entities evoked by a text and derive their IDs. What I have realized more recently is discussed in Section 6.5: namely, that the semantic problem of interpreting "one" anaphora[2] can be reduced to the already considered problem of identifying possible "set-type" resolvants for definite plural anaphora.

Before finishing this statement of my fundamental assumptions, I want to comment on where I see evoking and labeling discourse entities fitting into the whole process of understanding continuous text. First, most discourse entities are ones evoked by a noun phrase in its clausal context.[3] Now whether or not a discourse entity should be evoked (and if so, how it should be described) depends on clausal features - especially the combinatoric features presented in Section 6.3 - that often remain elusive, even after the clause is parsed and both general semantic and particular pragmatic knowledge is applied. That is, sentences often pose what might be called an "underconstrained combinatoric problem" [Bobrow and Webber 1980a]. What is required of semantic interpretation is to delineate the problem to be solved. What happens then depends on what is required: one

---

1. Combinatoric features are discussed in the next section. Briefly put, the ones I am considering are:

iteration "A window was tested in each house" implies the speaker is viewing the situation in terms of one testing per house.

dependency "A window was tested in each house" implies under one interpretation that the particular window depends on the particular house: a window associated with house1 was tested in house1, a window associated with house2 was tested in house2, etc. Under a different interpretation, the particular window is independent of the house, the same one tested throughout.

cardinality "Two windows were tested in each house" implies for any given house there were two windows tested, where the two are distinct from one another. Notice the sentence does not (on its own) imply anything about the cardinality of the entire window set.

2. as opposed to the *syntactic* problem of characterizing where "one(s)" can and cannot occur, a problem of interest to transformational grammarians, cf. Section 6.5.

3. Clauses may also evoke discourse entities of various sorts, as may verb phrases. For example,

Stir the dissolved yeast into the flour, then knead the dough for 10 minutes or until elastic.

The discourse entity describable as "the dough" is evoked by the first clause, or rather, the reader's understanding of it. However, I will be ignoring such examples in this discussion.

possibility is that the discourse/pragmatics component - using whatever discourse and pragmatic information is available to it - may be forced to solve the problem immediately in order to provide an appropriate response.

But what if no immediate response to the sentence is called for? What if one doesn't need to commit oneself one way or another? Then the combinatoric aspects of the sentence's interpretation can remain underconstrained - i.e., ambiguous. On the other hand, if the need to interpret later sentences requires a particular resolution or particular type of resolution, that can result in further constraints on the delineation. For example, in processing a definite anaphor, a listener may simultaneously (1) make explicit some or all the possible senses of a previous sentence; (2) formulate appropriate IDs for the entities that each sense, if correct, would evoke; (3) identify one of these entities as the intended resolvant of the definite anaphor; and (4) thereby identify the correct, intended sense of that previous sentence. What enables the listener to do all this is the fact that alternative possible interpretations do not lead to equally satisfying ways of resolving the anaphor.

6.3 Factors in Forming Discourse-dependent Descriptions

As I mentioned in the last section, it is necessary to take-account of certain combinatoric aspects of a sentence in order to form appropriate IDs for the discourse entities it evokes. To do this requires *inter alia*:[1]

> 1. distinguishing between definite and indefinite noun phrases and between singular and plural noun phrases.
>
> 2. distinguishing, for each modifier in a plural noun phrase, whether it conveys information about the entire set denoted by the plural noun phrase or about the individual set members. The same is true of the verb phrase/predicate.
>
> 3. resolving any ellipsed·verb phrases in the sentence.
>
> 4. identifying what has traditionally been called "quantifier scope assignments", although, as noted in Section 6.2, they may not be determinable when the sentence is first heard.

---

1. Other features are discussed in [Webber 1978a].)

After this, I shall show one way in which combinatoric aspects of a sentence can be articulated in a logical formalism, and hence provide a structural basis for forming appropriate discourse entity IDs. This is illustrated briefly in Section 6.4, after which I discuss the derivation of "generic set" discourse entities from specific ones and the use of both in understanding "one" anaphora.

6.3.1 The Definite/Indefinite Distinction

My reason for requiring distinct representations for definite and indefinite noun phrases is that while both can evoke discourse entities in the same context, the descriptions appropriate to them are quite different.[1] Looking first at simple singular noun phrases with no other quantified noun phrases around, compare the following examples.

D8-1 Wendy bought the yellow T-shirt that Elliot had admired.
   2 It cost twenty dollars.
D9-1 Wendy bought a yellow T-shirt that Elliot had admired.
   2 It cost twenty dollars.

In either case, the target of "it" has a unique description that both discourse participants share. In D8, it is the explicit description *the yellow T-shirt that Elliot had admired*. In D9, it is the derived description, something like "the just-mentioned yellow T-shirt that Elliot had admired, that Wendy bought." To see that only this description can be presumed to be shared, notice that D9 can be uttered truthfully if Elliot had admired several yellow T-shirts or even if Wendy had bought several such T-shirts. Thus it does not even presuppose that there is a unique yellow T-shirt that Elliot had admired that Wendy bought. But it does mention only one such T-shirt. As such, the above description applies uniquely to one entity - the one accessed by "it".

The point is that the entity evoked by a singular definite noun phrase can usually be described adequately by just that description (but cf. Section 6.3.2 on quantifier scoping). On the other hand, an adequate description of the entity evoked by a singular indefinite noun phrase depends on a conjunction of (1) the description inherent in the noun phrase (e.g. *yellow T-shirt that Elliot had admired*); (2) a predicate that embodies the remainder of the sentence (e.g. *which Wendy bought*); and (3) a predicate that relates that entity to the sentence evoking it (e.g. "which was mentioned in (or evoked by) sentence <k>"). This conjunctive

---

1. As I mentioned earlier, definite descriptions can be used in two ways: they can be used like definite pronouns to access entities presumed to be in the listener's discourse model or they can be used to evoke new entities into that model. It is the latter use of definite descriptions that is relevant here.

description forms the entity's initial description (ID).

Notice that forming the second conjunct requires all ellipsed verb phrases in the sentence be recovered. If not, a sentence like

D10-1 A woman whom Wendy knows is too.

would evoke a discourse entity which could only be described as *the just-mentioned woman whom Wendy knows who is too*. This is not very useful from the point of view of reasoning about entities.

However, a more important reason for requiring the recovery of ellipsed verb phrases is that doing so may reveal other noun phrases that should be associated with discourse entities. Failure to do so may result in subsequent definite anaphora failing to have referents. For example,

D11-1 John didn't bake a cake for Wendy. On the other hand, Elliot
did 0, but she didn't like it.
$0 =$ bake a cake for Wendy
$it =$ the "just-mentioned" cake that Elliot
baked for Wendy

If the ellipsed verb phrase has not been recovered by the time the *but* clause is being processed, there will be no way of accounting for the pronoun *it*. (Linguists have used the term "missing antecedent" [Grinder and Postal 1971] to describe this situation, in which the "antecedent" of a definite pronoun is not explicit, being somehow "contained" in an ellipsed constituent.)

The same characteristic behavior of definites and indefinites just discussed for singular noun phrases holds for plural noun phrases as well. The referent of the definite plural pronoun *they*, like the referent of a definite singular pronoun, must satisfy a unique description shared by speaker and listener. While both indefinite and definite plural noun phrases in context may evoke uniquely describable set entities, the procedure for forming their descriptions again differs in the two cases. Consider, for example, the following sentences. (Comments are in parentheses):

D12-1 I saw the guys from "Yes" on TV tonight. (I saw all of them.)
2 I saw the five guys from "Yes" on TV tonight. (I saw all of them
- that is, five.)
3 I saw all five guys from "Yes" on TV tonight. (Usually they're
only around in twos and threes.)
4 I saw some guys from "Yes" on TV tonight. (I didn't see them
all.)
5 I saw four guys from "Yes" on TV tonight. (There are more
than four guys in Yes.)

The first three sentences each contain a definite plural noun phrase. Corresponding to that noun phrase, a discourse entity will be evoked into the listener's discourse model which can be described appropriately as *the (set of) guys from 'Yes'*. (The second two sentences provide the cardinality of that set as well.)

This can be verified by following either of these sentences by "'They were being interviewed by Dick Cavett" and considering what is accessed by *they*. The last two sentences, on the other hand, each contain an indefinite plural noun phrase. The only appropriate description for the discourse entity that each of these noun phrases in context evokes is something like *the just-mentioned set of guys from 'Yes' that I saw on TV tonight.* This is because either sentence is consistent with there being other members of "Yes" whom I didn't see on TV tonight, as well as other members whom I did see but whom I don't mean to include in my statement. (The last sentence simply provides additional cardinality information about that set of guys from 'Yes' that I saw.)

6.3.2 Quantifier Scoping

The phenomenon to be discussed here has traditionally called "quantifier scoping" or "quantifier ordering", after its formulation in the first order predicate calculus. Early in the development of Transformational Grammar, it was found to pose a problem for the treatment of passivization as an "optional" (i.e., semantically neutral) transformation. The problem can be illustrated by the minimally different pair of sentences

- Each boy in the room speaks two languages.

- Two languages are spoken by each boy in the room.

Even though these two sentences differ only in their voice (active vs. passive), they have different immediate interpretations: the first allows for different languages per boy, and the second implies the same two languages, independent of boy. Because the traditional way of representing the two sentences logically has them differ in whether or not the universal quantifier ($\forall$) associated with the interpretation of *each boy in the room* is outside or inside the scope of the existential quantifier ($\exists$) associated with the interpretation of *two languages*, the problem has been called that of "quantifier scoping" or "quantifier ordering". If the universal is outside the scope of the existential ($\forall\exists$), then it can "distribute" over the existential and what VanLehn [VanLehn 1978] has called a "different/per" reading is allowed. (In theorem proving, this is called a <u>Skolem functional</u> dependency of the existential on the universal [Nilsson 1980].) If the universal is inside the existential ($\exists\forall$), then the existential is independent of the universal and van Lehn's "same/per" reading is implied.

What I want to comment on here is the importance of quantifier scoping/ordering to understanding anaphora in discourse. That importance arises from the different anaphoric properties of "same/per" and "different/per" readings, as shown in the following pairs of sentences.

D13-1 Mary showed each boy an apple.

2 The apple was a Mackintosh.

D14-1 Mary showed each boy an apple.

2 Then she mixed the apples up and had each boy guess which was his.

In example D13, understanding the anaphoric NP *the apple* follows from a "same/per" reading of the first sentence, while in example D14, understanding the anaphoric NP "the apples" follows from a "different/per" reading of that same first sentence. That is, only a "different/per" reading allows the possibility of a different apple per boy and hence a specifiable set of apples.

What this demonstrates is both that <u>something like</u> quantifier scoping is important for understanding anaphora in discourse *and* that the speaker's intended quantifer scope assignment (if s/he indeed has one) may only be made clear later in the discourse.

It is interesting to notice that such "same/per" and "different/per" readings are not limited to the interpretation of indefinite noun phrases; the same phenomenon arises with definite noun phrases as well. Consider the following case:

D15-1 In each car, the mechanic adjusted the radio antenna.

2 He had found them all 4 inches too short.

To understand the second sentence correctly, one must give a "same/per" reading to the description *the mechanic* - the same mechanic for all the cars - and a "different/per" reading to *the radio antenna* - a different one for each car. That is, one must see an <u>intrinsic</u> dependency between radio antennas and cars. (While world knowledge about mechanics, cars and radios may confirm the sensibility of these readings, it is also possible for a second sentence to require, say, a different mechanic per car as well, as in

D16-1 In each car, the mechanic adjusted the radio antenna.

2 Unfortunately for the drivers, the mechanics knew zip about radios.)

The reason for hedging above vis-a-vis "something like" quantifier scoping is that Bobrow and I have reason to advocate a reinterpretation of quantifier scoping in terms of the combinatoric features - dependency, iteration and cardinality. For example, we would distinguish a "same/per" and a "different/per" reading (of either a definite or an indefinite NP) in terms of whether or not the NP is seen to <u>depend</u> (either Skolem-functionally, intrinsically or explicitly) on some distributive quantifier (i.e., some <u>iterated</u> <u>description</u>). Our reinterpretation reflects the considerable (and growing) body of evidence that there is wide variation in people's grasp of quantified sentences: certain aspects of them seem to be understood easily and consistently, even when the sentences are presented with no context (e.g., "three <x>'s" implies. to people that there are at least three separate things describable as an <x>, never just one or two things, each describable in more than one way as an <x>). Certain other aspects people have trouble grasping at all [VanLehn 1978] - much less trying to select which of several alternative readings is intended (e.g., the data base queries below that [Thomas 1976] asked human subjects to answer.

- Print out any departments that sell every article that some company makes.

- Print the departments whose entire line of items is supplied by a single company.

Several subjects interpreted these queries in ways that bore little relation to any of the strict logical readings, while other subjects claimed they made no sense at all.)

We feel a better model for people's understanding of quantified sentences in discourse is one in which we can separate out those aspects of quantification that a listener will immediately understand in a given sentence and make a commitment to from those aspects which cannot be immediately understood, whose resolution will be postponed. Only when forced to by another task, like the need to act in response to the sentence or the need to understand a following one, will the listener attempt to resolve (partially, if not fully) these latter aspects. As presented in [Bobrow and Webber 1981], a combinatoric model allows for this separation.

Note though that the purpose of such a combinatoric model is to allow the discourse understander to postpone decisions about combinatoric features as long as possible, while still capturing all those aspects of meaning that can be immediately grasped. However in most cases, in order to describe the discourse entities that a clause gives rise to, some resolution is required, even if just to ascertain and compare its consequences with current discourse demands. The rules for deriving discourse entity descriptions presented in Section 6.4.4 are thus based on fully resolved forms. For a discussion in terms of perhaps only partially resolved combinatoric features, the reader is referred to [Bobrow and Webber 1981].

6.3.3 Member/Set Information

Plural noun phrases may provide information about two separate things: a *set* and its members. For example,

    D17-1 three dotted lines which intersect at point P
      2 the three dotted lines which intersect at point P

Dotted is a property of each individual line. *Three*, on the other hand, supplies information about the cardinality of the sets of lines which satisfy these descriptions. Moreover, the relative clause - *which intersect at point P* - does not directly restrict which individual lines belong to these sets, but rather specifies a property of appropriate sets of three lines. Prenominal, prepositional and clausal modifiers within a noun phrase may all be used to describe either a set as a unit or the set's individual members.

For handling anaphora, a distinction must be drawn between set and member information within a plural noun phrase, both for describing the entity it evokes and for describing those entities evoked by any embedded noun phrases. Consider the following sentences.

    D18-1 Three men who tried to lift a piano dropped it.
      2 The three men who tried to lift a piano dropped it.
      3 Three men who tried to lift a piano dropped them.
      4 The three men who tried to lift a piano dropped them.

In the first two sentences, the relative clause conveys information about the set of men as a unit. Thus *it* can be understood as accessing the discourse entity describable as *the just-mentioned piano which the just-mentioned three men tried to lift*. However, in the second two sentences, the relative clause conveys information about each member of the set. Thus *they* can be understood as accessing the entity describable as *the just-mentioned pianos, each of which one of the just-mentioned men tried to lift*.[1]

6.3.4 Three Uses of Plurals

Another factor in forming appropriate IDs for entities evoked by plural noun phrases involves distinguishing what the sentence is predicating of each set and what it is predicating of each individual set member. That is, I see <u>distributiveness</u> (i.e., an equivalent thing being predicated of each individual set member) as only

---

1. These four sentences hint at another distinction that must be made in order to identify discourse entities adequately - whether a noun phrase occurs embedded in a relative clause (as *a piano* does above) or in the matrix sentence. This is discussed at length in [Webber 1978c] and [Webber 1978b].

one of three distinct senses that a sentence containing a plural noun phrase can be used to convey. The three senses I call <u>distributive</u>, <u>collective</u> and <u>conjunctive</u>. Consider for example

- Three boys bought five roses.

This can be used to convey either:

1. that Boy1 bought five roses, Boy2 bought five roses and Boy3 bought five roses (*distributive reading*). Should the sentence have contained an explicit "each," this would clearly be the intended sense. However as [Stenning 1978] notes, "each" can be implied contextually as well - e.g.,

-How many roses did éach of your customers buy?

Well, ten boys bought 8 roses each.
Three boys bought 5 roses.
And one girl, she bought three dozen.

2. that three boys (formed into a consortium) bought five roses (*collective reading*).

3. that the total of rose-buying boys is three and the total number of roses, each of which was bought by some rose-buying boy, is five (*conjunctive reading*). This implies that the speaker either does not know or does not care to tell the listener how boys match up with roses. As it is the least commital interpretation, it may be the default when there is no contextual bias.

It is important for the listener to identify the intended sense because of their different implications. That is,

- If the example is understood distributively, it implies that each of the boys owns five roses as a result of the transaction.

- If it is understood conjunctively, then it implies that each of the boys owns at least one (or part of one) rose as a result.

- If it is understood collectively, then it does not imply that any individual boy owns any roses as a result. Only the consortium owns roses, and it owns five.

Distinguishing these implications is important not only for reasoning but for anaphora as well, as the following pairs of sentences show:

D19-1 The three boys ordered a large anchovy pizza.

2 Because of the heavy traffic, *it* was delivered cold.

D20-1 The three boys each ordered a large anchovy pizza.

2 Because of the heavy traffic, *they* were delivered cold.

Because English has a different pronoun for accessing a set than an individual, the distributive use of a plural must be distinguished from a conjunctive or collective use. Only when a plural is used to convey distributive quantification can it change the discourse entity evoked by a singular noun phrase within its scope from an individual to a set. This means that a different pronoun would be used to refer to it.

Specifically, in D19 *it* accesses a discourse entity appropriately described as *the just-mentioned large anchovy pizza that the boys ordered.* In D20, *they* accesses the set evoked by the same noun phrase, this time describable as *the set of just-mentioned large anchovy pizzas, each of which was ordered by one of the three boys.* The general issue is getting appropriate descriptions. In the original example,

Three boys bought five roses.

depending on which sense of *three boys* the speaker means to convey, the description appropriate to the discourse entity evoked by *five roses* will be something like

- the set of just-mentioned roses, each of which belongs to a set of five roses which one of these three rose-buying boys bought (distributive)

- the set of five roses, each of which one of the three rose-buying boys bought (in part or *in toto*) (conjunctive)

- the set of five roses which this rose-buying consortium of three boys bought (collective)

6.4 An Appropriate Formalism for Computing Descriptions

6.4.1 Noun Phrases in General

The attempt to capture both quantifier scope and predication in an adequate representation implies a formalism with logical operators. Unfortunately, a "flat" predicate calculus will not suffice: its structure is not rich enough to allow a distinction to be made between a predicate associated with a sentential verb phrase and a predicate associated with another part of the sentence. For example,

> *Some cotton T-shirt is expensive.*
> $(\exists x) . \text{Cotton}(x) \wedge \text{T-shirt}(x) \wedge \text{Expensive}(x)$

Without this distinction, it is impossible to effect different treatments for definite and indefinite noun phrases or to resolve ellipsed verb phrases [Webber 1978a], a necessary step in producing adequate IDs. Moreover, there is no way in a "flat" predicate calculus representation to distinguish a noun phrase embedded in a relative clause from one in a matrix clause. (This is another necessary distinction discussed in [Webber 1978a].)

One formalism that both contains the logical operators and allows the above distinctions to be made is an extension of *restricted quantification.*[1] In restricted quantification, a quantification operator (e.g. $\forall$, $\exists$). the variable of quantification and the class it ranges over (noted implicitly as a predicate) constitute a structural unit of the representation - i.e., $(Qx:P)$ where Q is a quantification operator; x, the variable of quantification; and P, a predicate. For example, *Every boy is happy* can be represented as

$$(\forall x:\text{Boy}) . \text{Happy}(x)$$

This is truth functionally equivalent to

$$\forall x . \text{Boy} (x) \supset \text{Happy}(x)$$

Similarly *Some boy is happy* can be represented as

$$(\exists x:\text{Boy}) . \text{Happy}(x)$$

which is truth functionally equivalent to

$$(\exists x) . \text{Boy}(x) \wedge \text{Happy}(x)$$

---

1. The formalism actually being used to implement these ideas is KL-ONE, a uniform language based on the idea of structured inheritance networks [Brachman 1978, 1979]. KL-ONE has several advantages over even a typed first-order predicate calculus (TOPC) formalism: being a non-linear representation, it allows for partial ordering of dependencies. (In the FOPC, left-to-right ordering rigidly defines dependencies.) Moreover, it will allow us to represent -- in terms of mappings -- all and only the combinatoric information currently known.[Bobrow and Webber 1980a]

To extend this notation to include relative clauses is quite simple. Semantically, a relative clause can be viewed as a predicate, albeit a complex one. One way to provide for arbitrarily complex predicates is through the use of the abstraction (or "λ") operator. For example, the noun phrase *a peanut* can be represented as

∃x:Peanut

while the noun phrase *a peanut that Wendy gave to a gorilla* can be represented as

∃x:λ(u:Peanut)[(∃y:Gorilla) . Gave(Wendy,u,y)]

This follows the same format as (Qx:P) as above. In this case

λ(u:Peanut)[(∃y:Gorilla) . Gave(Wendy,u,y)]

specifies a unary predicate which is true if its argument is a peanut that Wendy gave to some gorilla.

Notice that representing NPs in terms of (possibly complex) typed quantifiers in this way provides for both explicit and implicit dependencies between noun phrases - explicitly, by allowing the type-predicate of one variable to depend on the value of another, and implicitly, by quantifier ordering and attendant discourse-related or real-world knowledge.

6.4.2 Singular Noun Phrases

I argued in Section 6.3 that in order to form appropriate IDs, it was necessary to distinguish whether a noun phrase was singular or plural, definite or indefinite.[1] One way to do so is to use a typed existential quantificational operator ("there exists", or ∃) for indefinite NPs and another operator - ∃!, to be read "there exists a unique" - for definite NPs. Both are of the form

⟨operator⟩⟨variable⟩:⟨S⟩

where ⟨operator⟩ is either ∃ or ∃! and ⟨S⟩ is an open sentence in ⟨variable⟩. For example,

---

1. The following discussion contains a more uniform treatment of definite and indefinite noun phrases than that presented in [Webber 1978a]. However, it does not attempt to capture the notion of underconstrained combinatorics.

∃x: Hat   a hat
∃!x:λ(u:Hat)Saw(Sue,u)   the hat Sue saw
∃x:λ(u:Hat)Red(u)   a red hat

6.4.3 Plural Noun Phrases

As for the singular/plural noun phrase distinction, one can have the unmarked
case correspond to singular NPs, as above. However, the standard logical way to
specify a set via its defining property (or set of properties)[1] - i.e., where {u|the
arbitrary predicate P} represents the set of things u for which Pu is true - is
inadequate for representing all plural noun phrases, as it does not allow one to
predicate things about the sets themselves. This is because {u|Pu} always refers to
the maximal set of u's such that Pu is true. For example, this notation is
inadequate to represent noun phrases like

> three men who tried to lift a piano

> massed bagpipe bands

The sense of the former is *some* set of men, of cardinality three, who together tried
to lift a piano.

One way to remedy this deficiency is to introduce a way of getting at the
subsets of a given set, a way provided by the standard mathematical notion of a
power set. The power set of a given set is the complete set of its subsets. The
mathematical notation used to indicate the power set of the set A is 2^A. This
reflects the fact that the size of the power set of a set is 2 raised to the size of the
set. Corresponding to this, but in terms of predicates (whose extensions are sets)
rather than in terms of sets directly, one can use a function, set, which takes
predicates on individual x's to predicates on sets of x's. For example, if *Man* is a
predicate which is true if its argument is an individual man, then set(*Man*) is a
predicate which is true if its argument is a set of men. Similarly, if

> λ(v:Man)[(∃y:Piano) l (v,y)]

is a predicate true if its argument is a man who lifted a piano, then

---

1. A set may also be specified explicitly via a list of its members.

$$\lambda(v{:}set(Man))[(\exists y{:}Piano)L(v,y)]$$

is a predicate true if its argument is a set of men such that the set of them lifted a piano. On the other hand,

$$set(\lambda(v{:}Man)[(\exists y{:}Piano) . L(v,y)])$$

is a predicate which is true if its argument is a set of men, each of whom lifted a piano. [1]

All plurals (besides conjunctions like *Bob and Carol and Ted and Alice*) can now be represented with this set operator, the difference between definite and indefinite coming out in the choice of quantifier. For example,

> (i) $\exists x{:}\ \lambda(v{:}set(Man))[(\exists y{:}Piano)\ L(v,y)]$
> some men who (together) lifted a piano

> (ii) $\exists x{:}\ set(\lambda(v{:}Man)[(\exists y{:}Piano)\ L(v,y)])$
> some men who (each) lifted a piano

Definite plurals can be represented like definite singulars using the "unique existential" operator.

> (iii) $\exists!x{:}\ \lambda(v{:}set(Man))[(\exists y{:}Piano)\ L(v,y)]$
> the men who (together) lifted a piano
> (iv) $\exists!x{:}\ set(\lambda(v{:}Man)[(\exists y{:}Piano)\ L(v,y)])$
> the men who (each) lifted a piano

In (iv) the definiteness of the plural should be interpreted as indicating the *total* set of all and only those individuals (in the context) satisfying the given predicate.

Cardinality, if specified (e.g. *two men*, *the two men*, etc.), can be included in these representations simply by using the cardinality "| |" and equality "=" operators. For example, parallel to (i)-(iv) above are

> $\exists x{:}\ \lambda(v{:}set(Man))[(\exists y{:}Pig) . L(v,y) \wedge |v|=3]$
> "three men who (together) lifted a pig"

> $\exists x{:}\ \lambda(u{:}set(\lambda(v{:}Man)[(\exists y{:}Pig) . L(v,y)]))[|u|=3]$
> "three men who (each) lifted a pig"

---

1. I am assuming that predicates like L ("lift") can be applied to both individuals and sets, with the appropriate semantics falling out at evaluation. This notion of "semantic overloading" is well-known in the programming languages literature.

∃!x: λ(v:set(Man))[(∃y:Pig) . L(v,y) ∧ |v|=3]
"the three men who (together) lifted a pig"

∃!x: λ(u:set(λ(v:Man)[(∃y:Pig) L(v,y)]))[|u|=3]
"the three men who (each) lifted a pig"

At this point, the reader might be puzzled about the absence of universal quantifiers - ∀'s - thus far, given that in elementary logic, the standard practice is to use them to represent plural noun phrases. The standard example of this is

All men are mortal
∀x . Man(x) ⊃ Mortal(x)

However, this assumes that things are only attributable to individuals, and as I discussed earlier, English allows things to be attributed to sets as well. Adopting the above conventions permits a separation of the notions of focusing the listener on a set of things and of saying something about that set or about its individual members. Only when attributing some property to each member of some set, would one add in a universal quantifier. For example,

Three men ate a pizza.
(∃x:λ(u:set(Man))[|u|=3])(∃y:Pizza) Ate(x,y)

Three men each ate a pizza.
(∃x:λ(u:set(Man))[|u|=3])(∀w∈x)(∃y:Pizza) Ate(w,y)

The three men ate a pizza.
(∃!x: λ(u:set(Man))[|u|=3])(∃y:Pizza) Ate(x,y)

The three men each ate a pizza.
(∃!x: λ(u:set(Man))[|u|=3])(∀w∈x)(∃y:Pizza) Ate(w,y)

Now one might still choose to interpret sentences like "each man ate a pizza" simply in terms of a universal quantifier - i.e.,

Each man ate a pizza
(∀x: Man)(∃y: Pizza) Ate(x,y)

However, this misses the point that such sentences are rarely meant to imply true universality. Rather they imply that the predicate holds of every member of some more limited set that the speaker and listener jointly recognize. That is, "each ⟨x⟩" is more correctly interpreted as "each of the ⟨x⟩s" - i.e., in terms of a definite set and a universal quantifier over that set:

Each man ate a pizza.
(∃!w: set(Man))(∀x∈w)(∃y: Pizza) Ate(x,y)

As with other definite noun phrases, it is the task of pragmatics to figure out what accounts for the definiteness, including definiteness by virtue of being the total/universal set of things describable as an ⟨x⟩. In the following discussion - as in [Bobrow and Webber 1981] - I will be representing explicitly the definite set associated with "each NPs".

6.4.4 Deriving Discourse Entity IDs

6.4.4.1 IDs for Specific Discourse Entities

Following the example formalism presented in Section 6.4, the sentence representations we are interested in will have the form

$$Q . P \; x_1,...,x_n, d_1,...,d_k$$

where Q stands for a (possibly empty) sequence of typed quantifiers - the "quantifier collar" - and P, a (possibly complex) predicate applied to the variables of quantification $x_1,...,x_n$. For example, the sentence

Each boy gave a girl he knew three peaches

has one reading (i.e., the one in which *he* varies with *each boy*) which can be represented as

(∃!s: set(Boy))(∀x∈s) (∃y: λ(u:Girl) [Know(x,u)])
(∃z: λ(w:set(Peach))[|w| = 3]) Gave(x,y,z))

Here the representation for the clause is simply the open formula

Gave(x,y,z)

while the noun phrases correspond to elements in the quantifier collar. The variable x is shown to range over individual boys from the definite set indicated by "s", the variable y is shown to select, for each boy, an individual girl he knows, while the variable z ranges over sets of individual peaches whose cardinality is 3.

In this representation - a type of Prenex Normal Form - the open formula to the right of the quantifier collar can be viewed as a *pattern* - a way of describing a *set* of ground literal formulas by giving their *syntactic shape*. The literals in this set will vary according to how individual constants are substituted for the variables in the pattern. The quantifier collar, on the other hand, can be viewed as a *combinatoric specification* which determines what ordered combinations of constants can be assigned to the variables to instantiate or stamp out copies of the pattern. Among the combinatoric constraints on individual instantiations are the three earlier mentioned factors - dependency, distribution and cardinality. It is with respect to these three factors[1] that the rules for forming appropriate specific (as opposed to generic) discourse entity IDs can be specified.

In what follows, I will first present two rules for forming IDs where the evoking noun phrase (NP) is not dependent on any iteration, and then two rules for forming IDs when there is such a dependency. The IDs are formed by a procedure which moves across a clause representation left-to-right, applying whichever rule matches in order to identify the next discourse entity, and then rewriting the representation in terms of that entity in order to remove some of the quantificational complexity. (This should become clearer through the examples.)

One further note before beginning: in [Webber 1978a], I needed six rules in order to account for the same data as here. The current reduction comes from a more uniform treatment of definite and indefinite NPs - cf. Section 6.4.2 - and a treatment of "each" NPs as iterating over some definite (possibly discourse-definite) set - i.e., representing "each" NPs as a quantifier sequence of the form ($\exists!$ $\forall$). cf. Section 6.4.3

Non-iterated Contexts

Here we consider discourse entities evoked in the following two contexts

$$(\exists x : \langle type \rangle) . P(x)$$
$$(\exists!x : \langle type \rangle) . P(x)$$

where $\langle type \rangle$ is either a predicate on individuals or a predicate on sets. The relevant point is that the quantifier ($\exists$ or $\exists!$) is not within the scope of a distributive ($\forall$). Rule 1 below applies to singular and plural indefinites ($\exists$), Rule 2 to singular and plural definites ($\exists!$).

As for notation, I will limit myself to unary predicates, since any n-ary predicate can be rewritten as a unary one on the variable of interest by "lambda-fication" - i.e.,

$$P(x,y_1,...,y_k) \Rightarrow$$

---

1. disregarding other factors like tense, negation and modality [Webber 1978a].

$$\lambda(u)[P(u, y_1,...,y_k)] \, x =_{def} P'(x)$$

I will also not make explicit any quantifiers to the right of the one of interest, absorbing them rather into the predicate for simplicity - i.e.,

$$(\exists x Q) \quad Quant_2...Quant_k \quad . \quad P(x),... \quad \supset \quad (\exists x Q)$$
$$\lambda(u)[Quant_2...Quant_k . Pu,...] \, x \ =_{def} (\exists x Q) . P'(x)$$

Rule 1: The first rule applies in the following indefinite contexts (left column) to produce discourse entities with IDs as in the right column. (The clause being processed is labeled S and i stands for the iota function used in forming definite descriptions.)

$(\exists x Q) . P(x)$	$iX: Qx \wedge P(x) \wedge Evoke(S,x)$
$(\exists x: set(Q)) . P(X)$	$iX: set(Q)X \wedge P(X) \wedge Evoke(S,X)$
$(\exists x: set(Q))(\forall x \in X) . P(x)$	$iX: set(Q)X \wedge (\forall x \in X) P(x)$
	$\wedge Evoke(S,X)$

Rule 1 has the effect of associating with a clause like

> I saw a cat.
> $(\exists x: Cat) Saw(I,x)$

the discourse entity describable as

> "the cat I saw that was evoked by sentence S"
> $iX: Cat(x) \wedge Saw(I,x) \wedge Evoke(S,X)$

("Evoke" corresponds to the predicate discussed in Section 6.3.1.) Rule 1 also associates with a clause like

> I saw three cats.
> $(\exists x: \lambda(u{:}set(Cat))[|u|=3]) . Saw(I,x)$

the discourse entity describable as

> "the three cats that I saw that were evoked by S"
> $iX: \lambda(u{:}set(Cat))[|u|=3]X \wedge Saw(I,x) \wedge Evoke(S,X)$

and with the clause

Three cats each danced the tango.
(∃x: λ(u:set(Cat))[|u| = 3])(∀x∈X) . Tango(x)

the discourse entity describable as

"the three cats who each danced the tango
that were evoked by S"
iX: λ(u:set(Cat))[|u| = 3]X ∧ (∀x∈X) . Tango(x)
∧ Evoke(S,X)

Rule 2: The second rule applies in the following three definite contexts (left column) to produce discourse entities with IDs as in the right column.

(∃!x:Q) . P(x)	iX:Qx
(∃!x:set(Q)) . P(X)	iX:QX
(∃!x:set(Q))(∀x∈X) . P(x)	iX:QX

This rule is very simple, assigning to each discourse entity associated with an independent definite NP, simply that description. If the definite is meant to be anaphoric, then this new description must be compatible with ones already attributed to the entity so specified. If not, the ID is assigned to the newly evoked entity. Rule 2 is intended to cover all the following cases:

- I saw the cat who hates Sam.

- I saw the cats who hate Sam.

- I saw the three cats who hate Sam.

- The three cats who hate Sam each plotted mayhem.

But since its application and consequences are so simple, I will not bother to go through specific examples.

At this point, I want to take up the restriction in Rules 1 and 2 that the quantifier ∃ or ∃! appear at the left end of the wff. What about quantifiers "in the middle"? Because the clause is being processed sequentially left-to-right, this is not a problem. To see this, consider a wff of the form

$$(Hx_1:Q_1)(Hx_2:Q_2) ... P(x_1,x_2)$$

where H is either indefinite (∃) or definite (∃!), Q_2 may be dependent on x_1, and Q_1 and Q_2 may be predicates on either sets or individuals -- for example

Some boy kissed a girl he liked.
$$(\exists x_1: Boy)(\exists x_2:\lambda(u:Girl)\,[Liked(x_1,u)])\,K(x_1,x_2)$$

After the first quantifier $(\exists x_1: Boy)$ is processed and its associated discourse entity (e_1) identified, we can rewrite this wff in terms of e_1, thereby removing the first quantifier - i.e.,

$$(\exists x_2: \lambda(u:Girl)\,[Liked(e_1,u)])\,K(e_1,x)$$

That is, the wff schema given above can be rewritten as

$$(\exists x_2:Q_2)\,...P(e_1, x_2)$$

or if Q_2 depends on x_1, as it does in the "boy kiss girl" example,

$$(\exists x_2:Q_2(e_1))\,...P(e_1,x_2)$$

Thus, provided there is no distributive between the two quantifiers, each will in turn be leftmost and be matched by either Rule 1 or Rule 2. The two cases where a distributive is interposed between the two quantifiers will be taken up in the next section.

Iterated Contexts

Here we consider discourse entities evoked in the remaining two contexts

$$\text{indefinite: } (\forall y_1...y_k)(\exists x:\langle type\rangle)\,.\,P(x)$$

$$\text{definite: } (\forall y_1...y_k)(\exists! x:\langle type\rangle)\,.\,P(x)$$

where $\langle type\rangle$ is either a predicate on individuals or a predicate on sets, and may be a function of $y_1...y_k$. (In the definite case, it must be dependent on one or more of these variables in order for Rule 4 below to be applicable. Otherwise, the definite might just as well be to the left of the distributives, matching the context of Rule 2. The notations $(\forall y_1...y_k)$ and $(\exists y_1...y_k)$ are, respectively, short for

$$(\forall y_1 \in e_1)...(\forall y_k \in e_k)$$

and

$$(\exists y_1 \in e_1)...(\exists y_k \in e_k)$$

where $e_1...e_k$ are set-type discourse entities. How arbitrary wffs can be rewritten in the above rather general format will be justified after Rules 3 and 4 are presented.

Rule 3: The third rule applies in the following three indefinite contexts (left column) to produce the discourse entity IDs in the right.

$(\forall y_1...y_k)(\exists x:Q) . P(x)$ $(x|Qx \wedge (\exists y_1...y_k) . P(x)$
     $\wedge$ Evoke(S,X))

$(\forall y_1...y_k)(\exists X: set(Q)) . P(x)$ $(X | set(Q)X \wedge (\exists y_1...y_k) . P(X)$
     $\wedge$ Evoke(S,X))

$(\forall y_1...y_k)(\exists X: set(Q))(\forall x: X) . P(x)$ $(X | set(Q)X \wedge (\exists y_1...y_k)$
     $\wedge (\forall x \in X) . P(x) \wedge$ Evoke(S,X))

where P(x) stands for $\lambda(u)[P\ u, y_1,...y_k]x$ and Q may depend on one or more of the y's. The set notation [x | ...] should be interpreted as the set of all things for which the right-hand side description is true - i.e., the maximal set.

This rule has the effect of associating with the indefinite singular in a clause like

> Each cat ate a mouse it saw.
> $(\forall y \in c_1)(\exists x: \lambda(u:Mouse)[Saw\ y,u]) .$ Ate y,x

(where c_1 is the discourse entity associated with the definite set of cats) the discourse entity describable as

> the set of things each of which is a mouse and for each of which there is a cat who saw it and ate it and which was evoked by S
> $(x | (\exists y \in c_1)$ Mouse(x) $\wedge$ Ate(y,x) $\wedge$ Evoke(S,X))

and associating with the indefinite plural in a clause like

> Each cat ate three mice.
> $(\forall y \in c_1)(\exists x: \lambda(u:set(Mouse))[|u| = 3]) .$ Ate(y,x)

the discourse entity describable as

> the set of things, each of which is a set of three mice and for each of which there is a cat who ate them and which was evoked by S
> $(X | (\exists y \in c_1)$ set(Mouse)X $\wedge$ Ate(y,x) $\wedge$ Evoke(S,x))

and finally, associating with the indefinite plural distributive in a clause like

Each cat ate three mice, one by one.
$(\forall y \in c_1)(\exists x: \lambda(u:set(Mouse))[|u|=3])(\forall x \in X) . Ate(y,x)$.

the discourse entity describable as

the set of things, each of which is a set of three mice and for which there's a cat who ate each one of them and which was evoked by S
$[X|(\exists y \in c_1) set(Mouse)X \wedge (\forall x \in X) Ate(y,x) \wedge Evoke(S,X)]$

Rule 4: The fourth and final rule applies in the following three definite contexts (left column) to produce the discourse entity IDs in the right.

$(\forall y_1...y_k)(\exists!x:Q) . P(x)$ $[X|(\exists y_1...y_k) . Qx]$

$(\forall y_1...y_k)(\exists!x:set(Q)) . P(X)$ $[X|(\exists y_1...y_k) . set(Q)X]$

$(\forall y_1...y_k)(\exists!x:set(Q))(\forall x \in X) . P(x)$ $[X|(\exists y_1...y_k) . set(Q)X]$

This rule is intended to cover such cases as

- In each car the steering wheel was stuck.

- Each boy piled up his own books.

- In each car the two front wheels were under-pressured.

It has the effect of associating with the NP "the steering wheel" in the first clause

In each car the steering wheel was stuck.
$(\forall x \in c_1)(\exists!y: \lambda(u:S\text{-}Wheel)[Have u,x]) . Stuck y$

the discourse entity describable as

the set of things, each of which is the steering wheel of one of the cars
$[x| (\exists y \in c_1) . S\text{-}Wheel(x) \wedge Have(x,y)]$

where "S-Wheel" stands for *steering wheel*, c_1 is the discourse entity associated with the definite set of cars, and "Have" is a rough encoding of the implicit dependency relationship between steering wheel and car.

Rule 4 also associates with the NP *his own books* in the second clause

Each boy piled up his own books.

$$(\forall x \in c_2)(\exists!Y: \lambda(u:set(Book))[Have(u,x)]) \cdot P(x,y)$$

the discourse entity describable as

> the set of things, each of which is associated with some boy as
> his set of books
> $(Y | (\exists x \in c_2) \cdot set(Book)Y \wedge Have(y,x))$

where c_2 is the discourse entity associated with the definite set of boys and "P" stands for "piled up".

And finally, it associates with the NP "the front wheels" in the third clause

> In each car the two front wheels were underpressured.
> $(\forall x \in c_1)(\exists!Y: \lambda(u:set(F\text{-}Wheel))[|u|=2 \wedge Have(u,x)])$
> $(\forall y \in Y) \cdot Underpressured(y)$

the discourse entity describable as

> the set of things, each of which is associated with some car and
> is the set of two front wheels for that car
> $(Y | (\exists x \in c_1) \lambda(u:set(Wheel))[|u|=2]Y \wedge Have(Y,x))$

where c_1 is again the discourse entity associated with the definite set of cars.

Before winding up this presentation, I want to take up the restriction in Rules 3 and 4 that a distributive context can be represented simply as a quantifier collar of the form

$$(\forall y_1 \in c_1)...(\forall y_k \in c_k)$$

i.e., a form with no indefinite or definite existentials, which I have been abbreviating as

$$(\forall y_1...y_k)$$

Again, because the clause is being processed sequentially left-to-right, this restriction does not pose a problem. To see this, consider any of the following situations

- $(\exists y: set(Q_1))(\forall y \in Y)(\exists x:Q_2)...P(x),...$

- $(\exists y: set(Q_1))(\forall y \in Y)(\exists!x:Q_2)...P(x),...$

- $(\exists!Y: set(Q_1))(\forall y \in Y)(\exists x: Q_2)...P(x),...$

- $(\exists!Y: \text{set}(Q_1))(\forall y \in Y)(\exists!x: Q_2)...P(x),...$

which all have existentials ($\exists$ or $\exists!$) as well as distributive quantifiers ($\forall$) before the quantifier in question ($\exists x: Q_2$) or ($\exists!x: Q_2$). Notice that because of the way "each", "every", etc. are treated, every distributive is paired with an existential set that specifies the domain of the distribution. Q_2 may be a predicate on individuals or a predicate on sets, and in either case, may depend on y. (If Q_2 merely depends on Y_1, then it is simply a case covered by Rule 2 above.)

I showed earlier how simple existentials could be removed. Now for the existential-distributive pairs, by Rule 1 in the first two cases and Rule 2 in the second two, one can identify the discourse entity e_j associated with the leftmost pair and subsequently rewrite it as

$(\forall y \in e_j)$.

Rule 3 can now be used to remove any indefinite existentials in the scope of this distributive and Rule 4, any definite existentials in its scope, leaving the above form

$(\forall y_1 \in e_1)...(\forall y_k \in e_k)(\exists x:Q)...P\, x,...$

This concludes my presentation of the four rules needed to account for the specific discourse entities evoked by (disambiguated) quantified expressions. In the next section, I take up the issue of generic set entities.

6.4.5 IDs for Derived Entities: Generic Sets

Not all definite plural anaphora are intended to specify **particular** sets of $\langle x \rangle$s evoked by a text. Others seem intended to specify sets that one could characterize roughly as "the set of things describable as an $\langle x \rangle$". These set entities I have called "generic sets", although I do not mean to imply thereby that $\langle x \rangle$ need be any sort of "natural genus". For example, just as a definite plural anaphor may specify a particular sets of $\langle x \rangle$s like

D21-1 I see three Japanese cars outside.
  2 Do any of them belong to you?

them $\equiv$ the just-mentioned Japanese cars I see outside

D22-1 Last week Wendy again bought each boy a green T-shirt at Macy's.
    2 She's always buying them.

> *them ≡ the just mentioned green T-shirts, each of which Wendy bought at Macy's for some boy)*

a definite plural anaphor may also specify a generic set entity like

D23-1 I see seven Japanese cars in the parking lot.
    2 They're really selling like hot cakes.

> *they ≡ Japanese cars*

D24-1 Last week Wendy bought each boy a green T-shirt at Macy's.
    2 She gives them to everyone.

> *them ≡ green T-shirts*

The important questions regarding access to generic sets are thus:

> 1. When is a definite plural anaphor interpreted as specifying a generic set?

> 2. Is there a limit on the generic sets that a definite plural anaphor can specify, and if so, in what way is that limit related to the material present in the text and where it is located?>

Aspects of these questions are discussed in Sidner (Chapter 5 of this volume) and [Sidner 1979]. In particular, she shows that it is the elements in focus at any particular time that are the major (if not the only) textual source of generic set entities. Reflecting this, she augments her anaphor resolution heuristics for definite plural anaphora to try generic set resolvants based on the elements in focus at the particular time. The complementary problem that I have considered and want to discuss briefly here is that of characterizing this "based on" relation between focused elements and generic set entities and hence, the range of generic set entities that can and cannot be accessed.[1]

For example, the entity describable as *the set of just-mentioned green T-shirts, each of which Wendy gave to some boy* can give rise to an entity appropriately describable as *green T-shirts* as in D24 above, or even *T-shirts* as in D-23 below, but not *shirts, cotton things*, etc. If one of the latter is required to understand an utterance, it is distinctly bizarre, as in example D-25.

D25-1 Last week Wendy bought each boy a green T-shirt at Macy's.
2 She prefers them in more subdued colors, but these were on sale.
D26-1 The green T-shirt you gave me is lovely.
2 ?? But I prefer them with long sleeves and a button-down collar.
them ≡ *shirts*

I would like to claim that the listener can generate new generic-set entities, whose IDs are based on generalizations of a recent description the listener has either heard or derived. These generalizations will be limited to ones that the listener can, with some certainty, assume that the speaker assumes that s/he - the listener - can (and will) make. That is, they will rarely depend on world knowledge - even a type/inheritance hierarchy, since that cannot be assumed to be shared.

As for the descriptions that are subject to such generalizations, I agree with Sidner that they are related to notions of focus - what the speaker is talking about and in terms of. Such available descriptions can include not only (1) the IDs derived for and ascribable to all the focused discourse entities, but also (2) those descriptions in the text which don't evoke or access discourse entities. To see this, consider the following two examples.

D27-1 Wendy bought some T-shirts yesterday.
Usually she charges them, but yesterday, she paid cash.
them ≡ *T-shirts Wendy buys*
D28-1 Wendy wouldn't buy a green T-shirt, because they always run in the wash.
them ≡ *green T-shirts*

In D27 the generic set accessed by *them* is not describable by a generalization

---

1. There are other definite plural anaphors that seem to target entities corresponding to the "natural set" to which a given individual belongs, perhaps in a given context. Ellen Prince (personal communication) has pointed out the following example in a transcript of spoken narrative:

I went to pick up Jan the other day. You know, they live in that big house on Vine.

Here *they* seems to access Jan's natural "living" set - i.e., her family. However, I don't plan to discuss here the characteristics and boundaries of that inferential process that makes such entities (and not other ones) available to the listener and allows the speaker to correctly presume that availability.

of anything explicitly in the text. Rather it is describable by a generalization of the discourse entity ID *the just-mentioned set of T-shirts that Wendy bought yesterday*. In D28, on the other hand, no specific discourse entity is evoked by the indefinite noun phrase *a green T-shirt*, yet *they* is able to access the discourse entity describable as *green T-shirts*. Thus I believe that both explicit text descriptions (which don't necessarily evoke discourse entities) and discourse entity IDs are sources of generalizable descriptions and hence, of the discourse entities associated with them.

The accessibility of generic sets demands attention for several reasons. Most obviously, one must account for the instances of definite anaphora that seem to access them. Less obviously, it allows for a uniform account to be given of "one" anaphora, as I shall show in the next section. And finally, it is yet another instance of the generally intriguing problem of what inferences a speaker can assume a listener both capable of and likely to make.

6.5 One Anaphora

The anaphoric use of the work "one" (or "ones") is another phenomenon common to natural English discourse. On the surface, an anaphoric-"one" noun phrase is immediately recognizable in that it has the word "one(s)" taking the place of (at least) its head noun. For example,

- one that I heard long ago

- the striped one you got from Harry

- three small ones

Not all uses of "one" in English are anaphoric, of course: "one" is used by itself as a formal, non-specific third person pronoun e.g.,

- One is cautioned against harassing the bears

- One doesn't do that in polite company

or as a number - e.g.,

- One true faith, two French hens, ...

- We arrived at one p.m.

Although in most cases it is easy to distinguish anaphoric from formal or numeric "one" on surface syntactic grounds alone, it is possible for there to be syntactically ambiguous cases in text,[1] e.g.,

- Since anyone can choose his favorite number, I want one.

- Since John has a cat and I don't, I want one.

In linguistics, one can point to at least two significantly different approaches to "one" anaphora: the transformational approach (which is concerned with its syntax) and the text-level approach (which is more concerned with semantics). Since the approach that I will be presenting here differs from both of these, I will mention them both to provide a basis for comparison.

In transformational grammar, "one" anaphora has been discussed purely syntactically, as an intra-sentential **substitution** phenomenon. For example, Baker [Baker 1978] presents such an account in the context of deciding between two alternative structural analyses of noun phrases - the so-called "NP-S analysis" and the "Det-Nom analysis". The rewrite rules of these two analyses are roughly as follows:

NP-S

NP --> NP S
NP --> Det N

Det-Nom

NP --> Det Nom
Nom --> Nom S | Nom PP | Adj Nom
Nom --> N

Baker argues for the "Det-Nom analysis" because it seems to allow the simplest statement in terms of *structural identity* of what "one(s)" can substitute for. The statement that Baker arrives at is

X	NOM	Y	ADJ	NOM	Z
	the	Number	+count		
1	2	3	4	5	6

condition: $2 = 5$
$\Rightarrow$ 1, 2, 3, 4, one , 6
Number

where a NOM inherits its features (e.g. count, NUMBER, etc.) from those of its

---

head noun. Informally, the above transformation states that a NOM constituent preceded by an adjective or definite determiner, whose head is a count noun, can be replaced by "one" or "ones" (depending on whether the NOM is singular or plural in NUMBER) if an identical NOM appears earlier in the sentence. This transformation is meant to account for examples like

D29-1 I prefer the striped tie you got from your aunt to the paisley one.

The problem with this structural-identity account is not only that it is limited to individual sentences, but that it is not even an adequate syntactic account at that level. Consider for example is the following.

D30-1 If Mary offered you a new Porsche and Sally offered you a '68 Morgan, which one would you choose?

Under no analysis does this sentence meet the structural conditions of Baker's rule: rather *which one* means roughly "which member of the set consisting of the new Porsche Mary offered you and the '68 Morgan Sally offered you". Baker's approach has nothing to say about this.[1] In text linguistics, a particularly clear (albeit purely discursive) analysis of both definite pronoun and "one" anaphora is presented in [Halliday and Hasan 1976], where the primary concern is with the notion of "cohesion" - what makes a text hold together, what makes it more than a random set of sentences. According to the authors, both definite pronouns and "one(s)" can instantiate types of cohesive relations: the former, the relation of "reference", the latter, the relation of "substitution". "Reference", as Halliday and Hasan use the term, relates a text element like a definite pronoun and

> ...something else by reference to which it is interpreted in the given instance. Reference is a potentially cohesive relation because the thing that serves as the source of the interpretation may itself be an element of text [Halliday and Hasan 1976], pp.308-9.

Except for their terminology, Halliday and Hasan's general position on definite anaphora and its relation to the discourse is not all that far from that which I have been attempting to formalize.

"Substitution" on the other hand, is

---

1. Baker poses an additional constraint on "one" anaphora in [Baker 1979] - effectively, a "transderivational constraint" arbitrating between optional, applicable transformational rules. However, this still treats "one" anaphora purely intra-sententially and still does not address examples such as D30 above.)

a formal (lexicogrammatical) relation, in which a form (word or words) is specified through the use of a grammatical signal indicating that it is to be recovered from what has gone before. The source of recovery is the text, so that the relation of substitution is basically an endophoric one. It is inherently cohesive, since it is the preceding text that provides the relevant environment in which the presupposed item is located [Halliday and Hasan 1976]; p.308.

So unlike definite pronouns, "one(s)" establishes cohesion simply at the level of wording and syntactic structure. Thus except for not confining itself to the single sentence and being more concerned with the function of "one(s)" than with its formal syntax, Halliday and Hasan's account of "one(s)" anaphora still mirrors Baker's.

In [Webber 1978a], I took an approach to formalizing what a text makes available for "one"-anaphora that was not too far from Halliday and Hasan's. I based that work on the view that what "one" accessed was a "description" that the speaker felt was available to the listener. Such descriptions can be made available by the speaker's and hearer's shared spatio-temporal context, as in two people peering into a geology exhibit case and one saying to the other, "Even larger ones were found in the Mare Cambrium." However, a speaker can usually rely more on descriptions s/he has uttered being available to the listener. Hence, the most likely place to look for descriptions accessible to "one" anaphora is the text.

With more thought about the problems in my 1978a approach, I came to feel that a simpler account was possible. My current approach to anaphoric "one(s)" reduces it to the earlier-discussed problem of identifying the possible resolvants of definite plural anaphors. This approach is based on the intuition that "one" phrases always indicate to a listener selection from a set. That is, the interpretation of anaphoric "one" should be the same as the interpretation of "one of them". This reduces the problem to the (still non-trivial) one of identifying the set-type discourse entities (both specific and generic) that this implicit "them" can access.[1]

This way of treating "one" anaphora may seem fairly obvious here: however, its obviousness only follows from considering the sets a text makes available for access and realizing that these sets - both specific and generic - must also be "around" to provide an account of definite anaphora. As for the evidence,

---

1. Evidence for this approach also comes from Baker [Baker 1978]. His rewrite rules - given above - require the "one" constituent to be interpretable as having the feature "+count" - i.e., to be capable of specifying a set. A mass term X, except when interpreted as "types of X", does not specify a set. It is also not open to "one" anaphora, except in this "types of X" case - e.g.

I love red wine, especially ones that have been aged properly.

consider first some specific sets evoked by a text:

D31-1 All the wines in Dave's cellar are drinkable.

2 He bought them 10 years ago.

they ≡ *the wines in Dave's cellar*

D32-1 Sue gave each boy a green hat.

2 She had gotten them on sale.

them ≡ *the set of just mentioned green hats, each of which Wendy gave to some boy*

D33-1 I see a BMW, a Porsche, and an Audi outside.

2 Do they belong to you?

they ≡ *[the just-mentioned BMW I see outside, the just-mentioned Porsche I see outside, the just-mentioned Audi I see outside]*

Each of these can be the implicit set from which a "one" anaphor selects.

D34-1 All the wines in Dave's cellar are drinkable.

2 So bring me the ones he bought in Florence.

SELECT "ones" from: the wines in Dave's cellar

D35-1 Sue gave each boy a green hat.

2 Unfortunately the largest one was torn.

SELECT "one" from: *[the just-mentioned green hats, each of which Sue gave to some boy]*

D36-1 I see a BMW, a Porsche and an Audi outside.

2 Is one yours?

SELECT "one" from:

[the just-mentioned BMW I see outside, the just-mentioned Porsche I see outside, the just-mentioned Audi I see outside]

Notice that there may be additional stipulations given in the text concerning which member or members are to be selected - e.g., *bought in Florence, largest,* etc. However in these examples, selection from a specific set-type discourse entity does account for the data.

Next consider some generic set-type entities evoked by a text.

D37-1 All the wines in Dave's cellar are drinkable.

2 He buys them only from the best merchants.

them ≡ *wines*

D38-1 Sue gave each boy a green hat.
  2 Usually she pays $8 apiece for them.

D39-1 I saw 7 Japanese station wagons today.
  2 They must really be selling like hot cakes.

  they ≡ *Japanese station wagons*

Again, each of these generic sets can be the implicit set from which a "one" anaphor selects.

D40-1 All the wines in Dave's cellar are drinkable.
  2 So we don't need to open the ones he bought yesterday.

  SELECT "ones" from: *wines*

D41-1 Sue gave each boy a green hat.
  2 She gave Wendy one too.

  SELECT "one" from: *green hats*
  3 She gave Wendy a red one.

  SELECT "one" from: *hats*

D42-1 I saw 7 Japanese station wagons on Walnut Street and another one on Pine.

  SELECT "one" from: *Japanese station wagons*
  2 They were all smaller than the French one Jean bought.

  SELECT "one" from: *station wagons*

Notice that just as there may be more than one generic set entity derivable (via generalization) from a salient description, so may there be more than one generic set entity from which a "one" anaphor may select.

The final point I want to make concerns the ability of more subtle inferential processes to make additional set-type entities available to "one" anaphora. As noted in Footnote 16 (illustrated by the example repeated below), inferential processes can certainly make set-type entities accessible to explicit definite anaphora like *they*. However, as the example shows, such entities seem less available to the implicit "of them" in a "one" anaphor.

D43-1 I went to pick up Jan the other day.
  2 You know, they live in that big house on Vine.

  they ≡ *Jan's family*

D44-1 I went to pick up Jan the other day.
2 ?? You know, the older one broke his ankle?[1]

SELECT one from: *Jan's family*

Why this is the case is not clear. Intuitively, one could say that it was easier for a listener to take an explicit *they* via Jan to Jan's family, than it was to take "one" to an implicit *they* then via Jan through Jan's family to a selection from that set. As I noted earlier, I have not investigated the boundaries of the inferential processes which might make such associated "natural set" entities available. More to the point, no one I know of has as yet really investigated the actual distribution of "one" anaphora to look at the range of inferential processes assumed to be at work there. Whatever the results of such investigations may be though, I am sure that this unified approach to dealing with definite plural and "one" anaphora has the joint advantages of elegance and computational efficiency. We are currently at work on its implementation.[2]

6.6 Conclusion

I am writing this paper three years after completing and publishing the results of my thesis research. Since then the other authors represented in this volume have finished their research as well. I have thus been able to benefit from their investigations in rethinking my past research and composing this paper. I have also benefitted from their many useful comments on it.

What I have presented here is an approach to identifying what particular kinds of noun phrases make available to talk about next (definite anaphora) or in terms of next (one anaphora). In some way, this must be part of any speaker's knowledge of the language. If s/he wants to talk about (or in terms of) something and have the listener follow, s/he must obey the rules presented here at least more often than not. Sidner also presents similar rules, relating to sentence organization - some positions inviting the inference more than others that the associated entity will be talked about or in terms of next. McDonald's concern is to provide these types of knowledge for real time generation.

It is exciting to be working in this area, and it is my feeling that results of

---

1. I am aware that it seems perfectly fine to say "You know, the one who broke his ankle?". In that case, it would seem that "one" is selecting from the generic set of Jans that the speaker presumes the listener to know (and possibly confuse). How proper names evoke generic sets is an object of further study.
2. Work being carried out at Bolt Beranek and Newman Inc. and the University of Pennsylvania.

interest both psycholinguistically and computationally will continue to be produced.

BIBLIOGRAPHY

Aho, A. and Ullman, J. 1972 The Theory of Parsing, Translation, and Compiling Vol. 1, Englewood Cliffs, NJ: Prentice-Hall.

Aho, A. and Ullman, J. [1973] The Theory of Parsing, Translation, and Compiling, Vol. 2, Englewood Cliffs, NJ: Prentice-Hall.

Allen, J. 1979 *A Plan Based Approach to Speech Act Recognition*, TR 121/79, Department of Computer Science, University of Toronto, Toronto.

Allen, J.F., and Perrault, C.R. 1980 *Analyzing intention in utterances*, Artificial Intelligence 15(3): 143-178.

Austin, J.L. 1962 How To Do Things With Words, New York: Oxford University Press.

Baker, C.L. 1978 Introduction to Generative-Transformational Syntax, Englewood Cliffs NJ: Prentice-Hall, Inc.

Baker, C.L. 1979 *Syntactic theory and the projection problem*, Linguistic Inquiry 10(4): 533-581.

Baranovsky, S. 1973 *Some heuristics for Automatic Detection and Resolution of Anaphora in Discourse*, M.S. thesis, Dept. of Computer Sciences, University of Texas, Austin.

Barwise, J. and Perry, J. 1982 Situations and Attitudes, Cambridge, MA: Bradford Books.

Belnap, N.D., and T.B. Steel, 1976 The Logic of Questions and Answers, Yale University Press, New Haven, Conn.

Belnap, N.D., 1963 *An Analysis of Questions: Preliminary Report*, TM-1287/000/00, Systems Development Corp., Santa Monica, Ca..

Berwick, R. and K. Wexler 1982 *Parsing constraints and binding*, Proceedings of the First West Coast Conference on Formal Linguistics, Stanford University.

Berwick, B. and Weinberg, A. 1982 *The Role of Grammars in Models of Language Use*, Cognition, in press.

Bobrow, D.G. and Winograd, T. 1977 *An Overview of KRL, A Knowledge Representation Language*, Cognitive Science, 1(1):3-46.

Bobrow, R.J. and Webber, B.L. 1980a. *PSI-KLONE: Parsing and semantic interpretation in the BBN natural language understanding system*, Proc. 1980 Canadian Society for Computational Studies of Intelligence Conference, pp.131-142.

Bobrow, R.J. and Webber, B.L. 1980b. *Knowledge representation for syntatic/semantic processing*, Proc. 1st Annual Conference of the American Association for Artificial Intelligence, Stanford University, Stanford CA, pp. 316-323.

Bobrow, R.J. and Webber, B.L. 1981 *Parsing and semantic interpretation as incremental recognition*, Symposium on Human Parsing Strategies, University of Texas, Austin TX.

Brachman, R. 1978 *A structural paradigm for representing knowledge*, Technical Report 3605, Bolt Beranek & Newman Inc., Cambridge MA.

Brachman, R. 1979 *On the epistemological status of semantic networks*, in Associative Networks, ed. N. Findler. New York: Academic Press, pp. 3-50.

Brachman, R. J., Bobrow, R. J., Cohen, P., Klovstad, J. W., Webber, B. L. and Woods, W. A. 1979 *Research in Natural Language Understanding: Annual Report September 1, 1978 to August 31, 1979*, Bolt Beranek & Newman, Cambridge, Massachusetts.

Brady, Michael 1981 Computer Vision, Amsterdam: North-Holland.

Bresnan, J. 1978 *A realistic transformational grammar* in Linguistic Theory and Psychological Reality, ed. M. Halle, J. Bresnan, G. Miller, MIT Press, pp. 1-54.

Bronnenberg, W., Bunt, H., Landsbergen, S., Scha, R., Schoenmakers, W., and Van Utteren, E. 1980 *The Question-ANswering System PHLIQA1*, in Natural Language Question Answering Systems, ed. L. Bloc Munich, Germany: Hanser Publishing.

Brown, G.P. 1980 *Characterizing indirect speech acts*, Am. J. Comp. Linguistics 6(3-4):150-166.

Brown, R. H. 1973 *Use of Multiple-Body Interupts in Discourse Generation*, B.S. Dissertation, Massachusetts Institute of Technology.

Bruce, B.C. 1975 *Case systems for natural language*, Technical Report 3010, Bolt Beranek & Newman Inc., Cambridge MA.

Bruce, B.C. 1981 *Plans and social action*, Theoretical Issues in Reading Comprehension, ed. R. Spiro, B. Bruce, and W. Brewer. Hillsdale, NJ: Lawrence Erlbaum Associates, Publishers.

Burton, R.R. 1976 *Semantic grammar: An engineering technique for constructing natural language understanding systems*, BBN Report 3453.

Chafe, W. 1972 *Discourse Structure and Human Knowledge*, Language Comprehension and the Acquisition of Knowledge, ed. J.B. Carrol and R.O. Freedle. Washington: Winston, pp.41-69.

Charniak, E. 1972 *Toward a Model Of Children's Story Comprehension*, M.I.T. A.I. Lab TR-266, Cambridge, MA.

Chester, 1 1976 *The Translation of Formal Proofs into English*, Artificial Intelligence 7(3), pp.261-278.

Chomsky, N. 1955 The Logical Structure of Linguistic Theory reprinted in part 1975, New York: Plenum.

Chomsky, N. 1965 Aspects of the Theory of Syntax, Cambridge, MA: MIT Press.

Chomsky, N. 1973 *Conditions On Transformations*, in A Festschrift for Morris Halle, ed. S.R. Anderson and P. Kiparsky New York: Holt, Rinehart, and Winston.

Chomsky, N. 1975 Reflections on Language, New York: Pantheon.

Chomsky, N. 1976 *Conditions on Rules of Grammar*, Linguistic Analysis 2(4):303-351.

Chomsky, N. 1977 Essays on Form and Interpretation, New York:

North-Holland.

Chomsky, N. 1977 *On wh-movement* in Formal Syntax, ed. P. Culicover, A. Akmajian, T. Wasow, New york: Academic Press.

Chomsky, N. 1981 Lectures on Government and Binding, Dordrecht: Foris.

Chomsky, N. and Halle, M. 1968 The Sound Pattern of English, New York: Harper and Row.

Clark, H.H. and Marshall C. 1978 *Reference Diaries*, in Tinlap-2: Theoretical Issues in Natural Language Processing, 7:57-63, New York: Association for Computing Machinery and the Association of Computational Linguistics.

Clippinger, J. H. 1975 *Speaking with Many Tongues: Some Problems in Modeling Speakers of Actual Discourse*, in B. Nash-Webber and R. Schank, eds., Tinlap-1: Theoretical Issues in Natural Language Processing, New York: Association for Computing Machinery and the Association of Computational Linguistics, pp. 68-73.

Clippinger, J. H. 1978 Meaning and Discourse: A computer model of psychoanalytic speech and cognition Baltimore, MD: Johns Hopkins University Press.

Codasyl 1977 Data Base Task Group of CODASYL Programming Language Committee Report, ACM Publications, N.Y., 1971.

Cohen, P.R. 1978 *On knowing what to say: planning speech acts,* TR 118, Dept. of Computer Science, U. Toronto.

Cole, P., and Morgan, J.L. 1975 Syntax and Semantics, Vol. 3: Speech Acts, NY: Academic Press.

Collins, A., Brown, J.S., and Larkin, K. 1977 *Inference in text understanding*, Technical Report CSR-TR-40, Center for the Study of Reading, Champaign IL.

Cooper, W. and Paccia-Cooper, J. 1980 Syntax and Speech. Cambridge, MA: Harvard University Press.

Cooper, W. and Sorenson, J. 1977 *Fundamental frequency contours at syntactic boundaries.* Journal of the Acoustical Society of America. 62, pp. 683-692.

Davey, A. 1974 *Discourse Production* , Ph.D. Dissertation, Edinburgh University. (published as Discourse Production: A Computer Model of Some Aspects of a Speaker, Edinburgh: Edinburgh University Press, 1979.)

Denes and Pinson 1973 The Speech Chain: the Physics and Biology of the Spoken Language, Garden City, New York: Anchor Press.

Deutsch, B. 1974 *Typescripts of Task Oriented Dialogs,* Unpublished manuscript, SRI-International, Menlo Park, Ca.

Deutsch, B. 1975 *Establishing Context In Task-Oriented Dialogues,* Proceedings of the 13 Annual Meeting of ACL, AJCL Microfiche 35, p. 27.

Doyle, J. 1978 *Truth Maintainence Systems for Problem Solving,* M.I.T. A.I. Laboratory AI-TR-419, Cambridge, MA.

Ernst, G., and Newell, A. 1969 GPS: A Case Study in Generality and Problem Solving. New York: Academic Press.

Fahlman, S. E. 1979 NETL: A System for Representing and Using Real-World Knowledge. Cambridge: The MIT Press.

Fikes, R.E., and Nilsson, N.J. 1971 *STRIPS: A new approach to the application of theorem proving to problem solving,* Artificial Intelligence 2:89-205.

Fillmore, C. 1968 *The case for case,* in Universals in Linguistic Theory, ed. E. Bach and G. Harms, New York: Holt, Rinehart, and Winston, pp. 1-90.

Fillmore, C.F. 1971 *Lectures on Deixis,* Unpublished manuscript, Linguistics Department, University of California, Berkeley.

Fodor, J. 1975 The Language of Thought, New York: Thomas Crowell.

Fodor, J. 1982 The Modularity of Mind, unpublished manuscript.

Ford, M. and Holmes, V. 1978 *Planning units and syntax in sentence production* Cognition 6, pp. 35-53.

Genesereth, M. R. 1978 *Automated Consultation for Complex Computer Systems,* Ph.D. Dissertation, Harvard University,

Gerritsen, Rob, 1978 *SEED Reference Manual,* Version C00 - B04 draft, International Data Base Systems, Inc., Philadelphia, Pa., 19104.

Goldman, N. M. 1974 *Computer Generation of Natural Language from a Deep Conceptual Base,* Ph.D. Dissertation, Stanford University.

Gordon, D., and Lakoff, G. 1975 *Conversational postulates,* in Syntax and Semantics, Vol. 3: Speech Acts, ed. P. Cole and J.L. Morgan. New York: Academic Press, pp. 83-106.

Goudge, T. 1969, The Thought of C.S. Peirce, New York: Dover Publications.

Grice, H.P. 1975 *Logic and conversation,* Syntax and Semantics, Vol. 3: Speech Acts, ed. P. Cole and J.L. Morgan. New York: Academic Press, pp. 41-58.

Grinder, J., and Postal, P. 1971 *Missing antecedents,* Linguistic Inquiry 2(3):269-312.

Grosz, B., 1977 *The Representation and Use of Focus in Dialogue Understanding,* Technical Note 151, Artificial Intelligence Center, Stanford Research Institute, Menlo Park, Ca.

Grosz, B. 1978 *Focusing in Dialog,* Tinlap-2: Theoretical Issues in Natural Language Processing, 7:96-103, New York: Association for Computing Machinery and Association of Computational Linguistics.

Grosz, B. 1981 *Focusing and Description in Natural Language Dialogues,* in Elements of Discourse Understanding, A. Joshi, B. Webber, and I. Sag (eds.) Cambridge: Cambridge University Press. pp. 84-105.

Gruber, J. 1976 Lexical Structure in Syntax and Semantics. New York: North Holland.

Halliday, M. A. K. 1966 *Notes on transitivity and theme in English.* Journal of Linguistics 2:37-81.

Halliday, M. A. K. 1970 *Functional Diversity in Language as Seen from a Consideration of Modality and Mood in English.* Foundations of Language 6:322-361.

Halliday, M.A.K. and Hasan, R. 1976 Cohesion in English. London: Longman

Press.

Hankamer, J., and Sag, I. 1976 *Deep and surface anaphora*, Linguistic Inquiry 7(3):391-426.

Harris, L. R., December, 1978 *The ROBOT System: Natural Language Processing Applied to Data Base Query*, in Proceedings of the ACM 78, Washington D.C.

Hawkinson, L. 1975 *The Representation of Concepts in OWL*, Proceedings of the Fourth International Joint Conference in Artificial Intelligence, 4:107-114.

Hendrix, G. 1977 *Human engineering for applied natural language processing*, Proc. 5th Int. Jt. Conf. on Artificial Intelligence.

Hendrix, G. G., E. D. Sacerdoti, D. Sagalowicz, and J. Slocum, June, 1978. *Developing a Natural Language Interface to Complex Data*, ACM Transactions on Database Systems, Vol. 3, No. 2.

Higginbotham, J. 1980 *Pronouns and Bound Variables*, Linguistic Inquiry, 11(4), pp. 679-708.

Hintikka, J. 1963 Knowledge and Belief, Ithaca, New York: Cornell University Press.

Hobbs, J. R. 1976 *Pronoun Resolution*, Research Report #76-1, City College, City University of New York, New York.

Hobbs, J. R. 1977 *38 Examples of Elusive Antecedents from Published Texts*, Research Report #76-2, City College, City University of New York, New York.

Hobbs, J. R. 1979 *Coherence and Co-reference*, Cognitive Science. 3(1): 67-90.

Hornstein, N. 1981 *Two ways of interpreting quantifiers.* mimeographed, Columbia University.

Horrigan, M.K. 1977 *Modelling simple dialogs*, TR 108, Dept. of Computer Science, U. Toronto.

Hull, R. D., 1974 *A Logical Analysis of Questions and Answers*, Ph.D. Dissertation, University of Cambridge, Jesus College.

Isner, D. W. 1975 *Understanding "Understanding" Through Representation and Reasoning*, Ph.D. dissertation, University of Pittsburgh, Department of Computer Science.

Jackendoff, R. 1972 Semantic Interpretation in Generative Grammar, Cambridge, Ma: MIT Press.

Joshi, A. K. and R. Weischedel, 1977 *Computation of a subclass of inferences: Presupposition and Entailment*, in Am. J. of Comp. Linguistics.

Kaplan, R. and J. Bresnan, 1981 *Lexical-functional Grammar: A formal System for Grammatical Representation*, MIT Center for Cognitive Science Occasional Paper #13.

Kaplan, S.J., 1978 *On the Difference Between Natural Language and High Level Query Languages*, in Proceedings of the ACM 1978, Washington D.C.

Kaplan, S. J., 1979a *Cooperative Responses from a Portable Natural Language Data Base Query System*, Ph.D. Dissertation, U. of Pennsylvania, available as Stanford Heuristic Programming Project Report HPP-79-19, Computer Science Department, Stanford University, Stanford, Ca. 94305, July, 1979.

Kaplan, S.J., E.Mays, and A.K. Joshi, 1979 *A Technique for Managing the Lexicon in a Natural Language Interface to a Changing Data Base*, in Proceedings of the IJCAI 1979, Tokyo, Japan.

Karttunen, L. 1976 *Discourse referents*, in Syntax and Semantics, vol. 7., ed. J. McCawley. New York: Academic Press, pp. 363-386.

Karttunen, L., 1977 *Presupposition and Linguistic Context*, in Proceedings of the Texas Conference on Performatives, Presupposition, and Implicature, (A. Rogers, B. Wall, and J. P. Murphy, Ed.), Center for Applied Linguistics, Arlington, Va.

Katz, J. J. and Fodor, J. A. 1963 *The Structure of a Semantic Theory*, Language, 39(2):170-210.

Kayne, R. 1981 *ECP Extensions* Linguistic Inquiry 12(3), pp. 93-133.

Keenan, E.L., 1971 *Two Kinds of Presupposition in Natural Language*, in Studies in Linguistic Semantics, (C. J. Fillmore and D. T. Langendoen, Ed.), Holt,

Rinehart, and Winston, N.Y, pp. 45-52.

Keenan, E.L., and Hull, R.D., 1973 *The Logical Presuppositions of Questions and Answers*, in Prasuppositionen in Philosophie und Linguistik, (Petofi and Frank, Ed.), Athenaum Verlag, Frankfurt.

Kempen, I. 1977 *Building a Psychologically Plausible Sentence Generator*. presented at The Conference of Empirical and Methodological Foundations of Semantic Theories for Natural Language, March 1977; Nijmegen, The Netherlands.

Kempen, J. and Hoenkamp, E. 1980 *A Procedural Grammar for Sentence Production*. Technical Report Max-Plank Institute, Nijmegen, The Netherlands.

Krauwer, S. and L. des Tombes 1980 *Finite state transducers as a model of the language processor* Utrecht Working Papers in Linguistics, no. 19

Kroch, A. 1981 *Resumptive pronouns and the amnestying of wh-island violations*, Proceedings of the Chicago Linguistic Society, Chicago, Il.

Labov, W. 1966 *On the Grammaticality of Everyday Speech*. Proceedings of the Linguistic Society of America meeting, 1966, New York.

Lakoff, R. 1974 *Remarks on This and That*, Proceedings of the Tenth Regional Meeting of the Chicago Linguistic Society, ed. LaGaly,Fox and Ruck. Chicago: Chicago Linguistics Society, 10:345-356.

Lashley, K. 1951 *The Problem of Serial Order in Behavior*, in L.A. Jeffress (ed.) Cerebral Mechanisms in Behavior: The Hixon Symposium. New York: Wiley.

Lasnik, H. 1976 *Remarks on Co-reference*, Linguistic Analysis, 2(1):1-22.

Lehnert, W. 1977a *Human and computational question answering*, Cognitive Science 1(1), pp. 47-73.

Lehnert, W., 1977 *The Process of Question Answering*, TR 88, Dept. of Computer Science, Yale University.

Lewis, P. and R.E. Stearns 1968 *Syntax-directed transduction* Journal of the Association for Computing Machinery, 15:3, pp. 464-488.

Liberman, P. 1967 Intonation, Perception, and Language. Cambridge, MA: MIT Press.

Lightfoot, D. and Hornstein, N. 1981 Explanation in Linguistics, London: Longman.

Lockman, A. D. 1978 *Contextual Reference Resolution in Natural Language Processing*, Dept. of Computer Science TR-70, Rutgers University, New Brunswick, N.J.

Luria, S. E. 1975 Thirty-six Lectures in Biology, Cambridge, MA: MIT Press.

Mann, W. C., Bates, M., Grosz, B. J., McDonald, D. D., McKeown, K. R. and Swartout, I. in press. *The State of the Art in Text Generation. American Journal of Computational Linguistics* .

Mann, W. C. and Moore, J. 1981 *Computer Generation of Multiparagraph Text. American Journal of Computational Linguistics*, 7(1), pp. 17-29.

Marcus, M. 1980 A Theory of Syntactic Recognition for Natural Language. Cambridge: MIT Press.

Mark, W. 1981 *The Consul Project*. Technical Report, Information Sciences Institute, Marina Del Ray, California.

Martin, W. 1979 *Roles, Co-Descriptors and the Formal Representation of Quantified English Expressions*, Laboratory for Computer Science, TM-139, M.I.T., Cambridge, MA.

May, R. 1977 The Grammar of Quantification, PhD dissertation, MIT Department of Linguistics.

McAllester, D. A. 1978 *A Three Valued Truth Maintenance System*, MIT AI Lab Memo 473, Cambridge, MA.

McDonald, D.M. 1977 *Subsequent reference: syntactic and rhetorical constraints*, in Tinlap-2: Theoretical Issues in Natural Language Processing, 7:64-72, New York: Association for Computing Machinery and Association of Computational Linguistics.

McDonald D. D. 1980a Natural Language Generation as a Process of

Decision-making Under Constraints, PhD dissertation, MIT Department of Computer Science and Electrical Engineering.

McDonald, D. D. 1980b *A Linear-time Model of Language Production: Some Psycholinguistic Implications.* abstract in the proceedings of 18th Annual Meeting of the Association for Computational Linguistics, June 1980, University of Pennsylvania, pp. 55-57.

McDonald, D. D. 1981 *MUMBLE, A Flexible System for Language Production,* IJCAI-81, August 1981, University of British Columbia, p. 1062.

McDonald, D. D. (in preparation) *Natural Language Production by Computers: A Survey,* University of Massachusetts Technical Report.

McKeown, K.R., 1979 *Paraphrasing Using Given and New Information in a Question-Answering System,* in Proceedings of the 17th Annual Meeting of the Association for Computational Linguistics, pp.62-67.

McKeown, K. R. 1980 *Generating Relevant Explanations: Natural language responses to questions about database structure.* Proceedings of the First Annual National Conference on Artificial Intelligence, Stanford, CA, August 1980, pp. 306-309.

Meehan, J. R. 1976 *The Metanovel: Writing Stories by Computer.* Research Report 74, The Yale A.I. Group, Yale University, New Haven, Connecticut.

Minsky, M. 1974 *A Framework for Representing Knowledge,* in P. Winston (ed.) The Psychology of Computer Vision, New York: McGraw-Hill, pp. 211-227.

Montague, R. 1974 *The Proper Treatment of Quantification in Ordinary English,* in Formal Philosophy, ed. by Thomason, R., ps. 247-270, Yale University Press, New Haven.

Morgan, J. L. 1978 *Toward a Rational Model of Discourse Comprehension,* Tinlap-2: Theoretical Issues in Natural Language Processing, 7:109-114, New York: Association for Computing Machinery and Association of Computational Linguistics.

Nash-Webber B. and Schank R. 1975, Tinlap-1: Theoretical Issues in Natural Language Processing, New York: Association for Computing Machinery and the

Association of Computational Linguistics.

New York Times Corporation, 1973 *The Watergate Hearings - Break-in and Cover-up*, New York: Viking Press.

Nilsson, N.J. 1971 Problem Solving Methods in Artificial Intelligence, New York: McGraw-Hill.

Nilsson, N.J. 1980 Principles of Artificial Intelligence Palo Alto-CA: Tioga Press.

Partee, B. H. 1972 *Opacity, Co-reference and Pronouns*, Semantics of Natural Language ed. D. Davidson and G. Harman. Boston: Reidel, pp. 415-441.

Partee, B. H. 1978 *Bound Variables and Other Anaphors*, Tinlap-2: Theoretical Issues in Natural Language Processing, 7:79-85, New York: Association for Computing Machinery and Association of Computational Linguistics.

Perlmutter, D. M. and Postal, P. M. in preparation. Relational Grammar.

Perrault, C. R., Allen, J.F., and Cohen, P.R. 1978' *Speech acts as a basis for understanding dialogue coherence*, Tinlap-2: Theoretical Issues in Natural Language Processing. 7: New York: Association for Computing Machinery and Association of Computational Linguistics, pp. 125-132.

Perrault, C. R., and Allen, J.F. 1980 *A plan-based analysis of indirect speech acts*, J. Assoc. Comp. Linguistics 6(3), pp. 167-182.

Perrault, C. R., and Cohen, P. 1981 *It's for your own good*, Elements of Discourse Understanding, eds. A.K. Joshi, B.L. Webber and I.A. Sag. New York: Cambridge University Press, pp.217-230.

Postal, P. 1969 *Anaphoric Islands*, Papers from the Fifth Regional Meeting of the Chicago Linguistic Society, ed. Binnick, Davison, Green and Morgan. Chicago: Chicago Linguistic Society. 5:205-239.

Prince, E., 1978 *A Comparison of Wh-clefts and It-clefts in Discourse*, Language, 54, Vol.4.

Reichman, R. 1978 *Conversational coherency*, Cognitive Science, 2(4):283-327.

Reinhart, T. 1976 *The Syntactic Domain of Anaphora*, Ph.D. dissertation,

Department of Foreign Literature and Linguistics, M.I.T., Cambridge, MA.

Reiter, R., 1978 *On Closed World Data Bases*, in Logic and Data Bases, H. Gallaire and J. Minker (Eds.), Plenum Press, N.Y.

Resnick and Halliday 1966 Physics: Part I, New York: John Wiley.

Rieger, C. J. 1974 *Conceptual Memory: A Theory and Computer Program for Processing the Meaning Content of Natural Language Utterances*, Stanford Artificial Intelligence Lab Memo AIM-233, Stanford, CA.

Riesbeck, C.K. 1975 *Conceptual analysis*, in Conceptual Information Processing, ed. R.C. Schank. Amsterdam: North-Holland.

Roberts, B. and Goldstein, I. P. 1977 *The FRL Manual*. AIM-409, Artificial Intelligence Laboratory, Massachusetts Institute of Technology, Cambridge, Massachusetts.

Robinson, A. 1981. *Determining verb phrase referents in dialogues*, American Journal of Computational Linguistics, 7(1):1-16.

Rosenschein, S. J., October, 1976 *How Does a System Know When to Stop Inferencing?*, in American Journal of Computational Linguistics.

Ross, J. 1967 *Constraints on variables in syntax*, Ph.D. dissertation, MIT Department of Linguistics.

Sacerdoti, E.D. 1973 *Planning in a hierarchy of abstraction spaces*, Proc. 3rd Int. Jt. Conf. on Artificial Intelligence, pp. 412-422.

Sacerdoti, E.D. 1975 *The nonlinear nature of plans*, Proc. 4th Int. Jt. Conf. on Artificial Intelligence, pp. 206-214.

Sadock, J.M. 1974 Toward a Linguistic Theory of Speech Acts. New York: Academic Press.

Schank, R. 1975 Conceptual Information Processing. New York: American Elsevier.

Schank, R. and Colby, M. C., 1973 Computer models of thought and language, San Francisco: Freeman.

Schiffer, S.R. 1972 Meaning, London: Oxford University Press.

Schmidt, C.F., Sridharan, N.S., and Goodson, J.L. 1979 *The plan recognition problem: An intersection of artificial intelligence and psychology*, Artificial Intelligence 9(1), pp. 45-83.

Searle, J. R., 1969 Speech Acts, an Essay in the Philosophy of Language, New York: Cambridge University Press.

Searle, J.R. 1975 *Indirect speech acts*, in Syntax and Semantics, Vol. 3: Speech Acts, ed. P. Cole and J.L. Morgan. New York: Academic Press, pp. 59-82.

Shapiro, S. C. 1975 *Generation as Parsing from a Network into a Linear String*. *American Journal of Computational Linguistics*, Microfiche 35.

Shattuck-Hufnagel 1979 *Sentence production: a model based on speech errors patterns*, in Sentence Processing ed. W. Cooper and E. Walker, Hillsdale, NJ: Lawrence Erlbaum, pp. 295-342.

Shortliffe, E. H. 1976 Computer Based Medical Consultations: MYCIN. Amsterdam, The Netherlands: Elsevier North Holland Inc.

Sidner, C.L. 1978 *The Use of Focus as a Tool for Disambiguation of Definite Noun Phrases*, Tinlap-2: Theoretical Issues in Natural Language Processing, 7:86-95, New York: ACM and ACL.

Sidner, C. 1979 *Towards a computational theory of definite anaphora comprehension in English discourse*, Technical Report 537. MIT Artificial Intelligence Laboratory, Cambridge MA.

Silverman, H. 1975 *A Digitalis Therapy Advisor*, Technical Report 143, Project MAC, Massachusetts Institute of Technology, Cambridge, Massachusetts.

Simmons, R. F. and Slocum, J. 1972 *Generating English discourse from semantic networks*, Communications of the ACM 15, 10, 891-905.

Solan, L. 1978 *Anaphora in Child Language*, Ph.D. dissertation, Dept. of Linguistics, University of Massachusetts, Amherst, MA (available through the Graduate Linguistic Student Association, University of Massachusetts).

Steedman, M. J., and Johnson-Laird, P. N., June, 1976 *A Programmatic Theory of Linguistic Performance*, presented at the <u>Stirling</u> <u>Conference</u> <u>on</u> <u>Psycholinguistics</u>.

Stenning, K., 1978 *Anaphora as an approach to pragmatics*, in <u>Linguistic Theory</u> <u>and</u> <u>Psychological Reality</u>, eds. M. Halle, J. Bresnan, and G. Miller. Cambridge: MIT press.

Strawson, P.F. 1971 *Intention and convention in speech acts*, in <u>The Philosophy of</u> <u>Language</u>, ed. J.R. Searle New York: Oxford University Press, pp. 23-38.

Swartout, I. 1977 *A Digitalis Therapy Advisor with Explanations*, Technical Report Laboratory for Computer Science, Massachusetts Institute of Technology, Cambridge, Massachusetts.

Swartout, I. 1981 *Producing Explanations and Justifications of Expert Consulting Programs*, Technical Report 251, Laboratory for Computer Science, Massachusetts Institute of Technology, Cambridge, Massachusetts.

Thomas, J. C., 1976 *Quantifiers and question asking*, Technical report RC5866, IBM Thomas J. Watson Research Center.

Thompson, F.P., P.C. Lockeman, B.H. Dostert, R. Deverill, 1969 *REL: A Rapidly Extensible Language System*, in <u>Proceedings</u> <u>of</u> <u>the</u> <u>24th</u> <u>ACM</u> <u>National</u> <u>Conference</u>, N.Y., N.Y.

Van Lehn, K. A. 1978 *Determining the Scope of English Quantifiers*, AI-TR-483, Artificial Intelligence Laboratory, Massachusetts Institute of Technology, Cambridge, MA.

Walker, D. E. 1976 *Speech Understanding Research*, Final Technical Report, Project 4762. Artificial Intelligence Center, Stanford Research Institute, Menlo Park, CA.

Waltz, D. L., July, 1978 *An English Language Question Answering System for a Large Relational Database*, <u>Communications</u> <u>of</u> <u>the</u> <u>Assoc. Comp. Mach.</u>, 21(7), pp. 526-539.

Wasow, T. 1977 *Transformations and the Lexicon*, in <u>Formal</u> <u>Syntax</u>, ed. P. Culicover, A. Akmajian, and T. Wasow, New York: Academic Press.

Webber, B. L., 1978a *A Formal Approach to Discourse Anaphora*, Technical

Report 3761, Bolt Beranek and Newman, Inc. Cambridge, MA.

Webber, B. L., 1978b *Jumping ahead of the speaker: on recognition from indefinite NPs*, Sloan workshop on indefinite reference, University of Massachusetts, Amherst, Ma., December.

Webber, B. L., 1978c *Description formation and discourse model synthesis*, Proc. TINLAP-2, Assoc. Comp. Ling.

Webber, B. L., 1981 *Discourse model synthesis: preliminaries to reference*, Elements of discourse understanding, eds. A. K. Joshi, B. L. Webber, and I. A. Sag, Cambridge: Cambridge University Press.

Weischedel, R. M., 1975 *Computation of a Unique Class of Inferences: Presupposition and Entailment*, Ph.D. dissertation, Dept. of Computer and Information Science, University of Pennsylvania, Philadelphia, Pa.

Wilensky, R. 1978 *Focusing in the Comprehension of Definite Anaphora in Understanding Goal-Based Stories*, Ph.D. thesis. Yale University.

Williams, E. 1977 *Discourse and logical form*, Linguistic Inquiry, 8(1), pp. 101-139.

Willams, E. 1980 *Predication*, Linguistic Inquiry, 11(1), pp.203-238.

Winograd, T. 1972 Understanding Natural Language. New York: Academic Press.

Winston, P. H. 1980 *Learning and Reasoning by Analogy: the details*, AIM-520, Artificial Intelligence Laboratory, Massachusetts Institute of Technology, Cambridge, Massachusetts.

Woods, W. 1967 *The Semantics for a Question Answering system*, Ph.D. dissertation, Harvard University, Report NSF-19, Aiken Computation Laboratory, Harvard University. (reprinted by Garland Publishing, 1979)

Woods, W.A. 1970 *Transition network grammars for natural language analysis*, Comm. Assoc. Comp. Mach. 13(10), pp. 591-606.

Woods, W. 1973 *An Experimental Parsing System for Transition Network Grammars*, Natural Language Processing, ed. R. Rustin. New York: Algorithmics Press, pp. 111-154.

Woods, W. A., R. M. Kaplan, and B. Nash-Webber, 1972 *The Lunar Sciences Information System: Final Report*, BBN Report 2378, Bolt, Beranek, and Newman Inc., Cambridge, Mass.

Woods, W. A., et. al. 1976 *Speech understanding systems: final technical progress report*, Technical report 3438, Bolt, Beranek, and Newman Inc., Cambridge, Ma.

Woolf, V. 1957 A Room of One's Own. New York: Harcourt, Brace and Jovanovich.

Yngve, V. 1960 *A model and a hypothesis for language structure* Proceedings of the American Philosophical Society, 104, pp. 444-466.

Index